The Collected Works of Henry G. Manne

VOLUME 2 *Insider Trading*

Henry G. Manne

The Collected Works of Henry G. Manne

Fred S. McChesney

GENERAL EDITOR

VOLUME 2 Insider Trading

Edited and with an Introduction by Stephen M. Bainbridge

LIBERTY FUND

Indianapolis

This book is published by Liberty Fund, Inc., a foundation established to encourage study of the ideal of a society of free and responsible individuals.

The cuneiform inscription that serves as our logo and as the design motif for our endpapers is the earliest-known written appearance of the word "freedom" (*amagi*), or "liberty." It is taken from a clay document written about 2300 B.C. in the Sumerian city-state of Lagash.

Book design by Louise OFarrell, Gainesville, Florida

Printed in the United States of America

C 10 9 8 7 6 5 4 3 2 1
P 10 9 8 7 6 5 4 3 2 1

Library of Congress Cataloging-in-Publication Data
Manne, Henry G.
The collected works of Henry G. Manne / Fred S. McChesney, general editor.
p. cm.
Includes bibliographical references and index.
ISBN 978-0-86597-763-1 (set hbk. : alk. paper)—ISBN 978-0-86597-764-8 (set pbk. : alk. paper) 1. Corporations. 2. Corporate governance. 3. Insider trading in securities. 4. Social responsibility of business. 5. Law and economics. I. McChesney, Fred S. II. Title.
HD2731.M34 2009
343.73′07—dc22

2009018367

LIBERTY FUND, INC.
8335 Allison Pointe Trail, Suite 300
Indianapolis, Indiana 46250-1684

CONTENTS

ARTICLES AND ESSAYS

INTRODUCTION

Stephen M. Bainbridge

In the United States, early common law permitted insiders of a corporation to trade in their company's stock without prior disclosure of any material, nonpublic information they might possess. Over the last five decades, however, a complex federal prohibition of insider trading emerged as a central feature of modern U.S. securities regulation.

As the prohibition evolved, it typically was justified on vague notions of fairness or equity. As a California court recently put it, insider trading is "a manifestation of undue greed among the already well-to-do, worthy of legislative intervention if for no other reason than to send a message of censure on behalf of the American people."[1] To question the merits of regulating insider trading thus seemed little short of an attack on truth, justice, and the American way.

Henry Manne's 1966 book, *Insider Trading and the Stock Market,* therefore ranks among the truly seminal events in the economic analysis of law. One exaggerates only slightly to say that Manne stunned the corporate law academy by daring to propose the deregulation of insider trading. As we will see, the response by all too many traditionalist scholars was immediate and vitriolic.

Although Manne's policy prescriptions have found neither legislative nor regulatory acceptance, history has vindicated Manne's daring in at least one important respect. Although it is hard to believe at this remove, corporate law scholarship was moribund during much of the middle decades of the

1. *Friese v. Superior Court,* 36 Cal. Rptr. 3d 558, 566 (Cal. App. 2005).

last century. Manne's work on insider trading played a major role in ending that long intellectual drought by stimulating interest in economic analysis of corporate law. Whether one agrees with Manne's views on insider trading or not, one therefore must give him due credit for helping to stimulate the outpouring of important law and economics scholarship in corporate law and securities regulation in recent decades.

Manne's work on insider trading straddles what Richard Posner recently called the first and second generations of law and economics scholarship.[2] The first generation, which consisted of such scholars as Gary Becker, Guido Calabresi, Ronald Coase, and Aaron Director, blazed the trail by establishing the tools of microeconomics—most notably the rational choice model—as a methodology by which legal doctrines may usefully be examined. The second generation took these tools and ran with them, applying them to a host of legal doctrines. Their projects typically entailed translation of some legal principle into economic terms. They then applied a few basic economic tools—cost-benefit analysis, collective action theory, decision making under uncertainty, risk aversion, and the like—to the problem. Finally, they translated the result back into legal terms.

Manne was among those first-generation scholars who paved the way for law and economics to become an accepted jurisprudential methodology, but he also was one of the first and most important second-generation scholars. As Ronald Cass observes, "Manne was one of the first legal scholars . . . to use economics to generate a new insight into a legal issue and to do so in a way that dramatically changed discourse about that issue."[3] Indeed, Manne did it twice—once with respect to the market for the corporate control and again with respect to insider trading.

This volume collects all of Manne's extensive writings on insider trading over a span of forty-plus years. The works included range from traditional scholarship to newspaper op-ed columns. Read in sequence, they demonstrate Manne's continued engagement with this important field, as well as his willingness to change and evolve in response to constructive criticism

2. Richard A. Posner, "A Review of Steven Shavell's *Foundations of Economic Analysis of Law*," *Journal of Economic Literature* 44 (2006): 405.

3. Ronald A. Cass, "One Among the Manne: Changing Our Course," *Case Western Reserve Law Review* 50 (1999): 203, 204.

and new ideas. Although he was still making much the same basic policy recommendations in 2006 as he had back in 1966, he was constantly marshalling new theories and rationales in support of them. Manne never stood still as a scholar of insider trading.

Insider Trading and the Stock Market (1966) opens with a brief review of the moralizing that surrounded insider trading even in Manne's day. Although Manne acknowledges the importance of sound business ethics, he also insists on a rigorous and dispassionate analysis. Grandiose ethical pronouncements rooted only in fiat are to be replaced with careful economic analysis. Manne then moves to an extended review of the history of the insider-trading prohibition. As he demonstrates, at the time he was writing (the mid-1960s), neither state corporation law nor federal securities regulation comprehensively prohibited insider trading. All that was about to change, however, with the SEC's action against the insiders of the Texas Gulf Sulphur Company.

On November 13, 1963, TGS officers learned that the company might have struck a rich vein of ore at a mining site in Canada. Over the next several months, the company began buying up land in the area. Contemporaneously, various TGS insiders bought TGS stock and options. The SEC, seeking an injunction and other remedies, sued the officers for insider trading. In 1968, the Second Circuit held that insiders have a duty to disclose material nonpublic information they possess before trading or, if they cannot make such disclosure, to abstain from trading. Insiders who violate that rule by trading prior to public dissemination of the information violate SEC Rule 10b-5.[4]

Manne correctly anticipated that the SEC and the courts would use the *Texas Gulf Sulphur* case as a vehicle for imposing new restrictions on insider trading. He therefore used the case as a principal foil for both his legal and economic analysis. Indeed, the book is patently designed to provide an "analysis helpful to a court or legislature asked to resolve the issues posed by the *Texas Gulf Sulphur* case."

Manne identified two principal ways in which insider trading benefits

4. *SEC v. Texas Gulf Sulphur Co.*, 401 F.2d 833, 848 (2d Cir. 1968), *cert. denied*, 394 U.S. 976 (1969).

society and/or the firm in whose stock the insider traded. First, he argued that insider trading causes the market price of the affected security to move toward the price that the security would command if the inside information were publicly available. If so, both society and the firm benefit through increased price accuracy. Second, he posited insider trading as an efficient way of compensating managers for having produced information. If so, the firm benefits directly (and society indirectly) because managers have a greater incentive to produce additional information of value to the firm.

There is general agreement that both firms and society benefit from accurate pricing of securities. The "correct" price of a security is that which would be set by the market if all information relating to the security had been publicly disclosed. Accurate pricing benefits society by improving the economy's allocation of capital investment and by decreasing the volatility of security prices. This dampening of price fluctuations decreases the likelihood of individual windfall gains and increases the attractiveness of investing in securities for risk-averse investors. The individual corporation also benefits from accurate pricing of its securities through reduced investor uncertainty and improved monitoring of management's effectiveness.

Although U.S. securities laws purportedly encourage accurate pricing by requiring disclosure of corporate information, they do not require the disclosure of all material information. Where disclosure would interfere with legitimate business transactions, disclosure by the corporation is usually not required unless the firm is dealing in its own securities at the time.

When a firm lawfully withholds material information, its securities are no longer accurately priced by the market. If the undisclosed information is particularly significant, the error in price can be substantial. As Manne pointed out, in the *Texas Gulf Sulphur* case, when the deposit was discovered, Texas Gulf Sulphur common stock sold for approximately $18 per share. By the time the discovery was disclosed, four months later, the price had risen to over $31 per share. One month after disclosure, the stock was selling for approximately $58 per share. Pricing errors of this magnitude eliminate the benefits of accurate pricing. However, requiring TGS to disclose what it knew would have reduced the value of the information and thus the incentive to discover it.

Citing the gradual rise of Texas Gulf Sulphur's stock during the period in which the discovery was kept confidential, which he attributed to trading by insiders, Manne argued insider trading is an effective compromise between the need for preserving incentives to produce information and the need for maintaining accurate securities prices. As Texas Gulf Sulphur insiders traded, the stock price gradually rose toward the "correct" price. The process by which insider trading affects the stock market in this way is known as "derivatively informed trading."[5] Derivatively informed trading affects market prices through a two-step mechanism. First, those individuals possessing material nonpublic information begin trading. Their trading has only a small effect on price. Some uninformed traders become aware of the insider trading through leaks, tipping of information, or observation of insider trades. Other traders gain insight by following the price fluctuations of the securities. Gradually, these processes amplify the effect of the insiders' trades.

Absent insider trading and the resulting derivatively informed trading, the stock's price presumably would have remained in the $18 vicinity until the discovery was publicly disclosed and then rapidly risen to the correct price of nearly $60. Thus insider trading acted as a replacement for public disclosure of the information, preserving market gains of correct pricing while permitting the corporation to retain the benefits of nondisclosure. In addition, Manne argues, it did so without injuring investors.

Manne next turns to his argument that allowing insider trading was an effective means of compensating entrepreneurs in large corporations. The gist of this argument rests on a distinction Manne draws between corporate entrepreneurs and mere corporate managers. The latter merely operate the business according to previously established policies and guidelines. Because both the firm and the manager thus know what the manager will do and what his abilities are, salary is an appropriate method of compensation.

In contrast, Manne argues, an entrepreneur's services consist in large part of producing valuable new ideas. In order to properly incentivize such an entrepreneur, his compensation must have a reasonable relation to the value of his contribution. Because it is rarely possible to ascertain the in-

5. See generally Ronald Gilson and Reinier Kraakman, "The Mechanisms of Market Efficiency," *Virginia Law Review* 70 (1984): 549.

formation's value to the firm in advance, however, predetermined compensation, such as salary, is inappropriate for entrepreneurs. Instead, some form of *ex post* compensation based on the value of the new idea is necessary.

Manne asserted insider trading is an effective way to compensate corporate entrepreneurs for innovations. The increase in the price of the security following public disclosure provides an imperfect but comparatively accurate measure of the value of the innovation to the firm. By trading on the new information, the agent thus self-tailors his compensation to account for the information he produces, increasing his incentive to develop valuable innovations. Because insider trading provides the agent with a more certain and more precisely tailored reward than other compensation schemes, it provides incentives superior to bonuses, stock options, and other forms of performance-based compensation.[6]

In chapter 11, toward the end of *Insider Trading and the Stock Market,* Manne touches on a subject that remains a central issue today: the problems associated with attempting to create a workable prohibition of insider trading. In particular, as Manne recognized, the very name "insider" trading is a misnomer. As Manne details, many corporate outsiders have access to potentially valuable material, nonpublic information. Trading on the basis of such information by at least some such outsiders, such as stock market analysts and their clients, moreover, is clearly socially beneficial. The problem of sorting out which outsiders should be allowed to trade and which should not remains a key problem on which Manne's analysis offers useful insight.

"In Defense of Insider Trading" boiled down the arguments made at length in *Insider Trading and the Stock Market* to article length for the *Harvard Business Review.* The article illustrates Manne's penchant for academic entrepreneurialism. Unlike ivory tower academics content to watch their ideas collect dust on a library shelf, Manne long has played the dual role of

6. As David Haddock summarizes it, "Manne's point was simply that the opportunity to reap trading profits motivates insiders to create events on which they can trade. Those innovative efforts, in turn, can increase the value of the company for whom the insider works." David D. Haddock, "Academic Hostility and SEC Acquiescence: Henry Manne's Insider Trading," *Case Western Reserve Law Review* 50 (1999): 313, 314.

serious academic and public intellectual. As the latter, he has used both essays of this sort and newspaper op-ed columns to transmit his thesis to the public. In order to do so, Manne here embraces a more provocative tone—"as in most holy wars, self-righteousness and hypocrisy may be the true order of the day"—than one might find in staid academic journals. "In Defense of Insider Trading" thus not only offers a concise treatment of Manne's main claims, but also offers an example of his skills as a polemicist.

"Insider Trading and the Administrative Process" used insider trading as a case study of a larger problem: the gradual federalization of corporation law. Manne observed that SEC Rule 10b-5 was no longer evolving via accepted administrative procedures, but rather as though it were a legislative statute. It generally is accepted that courts may fill in the interstices of a statute via the interpretive process. In this limited sense, statutory interpretation can give rise to a form of federal common law. Precisely this process was taking place with respect to Rule 10b-5. Indeed, as William Rehnquist would observe some years later, Rule 10b-5 became "a judicial oak which has grown from little more than a legislative acorn."[7] Manne contends that this sort of judicial interstitial lawmaking is inappropriate with respect to administrative regulations such as Rule 10b-5.

Today, "Insider Trading and the Administrative Process" remains significant due to its treatment of the federalism issues raised by insider trading. In 1967, when Manne wrote this article, many observers believed courts were in the process of creating a de facto federal law of corporations through expansive judicial interpretations of Rule 10b-5. Indeed, as Manne pointed out, Rule 10b-5 already had preempted state corporation law insofar as insider trading was concerned.

Originally, insider trading was a matter of state corporation law fiduciary duties. Although *Texas Gulf Sulphur* and its progeny did not preempt de jure the body of state corporation law governing insider trading, they did so de facto. Since *Texas Gulf Sulphur,* insider trading has been regulated mainly by the federal government, principally via Rule 10b-5. Manne's contention that this development violated the rules governing the administrative process found acceptance by neither the SEC nor the courts. The

7. *Blue Chip Stamps v. Manor Drug Stores,* 421 U.S. 723, 737 (1975).

federalism issues Manne flagged in this article, however, remain just as pressing—and just as unresolved—today as they were in 1967.[8]

Manne's work met with what David Haddock aptly calls "vociferous hostility" from a number of more traditionally minded legal scholars.[9] Indeed, one might have thought Manne had insulted motherhood and apple pie. In "Insider Trading and the Law Professors," Manne replied to their arguments. Manne begins by pointing out the dearth of serious criticism of the SEC by legal academics prior to his work. As he observes, most prior legal academics held "a firm and unwavering conviction that what the SEC says is right." Today the reverse probably is true, thanks in large part to Manne's willingness to point out when the emperor had no clothes.

Turning to the merits, in "Insider Trading and the Law Professors" Manne offered his most complete defense against the various counterarguments lodged against *Insider Trading and the Stock Market.* Among the arguments Manne rebuffs in this article that one nevertheless still sees in the literature are the following:

- *Harm to investors.* Many of Manne's critics argued that an investor who trades in a security contemporaneously with insiders having access to material nonpublic information suffers in that the investor sold at the wrong price—a price that does not reflect the undisclosed information. If a firm's stock currently sells at $10 per share, but after disclosure of the new information will sell at $15, a shareholder who sells at the current price thus allegedly suffers a $5 loss. As Manne points out, however, this claim is fundamentally flawed. It is purely fortuitous that an insider was on the other side of the transaction. The gain corresponding to shareholder's "loss" is reaped not just by inside traders, but

8. See Stephen M. Bainbridge, "Insider Trading Regulation: The Path Dependent Choice between Property Rights and Securities Fraud," *Southern Methodist University Law Review* 52 (1999): 1589. Two essays are often singled out (including by Manne himself) as particularly hostile: John A. C. Hetherington, "Insider Trading and the Logic of the Law," *Wisconsin Law Review,* 1967, 720; Roy A. Schotland, "Unsafe at Any Price: A Reply to Manne, *Insider Trading and the Stock Market,*" *Virginia Law Review* 53 (1967): 1425.

9. Haddock, *Academic Hostility,* 314. Haddock offers the provocative suggestion that the hostility to Manne's policy prescriptions arose out of self-interest on the academic critics' part; after all, if adopted, his proposal would "reduce the demand for the services of legal experts, the legal academics directly, and those who are trained by the academics." Ibid., 315.

by all contemporaneous purchasers whether they had access to the undisclosed information or not.

- *Delay.* Manne's critics also claimed that, if insider trading were deregulated, it would create incentives for managers to delay the transmission of information to superiors. As Manne explains, however, given the rapidity with which securities transactions can be conducted in modern secondary trading markets, any such delay is likely to be trivial, especially since the manager often will wish to strike while the proverbial iron is hot.

- *Manipulation.* Manipulation of stock prices, as a form of fraud, harms both society and individuals by decreasing the accuracy of pricing by the market. Some of Manne's critics argued that if managers are permitted to trade on inside information they have a strong interest in keeping the stock pricing stable or in moving it in the correct direction while they are trading. Therefore, they have a strong incentive to use manipulative practices. Manne's principal response is that the costs of producing perfect compliance with a prohibition against insider trading are unacceptably high.

- *Investor confidence.* Like many modern proponents of the insider trading prohibition, Manne's critics argued that insider trading erodes investor confidence. If any investors believe that the SEC's enforcement actions have driven insider trading out of the markets, however, they require psychiatric rather than legal assistance. Nevertheless, the stock market remains robust. Manne thus concludes that insider trading does not seriously threaten the confidence of investors in the securities markets.

In addition to defending his prior arguments, Manne also makes an important positive clarification in this article: "All I am pleading for is a *rule of full disclosure.*" As Manne recognized in his analysis of the incentive effects of insider trading on corporate agents, the question of insider trading really can be seen as one about forms of compensation. Michael Dooley explained the importance of this insight on Manne's part as follows:

> Manne's principal argument was that insider trading was primarily a matter of contract between the corporation and its officers and directors. The parties might or might not agree to the use of confidential information as a form of compensation. . . . Taking its cue from state corporation law, the [SEC should] have realized that the common law has always adopted a hands-off approach with regard to the amount of explicit compensation paid to cor-

> porate executives. However, the agency has also taken a strict stance against hidden forms of implicit compensation and required divestiture of corporate opportunities, disgorgement of profits made from unauthorized use of corporate property and the like. This arrangement of rules—lenient with regard to explicit compensation and strict with regard to secret compensation—is eminently sensible. Shareholders are the best judges of the value of their executives' contributions to the corporation and are entitled to know how much they are paid. Shareholders might well, as Manne argued, be indifferent to the forms of compensation, but they would certainly be interested in the total amount of compensation paid to executives in addition to their announced salaries and bonuses.
>
> Since the SEC already had the authority to require disclosure of compensation, they had ample grounds on which to prosecute *Texas Gulf Sulphur* as a violation of the proxy rules. Subsequently, and without straining its authority, the agency might have amended the disclosure regulations under the proxy rules to require an *ex ante* announcement by the corporation as to whether insiders would be permitted to trade on inside information together with some sort of *ex post* settling up by the insiders themselves.[10]

It seems clear that Manne would have been eminently satisfied with such a result.

Manne's contribution of the insider trading entry to the *Palgrave Dictionary of Money and Finance* updated his arguments to take account of the extensive literature triggered by the publication of *Insider Trading and the Stock Market.* By this time (1992), a new generation of law and economics scholars had taken the ball and run with it, extending Manne's arguments or generating new arguments in favor of Manne's position. In this essay, Manne works their insights into the basic framework he had established back in the 1960s.

The next block of materials marks Manne's return to his role as a public intellectual. As an occasional op-ed columnist for the *Wall Street Journal,* he has written widely on current securities regulation issues. In a number of columns, reprinted here, he adapted his longstanding views of insider trading to various then-current issues of the day.

10. Michael P. Dooley, "Comment from an Enforcement Perspective," *Case Western Reserve Law Review* 50 (1999): 319, 321–22.

Manne's most recent work on insider trading, "Insider Trading: Hayek, Virtual Markets, and the Dog That Did Not Bark," is perhaps his most original contribution to the literature since the publication of *Insider Trading and the Stock Market* itself. Manne focuses on the three great issues that have animated insider trading scholarship over the last five decades: the impact of insider trading on the efficiency of the capital markets, the harm insider trading does to individual investors (if any), and the role of insider trading as a form of de facto executive compensation.

Manne's review of the recent literature leaves his mind unchanged with respect to the first two issues. As he puts it, "the idea that there is no direct harm [to investors] from the practice has held up very well," and no one has "seriously damaged the argument of the stock-pricing benefit of insider trading."

As Manne concedes, however, his argument that insider trading "could perform well as part of an executive compensation package" has been "forcefully attacked." Some commentators argued, for example, that even assuming the change in stock price accurately measures the value of the innovation, the insider's compensation is limited by the number of shares he can purchase. This, in turn, is limited by his wealth. Thus the insider's trading returns are based, not on the value of his contribution, but on his wealth.

Another objection made to the compensation argument is the difficulty of restricting trading to those who produced the information. Where information is concerned, production costs normally exceed distribution costs. Consequently, many firm agents may trade on the information without having contributed to its production.

A related objection is the difficulty of limiting trading to instances in which the insider actually produced valuable information. In particular, why should insiders be permitted to trade on bad news? Allowing managers to profit from inside trading reduces the penalties associated with a project's failure because trading managers can profit whether the project succeeds or fails. If the project fails, the manager can sell his shares before that information becomes public and thus avoid an otherwise certain loss. The manager can go beyond mere loss avoidance into actual profit making by short selling the firm's stock.

In "Hayek, Virtual Markets, and the Dog That Did Not Bark," Manne concedes that the compensation-based argument in favor of deregulating insider trading "is perhaps less robust than I and other proponents had originally assumed." Indeed, as Manne acknowledges, it is perhaps instructive that no company pre–*Texas Gulf Sulphur* had tried to use insider trading as a form of compensation. In sum, "Hayek, Virtual Markets, and the Dog That Did Not Bark" thus demonstrates Manne's willingness to remain engaged with the literature and to change his mind when presented with persuasive arguments.

Manne next reminds the reader, however, that very few companies pre–*Texas Gulf Sulphur* had voluntarily adopted proscriptions of insider trading. He therefore focuses attention on the question of why insider trading, as well as that of knowledgeable outsiders, was studiously ignored by the business and investment communities pre–*Texas Gulf Sulphur.* He argues that officers, directors, and controlling shareholders were unlikely to have remained silent in the face of widespread insider trading if they had believed the practice was harmful to their firm or to its investors. Instead, drawing on an analogy to the economic work of Friedrich Hayek, Manne argues that insider trading can help resolve the inefficiencies of information flows within large corporations by allowing the stock price to serve as a proxy for transmission of valuable information to top managers and large shareholders. In a sense, he argues, when managers trade on the basis of inside information, the stock price becomes akin to the sort of "prediction" markets widely used by corporations and policymakers in decision making.

Taken as a whole, the works in this volume, framed by Manne's groundbreaking book, *Insider Trading and the Stock Market,* will give readers not only a retrospective on Manne's forty-year-plus contributions to insider trading but also a fresh context for understanding the complex world of corporate law and securities regulation.

INSIDER TRADING AND THE STOCK MARKET

Preface

Probably no aspect of modern corporate life has been more roundly condemned than insider trading. Few people, even moderately well-informed about corporate affairs, can have failed to have heard some of this criticism. And none, it may be guessed, has heard this practice praised. The present work does, however, largely defend insider trading. And whether the reader agrees with the ultimate conclusion or not, he can hardly fail to recognize that the question is a complex and difficult one, deserving serious study rather than pat answers and off-hand solutions.

The major effort of this book is to offer an objective scheme of analysis, useful in describing and predicting the various effects of insider trading. The tone of this work is quite different from most of the previous literature. That literature, discussed in the first chapter, has been socially valuable in establishing a moral standard and a set of attitudes about corporate executives' conduct. The importance of this contribution should certainly not be ignored or belittled. Moral and ethical business standards have played a substantial role in the development of several areas of American business conduct. And one need only examine the unhappy consequences of dishonorable behavior by businessmen in certain underdeveloped economies to realize the commercial importance of a sense of responsibility and fair dealing.

But valuable as such attitudes may be, it is nonetheless imperative that we be willing to discuss various business practices objectively and disinter-

Insider Trading and the Stock Market (New York: The Free Press, 1966). Reproduced with permission of Henry G. Manne.

estedly. For no matter how useful an area or a practice may be as a vehicle for expression of moral concern, there is no substitute for the careful analysis necessary for formulating social policy. It is a fundamental weakness of most discussions of insider trading that they never push beyond a sense of moral outrage.

Our common-law courts, with their sometime genius for insight and wisdom in dealing with extremely complex issues, seem to have handled the problem of insider trading in a practical and sensible fashion. They recognized that there may be dangers to certain noninsiders attendant upon insider trading. By and large, the courts seem to have sensed these dangers and erected prophylactic barriers where possible. This legal background is discussed in Chapter 2, and a justification for the common-law rules, usually unarticulated in judicial opinions, is offered. There were, however, some problems with which these courts were not equipped to deal. Courts can act only on the parties before them in individual cases, and, as a practical matter of policing, this may be too inefficient or too costly to give the total protection needed. Thus it was generally believed that Congressional action was required to deal with certain specific forms of stock manipulation and with short-term insider trading. But at no time did Congress adopt a thoroughgoing and absolute prohibition on insider trading. Nor does such a rule exist at the date of this writing.*

* Editor's note: As of this writing (late 2006), Congress still had not legislatively defined insider trading. Instead, the definition of what constitutes illegal insider trading evolved through a series of judicial decisions, most notably three U.S. Supreme Court opinions: *Chiarella v. United States,* 445 U.S. 222 (1980); *Dirks v. SEC,* 463 U.S. 646 (1983); *United States v. O'Hagan,* 521 U.S. 642 (1997).

In the seminal *SEC v. Texas Gulf Sulphur Co.,* 401 F.2d 833 (2d Cir. 1968), *cert. denied,* 394 U.S. 976 (1969), decision to which Manne refers, the court established a policy of equality of access to information. Accordingly, virtually anyone who possessed material nonpublic information was required either to disclose it before trading or abstain from trading in the affected company's securities. If the would-be trader's fiduciary duties precluded him from disclosing the information prior to trading, abstention was the only option.

In *Chiarella* and *Dirks,* the Supreme Court rejected the equal access policy. Instead, the Court made clear that liability could be imposed only if the defendant was subject to a duty to disclose prior to trading. Inside traders thus were no longer liable merely because they had more information than other investors in the marketplace. Instead, a duty to

The last statement may surprise many readers. The implications of many recent newspaper stories in connection with the celebrated case of *Securities and Exchange Commission* v. *Texas Gulf Sulphur Co.* are that insider trading is illegal and that the purpose of that litigation is to prove whether the defendants are guilty of the practice. But that simply is not so. The real significance of the case lies in the rules that the courts *will* adopt. The question of what the Texas Gulf Sulphur officials did or do not do is of relatively little consequence compared to the fundamental legal rule against insider trading that the SEC is asking the courts to approve.

Nonetheless, new rules on insider trading have been developing at a rapid rate in the past five years. This legal development has not, however, been accompanied by parallel advances in the theory or analysis of this trading. A surprisingly large number of significant questions have hitherto gone unnoticed or untreated. For example, some of the issues or phenomena now

---

disclose arose only where the inside traders breached a preexisting fiduciary duty owed to the person with whom they traded.

The SEC believed that the *Chiarella/Dirks* framework failed to adequately police insider trading, especially in connection with takeovers. If an agent of a prospective takeover bidder traded in the stock of the prospective target, for example, there would be no liability under *Chiarella* and *Dirks*, because that person owed no duties to those with whom he or she traded. Accordingly, the SEC developed the so-called misappropriation theory to address such cases.

As with the traditional disclose or abstain rule, under the misappropriation theory trading on inside information becomes unlawful only in conjunction with a breach of fiduciary duty. It is not unlawful, for example, for an outsider to trade on the basis of inadvertently overheard information (*SEC v. Switzer*, 590 F. Supp. 756, 766 [W.D. Okla. 1984]). The fiduciary relationship in question, however, is a quite different one. Under the misappropriation theory, the defendant need not owe a fiduciary duty to the investor with whom he trades. Nor does he have to owe a fiduciary duty to the issuer of the securities that were traded. Instead, the misappropriation theory applies when the inside trader violates a fiduciary duty owed to the source of the information.

In *O'Hagan*, the Supreme Court validated the misappropriation theory as being designed "to 'protect the integrity of the securities markets against abuses by "outsiders" to a corporation who have access to confidential information that will affect the corporation's security price when revealed, but who owe no fiduciary or other duty to that corporation's shareholders.'"

Although Congress has never expressly adopted these standards, a number of statutes adopted in recent decades dealing with the penalties for insider trading implicitly endorse the judicial definition worked out in these cases.—S.B.

discussed for the first time include: the various techniques for insider trading other than the direct and immediate use of information in the stock market; the extent to which these practices actually occur in America; the actual effect of insider trading on stock market price movements; how barring or allowing insider trading would affect specific classes of individuals trading in the stock market, specifically short-term traders and long-term investors; whether the rewards of insider trading flow to the individuals who in some sense are responsible for producing the news; the distinctive features of inside information as a possible form of compensation for innovational activities in large corporations; the feasibility of preventing insider trading and the costs involved; and, finally, the possibilities and propriety of insider trading by government officials.

This book is offered primarily as a theoretical treatment of this fascinating subject. The reader will notice at many points a caveat to the effect that data on a particular point are needed but presently unavailable. Perhaps it is not the least contribution of this work that these areas are specified and analyzed. This is not to suggest, however, that empirical research is the only acceptable mode of proof in this area. Hopefully, the reader will find the conclusions convincing even though many are based on hypothesis. In this sense, however, these conclusions are tentative, and when all the data have been gathered, many of them may have to be modified.

Certainly the time has arrived for the Securities and Exchange Commission to establish a research office with responsibility for investigating issues like the ones raised in this book. Such agencies as the SEC were created and originally defended on the supposition that the regulation would be done by experts, knowledgeable and sophisticated about the area in their charge. But this expertise has frequently been notably absent. It is interesting to observe that the current position of the SEC, in the area of insider trading, is that the courts, with the aid of the Commission as a party litigant, are best equipped to guide this legal development. Thus no guidelines on insider trading have been issued by the SEC. The courts, in turn, show signs of assuming the SEC's expertise from their role in the litigation. Thus, while professing its faith in a common-law development of this area, the SEC substantially influences the direction of that change.

This book should furnish the Commission with an outline or guide for the conduct of the research it should be doing in this area. Hopefully, this research work will be begun before definitive and possibly damaging judicial holdings appear.

A word would seem to be in order about what may be the most common form of criticism of this book. From previous encounters it has appeared that thoughtful critics are largely concerned with the possibility that insider trading will put corporate managers in a conflict of interest position with shareholders. Undoubtedly, one can find specific instances of fraud, deceit, and manipulation that could be prevented by an effective rule against insider trading. But the important question that must be considered is whether the outlawing of all insider trading is the most appropriate sanction for this undesirable conduct. The answer seems to be in the negative, since traditional modes of administrative and criminal law enforcement are probably more appropriate and may be more efficient for dealing with these problems. At any rate, the burden of proof should rest on those who believe that drastic treatment is required. The time has come for the opponents of insider trading to justify their position with more than a few isolated scare stories.

My greatest debt for this work is to my students in seminars and classes in corporation law at The George Washington University, where I first began work on this subject. They have been at once my most ardent supporters and most severe critics. Several of these former students performed well as research assistants; and I should like especially to acknowledge the excellent help I received from Stuart M. Fischbein, Donn K. Jenkins, Steven A. Karsch, Timothy G. Greene, Morton H. Press, Matthew Rosen, and Radcliffe Welles. I also received extremely valuable suggestions, ideas, and criticisms from Armen A. Alchian, Joseph Aschheim, Joseph Bishop, Vartkes L. Broussalian, Eugene V. Rostow, and J. Fred Weston. Needless to say, none of the named individuals bears any responsibility for errors or weaknesses in this work. Mrs. Ella Louise Belk was my secretarial mainstay and a delight to work with. Parts of this book were earlier submitted to the Yale Law School in partial fulfillment of the requirements for the Degree of Doctor of the Science of Law.

I might add that the appearance of this book at a time when the Texas Gulf Sulphur litigation is much in the news is entirely coincidental. Early drafts of this work were completed, in substantially their present form, long before that action was brought. The book is entirely my own independent work and I have no connection, financial, legal, or otherwise, with Texas Gulf Sulphur or any of the litigants in that case or any other case dealing with insider trading.

Henry G. Manne

Washington, D.C.
March 1966

1 Background

Prior to the year 1910 no one had ever publicly questioned the morality of corporate officers, directors, and employees trading in the shares of corporations. There are several reasons why attitudes began to change early in the twentieth century. Part of the reason was simply a time lag between the dramatic, almost revolutionary development of the large publicly held corporation in the last quarter of the nineteenth century and the recognition of all the problems created by this institution. The functional relationship of shareholders in the corporation to each other had changed dramatically. No longer was it possible for each shareholder to demand in a personal and imperative way that his business associates deal with him fairly. In small enterprises social and psychological forces operate to maintain desirable interpersonal relationships, and individual policing is relatively easy and inexpensive. But these factors were missing in the large corporation with publicly traded shares. An open market for shares, with its greater assurance of liquidity for apprehensive shareholders, was the functional substitute for the older approach. Being less well understood than familiar forms, the open market has never been fully trusted, even by lawyers whose special province has always been the resolution of interpersonal conflicts.

The popular concept of morality in business in the late nineteenth century was very different from that of today. One need only read the classic descriptive works[1] to understand the change. Today an announcement that insiders are dealing in their company's shares is sufficient to cause an almost

1. The work which best conveys the ethos of the earlier epoch is Henry Clews, *Twenty-Eight Years in Wall Street* (New York: Irving Publishing Co., 1888).

audible gasp of public indignation. And yet in a survey by the *New York Times* in 1915,[2] 90 per cent of business executives interviewed admitted to trading regularly in their own company's shares. Today a comparable survey might find a few individuals admitting these transactions, but in all probability the percentage would be near zero.[3]

Law and Economics

From the beginning the subject of insider trading has been almost exclusively the province of lawyers and law professors. There is a rich economic literature that may be drawn on for understanding the problems, but economists, almost to the man, have remained silent on this specific question. In recent years, however, the legal literature has developed apace—in quantity, if not in quality. This fact has had a noticeable influence on developments in the whole area. The fundamental approach of lawyers to issues such as this one is quite different from that of economists. The lawyers' approach to most questions reflects the centuries-old tradition of viewing problems in the context of a case or lawsuit, the arena for settling disputes between two live human beings. Indeed, much of the common law (which is most of American law prior to the twentieth century) is the formalization of rules governing individuals in their personal relationships. Perhaps the only important exceptions to this statement in the common law are the archaic rules of real property and the uniquely developed commercial law.

Thus when lawyers, judges, and law professors are faced with issues of broad social or economic consequences, their tendency is to approach the

2. *New York Times Annalist,* 6 (1915), p. 65.

3. In a survey reported by Raymond C. Baumhart, S.J., "How Ethical Are Businessmen?" *Harvard Business Review* (July–August, 1961), p. 16, 42% of businessmen said they would buy shares in a company about to be acquired by their company under conditions indicating that the price would increase on announcement of the merger; 61% thought that other businessmen would buy under similar circumstances. At the time of this poll most businessmen would probably have believed such a practice to be legal because neither Section 16(b) of the Securities Exchange Act of 1934 nor Rule 10b-5 of the SEC would seem to have been applicable. Many refinements would be needed to make the cited poll meaningful. If businessmen were asked today, "Do you trade regularly on inside information about your company?", the percentage answering affirmatively would undoubtedly be very small.

subject with relationships between specific individuals in mind. Their acceptance or rejection of a practice will reflect their notion of the fairness of the transaction simply from the point of view of the two individuals involved. It is not difficult to see why lawyers have generally concluded that there is something unfair (primarily in the sense of "unequal") about insiders with undisclosed good news buying shares from existing shareholders

Economists think with a different tradition behind them. Theirs is perhaps the most scientific of the social sciences. Here the word *scientific* must connote objectivity and moral detachment, as well as systematic verification of results. Economists tend to view any controversy as reflecting a platonic, ideal conflict. The question for an economist is rarely one of the mutual fairness of a transaction between individual parties. He is not a specialist in matters of individual morality. *Fairness* ordinarily connotes to economists the propriety of allocation of resources or income among large, distinguishable bodies or groups of individuals. To the economist individuals are a fungible commodity, each substitutable for another. The economist, viewing the issue of insider trading, will ask how all shareholders are affected financially by the practice, whether it results in a desirable allocation of resources, and whether the return to insiders reflects a competitive or a monopoly gain.

Until fairly recent years, economic theory did not offer the necessary tools for dealing with this topic. Indeed only one major work has specifically dealt with information as a commodity.[4] Yet no market analysis of valuable information is possible without isolating it in this way. The absence of any accepted economic tools for analyzing this subject made the insider-trading area a fertile one for the lawyers' equity approach with its overtones of fairness and morality. Indeed, it is one of the greatest virtues of our legal system

4. Perhaps the major breakthrough in developing an economic theory of information was made by Anthony Downs, *An Economic Theory of Democracy* (New York: Harper & Bros., 1957). See also James M. Buchanan and Gordon Tullock, *The Calculus of Consent* (Ann Arbor: University of Michigan Press, 1962). As far as the author is aware, however, the theory developed in Chapters 4–7 of this book is the first attempt to construct a systematic model for the most active market for valuable information, that is, the stock market. The works of Becker, Machlup, and Van Den Haag on the economics of education and knowledge are not directly relevant. Education bears a relationship to information analogous to that of transportation or storage to tangible commodities.

that it performs this function when scientific explanation is lacking. But, as we develop greater understanding of underlying phenomena, the equity approach may become less appropriate for the solution to new legal issues.

The theory of the entrepreneur, the second major area of economic analysis that may be drawn on in analyzing insider trading, is perhaps more familiar to economists than is information theory. Here a rich economic literature exists, the pioneering work on which is largely associated with the names of Joseph Schumpeter and Frank Knight. Indeed, the present work is in large part an application of the theories of these two economists to the modern question of insider trading. As Schumpeter suggested, innovation is simply a new combination of existing factors.

Early Analysis of Insider Trading

The arguments against insider trading, interestingly enough, are not very old. Professor A. A. Berle, in an important statement on the subject in 1927,[5] gives the honor of being first in line to Professor H. L. Wilgus for his 1910 article[6] collecting the existing cases and commenting on the then fresh U.S. Supreme Court decision in *Strong* v. *Repide.*[7] Wilgus discussed the minority of cases that concluded that certain types of insider trading should not be allowed, but these cases, as was pointed out in a later article,[8] could probably have been decided on the basis of common-law fraud or deceit.

After reviewing the case holdings, Wilgus concluded that for a director to "take advantage of his position to secure the profits that all have won, offends the moral sense; no shareholder expects to be so treated by the director he selects; no director would urge his friends to select him for that reason; that the law yet allows him to do this, does more to discourage le-

5. Adolf A. Berle, Jr., "Publicity of Accounts and Directors' Purchases of Stock," *Michigan Law Review,* 25 (1927), p. 827.

6. H. L. Wilgus, "Purchase of Shares of Corporation by a Director from a Shareholder," *Michigan Law Review,* 8 (1910), p. 267.

7. 213 U.S. 419 (1909).

8. Roberts Walker, "The Duty of Disclosure by a Director Purchasing Stock from His Stockholders," *Yale Law Journal,* 32 (1923), p. 637. For some indication that this is still largely true, see Michael Conant, "Duties of Disclosure of Corporate Insiders Who Purchase Shares," *Cornell Law Quarterly,* 46 (1961), p. 53.

gitimate investment in corporate shares than almost anything else, and allows the fiction of corporate entity to obstruct instead of advance justice."[9] This quote constitutes almost the full extent of analysis in Professor Wilgus' article, which Berle seventeen years later said was the "most effectively expounded" statement of the position.[10] Wilgus did at least suggest the necessity of some argument beyond "offense to the moral sense." But, like most other arguments in this field, Professor Wilgus' were largely statements of conclusions. He offers no evidence, logical or empirical, to back them up.[11] His allegations are important, however, and they will be dealt with in this book. Special attention will be given in Chapter 7 to the charge that legitimate investment is discouraged by allowing insider trading.

To Berle, the "ablest exponent" of the opposing position was Robert Walker in 1923.[12] Again, however, the quality of the analysis is disappointing. Walker's principal argument was that the weight of precedent was on his side. Further, to oppose the moral position of his opponents, Walker criticized the courts for "leaving the safe human ground of fraud or deceit" and "establishing an abstract obligation, a commandment or ethical principle."[13] Walker offered some concrete arguments as well. For instance, he suggested that the rule proposed by Wilgus would catch those directors who were buying shares merely for investment and not speculating on inside

9. Wilgus, "Purchase of Shares," p. 297.

10. Berle, "Publicity of Accounts," p. 828.

11. An even less convincing example may be found in Clarence D. Laylin, "The Duty of a Director Purchasing Shares of Stock," *Yale Law Journal*, 27 (1918), p. 731. Professor Laylin argued that, because shareholders ultimately receive dividends and directors declare dividends, the directors therefore owe a fiduciary duty to shareholders, and a fiduciary relationship precludes their buying shares without disclosing their inside information. The difficulty with Professor Laylin's syllogism is that his conclusions do not follow from his premises. He has suggested a very narrow application of the fiduciary-duty doctrine in the context of dividend distributions. Indeed, such cases can be found. But by no stretch of the imagination can it be said that there is *therefore* a broader fiduciary duty covering all aspects of the relationship between insiders and shareholders. This kind of reasoning, involving the fallacy of the undistributed middle, while it may serve certain purposes for common-law courts, should be carefully avoided in complex social or economic questions. It should be noted, in passing, that this approach precludes any protection for non-shareholders buying from corporate insiders.

12. Walker, "Duty of Disclosure," p. 637.

13. *Ibid.*, p. 639.

information. And Wilgus, charged Walker, overlooked the fact that many outside stockholders were as smart as or smarter than the insiders with whom they dealt. These arguments seem disingenuous at best, but Walker did not really seem too concerned about the whole affair. He believed that most of the judicial sympathy with the minority rule he opposed occurred in states that were not financially important and that chartered few or no publicly held corporations. His argument was primarily directed against a broad fiduciary rule applicable in all cases of insider trading, including trading in listed securities. He approved a somewhat liberal application of the common-law fraud rule, and by implication he anticipated the modern notion of a fiduciary duty among shareholders in closely held corporations.[14]

Berle's Position

By 1927 Professor Berle indicated the desirability of converging two proposals then being made in the literature about corporations. One of these was the fiduciary concept proposed by Wilgus. The other was the concept of publicity of corporate financial accounts, generally associated with the name of Berle's mentor, William Z. Ripley,[15] and with that of Louis D. Brandeis.[16] Berle saw this convergence as the most appropriate answer to Walker's contention that a fiduciary relationship made no sense in anonymous transactions over a stock exchange. Now, Berle pointed out, the mechanical problems were solved. Regular disclosure about corporate affairs should be made before the insiders begin their trading.[17] In this way, problems of policing insiders would be minimized, while other market traders get the full value of the corporate information.

It is well-known history that the Ripley-Brandeis-Berle proposals for

14. See *Helms* v. *Duckworth,* 249 Fed. 2d 482 (D.C.C.A., 1957). The doctrine is by no means well-established, although several forces are presently converging for the development of such a rule. See Henry G. Manne's review of F. Hodge O'Neal and Jordan Derwin's "Expulsion or Oppression of Business Associates: Squeeze-Outs in Small Enterprises" in the *St. Louis University Law Journal,* 6 (1961), p. 567.

15. William Z. Ripley, *Main Street and Wall Street* (Boston: Little, Brown & Co., 1927).

16. Louis D. Brandeis, *Other People's Money* (Washington, D.C.: National Home Library Foundation, 1933).

17. Berle, "Publicity of Accounts," p. 827.

publicity of corporate accounts became an important feature of the Securities Exchange Act of 1934.[18] Berle was not explicit on how he would treat the use of special information, not a part of regularly published corporate accounts, that might provide the basis for corporate insiders' trading in listed securities. The implications are quite clear, however, that he sided with Professor Wilgus on this point, and Berle also attempted to justify his position.

> With neither power nor information, the stockholder becomes merely the beneficiary—*cestui*—of the corporate management. Deprive him of any right by way of fiduciary relation, and the business of investing in stocks becomes too hazardous to continue. More specifically, a corporate management which, as individuals, chooses to enter the open market and which at the same time exercises control over the release of information concerning corporate affairs, can deal with the current value of its securities, if not at pleasure, at least with tremendous effect; and the liquid value of the corporate securities held by the stockholder becomes a matter which the corporate management itself can determine.[19]

The assumption in the first sentence of this passage—that shareholders have *no* information—can never be wholly true. Shareholders certainly know how large a dividend they are receiving, and, at least in the case of listed securities, they can know the current and past market value of their own and others' securities.[20] If indeed they had no information, their status as *cestuis que trust* might be complete, but complete ignorance does not follow from the failure of an insider to disclose particular pieces of information on which he bases his trading. Furthermore, by suggesting the total dependence of shareholders on the insiders' information, Berle implies quite unfairly that shareholders are motivated solely by trading profits and not by long-term capital gains or dividends.[21]

18. We still do not have a detailed history of the provisions of the 1934 Act. Ralph F. De Bedts, *The New Deal's SEC* (New York and London: Columbia University Press, 1964) gives the broad outlines, but a full intellectual and political history remains to be written.

19. Berle, "Publicity of Accounts," pp. 830–31.

20. See Henry G. Manne, "Some Theoretical Aspects of Share Voting," *Columbia Law Review*, 64 (1964), pp. 1434–44.

21. In his 1927 article in the *Michigan Law Review* ("Publicity of Accounts"), Berle cited Ripley's *Main Street and Wall Street* as supporting his idea that insider trading should be

Berle's second quoted sentence, suggesting that trading is "too hazardous to continue" without a fiduciary duty, can mean one of two things. It can mean that the risks of such trading are so great to outside shareholders that they will leave the market—a result that we do not want. But this cannot be completely true, or the shareholders whom Berle was seeking to protect would not be in existence at the time he wrote. That is, if the risk was in fact too hazardous for some individuals to assume consciously (and no one suggests that the shareholders of the period were unaware that insiders were allowed to trade freely), presumably those individuals were not shareholders. But shareholders were willing to assume these risks, consciously and in large numbers. Since they were there, "too hazardous to continue" cannot refer to the existence of outside shareholders in the market.

Alternatively, the statement might refer to particular individuals who stay out of the market because they feel that insider trading increases their risk of loss. The problem then would lie in the decrease in market liquidity resulting from the smaller number of individual traders. But Berle has no evidence to substantiate this proposition. In the first place, it is possible that insiders who are trading add more liquidity than they frighten away. More important, however, the argument assumes that insider trading actually increases the risk of loss to outside shareholders. As we shall see in Chapter 7, it is doubtful that this is generally true. Furthermore, to the extent that insider trading does in certain instances injure some particular individuals, unidentifiable in advance, financial advantages flowing to all shareholders more than compensate for this loss.

It is possible that behind Berle's thinking was the "bumpkin" theory of outside shareholders. That is, these people should be treated somewhat as wards in chancery or profligates who would waste their valuable assets while

---

forbidden. A careful reading of Ripley's book (p. 205), however, discloses that his strongest reason for favoring full disclosure is his belief that companies that hide information have more speculative securities than those which do not. As we shall see in Chapter 6, this is a very questionable proposition. Even if it were completely true, it is not a strong argument. We are not told what "speculative securities" are, nor why they are bad. Furthermore, Ripley implied a causal connection between insider trading and rapid share-price fluctuations, with no attempt to substantiate this implication.

their needy families starve and languish at home. No one, it must be acknowledged, has explicitly made this argument.

In the last part of his argument, Berle may have been implying some relationship between insider trading and the danger of manipulation of corporate affairs. Certainly this relationship was frequently alluded to in the congressional hearings[22] on the Securities Exchange Act of 1934. But again this causal relationship should not be assumed. As we shall see in the discussion in Chapter 10, only very rarely is there any reason to believe that insider traders have an incentive to manage corporate affairs contrary to the interests of all shareholders.

The 1933–1934 Congressional Hearings

To the politically uninitiated it might seem that there exists one treasure trove of analysis of insider trading. For weeks and months during 1933 and 1934, in some of the most spectacular legislative hearings ever held in Washington, the greats of the financial, industrial, and commercial communities were put through searing examinations of their practices. In the Senate hearings many important and famous men willingly or grudgingly conceded that they traded in the stock market with inside information. The Senate Committee on Banking and Currency and its chief counsel, Ferdinand Pecora, waxed indignant. But one looks in vain for an analysis as to why this trading was deemed evil. No one could deny that prior to 1933 insider trading, both in promotional stocks and existing issues, occurred regularly. But the bankers and executives involved were not the proper witnesses to make a logical case for a strong rule against insider trading. The witnesses should have been Berle, Brandeis, and others who maintained the undesirability of the practice.

For one brief moment during the course of the 1933 Senate hearings, one such witness testified on insider trading. Thomas G. Corcoran, one of the draftsmen of the bill under consideration, stated in reference to the present Section 16(b) of the Securities Exchange Act:

22. *Stock Exchange Practices, Hearings Before the Committee on Banking and Currency*, U.S. Senate, 73d Cong., 1st Sess., 1933 (10 volumes).

> That [Section 16(b)] is to prevent directors receiving the benefits of short-term speculative swings on the securities of their own companies, because of inside information. The profit of such transaction under the bill would go to the corporation. You hold the director, irrespective of any intention or expectation to sell the security within six months after, because it will be absolutely impossible to prove the existence of such intention or expectation, and you have to have this crude rule of thumb, because you cannot undertake the burden of having to prove that the director intended, at the time he bought, to get out on a short swing.[23]

Corcoran noted a few moments later that the New York Stock Exchange was aware of "these evils, and despairing of effective prosecutions under the laws of all States . . . have [*sic*] urged that this situation be cured by the passage of a Federal law governing the incorporation of companies."[24] As Corcoran characterized it, the objection of the stock exchange to "these provisions is that they put a heavier burden on listed companies, because the directors of such companies cannot cheat their stockholders, than it does on unlisted companies, which will still be in the position where the directors can cheat their stockholders."

Senator Thomas Gore of Oklahoma asked Corcoran if the Section was "aimed at the general evil of officers and directors rigging their stock up and down, and squeezing out their own stockholders."[25] Corcoran replied that it was, and that was the end of the discussion of what was wrong with insider trading. Even so, Senator Gore's implication that Section 16(b) was designed to prevent fraud and manipulation has not been accepted by courts or commentators, and other Sections of the Act were explicitly stated to be for that purpose.[26]

23. *Ibid.*, p. 6557.
24. *Ibid.*, p. 6559.
25. *Ibid.*
26. U.S. Senate Report No. 1455, 73d Cong., 2d Sess., 1934. Cf. Sections 9 and 10 of the 1934 Act. Section 16(b) begins with the words "for the purpose of preventing the unfair use of information which may have been obtained by such beneficial owner, director, or officer by reason of his relationship to the issuer. . . ." These introductory words are peculiar and it has been argued that these words are *limiting*, requiring some proof that the use of the information by an insider is in fact unfair. This contention was denied in *Smolowe* v. *Delendo Corp.*, 136 Fed. 2d 231, 236 (2d Cir., 1943), *cert. denied*, 320 U.S. 751. The denial is extensive and commonly accepted today as correct. The introductory words were

The 1934 Report of the Senate committee stated:

> Among the most vicious practices unearthed at the hearings before the subcommittee was the flagrant betrayal of their fiduciary duties by directors and officers of corporations who used their positions of trust and confidential information which came to them in such positions, to aid them in their market activities. Closely allied to this type of abuse was the unscrupulous employment of inside information by large stockholders who, while not directors and officers, exercised sufficient control over the destinies of their companies to enable them to acquire and profit by information not available to others.[27]

The House Report was simply more of the same: "Men charged with the administration of others' money must not use inside information for their own advantage."[28] Why not? We are never told. To call insider trading a breach of a fiduciary duty was simply conclusionary, as there was no law prior to 1934 generally considering it to be such. And to say that the practice was vicious or unscrupulous was also not a reasoned answer. Worse than that, the emotional tone of the arguments probably intimidated anyone who tried to defend the practice or even make cogent inquiries.

Recent Discussions

The low quality of analysis found in the 1933–1934 hearings and reports has characterized subsequent investigations into the subject as well. In 1963 the Special Study of Securities Markets of the SEC begged the same questions as did the earlier efforts.[29] After stating that the keystone of the entire structure of federal securities legislation was disclosure and pointing out that Section 16 was consistent with this disclosure philosophy, the Study forthwith recommended the extension of this Section to securities not previously

---

said to aid constitutionality and guide the SEC in its rule-making, but did not require a showing of unfairness or damage in every case otherwise covered by Section 16(b). See Louis Loss, *Securities Regulation* (Boston and Toronto: Little, Brown and Co., 1961), p. 1041.

27. *Ibid.*

28. H.R. Report No. 1383, 73d Cong., 2d Sess., 1934, p. 13.

29. *Report of Special Study of Securities Markets of the Securities and Exchange Commission,* House Doc. No. 95, Part 3, 88th Cong., 1st Sess., 1963.

covered. This approach was fundamentally that of the New York Stock Exchange in 1933, that is, that the only thing wrong with rules against insider trading is that they did not cover unlisted as well as listed stocks. This time Congress obliged.[30]

At one point the Special Study was almost led into some analysis of insider trading. While considering the question of broker-dealers who sit on corporate boards of directors, the Study noted the complexities faced when information gained from this position was used either personally or for customers to whom a fiduciary obligation was owed.[31] But that problem, complex as the Special Study said it was, was not carefully analyzed or, for that matter, really faced at all. With an almost audible sigh of relief that such an alternative was available, the Special Study concluded that this was "the kind of area in which the self-regulatory agencies, with support from governmental agencies where violations of legal duties are involved, can be instrumental in defining and effectuating higher ethical standards."[32] The matter then was left up to the SEC by the Special Study.

Actually since the early attempts to deal with the subject of corporate insider trading, the matter has generally been assumed to be closed. In 1961, Professor Louis Loss could state that the "purpose of §16(b)—prevention of the unfair use of information by corporate insiders—does not, of course, admit of dispute."[33] And a young SEC lawyer, writing in a law review in 1964, stated that "the policy in favor of providing public investors with all available information that might be material to their investment decisions—a policy too obvious to require further elaboration—far outweighs any policy in favor of allowing corporate insiders to trade freely, *on the basis of inside information*, in the securities of their corporations—a policy for which it is difficult to conceive of any justification."[34]

30. *Securities Acts Amendments of 1964*, 78 Stat. 565 (1964).

31. *Report of Special Study of Securities Markets of the Securities and Exchange Commission*, Part 1, pp. 438–39.

32. *Ibid.*, p. 440. "Self-regulatory agencies" would include the registered stock exchanges and the National Association of Securities Dealers.

33. Loss, *Securities Regulation*, p. 1088. The arguments against Section 16(b), even by representatives of the securities industry, are, according to Loss, directed against the method by which 16(b) seeks to achieve its purpose, not the purpose itself.

34. Michael Joseph, "Civil Liability Under Rule 10b-5—A Reply," *Northwestern University Law Review*, 59 (1964), p. 183.

Cary's Position

Other statements to similar effect, though far more influential, have come from Professor William Cary, who was Chairman of the SEC from 1961 to 1965.[35] On no less than four different occasions during his tenure as chairman, Professor Cary concluded that full disclosure is so important that insiders who could not disclose material facts about corporate affairs should forego any transaction in the stock at that time, for whatever reason the transaction might be entered into. In his opinion, *In the Matter of Cady, Roberts & Co.*, Cary states: "So many times that citation is unnecessary, we have indicated that the purchase and sale of securities is a field in special need of regulation for the protection of investors."[36] Cary further states that the SEC "antifraud provisions[37] are not intended as a specification of particular acts or practices which constitute fraud, but rather are designed to encompass the infinite variety of devices by which *undue advantage* [italics mine] may be taken of investors and others."[38]

Apparently among the infinite variety of devices by which undue advantage may be taken of investors is the use of valuable information in insider trading. Although in this opinion Cary did not state why insider trading was unfair, on other occasions he has attempted to explain why he felt it was an evil.

> A manager should receive corporate information not for his own personal emolument, but to assist the corporation in its operations. The use of inside

35. *In the Matter of Cady, Roberts & Co.*, SEC Release No. 6668, *CCH Federal Securities Law Reporter* (1961), p. 81018; "Corporate Standards and Legal Rules," *California Law Review*, 50 (1962), p. 415; "The Direction of Management Responsibility," *The Business Lawyer*, 18 (1962), p. 32; "Recent Developments in Securities Regulation," *Columbia Law Review*, 63 (1963), p. 864. All of these are cited in David S. Ruder, "Pitfalls in the Development of a Federal Law of Corporations by Implications Through Rule 10b-5," *Northwestern University Law Review*, 59 (1964), p. 210.

36. *CCH Federal Securities Law Reporter* (1961), p. 81015.

37. There is a subtle borrowing from the general acceptability of common-law fraud rules in this choice of terms. None of the rather strict logic underlying the elements of common-law fraud can be found in the Commission's, or indeed many courts', interpretation of Rule 10b-5. Cf. William Prosser, *Handbook of the Law of Torts*, 3d ed. (St. Paul: West Publishing Co., 1964), p. 700.

38. *CCH Federal Securities Law Reporter* (1961), p. 81016.

> information by a director or other manager to trade in shares is the securing of additional compensation in a covert fashion, and should be condemned. (It further, of course, infects the integrity of the market.)[39]

Close analysis of this statement is certainly required. Cary implies that managers have contracted for a specific compensation and that they have no claim on anything else of value from the corporation.[40] If there were in fact some prohibition in the employment contract, or in existing law, against all forms of insider trading, then indeed it would be fair to make this statement as quoted. But this statement was not a correct description of the law on the subject, nor was it offered as such. It was offered as a logical argument for a change in the existing rules.

The phrase "securing of additional compensation" implies that the insider is recovering more than he has contracted for. But this is a question of his employment-contract terms—express, implied, or omitted—and what the law on insider trading was at the time he entered into his employment contract. If there are no prohibitions other than Section 16(b) of the 1934 Act and some liberalized fraud concepts operating, then there can be no implied provision prohibiting the insider from trading in his employer's shares when he possesses "inside information." If there is no provision, expressed or implied, in the contract forbidding this share trading, it cannot be said to be proscribed by the contract. And it cannot be assumed that silence on such a topic implies proscription. Strong reasons should be advanced for so restricting insiders by implication. Cary's statement displays conviction but not proof.

As a further mark of Cary's strong feelings on this subject, we should notice that insider trading (that is, trading with information not publicly disclosed) allows covert compensation and "infects the integrity of the market." Trading with inside information does appear to be covert; we shall see

39. *California Law Review,* 50 (1962), p. 415.

40. Cary himself has cited contradictory evidence when he noted that 42% of businessmen interviewed in the *Harvard Business Review* poll (cited in footnote 3) said they would buy shares of a company being merged into theirs before public disclosure; 61% thought others would buy. Cary said this was a "surprising, and perhaps shocking, number of executives [who] feel that it is perfectly reasonable conduct to use inside information for their personal benefit." *The Business Lawyer,* 18 (1962), p. 33.

that as a practical matter this must be so. But this is a long way from suggesting that shareholders are unaware that corporate insiders trade in the securities market. That proposition, if true, would certainly be the most frightening thing yet discovered about public participation in the stock market. Finally, we are told neither what the "integrity of the market" is nor how insider trading infects it.

Cary was obviously troubled by his own strong insistence that insider trading was wrong. In another place he does attempt to justify his position. He states:

> I should like to suggest reasons for compelling disclosure on a broad basis. First, should not any corporation in whose shares there is a public interest, be required to disclose all material information? Secondly, corporate managements themselves seem to suggest that the modern corporation has a duty to disclose everything to almost everybody. Quite frequently we read the following in a company annual report:
>
> > In addition, [a corporation] has civic responsibilities to the various communities where its affiliates operate, financial responsibilities to the educational institutions from which it draws many of its key employees, and—under many categories—responsibilities to governments.
>
> If the company really believes, and says, it has a responsibility to these numerous groups, must it not at least account to these groups by full disclosure?
>
> Finally, another reason for disclosure is the continuing and increasing relationships of many corporations with the government (both federal and local). They are frequently dependent on government contracts, financing, etc. Does not this tend to give these corporations a special character? I would suggest that these government contacts impose on management most serious responsibilities. These contacts with the agencies of the public are perhaps a strong reason for disclosure to the public. They further suggest the need for management voluntarily to pursue higher standards or be confronted with a Congressional investigation and subsequent demand to do so.[41]

Apart from the obvious *non sequitur* in the third paragraph and the rather threatening tone of the last, the argument for disclosure still seems to miss a crucial point about insider trading. Cary confuses two different

41. *Ibid.*, p. 34.

concepts of disclosure in the quoted passage. One is the actual announcement of various activities, as required by law. The other, with which we are immediately concerned, is disclosure of information *before it is traded upon by insiders.* Ultimately, most information used by insiders is disclosed; otherwise the insiders may make no profit from it. But the question of insider trading requires concern only with the *timing* of a disclosure, not its ultimate occurrence. And the proper time for any disclosure will vary with the purpose for which it is being made. Since these purposes, some of which are listed by Cary, show great variety, it is illogical to conclude that one disclosure time is appropriate for all. Further, the mere fact that disclosure is required for one specific purpose tells us nothing about whether it should be made at another time for a different purpose.

Conclusion

This exercise could be continued indefinitely. Over and over one finds statements that insider trading without disclosure is indefensible and unfair, that shareholders are being duped or defrauded, that undue advantage is taken of them, and that they are being subjected to unfair risk. We are told that business ethics must be improved, that shareholders do not expect their managers to trade before disclosure, and that it is a violation of their fiduciary duty to trade in this fashion.

All of these can be lumped under the general heading of "it's just not right" propositions,[42] and, if repetition were a form of scientific proof, undoubtedly the case against insider trading would long ago have been proved. Unfortunately, however, these disputations have merely served to conceal the fact that in the literature on insider trading almost no careful analysis of the subject exists.[43] This is not to say that moral standards do not play

42. This expression originated with an anonymous lady law student, who, during a classroom discussion of the subject, stamped her foot and angrily declaimed, "I don't care; it's just not right."

43. There are two exceptions to the rather bleak picture generally presented by the legal literature on insider trading. The first of these is Victor Brudney, "Insider Securities Dealings During Corporate Crises," *Michigan Law Review,* 61 (1962), p. 1. This is a thoughtful and analytical survey of many of the policy issues involved in the question of insider

an important role in the business community. Indeed, unless there is broad-based agreement on various standards of ethical conduct, free markets do not seem to function very effectively. But no amount of moral exhortation can substitute for the rigorous analysis necessary to understand the problem of insider trading. If we can understand the institutions, practices, and consequences of insider trading, we may then make more appropriate moral judgments.

---

trading. Professor Brudney's strongest objections seem to be (1) the possibility of manipulation by insiders to maximize their trading profits and (2) the inappropriateness of inside information as a form of compensation. Each of these objections is discussed in Chapter 10.

The author of the second work is both an economist and a lawyer, and it is not surprising that his conclusions differ somewhat from those of Berle or Cary. Professor Michael Conant has argued in "Duties of Disclosure of Corporate Insiders Who Purchase Shares," *Cornell Law Quarterly,* 46 (1960), p. 53, that the value of this information belongs as a matter of traditional fiduciary-duty law to the corporation and not to the individual outside shareholder. Thus, he would extend the policy of Section 16(b) of the Securities Exchange Act to cover all insider transactions, and the corporation would be entitled to recover the insider's profits. The law, however, does not bear out Professor Conant's position, and the one case he cites for it, the *Brophy* case, discussed in Chapter 3, can easily be explained on other grounds.

But by far the most interesting aspect of Professor Conant's article is his statement (p. 57) of why we should *not* allow outsiders to recover profits from insiders with whom they have dealt:

> In the free market, the less informed party to the sale of a tangible item may inspect and ask questions. If the item sold is an intangible, he may ask questions. If he does not bother to inspect or ask questions, he has assumed the uncertainty that the other party may bargain with superior information. The corporate stockholder selling his shares to an officer or director is in such a position. The insider is likely to have more information about the corporation's prospects than the ordinary shareholder. The shareholder is free to ask the insider for a summary of facts on which he bases his purchase. In this case, the law of fraud requires a complete answer by the insider, for speaking a half-truth under the circumstances would be equivalent to misrepresentation. If the shareholder does not bother to ask questions, he assumes the uncertainty that the insider may deal with superior knowledge.

2 The Traditional Legal Context

The common law on insider trading reflects a fundamental tension characteristic of American corporation law. This tension results from the law's effort to cover both large, publicly held corporations and small, closely held ones with one set of rules. Most of our traditional corporate legal norms, both statutory and common law, were designed for the large corporation. Indeed, most of them developed during the era when the corporate form was rarely used for smaller business associations. As the corporate form became popular for small ventures and began to replace the familiar partnership, pressures on these legal rules intensified.[1]

The legal attitude toward protection of shareholders in large corporations has clearly reflected the free-market philosophy underlying our corporation laws. With an active and open market for corporate shares, there is little for law and courts to do. Aggrieved shareholders can sell their shares at the market price, and this price will be determined by the total market's appraisal of the worth of the securities. The identity of individuals participating in such a market need not be known, since market forces will determine the price. Because corporate managers are assumed to operate the

1. Carlos D. Israels, "The Close Corporation and the Law," *Cornell Law Quarterly,* 33 (1948), p. 488; George D. Hornstein, "Stockholders' Agreements in the Closely Held Corporation," *Yale Law Journal,* 59 (1950), p. 1040; William L. Cary, "How Illinois Corporations May Enjoy Partnership Advantages," *Northwestern University Law Review,* 48 (1953), p. 427; and F. Hodge O'Neal, *Close Corporations* (Chicago: Callaghan & Co., 1958), 2 vols. Additional sources are cited in Ralph J. Baker and William L. Cary, *Cases and Materials on Corporations,* 3d ed. (Brooklyn: The Foundation Press, Inc., 1959).

business consistent with the interests of the shareholders, presumably there is little danger to other shareholders because insiders are trading.

It is not surprising then that prior to 1909 the overwhelming number of states that had considered the matter concluded that there was no obligation on the part of an insider buying shares to disclose information known only to him. This was the so-called majority rule, holding that directors and officers of a corporation may deal at arm's length with the company's shareholders. This is still termed the majority rule, though it is no longer that in fact.

The only limitation on insiders purchasing shares in a majority-rule state is the one operating on any contracting party at common law: He could not retain any gains resulting from fraud. But fraud cases are extremely difficult to prove. There must normally be an affirmative misrepresentation. It must be recognized as such by its perpetrator and relied upon as true by the victim. The latter's reliance must be reasonable under the circumstances, and he must prove actual damages. Some of these elements are extremely difficult to prove in a normal stock-exchange transaction. The insider will ordinarily not make any statement. Consequently the affirmative misrepresentation will not appear. Further, the courts have held that in an exchange transaction it was not reasonable for an outsider to rely upon silence as an indication that the status quo would continue. The common-law-fraud doctrine seemed tailor-made for a laissez-faire, market economy in which few restraints on business dealing were evident.

The Minority Rule

Only three states early declined the majority rule. Georgia in 1903[2] and Kansas in 1904[3] adopted the *minority rule,* and Nebraska followed in 1916.[4] It is interesting to note that in 1911 Kansas became the first state to adopt a Blue-Sky Law, requiring full and truthful disclosures in the public *sale* of securities. The minority rule created a fiduciary relationship between corporate

2. *Oliver* v. *Oliver,* 118 Ga. 362, 45 S.E. 232 (1903).
3. *Stewart* v. *Harris,* 69 Kan. 498, 77 Pac. 277 (1904).
4. *Jacquith* v. *Mason,* 99 Neb. 509, 156 N.W. 1041 (1916).

directors and officers on the one hand and selling shareholders on the other. Under this rule full disclosure of all relevant facts was required before the fiduciary could deal with his beneficiary. Legal analogies were found in the relationships between a trustee and his beneficiary, between a principal and an agent, and among the members of a partnership. However, since one had to own shares to gain the protective relationship, only share purchases by insiders from existing shareholders and not sales to outsiders were covered by the rule. Blue-Sky Laws do, of course, cover many sales to outsiders, including many sales by corporate insiders in so-called secondary offerings.

The fiduciary relationship is an equitable concept signifying that a special degree of care or concern must be demonstrated by the fiduciary for the beneficiary. It is usually counterposed to the notion of an arm's-length transaction, the prototype of which is the sale in an open market to a perfect stranger. Fiduciary duties are generally found to exist when the relationship of the parties precludes the desirability of arm's-length dealing. The most obvious case is that of one individual entrusted with the property of another to manage it in the latter's interest. This trustee may not then deal with the owner in relation to the property as if they were strangers in the marketplace. If, for instance, the trustee wishes to buy the property for himself, his interest is in conflict with that of the owner, and the fiduciary duty requires full disclosure on his part. If this is not forthcoming, he will not be allowed to realize any profit from his breach of duty. And in his regular management of trust property, the trustee is subject to constant overseeing by courts of equity.

An employment contract also creates a fiduciary relationship. An agent, among other duties, must deal fairly with his principal, refrain from developing competing interests, preserve his principal's business secrets, and make full disclosure of any self-interest in dealing with his principal.[5] These rules are basically employment-contract provisions implied by law. They are implied because contracting parties rarely spell out such ideas explicitly, though both parties would probably have agreed in advance to their desirability.

5. American Law Institute, *Restatement of the Law Second,* Agency 2d (St. Paul: American Law Institute Publishers, 1958), Sections 387–98.

It is, of course, quite possible to provide explicitly for full disclosure or some other aspect of fiduciary duty even when the law would not imply it. Somewhat surprising, there is only one reported case of a provision of this kind being used.[6] In that case, each of the two shareholders agreed to "give to the other party full information of all transactions relating to the business of the corporation. . . ." The parties also agreed to divulge "any information . . . which may be conducive to the profitable operation of the corporation." This is an extremely unusual provision, but the court showed no hesitation or difficulty in enforcing it when the defendant purchased the plaintiff's shares without disclosing the negotiation of a very profitable lease. Provisions of this sort, whether in articles of incorporation or in separate shareholders' agreements, could be extremely valuable planning devices for small corporations. Surprisingly, they are almost unknown to attorneys or businessmen.[7]

Strict fiduciary standards have long been applied to the dealings of one partner with another. Business relationships of two, three, or more individuals, working closely together and relying heavily on the integrity of each other, probably function more satisfactorily because the law implies the fiduciary obligation. The dependencies are too great and the relationships too personal to allow reliance solely on the disciplinary forces of the market. Consequently, partnership law implied the fiduciary standard in every partnership contract. This provision operated as an open invitation for equity courts to oversee and supervise the relationships of partners. A famous quotation from Judge Benjamin Cardozo epitomizes the standards required.

> Joint adventurers, like copartners, owe to one another, while the enterprise continues, the duty of the finest loyalty. Many forms of conduct permissible in a workaday world for those acting at arm's length, are forbidden to those

6. *Sher* v. *Sandler*, 325 Mass. 348, 90 N.E. 2d 536 (1950). There have been at least two other kinds of situations in which courts deduced the existence of a fiduciary duty from extraneous private agreements. In *Helms* v. *Duckworth*, 249 Fed. 2d 482 (D.C.C.A., 1957), the court implied a fiduciary relationship from a survivor purchase agreement between the only two shareholders in a small corporation. In *De Boy* v. *Harris*, 207 Md. 212, 113 Atl. 2d 903 (1955), the court found that the fiduciary relationship of a joint-venture partnership survived incorporation when there was no express dissolution of the partnership.

7. See Henry G. Manne's book review, *St. Louis University Law Journal*, 6 (1961), p. 567.

bound by fiduciary ties. A trustee is held to something stricter than the morals of the market place. Not honesty alone, but the punctilio of an honor the most sensitive, is then the standard of behavior. . . .[8]

The Special-Facts Rule

So long as the corporate form was used only for enterprises with large numbers of nonmanaging shareholders, the problem of insider trading never seemed important. During the period of special chartering of corporations, some direct surveillance and control of the use of the corporate form was possible.[9] But by 1875 this period had ended and general incorporation acts available to a minimum of three incorporators prevailed in every state. By 1900 the proliferation of small corporations had begun, although it was not until the 1940's with their substantial income-tax rates that the form became extremely popular for small businesses. By 1909 the need for some coalescence of the majority and minority rules had become clear, and in that year the Supreme Court of the United States decided *Strong* v. *Repide.*[10]

The defendant in that case was the general manager of a corporation which owned land in the Philippine Islands. He owned approximately 75 per cent of the shares and acted with complete authority to negotiate the sale of the company's lands to the United States government. During the course of these negotiations, the defendant, through an agent who did not identify his principal, approached the plaintiff to buy her small, minority interest. Because of the government's failure to police guerrilla activity in the area, the land had become nearly worthless, and the plaintiff sold her shares for approximately one tenth of their value after the government purchase.

The Court found that the plaintiff would not have sold if she had known that the defendant was the purchaser. The Court stated that the matter

8. *Meinhard* v. *Salmon,* 249 N.Y. 458, at p. 464, 164 N.E. 545, at p. 546, 62 A.L.R. 1 (1928).

9. For the best available discussion of legislative controls during the period of special chartering, as well as a superb corporation-law history, see John William Cadman, Jr., *The Corporation in New Jersey: Business and Politics, 1791–1875* (Cambridge, Mass.: Harvard University Press, 1949).

10. 213 U.S. 419 (1909).

could not be determined simply by the bare relationship existing between a director and a shareholder. "That the defendant was a director of the corporation is but one of the facts upon which the liability is asserted, the existence of all the others in addition making such a combination as rendered it the plain duty of the defendant to speak."[11] The Court laid heavy stress on the affirmative steps taken to conceal the identity of the defendant, speaking of this as "strong evidence of fraud." And the fact that a pending sale of surrounding lands to the government was a matter of common gossip in newspaper stories was brushed aside, as only the defendant was in a position to know accurately the state of negotiations.

Thus was born the so-called special-facts rule, which is without question the prevailing approach in the states today.[12] This rule is a long way from a thoroughgoing prohibition on insider trading. For example, no case has ever found an insider liable for a transaction that took place over an organized stock exchange. This seems to be an implicit recognition by common-law courts that specific regulation is needed only in those instances when an active market for corporate securities does not guarantee to shareholders sufficient protection against fraud. A leading case[13] recognized this fact implicitly when it stated that mere silence does not usually amount to a breach of duty. "Purchases and sales of stock dealt in on the stock exchange are commonly impersonal affairs. . . . Business of that na-

11. *Strong* v. *Repide,* 213 U.S. 419, 431 (1909).

12. See Louis Loss, *Securities Regulation,* 2d ed. (Boston and Toronto: Little, Brown & Co., 1961), pp. 1446–48, with authorities cited. Other collections of cases may be found in Baker and Cary, *Cases and Materials on Corporations,* pp. 553–63; and Michael Conant, "Duties of Disclosure of Corporate Insiders Who Purchase Shares," *Cornell Law Quarterly,* 46 (1961), pp. 57–58.

13. *Goodwin* v. *Agassiz,* 283 Mass. 358, 186 N.E. 659 (1933). In this case the plaintiff, an experienced businessman, sold shares in a mining company over the Boston Stock Exchange to the defendants, who were officers and directors of the corporation. The insiders were buying because of their confidence in a new geological theory suggesting heavy copper deposits in an area in which the corporation was interested. Not long before this theory came to their attention, the company's previous explorations had proved unsuccessful, and this had been publicized in local newspapers. The court did not expressly hold that a transaction across an exchange always insulates insiders from liability. It merely found that in this case the circumstances did not indicate the need for special protection for the plaintiff.

ture is a matter to be governed by practical rules. Fiduciary obligations of directors ought not to be made so onerous that men of experience and ability will be deterred from accepting such office."[14] The Court did recognize that parties may stand in such relation to each other that an equitable responsibility arises to communicate facts, but the implication was clear that such a relationship would be difficult to find in the normal stock-exchange transaction.

The special-facts rule seems to require some relationship between the parties indicating a substantial danger of fraud.[15] The courts might, therefore, compare the financial sophistication of the parties and, if the disparity is too great, give the plaintiff the benefit of the rule. Reasonable reliance by the shareholder on the insider's intimation of assistance might also be considered. Many cases granting relief involve a director's seeking out the individual shareholder to induce a sale of his securities. And cases involving so-called incorporated partnerships, where two parties hold all shares of the corporation, are not uncommon. The conditions discussed are generally characteristic of closely held corporations, where the opportunities for subtle misstatements or misleading acts are often very great, though the proof of fraud may be extremely difficult. It does appear, therefore, that courts in their application of the special-facts rule have attempted to limit it to those cases in which the possibility of undue influence was greatest.

Another variable in the special-facts equation is the information withheld. Matters of opinion, as opposed to fact, are not covered, though half-truths are, once disclosure is begun. The failure to disclose any significant information may be the basis for liability, but the likelihood of liability seems greater if the undisclosed information involves a merger, consolidation, dissolution, or sale of substantially all of the corporation's assets.[16]

14. *Ibid.*, p. 661.

15. For a cataloging of such circumstances, see F. Hodge O'Neal and Jordan Derwin, *Expulsion or Oppression of Business Associates: "Squeeze-Outs" in Small Enterprises* (Durham: Duke University Press, 1961). This book deals with a variety of problems in small businesses and not with the special-facts rule as such. It illustrates dramatically, however, the dangers for noncontrolling shareholders in smaller corporations with no active market for their securities.

16. See Baker and Cary, *Cases and Materials on Corporations*, p. 560, and "Insider Li-

There is one final indication that the special-facts rule developed as a substitute for market protection when the market is not operating effectively. Only existing shareholders who sell shares to insiders receive any protection from the rule. Outsiders buying from insiders are never covered. It can be argued that the outsider has the world to choose from in making his purchases. Thus he does have the protection of the marketplace in his transactions. Ordinarily he will not stand in a peculiar relationship to a corporate insider raising the dangers of subtle fraud. The existing shareholder, on the other hand, is frequently locked in. No active market for his shares exists, and he may be especially susceptible to the pessimistic sales pitch of an insider.

The common-law approach to insider's trading in the shares of large corporations with listed securities was clear. No doctrine of common law impeded their trading with undisclosed information. As the Supreme Judicial Court of Massachusetts in *Goodwin* v. *Agassiz* stated: "Law in its sanctions is not coextensive with morality. It cannot undertake to put all parties to every contract on an equality as to knowledge, experience, skill and shrewdness. It cannot undertake to relieve against hard bargains made between competent parties without fraud."[17]

Brophy v. *Cities Service Co.*

The cases discussed up to this point have all involved an allegation of injury by an individual shareholder in a private action to recover damages.*

---

ability Under Securities Exchange Act Rule 10b-5: The *Cady, Roberts* Doctrine," *University of Chicago Law Review,* 30 (1962), p. 124.

17. *Goodwin* v. *Agassiz,* 283 Mass. 358, at p. 363, 186 N.E. 659, at p. 661 (1933).

* Editor's note: The special circumstances and minority rules continued to pick up adherents during the decades after 1930. See, e.g., *Broffe v. Horton,* 172 F.2d 489 (2d Cir. 1949) (diversity case); *Childs v. RIC Group, Inc.,* 331 F. Supp. 1078, 1081 (N.D.Ga. 1970), *aff'd,* 447 F.2d 1407 (5th Cir. 1971) (diversity case); *Hobart v. Hobart Estate Co.,* 159 P.2d 958 (Cal. 1945); *Hotchkiss v. Fischer,* 16 P.2d 531 (Kan. 1932); *Jacobson v. Yaschik,* 155 S.E.2d 601 (S.C. 1967). For an especially useful discussion of state common law, along with a holding "that a director, who solicits a shareholder to purchase his stock and fails to disclose information not known to the shareholder that bears upon the potential in-

Somewhat different are the cases proceeding from the theory that the stock trading has injured the corporation, thus allowing a corporate rather than an individual recovery. Only the Securities Exchange Act of 1934 and one common-law case have ever maintained this position. The case, *Brophy* v. *Cities Service Co.,*[18] decided by the Delaware Court of Chancery in 1949, has never been cited on the merits in any subsequent case. Its facts are somewhat novel, and the opinion is far from convincing.

In that case a Mr. Kennedy, the confidential secretary of the president of Cities Service oil company, was privy to information concerning the corporation's purchases of its own shares in the open market. He would purchase before and sell after completion of the corporation's projected transactions. The court reasoned that the information belonged to the corporation and that it was a violation of his fiduciary duty to the corporation for Kennedy to use this property for his own benefit. In answer to the argument that no damage to the corporation was shown—presumably because his share purchases were not large enough to affect the market price—the court said that no damages need be shown when a beneficiary is merely recovering illicit profits made by his fiduciary.

It can be inferred from the opinion that Kennedy had not been expressly authorized by a competent officer to trade in the corporation's shares. If

---

crease in the value of the shares, shall be liable to the shareholder," see *Bailey v. Vaughan,* 359 S.E.2d 599, 605 (W.Va. 1987).

Perhaps surprisingly, however, a number of states continue to adhere to the no-duty rule. See, e.g., *Goodman v. Poland,* 395 F. Supp. 660, 678–80 (D.Md. 1975); *Lank v. Steiner,* 224 A.2d 242 (Del. 1966); *Fleetwood Corp. v. Mirich,* 404 N.E.2d 38, 46 (Ind. Ct. App. 1980); *Yerke v. Batman,* 376 N.E.2d 1211, 1214 (Ind. Ct. App. 1978); *Gladstone v. Murray Co.,* 50 N.E.2d 958 (Mass. 1943); cf. *Treadway Cos., Inc. v. Care Corp.,* 638 F.2d 357, 375 (2d Cir. 1980) (restating no liability rule as applied by New Jersey state courts, albeit subject to the caveat that New Jersey might no longer follow this rule).

Insofar as stock market transactions are concerned, moreover, *Goodwin v. Agassiz* apparently remains the prevailing view (William Meade Fletcher et al., *Fletcher Cyclopedia of the Law of Corporations,* Perm. ed. [St. Paul, Minn.: West, 1986], vol. 3A, par. 1168.1). But see American Law Institute, *Principles of Corporate Governance: Analysis and Recommendations* § 5.04 (1992) (opining that a duty to disclose exists in both face-to-face and stock market transactions). Somewhat amusingly, the only state law support offered by the Reporter for the proposition that this duty extends to secondary market transactions is a "but see" cite to *Goodwin.* See id. at 282.—S.B.

18. *Brophy* v. *Cities Service Co.,* 31 Del. Ch. 241, 70 Atl. 2d 5 (1949).

such permission had been given, it could certainly have been argued forcefully that his profits constituted part of his compensation under his employment contract. There is, however, some mystery about the facts. We are told that four directors of the corporation had previously been joined in the same action and that they had been dropped as defendants. But we are not told why they were dropped. Conceivably, the court viewed the entire transaction as a conspiracy to avoid liability under Section 16(b) of the Securities Exchange Act. If this is so, however, there is no mention of it in the opinion.

But it is not difficult, logically, to imply a trading prohibition from all the surrounding facts. There is always an implied provision in any employment contract that the employee will not act on his own self-interest to the detriment of his employer. We need only find some injury to the corporation from Kennedy's transactions. The court stated that it could not infer loss to the corporation from the general allegations in the complaint. And yet these allegations were sufficient to allow the court to deduce the necessary conclusion: the defendant's purchases must have damaged the corporation. A consideration of the effects of share purchases by the corporation and Kennedy will show why this is so.

As a corporation proceeds with its purchases, the price of the stock will rise. This rise will continue until the projected number of shares has been purchased. Any unusual purchases made before the corporation begins its buying will simply push the projected price curve of corporate purchases that much higher. The corporation lost the opportunity to buy in those shares that Kennedy purchased at the lower price. The loss to the corporation was the difference between what Kennedy paid for his shares and what the corporation paid for its last purchase of the same number of shares. Thus, no matter how small Kennedy's purchases were and how insignificant the effect of his purchases was on market price, if corporate purchases increase the market price, the corporation was damaged by Kennedy's trading.

Unfortunately, the court in the *Brophy* case did not engage in any analysis of potential loss. It merely characterized Kennedy's position as being confidential and concluded that he could not, therefore, profit by his information. If the court had offered a sound analysis, the case could not be deemed to create a general rule against insider trading. Subsequent judicial disregard of the opinion strongly suggests dissatisfaction with the opinion as written. The result in the *Brophy* case does seem correct, but no convincing reason was offered by the judge for his conclusion.[19]

Section 16(b) of the Securities Exchange Act of 1934

In an explicit effort to equalize the bargaining position of insiders and other market investors, Congress adopted Section 16(b) of the Securities Exchange Act of 1934,[20] termed the *insiders' short-swing profit rule.* The Sec-

19. The *Brophy* case suggests an intriguing problem under Rule 10b-5, discussed in the next chapter. Cases have decided that corporations as well as individuals can violate the rule. Consequently, any time a corporation goes unannounced into the market to purchase its own shares, and these purchases have the effect of raising the market price, a violation of 10b-5 might automatically follow. If, of course, the corporation announced in advance that it was going to purchase shares, the cost would be substantially greater, *as would the ultimate loss to those shareholders of the corporation who were not in the market to sell their shares.* See Chapter 6.

20. As amended to August 20, 1964:

> Section 16. (a) Every person who is directly or indirectly the beneficial owner of more than 10 per centum of any class of any equity security (other than an exempted security) which is registered pursuant to section 12 of this title, or who is a director or an officer of the issuer of such security, shall file, at the time of the registration of such security on a national securities exchange or by the effective date of a registration statement filed pursuant to section 12(g) of this title, or within ten days after he becomes such beneficial owner, director, or officer, a statement with the Commission (and, if such security is registered on a national securities exchange, also with the exchange) of the amount of all equity securities of such issuer of which he is the beneficial owner, and within ten days after the close of each calendar month thereafter, if there has been a change in such ownership during such month, shall file with the Commission (and if such security is registered on a national securities exchange, shall also file with the exchange), a statement indicating his ownership at the close of the calendar month and such changes in his ownership as have occurred during such calendar month.
>
> (b) For the purpose of preventing the unfair use of information which may have been obtained by such beneficial owner, director, or officer by reason of his relationship to the issuer, any profit realized by him from any purchase and sale, or any sale and purchase, of any equity security of such issuer (other than an exempted security) within any period of less than six months, unless such security was acquired in good faith in connection with a debt previously contracted, shall inure to and be recoverable by the issuer, irrespective of any intention on the part of such beneficial owner, di-

tion was not designed to protect corporate shareholders in what might be considered their contract expectations. Indeed, a shareholder who sold to an insider liable under the Act still has only his common-law protections.

---

rector, or officer in entering into such transaction of holding the security purchased or of not repurchasing the security sold for a period exceeding six months. Suit to recover such profit may be instituted at law or in equity in any court of competent jurisdiction by the issuer, or by the owner of any security of the issuer in the name and in behalf of the issuer if the issuer shall fail or refuse to bring such suit within sixty days after request or shall fail diligently to prosecute the same thereafter; but no such suit shall be brought more than two years after the date such profit was realized. This subsection shall not be construed to cover any transaction where such beneficial owner was not such both at the time of the purchase and sale, or the sale and purchase, of the security involved, or any transaction or transactions which the Commission by rules and regulations may exempt as not comprehended with the purpose of this subsection.

(c) It shall be unlawful for any such beneficial owner, director, or officer, directly or indirectly, to sell any equity security of such issuer (other than an exempted security), if the person selling the security or his principal (1) does not own the security sold, or (2) if owning the security does not deliver it against such sale within twenty days thereafter, or does not within five days after such sale deposit it in the mails or other usual channels of transportation; but no person shall be deemed to have violated this subsection if he proves that notwithstanding the exercise of good faith he was unable to make such delivery or deposit within such time, or that to do so would cause undue inconvenience or expense.

Subsections (d) and (e) provide certain exemptions for brokerage and arbitrage transactions. Certain relevant definitions appear in Section 3(a) of the 1934 Act:

(9) The term "person" means an individual, a corporation, a partnership, an association, a joint-stock company, a business trust, or an unincorporated organization.

(10) The term "security" means any note, stock, treasury stock, bond, debenture, certificate of interest or participation in any profit-sharing agreement or in any oil, gas, or other mineral royalty or lease, any collateral-trust certificate, pre-organization certificate or subscription, transferable share, investment contract, voting-trust certificate, certificate of deposit, for a security, or in general, any instrument commonly known as a "security"; or any certificate of interest or participation in, temporary or interim certificate for, receipt for, or warrant or right to subscribe to or purchase, any of the foregoing; but shall not include currency or any note, draft, bill of exchange, or banker's acceptance which has a maturity at the time of issuance of not exceeding nine months, exclusive of days of grace, or any renewal thereof the maturity of which is likewise limited.

(11) The term "equity security" means any stock or similar security; or any security convertible, with or without consideration, into such a security, or carrying any warrant or right to subscribe to or purchase such a security; or any such warrant or right;

The Section was designed only to prevent insiders from profiting from inside information, and the inhibiting device chosen was not a suit by the injured shareholder but rather a suit by the corporation or a derivative suit on its behalf. Prior to the 1964 amendments, the provisions of Section 16 applied only to the insiders of corporations that had an equity security registered on an exchange. Since 1964, however, they apply to any corporation engaged in interstate commerce or whose securities are traded through the mails if it has total assets exceeding $1 million and five hundred or more record holders of an equity security.[21]

At first glance Section 16 would seem to be an effective device for preventing insider trading. Insiders are required by 16(a) to report any changes in their holdings of corporate securities, and this information is readily available to lawyers attracted by the promise of relatively large and easy fees.[22] The proof required for a successful 16(b) prosecution is the height of simplicity. The plaintiff need merely show that during any six-month period the insider sold corporate securities at a higher price than he paid during the same period. A variety of procedural problems have arisen,[23] but the courts have generally shown considerable sympathy with the stated congressional policy in their interpretation of the Act.[24]

But with all these advantages, Section 16 has still probably not had an appreciable effect on the total amount gained by insiders as a result of their possessing inside information. There are two fundamental reasons why this

---

or any other security which the Commission shall deem to be of similar nature and consider necessary or appropriate, by such rules and regulations as it may prescribe in the public interest or for the protection of investors, to treat as an equity security. . . .

(13) The terms "buy" and "purchase" each include any contract to buy, purchase, or otherwise acquire.

(14) The terms "sale" and "sell" each include any contract to sell or otherwise dispose of.

21. *Securities Exchange Act of 1934,* Section 12 (g)(1)(A). The figure is actually 750 shareholders for approximately two years after the amendment was adopted and then it changes to 500. Sec. 12(g)(1)(B).

22. Loss, *Securities Regulation,* pp. 1051–55.

23. *Ibid.,* pp. 1044ff.

24. See, for example, *Smolowe* v. *Delendo Corp.,* 136 Fed. 2d 231 (2d Cir., 1943), and *Gratz* v. *Claughton,* 187 Fed. 2d 46 (2d Cir., 1951).

is so. The statute has no effect on any attempt to make profits at the end of a six-month period. Since securities must be held for six months in order to qualify for capital-gains treatment under the Internal Revenue Code, many corporate insiders, buying before disclosure of important information, would hold them for the six-month period in any event. If shares have been held for six months, sales may be made without violating the Section. Short sales by insiders, however, are always prohibited.

But there is a second and far more fundamental reason why Section 16 cannot be effective in preventing insider trading. The coverage of the Section is limited to specifically designated insiders trading in the securities of the corporation to which they bear the specified relationship. The Section touches upon only one of the several methods by which valuable information may be exploited.

For instance, the prohibition of the Section does not necessarily cover trading in the securities of a controlled subsidiary by an officer, director, or 10 per cent shareholder in the parent company if the individual trading is not an officer, director, or 10 per cent shareholder of the subsidiary. It would seem that only if the individual actually controls the parent corporation would he be considered the beneficial owner of the control shares for purposes of the 10 per cent limitation.[25]

Much more important, however, the entire, complex system for the exchange of information to other individuals is left completely untouched by the Section because it covers only immediate uses of information by insiders buying and selling securities. As Professor Louis Loss says: "There is also no guarantee against evasion by mutual 'back-scratching' of insiders in differ-

25. See *Opinion of the General Counsel*, Securities Exchange Act Release No. 1965 (1938) and *Boston & Maine R.R. Co.* v. *Hillman, CCH Federal Securities Law Reporter*, par. 90813 (S.D.N.Y., 1957). Perhaps in an effort to aid the SEC in "plugging" this hole, the New York Stock Exchange has recently forbidden directors of a listed company to own shares in a controlled subsidiary; see *Wall Street Journal* (Aug. 30, 1965), p. 22, col. 2. Clearly, under the doctrine of the *Blau* case, discussed later in this chapter, the Commission would have no authority to extend the application of 16(b) in this fashion. Presumably, however, the New York Stock Exchange is not limited by the same constraints that guide the SEC, as it is a private rule-making body. If the Exchange wins its current legislative fight to gain exemption from the antitrust laws, its status as a private rulemaker should be re-examined. Cf. *Steele* v. *Louisville & Nashville R.R. Co.*, 323 U.S. 192, especially at 198 (1944).

ent corporations, or by trading through relatives or friends."[26] However, it should not be denied that the Section has had considerable influence in forming the moral values voiced and held by the business community.

Blau v. Lehman

That the SEC has long chafed under the restrictive applicability of Section 16 is illustrated by the 1962 decision in *Blau* v. *Lehman.*[27] This was the Supreme Court's first opportunity to construe Section 16(b) of the 1934 Act. The case involved a partner in the investment-banking firm of Lehman Brothers—a Mr. Thomas, who had succeeded another Lehman partner, John Hertz, on the board of directors of the Tide Water Associated Oil Company. The banking firm, according to the opinion, using information generally available to the public and without consulting Thomas, bought and sold Tide Water shares and realized a short-swing profit. The petitioner, and the Securities and Exchange Commission as *amicus curiae,* argued that the firm of Lehman Brothers was a director of the corporation within the meaning of the Act and that consequently the entire profits of the banking firm, and not merely the partnership share of Thomas, should be recovered by the corporation. The Court concluded that the partnership could be liable if it had designated or deputized an individual to be its representative on a board or if he was active in making partnership trading decisions. But such liability did not automatically follow in the case at hand.

The Court was unimpressed with the argument of the petitioner and the Commission that the Section should be extended to include anyone realizing short-swing profits that might be based on inside information. The Court noted that Congress had considered and rejected draft provisions extending the Section's liability to anyone, insider or not, "to whom such unlawful disclosure" was made. Furthermore, Congress had left the Act unamended after a 1952 Court of Appeals case[28] limited the Act to the designated insiders. The Court said: "Congress . . . might amend § 16(b) if the

26. Loss, *Securities Regulation,* p. 1043.
27. 368 U.S. 403 (1962).
28. *Rattner* v. *Lehman,* 193 Fed. 2d 564 (2d Cir., 1952).

Commission would present to it the policy arguments it has presented to us, but we think that Congress is the proper agency to change an interpretation of the Act unbroken since its passage, if the change is to be made."[29]

The core of the opinion involves defining the word *director.* This word is defined in the Act to include "any person performing similar functions" to those of a director, and the statutory definition of *person* includes a partnership.[30] But the Court refused to apply the entity theory of partnership,[31] under which any partner's act would be the act of the partnership. They concluded that the definitional sections allow a partnership to be treated as an entity but do not require it in every case. They held that Congress did not intend that partnerships be included automatically whenever one partner was a statutory insider.

In his dissenting opinion, Justice William O. Douglas, while berating the pursuit of the entity-aggregate will-o'-the-wisp, concluded that it was easier in this case "to make this partnership a 'director' for purposes of § 16 than to hold the opposite."[32] He was particularly disturbed by what seemed to him to be the exclusion of the most important segment of the financial community from the coverage of Section 16(b). Justice Douglas then went on to repeat the usual arguments about the abuses of trading in inside information. His opinion is replete with such words as *fiduciaries, vicious, predatory,* and *flagrant betrayal.* He reminds us again of Brandeis' admonitions and the fact that the hearings leading to the Securities Exchange Act of 1934 were filled with stories of personal gain by insiders. (For the full text of the *Blau* v. *Lehman* opinion, see the Appendix, pages 202–12.)

A Rationalization of Section 16(b)

The majority opinion in the *Blau* case is in the tradition of pre-existing law on the subject of insider trading. It was Douglas who missed the point of Congress' refusal to outlaw all insider trading. The touchstone in all prior

29. *Blau* v. *Lehman,* 368 U.S. 403, 413 (1962).

30. See definition Sec. 3(a)(9) in footnote 20.

31. See Floyd R. Mechem, *Elements of the Law of Partnership,* 2d ed. (Chicago: Callaghan and Co., 1920), pp. 8–13.

32. *Blau* v. *Lehman,* 368 U.S. 403, 416 (1962).

law, statutory or common law, was the concept of fraud, not fiduciary duty. Section 16(b) can be rationalized as an antimanipulation device but not as an effective prohibition of insider trading. It cannot succeed at the latter task, but it may be quite effective for the former. Since insiders are left free to exchange their information, the Section may have had little economic effect. On the other hand, because the Section dictates that information *must* be exchanged in most instances before it can be used, insiders will have little incentive to manipulate corporate affairs for their own trading purposes and contrary to the interest of all shareholders.[33] It is one thing to manipulate corporate affairs when the insider can quickly exploit this information by himself. It is quite another matter to engage in manipulation for the immediate benefit of a third person. If manipulation of corporate affairs for trading purposes does occur in American corporations, Section 16(b) has probably been an effective device for minimizing it.

Neither legislative history nor the subsequent literature on the Section has viewed Section 16 as another of the antimanipulation devices Congress included in the 1934 Act.[34] But Congress' refusal to include a general prohibition on insider trading and its apparent concern with deceptive practices suggests that this explanation of Section 16 may be correct. The Supreme Court's opinion in *Blau* v. *Lehman* is consistent with this explanation. The opinion is, like the common-law cases traced back to *Strong* v. *Repide,* logical and respectable. Section 16 filled what may have been an important gap in the law's treatment of insider dealing, and the *Blau* decision limited that Section to serving this antimanipulation purpose.

The defeat for the Securities and Exchange Commission was unmistakable. The Commission's plea for an assumption of guilt was met by the Supreme Court's demand for specific evidence that the director might be involved in a scheme that the Section was designed to prevent. As is often true, effective law in an area turns on questions of the burden of proof. So

33. See Chapter 10.

34. Senator Gore, as noted on p. 18, indicated his belief that 16(b) was an antimanipulation or antifraud provision. But this contention was specifically denied in *Smolowe* v. *Delendo Corp.*, 136 Fed. 2d 231 (2d Cir., 1943).

long as there is no presumption of wrongdoing when information exchanges are possible, the job of policing Section 16(b) will remain extremely difficult. The *Blau* opinion signaled the limit to which the SEC could push the Section. But long before this limit was set, a new, more radical, and far less defensible development was well under way.

3 Developments Under SEC Rule 10b-5

As the Supreme Court reminded us in *Blau* v. *Lehman,* Congress expressly declined to adopt a broad rule against all trading with inside information. In Section 17(a) of the Securities Act of 1933, Congress did provide a stringent antifraud rule in connection with the sale of securities. From its context and legislative history, this Section appears to have been designed as a catchall for undesirable stock promotional practices not otherwise covered in the Act.[1] In 1936, Congress amended the Securities Exchange Act of 1934 to include a general antideception section, now Section 15(c)(1), applicable to brokers and dealers in their purchases or sales of over-the-counter stocks.[2] This Section gave the Securities and Exchange Commission broad powers to make rules for the regulation of broker-dealers, perhaps broad enough to prohibit insider trading in unlisted securities, though this has never been done explicitly.[3]

The 1934 Act also contains a general provision, Section 10(b), dealing with purchases or sales of securities. This Section makes it unlawful:

> To use or employ, in connection with the purchase or sale of any security registered on a national securities exchange or any security not so registered, any manipulative or deceptive device or contrivance in contravention of such rules and regulations as the Commission may prescribe as necessary or appropriate in the public interest or for the protection of investors.

1. See Loss, *Securities Regulation,* p. 1423.

2. *Ibid.*, p. 1425.

3. Interestingly, Section 16(d) of the 1934 Act was amended in 1964 to exempt broker-dealers from the coverage of 16(b) when they are directors of companies for whose shares they maintain a market.

Again, the legislative history of this Section, though very meager, suggests that Congress recognized the possibility of manipulative or deceptive devices other than those specifically treated in Section 9 of the Act.[4] It is under this Section 10 that the major legal developments prohibiting insider trading have occurred.

In 1942, rebuffed in its legislative effort to extend Section 17(a) of the 1933 Act to purchases as well as to sales of securities,[5] the Commission promulgated Rule X-10B-5.[6] This Rule is a combination of the jurisdictional coverage of Section 10(b) of the 1934 Act ("any person" and "purchase or sale") with the substantive aspects of Section 17(a) of the 1933 Act. The Rule, like its parent statutory Sections, is not remarkable for its clarity, logic, organization, or precision.

> It shall be unlawful for any person, directly or indirectly, by the use of any means or instrumentality of interstate commerce, or of the mails, or of any facility of any national securities exchange,
>
> 1. to employ any device, scheme, or artifice to defraud,
>
> 2. to make any untrue statement of a material fact or to omit to state a material fact necessary in order to make the statements made, in the light of the circumstances under which they were made, not misleading, or
>
> 3. to engage in any act, practice, or course of business which operates or would operate as a fraud or deceit upon any person, in connection with the purchase or sale of any security.

Litigation Under Rule 10b-5

Rule 10b-5 was born of one section aimed at fraudulent stock issues and another aimed largely at deceptions by brokers. Consequently, it is not surprising that for the first five years after its promulgation, about its only use was in broker-dealer disciplinary actions by the SEC. The first judicial rec-

4. In fact this Section was originally numbered 9(c), but in a later draft it became 10(b). See Loss, *Securities Regulation,* p. 1424. Section 9 applies only to listed securities, and the move may have been aimed merely at authorizing rules against manipulative practices in over-the-counter stocks.

5. *Ibid.,* p. 1426.

6. *Code of Federal Regulations,* Vol. 17, Sec. 240.10b-5. This was originally promulgated as Rule X-10B-5 and is now simply Rule 10b-5.

ognition of its applicability to insider trading in a private civil action came in 1947.[7] And it was another five years before a truly important decision occurred, in *Speed* v. *Transamerica Corp.*[8]

In the *Speed* case a tobacco company had a cigarette-tobacco inventory that had greatly appreciated in value during World War II, and this was common knowledge in financial and tobacco circles. It was not known, however, that the controlling shareholder had devised a liquidation plan whereby this appreciated value could be realized in spite of price controls on cigarettes. It was the controlling shareholder's failure to disclose to the plaintiff minority shareholder his intention to liquidate the corporation under this plan that a Federal District Court considered actionable. Without knowledge of the plan, knowledge that tobacco inventories had appreciated was not important. Judge Paul Leahy referred to 10b-5 as follows:

> The rule is clear. It is unlawful for an insider, such as a majority stockholder, to purchase the stock of minority stockholders without disclosing material facts affecting the value of the stock, known to the majority stockholder by virtue of his inside position but not known to the selling minority stockholders, which information would have affected the judgment of the sellers. The duty of disclosure stems from the necessity of preventing a corporate insider from utilizing his position to take unfair advantage of the uninformed minority stockholders. It is an attempt to provide some degree of equalization of bargaining positions in order that the minority may exercise an informed judgment in any such transaction. Some courts have called this a fiduciary duty while others state it is a duty imposed by the "special circumstances." One of the primary purposes of the Securities Exchange Act of 1934 . . . was to outlaw the use of inside information by corporate officers and principal stockholders for their own financial advantage to the detriment of uninformed public security holders.[9]

Judge Leahy's language clearly went beyond anything suggested in earlier cases. It might be noted, however, that this was still not a transaction across an exchange, and it did involve the sale of substantially all the assets of the corporation. And, most important, Transamerica had approached the mi-

7. *Kardon* v. *National Gypsum Co.*, 73 Fed. Supp. 798 (D.C.E.D. Pa., 1947).
8. 99 Fed. Supp. 808 (D. Del., 1951).
9. *Speed* v. *Transamerica Corp.*, 99 Fed. Supp. 808, 828–29 (D. Del., 1951).

nority shareholders personally to make an offer for their shares. Thus it is not surprising that many commentators, even after the *Speed* case, continued to believe that Rule 10b-5 was basically designed only to extend the special-facts rule of *Strong* v. *Repide* to all cases involving security transactions within interstate commerce.[10] Most of the provisions of the Securities Exchange Act of 1934 applied only to corporations with securities registered on an exchange.[11] Rule 10b-5, however, like Section 10(b) of the Act, applied to "any person" so long as the transaction fell within the purview of congressional powers.

Some Unanswered Questions

After the *Speed* decision the pace of 10b-5 civil actions involving insider trading began to quicken,[12] until in 1965 it reached almost flood proportions.[13] This mushrooming volume of cases does not, however, represent a coherent development of the law. Only in June, 1964, for example, did the Supreme Court of the United States apparently decide that a private right of action is permitted by the Act.[14] Many, many issues remain unsettled. The basic

10. Norman D. Lattin, *The Law of Corporations* (Brooklyn: The Foundation Press, Inc., 1959), pp. 274–75.

11. This was changed in the 1964 amendments to cover any corporation with assets of $1 million and 750 shareholders operating in interstate commerce or whose securities are traded in interstate commerce or by use of the mails. The Securities Exchange Act of 1934, Sec. 12(g)(1)(A). By Sec. 12(g)(1)(B) the requirement for 750 shareholders is reduced to 500 after two years.

12. See David S. Ruder, "Civil Liability Under Rule 10b-5: Judicial Revision of Legislative Intent?" *Northwestern University Law Review*, 57 (1963), p. 627, and Appendix, p. 687. The acceleration of use of 10b-5 is dramatically illustrated by comparing Shepard's *United States Citations—Statutes, Edition Supplement 1943–1964* (covering cases until 1962) with the July, 1965, *Supplement*. In approximately the last two years 10b-5 has been cited in well over half again as many cases as it was in the previous twenty years of its existence.

13. See Daniel B. Posner, "Developments in Federal Securities Regulation," *The Business Lawyer*, 20 (1965), p. 595.

14. *J. I. Case Co.* v. *Borak*, 377 U.S. 426 (1964). This case involved a civil action for an alleged violation of the SEC's proxy-solicitation rules promulgated under Section 14(a) of the Securities Exchange Act. However, the broad language used in the opinion left no doubt that civil actions under Rule 10b-5 were approved as well. The Court, while noting that the statute makes no specific reference to a private right of action, concluded that "it

validity of the promulgation of Rule 10b-5 has not been carefully tested. Its applicability to nonbroker-dealers has not even been questioned. Many issues raised by the fraud–fiduciary duty dichotomy are in doubt. For instance, the cases disagree on the necessity for *scienter*, or knowledge by the defendant that a misrepresentation is being made; the necessity for reliance by the plaintiff, with the subordinate question of whether he must show "due care" in replying; the necessity for "some semblance of privity," that is, some relationship between the alleged violator of the rule and the plaintiff; whether damages need to be shown (generally true on a fraud theory) or whether the defendant's profits may be recovered (characteristic of fiduciary-duty actions); and the necessity that the undisclosed information be material.[15]

Other questions peculiar to the use of undisclosed information abound. Are customers for whom a broker buys with inside information liable? Is the danger of liability greater for directors than for others who receive undisclosed news? May tips and rumors be played with impunity, or is there a danger if they prove true? Are security analysts in danger if a theory proves correct? Can insiders ever purge themselves of all inside information? Any thoroughgoing restriction on insider trading raises all these questions and more. But the decided cases have barely begun to raise the questions, and already the answers are in hopeless confusion.

In the Matter of Cady, Roberts & Co.

Undoubtedly the most important opinion up until 1966 under Rule 10b-5 is a 1961 opinion by the Securities and Exchange Commission, *In the Matter of Cady, Roberts & Co.*[16] This was an action to discipline a broker and his

is the duty of the courts to be alert to provide such remedies as are necessary to make effective the Congressional purpose."

15. Discussions of these and many other issues may be found in the following: Loss, *Securities Regulation*, pp. 1448–74; Posner, "Developments in Federal Securities Regulation" (1965); Ruder, "Pitfalls in the Development," p. 185; Daniel B. Posner, "Developments in Federal Securities Regulation," *The Business Lawyer*, 19 (1964), p. 593; Ruder, "Civil Liability Under Rule 10b-5."

16. *CCH Federal Securities Law Reporter* (1961), par. 76803.

firm for a violation of Rule 10b-5; it did not involve any issue of money damages for aggrieved stock buyers.

A registered representative of Cady, Roberts, J. Cheever Cowdin, was a director of the Curtiss-Wright Corporation. There had been a great rise in the price of that company's shares as a result of considerable ballyhoo about a new engine under development. Shortly thereafter, the board of directors substantially cut the dividend of the company. During the period of rising prices, a broker and partner in Cady, Roberts, Robert M. Gintel, had been buying shares for approximately thirty discretionary accounts of firm customers, one of whom was his wife. The day before the dividend was cut, he began selling shares from these discretionary accounts. In the two days before the transactions in question he had sold over half these holdings.

After the dividend decision by the board of directors, the meeting was recessed. Cowdin telephoned a message for Gintel that the dividend had been cut. Upon receiving this information, Gintel entered substantial sell orders for some[17] of his discretionary accounts, and he sold a substantial block of shares short for some accounts.

The dividend action occurred at approximately 11:00 A.M., at which time the standard authorization for transmission of this information to the New York Stock Exchange was given. For reasons never explained, but presumed to be inadvertent, the New York Stock Exchange did not receive this information for nearly one-and-a-half hours. The Dow Jones financial news service was not given the information for approximately forty-five minutes, again presumedly through inadvertence.

Regardless of the reasons for those delays, the associates of Cady, Roberts & Company acted with alacrity and efficiency. Gintel's orders were executed fifteen and eighteen minutes, respectively, after the dividend action. The stock, needless to say, plummeted on the later publication of the news. Gintel's actions were found to be a willful violation of Section 17(a) of the Securities Act of 1933, of 10(b) of the Securities Exchange Act of 1934, and of Rule 10b-5.

In his opinion in *Cady, Roberts,* Chairman Cary stated that liability under

17. The opinion makes no attempt to explain why Gintel did not sell out all of his discretionary accounts. For a possible explanation see Chapter 5.

10b-5 rests on two principal elements: "the existence of a relationship giving access, directly or indirectly, to information intended to be available only for a corporate purpose and not for the personal benefit of anyone, and second, the inherent unfairness involved where a party takes advantage of such information knowing it is unavailable to those with whom he is dealing." Presumably both these elements and not merely the latter must appear to establish liability, since Chairman Cary states further: "our task here is to identify those persons who are in a special relationship with a company and privy to its internal affairs, and thereby suffer correlative duties in trading in its securities."

The Commission had no difficulty in finding the requisite special relationship existing between Curtiss-Wright, Cowdin, Gintel, and Cady, Roberts.[18] But the prohibition on trading was extended to those selling for discretionary accounts managed for third parties with no special relationship with the company.[19]

The Commission clearly rejected the suggestion, made in a variety of ways by the respondents, that Rule 10b-5 was not intended to extend beyond the special-facts rule in state law. For instance, the special-facts rule is limited to shareholders selling to insiders and does not extend to those buying from them. Further, as indicated previously, no special-facts case ever found liability in a transaction over an exchange, and some "semblance of privity" always had to be shown. The Commission replied that cases under the common-law special-facts rule had no relevance here, since purchasers as

18. Query whether the Supreme Court in its subsequent opinion in *Blau* v. *Lehman* did not weaken the legal effect of the relationship so readily found incriminating by the Commission? It can be argued, however, that the necessary relationship under 10b-5 is a matter to be determined under all the existing circumstances, whereas the relationship necessary for liability under Section 16(b) is determined by the statute.

19. The Commission's ruling also prohibited soliciting and executing other orders. Query whether this means that if a customer of Cady, Roberts had at the precise moment but by sheer coincidence asked his broker Gintel to sell his Curtiss-Wright shares that Gintel would not be allowed to do so?

Another important and difficult question presented by the case is whether it is intended to have application to situations not involving such direct use of valuable information. If Gintel had merely called a friend at another brokerage house in no way connected with Curtiss-Wright and advised him to sell, would the second broker also be subject to disciplinary action?

well as buyers over an exchange were intended to be protected by the Act, and that privity was not required in an action by the Commission to discipline a broker.[20]

The opinion in *Cady, Roberts* is important for several reasons. It laid to final rest the belief that Rule 10b-5 was still circumscribed by the older special-facts approach. The case itself involves only a disciplinary action by the Commission against a broker, but the underlying logic would certainly seem applicable to a private civil action. And even though the opinion requires the existence of some "special relationship" giving access to information, its general tone as an attack on all insider trading was unmistakable. This opinion undoubtedly provided a good part of the confidence with which the SEC took its next and most radical step. (For the full text of *Cady, Roberts,* see the Appendix, pages 212–19.)

Texas Gulf Sulphur Company

In April, 1965, the SEC brought insider trading to the public's attention with the most dramatic disclosure since the Pecora hearings in 1933. *SEC* v. *Texas Gulf Sulphur Company* became the focus of attention for the whole subject of insider trading. This case, which went to trial on May 9, 1966, presents in almost classic terms all of the factors that must be considered in a comprehensive treatment of insider trading. The resolution of the questions in this case may determine the law in this field for many years to come. This case is so important and so illustrative of the fundamental issues involved in insider trading that a summary of the available facts is presented here.[21]

20. This would seem to suggest that the Commission was setting up a different standard in an action to discipline a broker than would operate in a civil action for damages. Cf. "Broker Silence and Rule 10b-5: Expanding the Duty to Disclose," *Yale Law Journal,* 71 (1962), p. 742. But see F. Arnold Daum and Howard W. Phillips, "The Implications of Cady, Roberts," *The Business Lawyer,* 17 (1962), p. 950. For an earlier argument that 10b-5 establishes a gradation of duties with the most severe ones running against insiders and brokers but with rank outsiders left only with their common-law liabilities, see "The Prospects for Rule 10b-5: An Emerging Remedy for Defrauded Investors," *Yale Law Journal,* 59 (1950), p. 1143.

21. The sources for this summary of facts other than those specifically mentioned in the text are Robert Sheehan, "Great Day in the Morning for Texas Gulf Sulphur," *Fortune*

The Texas Gulf Sulphur Company was founded in 1909 and taken over in 1916 by Bernard Baruch, J. P. Morgan, and other financial interests. Until the mid-1950's, Texas Gulf was the world's leading producer of sulphur. By this time, however, several factors had combined to depress the price of Texas Gulf stock. The world demand for sulphur was very low, and Texas Gulf was a one-product company. Texas Gulf had lost many millions of dollars in unsuccessful efforts to develop new sulphur deposits. Younger corporations with less complacent management were making successful bids for a growing share of the sulphur market.

In 1959 a new team of managers took over the direction of Texas Gulf's affairs. The company embarked on a venturesome and imaginative program of diversification, exploration, and development. The company entered the booming potash and phosphate fields and pioneered the development of an important new mining process for sulphur. As part of the Company's ambitious program of prospecting for mineral deposits, a company geologist, in a helicopter equipped with magnetic surveying equipment, discovered the first sign of valuable new deposits in Timmins, Ontario, in 1959. It was not until some time in late 1963, however, that the company made the first drilling that indicated the possible presence of a rich vein of copper and zinc. This was the famous Timmins ore find, presently estimated to contain 55 million tons of copper, zinc, and silver.

When the first successful drill-hole was completed, the geologist in charge instituted tight security measures for his crew. No one was allowed to leave the camp site. Various schemes, such as fake drill cores and the removal of the drilling rig to another location, were employed to prevent the truth from leaking out. It is alleged by the SEC that at this time the geologist called the president of the company in New York. The SEC's com-

---

(July, 1964), p. 137, and *The Wall Street Journal* (Eastern Edition), Mar. 9, 1965, p. 4, col. 2; Apr. 20, 1965, p. 3, col. 3; Apr. 21, 1965, p. 4, col. 2; Apr. 22, 1965, p. 28, col. 1; Apr. 23, 1965, p. 3, cols. 3–4; Apr. 27, 1965, p. 1, col. 8; July 8, 1965, p. 30, col. 2; July 9, 1965, p. 5, col. 1; and Aug. 4, 1965, p. 24, col. 2. It is interesting to note, according to the last cited report, that Texas Gulf and its officials defended their action primarily on the grounds that they were not engaged in insider trading, that the statement of Apr. 12, 1965, was necessary and correct under the circumstances, and that factors other than the Timmins strike affected the stock's price.

plaint further alleges that from this time until April 16, 1964, various officers, directors, and employees of the company, knowing this information and the fact that it had not been released to the public, bought shares on the open market, bought calls on the company shares, or were given stock options by the company. Another list of individuals, not connected officially with the company, were named in the SEC's complaint as having received information about the find and having purchased shares of Texas Gulf before public disclosure. These persons were not made defendants in the suit, although some have been named in subsequent private civil actions.

By March, 1964, New York and Washington, and undoubtedly other areas of the United States and Canada, were rife with rumors about Texas Gulf Sulphur. The price of the shares had risen from $17.375 on November 10, 1963, to $29.375 by mid-April, 1964. It subsequently reached a high of 71 in the period before the SEC's suit was filed on April 19, 1965.

On April 12, 1964, the company announced that it was indeed prospecting in the Timmins area but that preliminary indications were that more drilling would be required for proper evaluation of this prospect. The announcement continued: "The drilling to date has not been conclusive, but the statements made by many outside quarters are unreliable and include information and figures that are not available to Texas Gulf." The rumors were termed "unreliable" and "premature and possibly misleading" and were said to have originated with speculators not connected with the company. But on April 16, 1964, four days later, Texas Gulf officials announced a "major ore discovery" of about twenty-five million tons of copper, zinc, and silver. These officials subsequently explained that, as of April 12, only one good core had been discovered, whereas by the 16th there were seven cores that accurately indicated the extent of the discovery. Company officials have also claimed that the April 12 statement resulted from careful consideration of the entire situation. While not wanting to mislead the public with any unproved claims, they also did not want the public misled by rumors. As soon as the facts were available, the statement of April 16 was made.

Among the defendants was a director, Thomas G. Lamont, who was also a director of the Morgan Guaranty Bank. He was not initially charged with purchasing any shares for himself, but rather with having caused the bank to purchase Texas Gulf stock for various clients for whom Morgan Guaranty acted as trustee or agent, including a hospital and the bank's own employees' profit-sharing fund. Lamont is alleged merely to have advised an official at Morgan Guaranty on the 16th to "look at the news ticker for news pertaining to Texas Gulf." Lamont also claimed that the information had been released earlier by a Canadian mining paper.

Another party who was named as having traded on the inside information but was not sued as a defendant was Herbert Klotz, then an assistant secretary of the Department of Commerce. Klotz, previously associated with a Washington, D.C., investment-banking house, forthwith resigned from his government position. He claimed that his only source of information was a secretary in the Department of Commerce who was a family friend of the Texas Gulf geologist at Timmins. Klotz said he noticed heavy trading with a price increase and, therefore, played the tip. The geologist admitted recommending Texas Gulf stock to friends based on the general improvement in the company's affairs, but he maintains that he told no outsiders about the discovery at Timmins.

In April of 1965, the Securities and Exchange Commission filed suit in the United States District Court for the Southern District of New York against Texas Gulf Sulphur Company and a number of individual defendants. The complaint itemizes purchases of shares and calls or the receipt of stock options by the defendants between November 12, 1963, the discovery date, and April 16, 1964. Each of the many paragraphs of the complaint stated that the individuals acted on "knowledge and information of material facts . . . not generally known to the investing public . . . without disclosing to the seller the aforementioned material facts." Interspersed chronologically with allegations of purchases by defendants are a series of allegations relating to purchases by third persons informed about the discovery by a named defendant.

After describing the allegedly misleading press release of April 12, 1964, and the correct announcement on April 16, the complaint alleges that during this period "numerous stockholders of defendant TEXAS GULF sold their shares of defendant TEXAS GULF stock at prices at which they would not have sold their shares, had they known the material facts which were known to, but not made available to them by, defendant TEXAS GULF." This suggests the possibility of liability of the corporation to these shareholders, perhaps in civil actions as there is no prayer for damages from the company.[22] The complaint indicates that during the relevant time period, defendants purchased an aggregate of 9,100 shares of Texas Gulf Sulphur stock and calls on 5,200 shares and that they received options to purchase an aggregate of 31,200 shares.[23] During the same period, persons who allegedly bought on the advice of defendants purchased 12,100 shares and calls on 14,100 shares. This indicates that 21,200 shares were purchased and 50,500 shares were covered by options or calls during the relevant time period. The 21,200 shares represent less than 10 per cent of the approximately 261,000 shares traded during the twenty-two-week period in question. In the ensuing three weeks after the announcement was made, purchases totaled approximately 557,000 shares, and the price approximately doubled.

The SEC prayed for several kinds of equitable relief. First, they asked that the individual defendants be enjoined from violating Rule 10b-5 in the following ways:

> (a) engaging in the purchase and sale of securities on the basis of information with respect to material facts relating to defendant TEXAS GULF acquired by said defendants in the course of their corporate duties or employment with defendant TEXAS GULF which information had not been made available to defendant TEXAS GULF, its stockholders and other public investors; (b) making available such information, directly or indirectly, to other persons for the purpose of permitting or allowing such other persons to benefit from the receipt of such information through the purchase and sale of securities; and (c) engaging in other conduct of similar purport and object.

Next, the SEC requested an order directing certain of the named defendants "to offer rescission to the person from whom each of these defendants

22. Civil actions against the corporation did in fact follow soon after the SEC's action. See *The Wall Street Journal,* Apr. 26, 1965, p. 5, col. 1. Some private actions were filed prior to the SEC's suit. See *The Wall Street Journal,* Apr. 21, 1965, p. 4, col. 2, and July 14, 1965, p. 1, col. 8.

23. Actually the number of shares purchased by the insiders seems small if they really intended to make a killing with inside information. This suggests one of three possibilities: the SEC has not yet uncovered all of the insiders' trading or giving of information to outsiders (see Chapters 5 and 11); or the insiders did not feel confident of the value of their information (see Chapters 6 and 7); or these insiders simply were not trading on the Timmins information in any substantial amount.

purchased stock and options or calls to purchase TEXAS GULF stock during the period from November 12, 1963, to April 17, 1964." The Commission also demanded restitution by certain named defendants to the individuals who sold stock to parties advised by the defendants. That is, the sellers to those receiving information from the insiders would receive restitution directly from the insider, not from the purchaser of the stock. The SEC also requested the cancellation of unexercised stock options and the return of profits or stock if they had been exercised.[24] And finally, the SEC requested that Texas Gulf Sulphur be permanently enjoined from disseminating false or misleading statements concerning its activities.

Several things must be noted about the SEC's prayer. The first remedy is limited to defendants' trading on facts learned "in the course of their corporate duties or employment." They are enjoined either from using this information directly in the market or from passing this information along to other individuals. Individual defendants who purchased shares are to offer rescission to the individuals from whom they purchased and restitution to those from whom their friends purchased. The corporation, however, is not charged in this complaint with any financial responsibility to those who relied on its statements.

The prayer for restitution to individuals selling to those who bought on the advice of insiders is most peculiar. The complaint does not even limit this liability to cases of sales to first-level advisees. Texas Gulf's geologist at Timmins is alleged to have advised a Miss Atkinson, a secretary in the Department of Commerce, who in turn told two individuals, whose shares are also included in the request-for-restitution order. One of these two was Assistant Secretary of Commerce Herbert Klotz, who is alleged merely to have worked in the same office as Miss Atkinson. There is no attempt to include individuals advised by second-level advisees, though it is well-known that these did exist.

In going beyond liability to the persons who sold to insiders, the SEC has perhaps made the most unusual proposal. Clearly, the number of shares an

24. Most of the company officials voluntarily returned to the company their stock options granted after Nov., 1964, or transferred to the company at cost the stock already taken under such options. See *The Wall Street Journal*, Aug. 4, 1965, p. 24, col. 2.

advisee purchases or causes others to purchase cannot be controlled by the insider. Thus, as the advisee and his friends become richer, it is more and more in their power to bankrupt the insider-adviser if civil actions are brought against him by those who sold to the advisees. It may well be that advisees will also be made liable for rescission or restitution by the opposite party to their particular transactions, but this too is very troublesome. There must be some limits to this notion. A certain number of fundamentally unreliable tips will in fact prove to be correct. It would be the height of absurdity to hold speculators on low-reliability advice liable on the few occasions when their gambles paid off. But it would seem equally strange to make the insider who told the first outsider an insurer for every seller's loss.[25]

Some question might also be raised about the SEC's paternalistic concern with the sellers of calls to corporate insiders. From all indications, the individuals who make markets in puts and calls are among the most sophisticated market traders in existence. It is probably safe to say that their sophistication about market transactions exceeds that of their self-appointed protector, the SEC. While a number of individual stock sellers have brought private actions against the Texas Gulf insiders, some members of the put and call industry in New York might be somewhat embarrassed at even being included in the SEC's protective complaint. These firms or individuals would not ordinarily bring an action against insiders for purchasing calls with undisclosed information. It is a safe bet that call dealers are well aware that insiders constitute a substantial number of their customers and that they do not buy calls on their own company's stock without some information or highly reliable belief that has not been disclosed in the market. If the dealers are uneasy about the risks they are taking, it is simple enough for them to cover their own sales of calls by buying the stock in the market or by selling a put.[26] It might have been more sensible for the SEC to have

25. For additional analysis of the SEC's complaint and some astute observations about insider trading, see Jack M. Whitney II, "Section 10b-5: From Cady, Roberts to Texas Gulf: Matters of Disclosure," *The Business Lawyer*, 21 (1965), p. 193. Also see William H. Painter, "Inside Information: Growing Pains for the Development of Federal Corporation Law Under Rule 10b-5," *Columbia Law Review*, 65 (1965), p. 1361.

26. See Chapter 6.

treated these call brokers in the same way as advisees of the insiders. That is, the Commission might have demanded restitution for any individuals who sold shares to these call brokers rather than for the brokers themselves.

If law is to perform its function in our society, it must conform to new problems and even new attitudes. But it is crucial that courts know precisely what issues are involved before they make changes with important social, political, or economic consequences. There is in today's literature, however, very little analysis helpful to a court or a legislature asked to resolve the issues posed by the *Texas Gulf Sulphur* case. The SEC has shown little disposition to do the necessary study, though presumably that is why specialized agencies were created.[27]

27. See Ralph F. Fuchs, "Agency Development of Policy Through Rule-Making," *Northwestern University Law Review,* 59 (1965), p. 781, especially pp. 795ff. The SEC's actions in regard to Texas Gulf Sulphur call to mind that agency's much-criticized position in the second *Chenery* case, *Securities and Exchange Commission* v. *Chenery Corporation,* 332 U.S. 194 (1947). See especially Mr. Justice Robert Jackson's dissent, at 212–18. Also see *Securities and Exchange Commission* v. *Chenery Corporation,* 318 U.S. 80 (1943) and authorities cited in Fuchs, pp. 793–94. It is interesting to note in this connection that about six weeks before filing its complaint against Texas Gulf *et al.,* the SEC "deferred indefinitely" action on a proposed regulation to require disclosure of certain insider dealings. See *The Wall Street Journal,* Mar. 8, 1965, p. 3, col. 4. The SEC apparently does not feel that it is necessary to develop rules and regulations concerning insider trading. For the view that it is appropriate to have this field of law developed in a series of judicial determinations, see Arthur Fleischer, Jr., "'Federal Corporation Law': An Assessment," *Harvard Law Review,* 78 (1965), p. 1146.

Professor Loss has also implied that the SEC should not play solely the role of poor man's complainant. He said that "the Commission is in a peculiarly good position, since it is not bogged down entirely the way courts are in deciding only cases, to shepherd this development along, modulating the sanctions and then ultimately, from time to time, codifying the developments in statements of policy, which I think the courts would be delighted to have and would very largely respect." William L. Cary, Carlos Israels, and Louis Loss, "Recent Developments in Securities Regulation," *Columbia Law Review,* 63 (1963), p. 867.

4 The Market for Valuable Information: An Introduction

In many respects the entire stock market is a complex arrangement for the marketing of information. In an investment market characterized by great risk a high premium will normally be paid for reliable information. In a market more stable and less subject to fluctuations, the difference in rate of return to the more-informed and the less-informed participants becomes smaller. The market for United States government bonds illustrates this kind of relatively stable market. As a market is subjected to more uncertainty, information about the possibility of change and its actual occurrence become more valuable. The different amounts of profit of different individuals will reflect their different degrees of sophistication and the reliability of their information. The stock market is, par excellence, the arbiter of the value of information.

The information necessary for successful investment or trading in the stock market is a fairly complex matter. It is not, as is almost true of Government bonds, simply a matter of knowing what return is offered. First, there are two broad categories of information which must be distinguished. The first of these comprehends what might be called financial sophistication, and the second involves the specific bits of data representing news of change. The first category may be likened to the knowledge of a static or unchanging system. Its content is simply knowledge of all relevant events of the past.[1] There may be large differences of opinion about the meaning

1. In this respect the first category of information may be analogized to a balance sheet that reflects all past financial occurrences. Second-category information, to follow the

or even the occurrence of these past events, but all the information that can be made available is included in this category.

Information in the second category reflects the existence of change. It is information that, in a realistic sense, cannot be predicted in advance, even in a probability sense. To the extent that a particular bit of information can be predicted, its value lies in the first category rather than in the second. As we shall see, however, neither type of information can be successfully exploited without the other. And it should also be observed that this dichotomy of what we shall term *first-* and *second-category information* is a construct designed solely to aid in the exposition of various facets of the insider-trading question. The distinction is not a necessary one for other purposes, and actually distinguishing between the categories might be extremely difficult or impossible in many instances. Nonetheless, the theoretical distinction is important for present purposes, because it allows us to understand why different techniques for marketing information have developed.

First-Category Information

Several levels of first-category information must be considered. The most fundamental level includes knowledge of the existence and nature of the stock market, alternative forms of investment, how to deal with stock brokers, how individual circumstances may dictate different investment or financial policies, the various tax consequences of different choices, and the basic institutional arrangements of the economy. The next level covers the fundamentals of finance and includes basic sophistication about balance sheets, income statements, stock market reports, and financial news generally.

A higher level of information in the first category is knowledge of the manner in which specific events that may occur in the world affect the stock market. For example, we should include here knowledge of how the following events would affect the stock market: a change in Federal Reserve Board interest policies, either restricting or expanding the amount of credit; a change in the tax laws, perhaps affecting capital-gains treatment or depre-

analogy through, would constitute events that would cause a change in the asset or liability entries in an existing balance sheet. A more apt analogy for first-category information is to the Schumpeterian stable economic system discussed in Chapter 8.

ciation allowances; international developments that may affect both the supply of and demand for different commodities.

At the next higher level it must be understood how various changes, such as those just listed, will affect not only the stock market in general but particular industries and particular companies. For instance, knowledge of how the announcement of a huge iron-ore discovery will affect market price may be necessary to evaluate the find properly. Knowledge of conditions in the electric-power industry will certainly be crucial to evaluating information about nuclear-power generators. And knowledge of a huge order from a foreign country may be worthless if it is not known whether sufficient bottoms are available for shipment.

Sophistication about conditions in an industry or a particular company is not as easily acquired as are the lower levels of sophistication. The more fundamental information may be had simply by paying the tuition costs at a university or by reading a book or newspapers. Occasionally the mere expenditure of time observing the world will be sufficient. But knowledge of particular industries and companies is not so cheaply come by. Typically it is gained as a by-product of employment within the industry or the company.

This education is not ordinarily hidden or confidential, but full sophistication about an industry is peculiarly available to those within it and rarely available to those on the outside. This is perhaps even more true of particular companies than it is of whole industries, because knowledge of the value of specific bits of information is less circumscribed by unknown details at the industry level than it is within a particular company. Knowledge that the demand for steel is up appreciably can be exploited by buying stock in all steel companies, even though some individual companies may not participate in the gain, perhaps because, unlike other companies, they are already operating at full capacity.

First-category education or sophistication about an industry or a firm cannot generally be considered inside information in the sense we shall use that term. It may be purchased in a variety of ways, and as already noted, it may be gained as part of an employment contract.[2] Securities analysts and

2. In this respect it is similar to true inside information, which typically is initially acquired only by employees. But no one has ever suggested that the experience or so-

investment advisers are in the business of collecting this kind of information in order to sell it, preanalyzed or not, to their customers. This information is frequently available in trade journals, the financial press, and in published data about particular companies, including the monthly 8-K reports that must be filed with the Securities and Exchange Commission. To a considerable extent the principal costs necessary to gain this kind of information are those involved in collecting it, storing it, and transmitting it to the ultimate purchaser. There is, however, little loss in its value if it is known to everyone, and small gain if it is known to only a few.

A Case Study in the Marketing of First-Category Information

The case of *Securities and Exchange Commission* v. *Capital Gains Research Bureau, Inc.*[3] involves an overt market for first-category information. There is no suggestion that inside information was involved. The Capital Gains Research Bureau, Inc., was an investment advisory service that engaged in a practice known in the trade as *scalping.* The advisory firm purchased a company's shares for its own account shortly before recommending the same security to its clients without disclosure of its own interest. Then the firm would sell upon a rise in market price following the recommendation.[4]

---

phistication gained from a job, apart from trade secrets, cannot be exploited exclusively by the employee when he seeks to market its value by taking a higher-paying job. Probably jobs that allow the individual to invest part of the return in himself in this fashion pay less in tangible compensation than comparable jobs that do not. Furthermore, an individual may choose to work harder for the same pay in order to guarantee advancement. This too represents a form of investment, while the laggard may be said to be consuming the full value of his position currently.

3. 375 U.S. 180 (1963).

4. In the Supreme Court's opinion the last part of this sentence appears as "immediately selling the shares at a profit upon *the* [italics mine] rise in the market price following the recommendation." If the use of *the* rather than the indefinite article *a* was conscious, it implies the Court's belief that the rise resulted from the recommendation itself and not from the disclosure of first-category information about the company. But if the former is true, a species of real fraud is implied, though the Court explicitly denies that. But this *the* may be more indicative of what the Court really thought was happening than is the rest of the opinion.

The SEC sought an injunction under Section 206 of the Investment Advisers Act of 1940, alleging that scalping "operated as a fraud or deceit" upon firm clients. The phrase *operates as a fraud* is given the same broad meaning it regularly receives in interpretations of Rule 10b-5. There is no evidence mentioned in the opinion that the advisory firm may have been engaged in manipulative practices such as touting stocks contrary to the adviser's belief or attempting to raise prices artificially in order to unload holdings at a profit. The Supreme Court's opinion, written by Mr. Justice Arthur Goldberg, emphasized that under the standard of fraud that Congress enacted in the 1940 Act, it was not necessary to show any dishonesty or intent to defraud. As he stated several times, the fundamental purpose of the Act was to achieve a "high standard of business ethics in the securities industry."[5]

Justice Goldberg examined select bits of testimony given in the hearings leading to the adoption of the Investment Advisers Act of 1940. These statements by members of the investment-advisory industry condemned investment counselors' trading in securities in which their clients were interested.[6] A report of the SEC on practices of investment companies concluded that "all conflicts of interest between the investment counsel and the client" should be removed.[7] Both the SEC and investment advisers condemned affiliations by investment advisers with investment bankers or corporations. Their stress was "not limited to deliberate or conscious impediments to objectivity"; the emphasis was said to be on "subconscious motivation."[8]

Perhaps Goldberg was naive in accepting the statements of competitors in an industry as to the meaning of high business ethics. Even from the carefully selected evidence included in the *Capital Gains* opinion, it seems that the Investment Advisers Act of 1940 may have been designed, consciously or unconsciously, to prevent competition in the investment-advisory industry. Cries of unethical conduct by competitors should be treated with a

5. *Securities and Exchange Commission* v. *Capital Gains Research Bureau, Inc.*, 375 U.S. 180, 186 (1963).

6. *Ibid.*, p. 189.

7. *Ibid.*, p. 187.

8. *Ibid.*, p. 188.

severe dose of skepticism. They are a common sign of requests for government aid in subduing obstreperous competitors.[9]

Justice Goldberg did find it incumbent on himself to establish an hypothesis under which scalping might injure clients. This is his explanation:

> An adviser who, like respondents, secretly trades on the market effect of his own recommendation may be motivated—consciously or unconsciously—to recommend a given security not because of its potential for long-run price increase (which would profit the client), but because of its potential for short-run price increase in response to anticipated activity from the recommendation (which would profit the adviser). An investor seeking the advice of a registered investment adviser must, if the legislative purpose is to be served, be permitted to evaluate such overlapping motivations, through appropriate disclosure, in deciding whether an adviser is serving "two masters" or only one, "especially . . . if one of the masters happens to be economic self-interest." *U.S.* v. *Mississippi Valley Co.,* 364 U.S. 520, 549.[10]

The last sentence is the heart of the opinion, and yet it leaves much explanation to be desired. Goldberg seems to be saying that there are two possible reasons why prices may increase after a recommendation. The first of these is that the recommendation is based on solid fact and that the price increase will stick, thus allowing the advisee to realize a long-term gain. The alternative is that the price rises merely because of the recommendation, and it will not stick because truth will out and the price will drop back. Disclosure of stock purchases by the advisory firm will, according to Goldberg's logic, allow the investor to evaluate these possibilities. Aside from the dubiousness of the last proposition and the fact that there was no evidence whatever that Capital Gains Research Bureau, Inc., acted in bad faith in its recommendations, it is essential in analyzing the practice of scalping to recognize certain aspects of the market for valuable information. (The text of the *SEC* v. *Capital Gains* opinion may be found in the Appendix, pages 219–32.)

9. See Lawrence M. Friedman, "Freedom of Contract and Occupational Licensing 1890–1910: A Legal and Social Study," *California Law Review,* 53 (1965), p. 487, and Thomas G. Moore, "The Purpose of Licensing," *The Journal of Law and Economics,* 4 (1961), p. 93.

10. *Securities and Exchange Commission* v. *Capital Gains Research Bureau, Inc.,* 375 U.S. 180, 196 (1963).

Let us assume that the stock recommendation was made in the good-faith belief that it was true and that the investment adviser took a prior position in the security with the intention of selling after his recommendation was made. For example, the adviser may have concluded that the stock of a given company should increase from 50 to 52. But he may realize that others will not share his confidence and that the total number of shares he can cause his clients to purchase is only sufficient to raise the price of the security from 50 to 51½. Assuming that his recommendation is correct, or merely that he has confidence that it is, he must believe that there is an additional profit to be made by purchasing shares in this corporation. If he waits to purchase shares until after he has made his recommendation to his customers, the information will be given to others and the price will quickly reach 52. His customers, on the average, will still have realized something less than the full $2 gain, though presumably they are satisfied with the value they are receiving. Unless they can resell the advice, they are indifferent whether the adviser or various third persons using his information realize additional profit.

The analysis is not altered in any important respect if we conclude that the customers themselves could have realized the additional profit. Whether the unpaid-for additional value goes to third parties or to his clients is a matter of indifference to the investment adviser. He will be concerned to make sure that his customers are satisfied with his service, but he will be equally concerned to prevent them or others from receiving his service for less than it is worth to them. Thus it may be true that he takes a market gain at the expense of his customers. However, this conclusion in no way implies that he has done anything wrong, and any attempt on the part of courts or others to determine whether information buyers are receiving full value must necessarily end up in a morass of indeterminacy.

Failure of the investment adviser to disclose to his customers that he has taken a position does not imply that they have been misled in any way that damages them, since they have no way of knowing in advance the value of the bits of information they have purchased. If they are satisfied in retrospect and continue to deal with the same information seller, there is no basis for saying that they have been harmed. For this reason a simple "label" requirement indicating that the adviser may be trading in his recommended stocks[11] seems in no way harmful, although it probably adds nothing to the knowledge that customers in this market really want. Performance will speak far louder than labels.

Second-Category Information

We turn next to second-category information, that is, knowledge of specific events or of the probability of future events that will ultimately cause a change in share prices. This information may or may not be inside information, as we shall use that term, because the distinction is purely a functional one depending on how the news is treated. For example, a disclosure in the newspapers that the government is about to step up procurement of aircraft represents a change from previous conditions. This is a specific bit of information which, if properly understood, has a value in the marketplace. But it cannot be considered inside information if it is publicized to all interested parties before it is acted upon in the stock market. This remains true even though opinions will differ about the impact of the order upon particular companies. Non-inside, second-category information might typically include news of such matters as government financial, tax, and credit policies; changes in the general market demand for a specific product; nationalization of foreign holdings by proclamation; loss of an important plant or building as a result of fire or natural causes; and other matters that in the ordinary course of events can be known to outsiders just as quickly as they will be known to officials within affected industries or companies.

Often non-inside news of important changes affecting stock prices will be published in general newspapers, the financial press, or trade journals as soon as it is available. And certain portions of this information may be discovered simultaneously by many interested parties, thus preventing any one individual from making a substantial profit from it. An example would be a general upturn in the demand for steel recognized by officials in many

11. This appears to be all the SEC was asking for. *Securities and Exchange Commission v. Capital Gains Research Bureau, Inc.*, 375 U.S. 180, 181 (1963). The Court on p. 201 refers to "disclosure of material facts," which might conceivably be construed to require a statement not merely that scalping was involved but how many shares the advisory firm had purchased and whether it intended selling after a price rise.

different steel companies at about the same time. This information may have some small trading value, but, for reasons we shall examine in Chapter 7, it is very unlikely that any substantial amount of true insider trading will be based on it. This kind of information rather quickly becomes first-category information and is reflected in the market value of affected stocks.

To constitute the inside information that is the subject of this book, two conditions seem necessary. The event must be one that, if all other factors were held constant, would substantially affect the price of a company's shares. But the news must also be capable of physical exploitation in the market by some individuals before the matter becomes public knowledge. That is, it must be possible for some individual or select group of individuals to buy or sell shares before the effect of the news has been substantially reflected in the market.

Certain events or developments lend themselves peculiarly to exploitation by insiders. Not surprisingly, many of these are items that corporate employees or others close to the corporation will have produced. Higher earnings or the concommitant dividend increase are clear examples. New products or inventions, new ore discoveries, oil finds, or successful marketing or management techniques also will generally be known first to those in the company responsible for the development. And news of merger offers, tender-bids, or important contracts, though perhaps originating with an outsider, will also be partially within the control of corporate officials.

Inside information may cover knowledge of the probability of a particular occurrence, as well as knowledge of an actual occurrence. Thus, as an executive is approached about a merger that he believes can be effectuated on profitable terms, he has valuable information even though the certainty of occurrence is less than 100 per cent. The value of his information must, in fact, be discounted by the probability of nonoccurrence. This explains why insiders may frequently make investments that do not yield a quick capital gain. Nonetheless, if the decision is based on some specific knowledge, then no matter how uncertain it is that a benefit will be realized or how much judgment or first-category information is involved in the conclusion, an element of true inside information will be present.[12]

12. This fact, that insider trading involves aspects of uncertainty and first-category as

There are still other reasons why insiders may not realize 100 per cent of the potential value of a bit of information. Insiders often do not have exclusive control of inside information. Not all the information that insiders do control is necessarily of their own making. Knowledge of an important contract or take-over bid is automatically shared with at least one other party. And many significant pieces of information are windfalls to the individuals who first learn of them. For instance, by virtue of the explorations of one mining company in an area, the value of neighboring holdings may appreciate tremendously. This fact may be successfully exploited in the stock market before the news is publicized. Unexpected adverse developments may likewise constitute the content of true inside information. Again the only test is the purely functional one of whether the news can be exploited in the stock market before it becomes first-category information.

Although the point will be discussed at some length in the next chapters, it should be noted now that stockholders in a corporation do not have to be aware of developments in order to share the benefits. Ultimately the information will be reflected in a higher share price. So long as they hold their shares and do not sell before this happens, the information will become first-category information and work to their benefit. But to exploit second-category information, one must either buy the stock or pass the information to someone else who will buy the stock. In either case, the share price will increase in an amount determined by the value of the information. At that point the information becomes first-category information, and anyone remaining an investor will, through this process, have realized the value with no additional expenditure of money or time.

Thus the value of first-category information may be acquired at almost no cost. But the acquisition of second-category information is a very different story. It normally cannot be acquired without cost, and hot tips are usually worth what is paid for them. But because the value of second-category information tends to be highly ephemeral, its acquisition and transmission are quite complex. The next three chapters are concerned with the institutional and analytical aspects of the market for this information.

---

well as second-category information, necessarily complicates any effort to restrain trading in true inside information. See Chapter 11.

5 Mechanisms for Marketing Inside Information

In the last chapter we distinguished several different types of valuable information and examined certain of the mechanisms available for its profitable exploitation. In this chapter we will deal with those institutionalized marketing devices that are peculiarly appropriate for exploiting true inside information. Unfortunately it is extremely difficult to find helpful and reliable data in this area. One of the reasons is the reticence of insiders and others to talk about what today may be illegal activity. Gone is the day when 90 per cent of corporate directors interviewed in a newspaper poll would state that they speculated in the stocks of their own company. Now polite businessmen simply do not discuss the matter, and it is deemed bad taste in some circles even to mention it.

But all of the difficulty does not lie in the reticence of insiders to talk about their market transactions. A more fundamental difficulty may be their failure to understand that they are in fact engaging in this kind of activity. The truth of certain economic relationships is often not recognized by the parties involved. Luckily for them, understanding is not a prerequisite to gain.[1]

1. For examples of what may have been honest misunderstandings of the various institutional arrangements, see the testimony of George Whitney, a partner in the firm of J. P. Morgan & Co., in *Hearings Before the Committee on Banking and Currency of the United States Senate,* 73d Cong., 1st Sess., 1933, p. 172. For an interesting theoretical explanation of why understanding is not a prerequisite to gain, see Armen A. Alchian, "Uncertainty, Evolution, and Economic Theory," *Journal of Political Economy,* 58 (1950), p. 211, reprinted in American Economics Association, *Readings in Industrial Organization*

As was suggested in the last chapter, there are fundamentally three different ways in which valuable information about stock market prices may be profitably exploited. The first of these, direct sale for money, is of almost no practical importance in connection with pure inside information. Although there are no cases directly on the point, it is very likely that a court would hold the direct sale of insider information by an insider to be a breach of fiduciary duty. Perhaps the closest legal analogy would lie in those cases holding that a sale of corporate office without a transfer of control is illegal,[2] even though analytically the two situations bear little resemblance. In each case there is a sale of something peculiarly associated with the corporation itself. More important, in each case the intangible is something not normally sold in this fashion. There are other cases involving the sale or transmission of valuable information, such as trade secrets sold to competitors or customer lists sold or used by a former employee. The law is generally quite clear in prohibiting these practices,[3] and these cases might be relied upon to prevent sales of stock-market information. However, the harm to the employer is readily apparent in these cases, but it is not with the sale of inside information.

Exploiting Information by Stock Purchases

The second method by which the value of information may be exploited is by buying stocks.[4] Interestingly enough, a purchase of stock can have pre-

---

and Public Policy, Vol. 8, eds., Richard B. Heflebower and George W. Stocking (Homewood, Ill.: Richard D. Irwin, Inc., 1958).

2. *Bosworth* v. *Allen,* 168 N.Y. 157, 61 N.E. 163 (1901); *Essex Universal Corporation* v. *Yates,* 305 Fed. 2d 572, 575 (2d Cir., 1962); Fletcher, *Cyclopedia Corporations,* Section 902 (Chicago: Callaghan and Co., 1954).

3. The classic cases are *E. I. DuPont de Nemours Powder Co.* v. *Masland,* 244 U.S. 100 (1917), a case involving a trade secret; *Colonial Laundries, Inc.* v. *Henry,* 48 R.I. 332, 138 Atl. 47 (1927), a case involving a customer list.

4. At many points in the ensuing discussion reference will be made only to the exploitation of good news and not to use of bad news. It is true, of course, that profits can be made by selling on bad news as easily as by buying on good, but at this point it is simply a matter of convenience to use only one illustration instead of two. In Chapters 6 and 10, where it is important to distinguish good from bad news, specific consideration will be given to each.

cisely the same effect as a direct sale of the information. In any normal sale, in which all interests in the item sold are transferred to a buyer, there is no value left to the seller. He has exchanged any claim to that value for something else, which to him is of equivalent or higher value. So it is in the stock market. As those with valuable information purchase shares, *ipso facto,* they tend to make the price or value of all shares rise. Assuming perfect knowledge on their part and that all other variables affecting price remain constant, insiders would continue to buy shares until the aggregate market price of all outstanding shares has increased by an amount equal to the value of the information.[5]

At this point, the information itself has become valueless. Its disclosure will add nothing to the market price (assuming other holders will understand its value). The knowledgeable individuals buying stock before this price is reached have, therefore, in a real sense disposed of the value of their information in exchange for an appreciation in the value of their shares. At the same time, the market value of the shares held by people who may know nothing whatever of the new information has increased. The insider has, in effect, transferred part of the value of his information to the public. Anyone holding shares in the company has now benefited proportionately by this underlying reality whether he has particular knowledge of it or not.

The transaction described is not, in any ordinary sense, a sale of the information. To constitute a sale, those receiving the benefit of the item sold (here, the information) would have to give up something in return. But the benefit of this information is available at no additional cost to those who

5. Aggregate price must, perforce, be measured by market price, but market price represents only the price of the marginally offered share. Only if the supply curve is completely elastic will the marginal price accurately reflect aggregate market price. That is, all shares would have to be offered at the same per-share price as the "next" share to be offered. But most supply curves can be assumed to have some inelasticity. And as no one's knowledge of the slope of the supply curve is perfect, the statement in the text (that insiders would buy until the aggregate market price of all outstanding shares has increased by an amount equal to the value of the information) represents only an ideal situation. The two would coincide in fact only when the outstanding shares would be offered at the market price and the information possessor purchased all of them. This may occasionally happen with certain public tender-bids for shares. See Henry G. Manne, "Mergers and the Market for Corporate Control," *Journal of Political Economy,* 73 (1965), p. 116.

hold their shares.[6] This results because there has been a creation of new value. The insiders' gain is not made at the expense of anyone. The occasionally voiced objection to insider trading—that someone must be losing the specific money the insiders make—is not true in any relevant sense. The fallacy results from a failure to analyze adequately the nature of the insiders' gain and the fact that the shareholders participate in the new value in proportion to their shareholdings.

A simple analogy may help clarify the point. If an individual makes an invention and secures a patent on it, he is protected in his ownership of the information involved in the patent. He may now sell this information directly, either by licensing others to use his patent or by an outright sale of the patent itself. But, consider an individual who has developed a valuable idea on which no patent is obtainable. Occasionally such ideas are directly marketable, though the law provides little protection for nonpatentable ideas.[7] If direct marketing of the idea itself is not feasible, the holder has two alternatives. He may either suppress the idea, or he may secure a right in some marketable property to which the value of the idea can be attached. Thus, if his idea is that there is a huge demand for an item he calls *hula-hoops,* and hula-hoops are nonpatentable, he may go into the business of selling circular tubes of plastic. Others will undoubtedly follow if his idea is successful, and he consequently earns less than he would make if the idea had been patentable. Nonetheless, he has exchanged the value of his information or idea for the increased value of the property (in this case, plastic tubing) to which the information value has been attached.

Basically the same phenomenon occurs in the case of scientists and research workers who have agreed as part of their employment contract that all patents belong to the company. This common provision would seem at

6. The statement is not completely accurate, as there is an opportunity cost involved in holding the shares, but for the long-term investor, this must be very small and probably negligible.

7. *Bristol* v. *Equitable Life Assurance Society of the U.S.,* 132 N.Y. 264, 30 N.E. 506 (1892); *Stein* v. *Morris,* 120 Va. 390, 91 S.E. 177 (1917). See also Harold C. Havighurst, "The Right to Compensation for an Idea," *Northwestern University Law Review,* 49 (1954), p. 295, and William Prosser, *Handbook of the Law of Torts,* 3d ed., sec. 124 (St. Paul: West Publishing Co., 1964).

first glance to prevent the inventor from benefiting financially—apart from any bonuses his company may give him—from significant discoveries he makes. But if the invention is important enough to affect the market value of the company's shares, the inventor may secure a part of the value of his invention by purchasing shares of his employer's stock. Even if the inventor has no proprietary interest in the patent, he may be able to secure for himself a large part of the value of his invention, if he moves quickly enough in the stock market. This phenomenon will be discussed in more detail in the next chapter.

Information Exchanges

There is still a third mechanism for marketing valuable inside information. Ultimately any information will be exploited by a purchase of shares, but a different market for information exists at a more preliminary stage. Just as the direct sale of information is logically possible, so information may be exchanged before it is acted upon by a share purchase or sale. An exchange or barter system has some advantage over either direct sales of information or insider share purchases, since the first is probably illegal and the second is somewhat constrained by various legal rules and moral precepts. It is probable that a market for the exchange of valuable information operates on a large scale in the United States. Aspects of this market have been examined, investigated, discussed, and even litigated on countless occasions. And yet, only rarely in the voluminous literature in learned journals, congressional hearings, SEC studies, and reported cases has it ever been noted that a simple economic exchange phenomenon is involved.[8] This rare recognition has not been sufficient to dispel the confusion surrounding this basic notion.

The exchange or barter system for valuable information operates in ways

8. At many points during the Senate Hearings on Stock Exchange Practices in 1933, as well as in his book, *Wall Street Under Oath* (New York: Simon & Schuster, 1939), Ferdinand Pecora remarked that preferred lists and bargain shares seemed to evidence a reciprocity agreement among underwriters. However, these were merely innuendoes suggesting something evil rather than any attempt to understand a comprehensive market for information.

ranging from the most informal to the most sophisticated, complex, and highly institutionalized. The most informal level would comprehend, for example, two executives who are members of the same golf club. One may be a director of an automobile-manufacturing company and the other a director of a steel company. Over the years it would not be unusual at all for these two friends to give each other information, or advice based on reliable information, about their respective companies. If the two companies generated approximately the same quantity of valuable information over a period of years, measured in dollar terms, each of the men might be made better off financially by this practice, even though they did not recognize it as an exchange. The direct use of insider information for short-swing profits on listed securities was made illegal in 1934. But a careful study might reveal that the estates of executives in the companies covered were built up, not by ownership of their own company's shares but rather from trading in the shares of several other companies. The necessary data would not be difficult to obtain from tax returns, and yet the existing research in this area has not produced a single helpful statistic.[9]

Problems with a Barter Market

There are numerous difficulties in even simple bartering. It is very cumbersome and not apt to be satisfactory to both parties over a period of time. Each party may feel that he is giving more than he is receiving. And if one individual tries to ration the flow of information to his friend, he is apt to find that they are engaged in an implicit bargaining situation that neither party relishes or quite understands. It is not likely that memberships in

9. The New York Stock Exchange publishes annual figures in broad categories of those who own corporate shares, and the attention of most writers has focused on share ownership rather than on trading. See, for instance, Adolf A. Berle, Jr., and Gardiner C. Means, *The Modern Corporation and Private Property* (New York: The Macmillan Co., 1933), p. 51, and Lewis H. Kimmel, *Share Ownership in the United States* (Washington, D.C.: Brookings Institution, 1952). The SEC does maintain statistics on ownership and changes in ownership of their own companies' shares by corporate insiders. But for the reasons suggested in the text, such data is of little assistance in knowing the extent to which all stock trading reflects exploitation of undisclosed information. Cf. Louis Loss, *Securities Regulation* (Boston and Toronto: Little, Brown and Co., 1961), p. 1043.

country clubs, golf foursomes, or other voluntary social groups are determined by a one-for-one exchange of valuable information. But cultural, religious, political, moral, and economic attitudes and values are constantly exchanged through such mechanisms. It is neither crass nor undemocratic to suggest that individuals, in choosing their voluntary associations, will look for individuals with whom the exchange of these values will not be one-sided. Valuable business information is simply another of the factors that, either consciously or unconsciously, may be included in the equation.

Barter is an inefficient method of exchange, and often it cannot be done on a large enough scale to allow the full exploitation of certain kinds of information. In the fellow-golfers example, one of the two executives might know a certain bit of information sufficient to make the price of his company's shares rise from 50 to 55. Before announcing this information to anyone not already privy to it, he would exploit it to the fullest extent of his own financial abilities. However, this may not be sufficient to account for the full value implicit in the information. He may, for instance, only be able to account for a rise in the stock-market price from 50 to 51. If he turns the balance of the value over to his golfing acquaintances, they may only be able to raise the price to 52. There would still be substantial value in the information, and it is not reasonable to assume, *a priori,* that individuals are willing to lose such a valuable commodity or give it away when efficient exchange devices are readily available.

If an insider chooses to distribute valuable information on the informal basis suggested, he runs into some additional difficulties. There will often be a time lag before he can reach his friends, and during this time the information, usually a very volatile commodity, may be fully exploited by others who have it. Also, the friends will tell their friends, and the information may spread very quickly. Thus, with each additional disclosure, the first executive's control over the remaining value of the information may be lost very rapidly.

Selection of Corporate Directors

A somewhat refined version of the golfers' exchange may explain the selection of certain individuals to sit on boards of directors. The reason for many of these appointments has long been one of the nagging academic questions about the business world.[10] Without for a moment suggesting that there are not myriad other factors that enter into these selections, it is interesting to note the possibility of using such appointments as information-exchange devices. In effect, the party with whom the exchange relation is sought is made a kind of "junior insider," placed there primarily to capitalize on his position for his own benefit. By virtue of his being a director, this individual will normally be privy to considerable information about the company and perhaps its industry. If, incidentally, he brings valuable skill to the running of the company, so much the better. Admittedly, all appointments cannot be explained on this basis. It is possible, however, that careful empirical research might establish many directorships as information-exchange appointments.[11]

10. Monopolistic collusion has been suggested as a possible explanation for many directors' appointments. See Louis D. Brandeis, *Other People's Money* (Washington: National Home Library Foundation, 1933), p. 35, and T.N.E.C., *Bureaucracy and Trusteeship in Large Corporations,* Monograph No. 11, 76th Cong., 3d Sess., 1940, pp. 6–8. This charge is more characteristic of the 1930's than of the 1960's, and, from what we know of how directors actually function, this would seem to be a crude and inefficient device for accomplishing the alleged purpose. The charge has also been made that control over directorships has been used by investment bankers as an aid in maintaining a monopoly position. See *United States* v. *Morgan,* 118 Fed. Supp. 621, 702 (S.D.N.Y., 1953).

11. Some of the raw data suggesting this hypothesis can be found in two sources, the *Senate Hearings on Stock Exchange Practices in 1933* and the SEC's *Special Study of Securities Markets,* Part 1, House Doc. No. 95, Part 1, 88th Cong., 1st Sess., 1963. In the first source see, for example, pp. 29–33 for testimony and questioning of J. P. Morgan and pp. 1208–9 for testimony and questioning of Otto Kahn. In the *Special Study* see pp. 429–31 for discussion of directorships held by broker-dealers and their motives for going on boards. The following from p. 429 is of interest:

> Of 4,964 firms replying to the questionnaire, 476 stated that members were directors of one or more companies whose stock was traded on an exchange, and 995 that they were directors of one or more companies whose stock was traded only over the counter. Many of these firms had only one or two directorships, but 101, including several of the largest underwriters and commission houses, were represented on the boards of at least 10 companies. For example, members of Bache & Co. were directors of 23 listed and 29 over-the-counter companies; Kidder, Peabody & Co., 23 listed and 29 over-the-counter companies; Lehman Bros., 58 listed and 23 over-the-counter companies; and Paine, Webber, Jackson & Curtis, 24 listed and 29 over-the-counter companies. In addition to these large, well established firms, several of the newer and

Another question about directors that has long troubled scholars in the field is: Why do directors not direct?[12] We may now offer a strong hypothesis. To the extent that appointments are made in order to make valuable information available to directors, we should not expect those directors to direct. Nor should we even expect them to be very interested in most corporate affairs. Interest on their part might signify either a demand for more information than the director "deserves" or a threat to the present control group. Too much interest from outside directors must frequently result in a termination of the relationship. There should be little mystery as to why many directors do not direct.

The same concept of an exchange of information may help to explain

---

> smaller underwriting houses which specialized in bringing out new issues in recent years had members on the boards of directors of several over-the-counter companies. For example, Globus, Inc., had 17 such directorships.

And consider the following from p. 433:

> The basic conflicts which are highlighted by the *Cady, Roberts* case stem from the fact that a director, by virtue of his office, may have access to corporate information not contemporaneously available to the general public. A representative of a broker-dealer sitting on the board of directors of a company may have difficulty resolving loyalties and duties to the company, his customers, and stockholders of the company who are not his customers. . . .
>
> Carl M. Loeb, Rhoades & Co. also tries to distinguish secret information which it receives through members who serve as directors, from that which may be disclosed. A partner of the firm told the Special Study:
>
> I ascertain from management in most cases, or in all cases, if I am going to make this information available to anyone. I say, "Is this information available generally to any part of the investing public that wants to find it?"
>
> * * * If that is the situation, I do not wait 6 months until the public report comes out on the company. If this is not secret information and you are sure this is information that would be available in like manner, you do not try to jump the market but, at the same time, you do not want to stand back and look stupid.
>
> This is a very difficult area to move in. This is why we have this policy of not tying our trading department's hands with inside knowledge, because what is inside knowledge to me is already on the street in about 9 cases out of 10.
>
> That is why we get the company to release the information as soon as possible, to remove the problem.

12. William O. Douglas, "Directors Who Do Not Direct," *Harvard Law Review,* 47 (1934), p. 1305; Horace B. Samuel, *Shareholders' Money* (London: Sir Isaac Pitman & Sons, Ltd., 1933), p. 124.

and perhaps soften the old criticism of the famous stock pools of the 1920's and earlier. Most pools had a great many corporate executives and directors among their members. Typically these individuals were privy to advance inside information about a corporation. Most pools came into existence when there were prospects of a merger, a favorable earning statement, or other encouraging news.[13] If the manager of the pool were also the insider with valuable information, the pool became not only an efficient device for disseminating information but also a foolproof way of policing the information the pool sought to exploit. The pool was possibly the most efficient device ever discovered for the exchange of valuable information. Unfortunately, the device lent itself easily to fraudulent market manipulation,[14] and the antimanipulation provisions of the Securities and Exchange Act of 1934 were the result.[15]

A Clearinghouse for Information

As we have seen, the individual or individuals initially possessing valuable information are rarely able to exploit fully the value of that information by purchases in the stock market or by direct sales of the information. They may be left with information that others, who are able to exploit it, would like to have. If these latter individuals at other times have information they cannot exploit directly, the necessary conditions for a beneficial exchange exist, and we should expect the exchange to occur. As we have seen, this can be done informally and on a small scale by direct barter. For the large-scale exchange mechanisms, however, we shall have to look elsewhere.

Basically what is needed for the effective functioning of this market is some sort of clearinghouse operation. This clearinghouse would have to perform at least four distinguishable functions. It would have to be a repository of valuable information or its value. The clearinghouse might, in

13. Sen. Report No. 1455, 73d Cong., 2d Sess., 1934, p. 36.

14. Some of the reasons why pools could be easily converted into devices for fraudulent manipulation will become clearer in Chapter 7. Basically, the argument is that many outside shareholders respond to stock-price movements rather than to fundamental data about corporate affairs. Additional discussion of pools appears in Chapter 10.

15. Sec. 9, *Securities Exchange Act of 1934,* as amended, 15 U.S.C. 78i (1965).

this respect, be viewed as an information retailer who buys wholesale. Secondly, whoever performs this clearinghouse function should be in a position to determine which individuals are entitled to share in the value of information collected. That is, the functionary should be able to identify those individuals who, as a result of "depositing" valuable information, have gained some claim against the total pool. And, naturally, he should also be able to determine the amount of the claim held by these parties. Presumably, over some period of time the amount any individual might claim from the pool would be determined by the amount of information he has furnished. Finally, some method should be available for assuring that the people withdrawing information or its value are in fact entitled to it and that there is no substantial leakage to those who are not entitled.

Is anyone or any institution performing all of these functions in the modern American economy? A firm answer cannot be given to this question, as too many of the details would be or are carefully guarded secrets. But one group is certainly in a position to perform the functions mentioned if it wishes. The special relationship of investment bankers, underwriters, and large brokerage houses to the American corporation has long been a subject of controversy, analysis, and even litigation.[16] These multifaceted organizations undoubtedly perform many different services for American businesses. They are financial advisers, management counselors, executive and director finders, merger arrangers, underwriters, and many other things. They may be, in addition, the clearinghouses par excellence for valuable information. Let us examine then how these functionaries (for convenience we shall refer to them simply as investment bankers)[17] can perform the functions necessary for operating a clearinghouse for information.

16. Brandeis, *Other People's Money; Stock Exchange Practices;* Roscoe T. Steffen, "The Investment Bankers' Case: Some Observations," *Yale Law Journal,* 64 (1954), p. 169; William Dwight Whitney, "The Investment Bankers' Case—Including a Reply to Professor Steffen," *Yale Law Journal,* 64 (1955), p. 319, Roscoe T. Steffen, "The Investment Bankers' Case: Observations in Rejoinder," *Yale Law Journal,* 64 (1955), p. 863; William Dwight Whitney, "The Investment Bankers' Case: Surrejoinder," *Yale Law Journal,* 64 (1955), p. 873; *United States* v. *Morgan,* 118 Fed. Supp. 621 (S.D.N.Y., 1953).

17. Merrill Lynch, Pierce, Fenner & Smith is the principal illustration of a firm ordinarily called a brokerage house but playing an increasingly important role in underwriting

Investment Bankers as Information Repositories

A successful clearinghouse should be able to receive and store the necessary information. One method of doing this we have already mentioned: the placement of representatives on corporate boards of directors. Although this practice may not be as common as it was in years gone by, the figures are still impressive. The SEC's Special Study[18] reported that 1,471 registered broker-dealer firms stated that members were directors of one or more publicly traded companies. Of this number, 101 were represented on the boards of at least ten companies. Lehman Brothers led the list with directorships on fifty-eight listed and twenty-three over-the-counter companies.

But these figures do not tell the whole story, as it is not necessary for representatives of these firms to be directors in order to gain information. As the SEC's Special Study states:

> It should also be pointed out that underwriting firms, whether or not they have a representative on a company's board of directors, often retain a special relationship which enables them to obtain information concerning the company which the general public does not have. In the first place, the requirement in an underwriting agreement of regular financial reports to the managing underwriters, as distinguished from the general body of stockholders, may give a firm a considerable advantage in the market. Secondly, a firm with an underwriting relationship is likely to be among the first to be advised of any corporate developments.[19]

Today it is generally believed that the position of investment bankers in controlling large corporations is substantially weaker than it was thirty years ago. Some writers declare that control has passed from banker hands into management hands.[20] Whether or not this is true in any meaningful sense, it

---

and other investment-banking functions. See T. A. Wise, *The Insiders* (New York: Doubleday & Co., Inc., n.d.), pp. 65–66.

18. *Report of Special Study of Securities Markets of the Securities and Exchange Commission,* Part 1, p. 429.

19. *Ibid.,* p. 433.

20. Robert A. Gordon, *Business Leadership in the Large Corporation* (Berkeley and Los Angeles: University of California Press, 1961), pp. 214–21; Andreas G. Papandreou, "Some Basic Problems in the Theory of the Firm," *A Survey of Contemporary Economics,* Vol. 2, ed., Bernard F. Haley (Homewood, Ill.: Richard D. Irwin, Inc., 1952), p. 183.

cannot be denied that investment bankers remain one of the important creative forces in American business. Whether their actions take the form of arranging a merger, financing important new industrial developments, or arranging the spin-off of an unprofitable subsidiary, they are privy at an early stage to important information. The illustrations could be continued at length. Regardless of the power of management, the investment-banking fraternity is uniquely situated to be a repository of valuable information and to serve the first of the four functions necessary for an information clearinghouse.

Investment Bankers as Distributors of Information

The next function is that of determining who is entitled to share in the value of information produced. There are several ways in which investment-banking houses may perform this function. If a house controls a given corporation or exercises substantial influence, it will be able to name members to the corporation's board of directors. These need not be members of the firm itself but rather individuals whom the bankers recognize as entitled to share in valuable information. It must be repeated that there are many other reasons why a particular individual may be named to a board of directors, but one factor likely to be considered is whether or not the individual chosen should be given access to the information normally available to directors.[21]

The function of deciding who is entitled to information may be quite complex. The problem is compounded by the unlikelihood that actual books would be kept today. The old pools undoubtedly did just that. The problem is one of knowing who is responsible for having "deposited" valuable information previously with the bankers. No simple answer will ordinarily be available. It may be almost impossible to know, for example, who actually engineered a certain merger or who was responsible for the bankers' knowing about new industrial developments. The bankers must of necessity have close, personal associations with corporations and their

21. This discussion has some implications for the subject of cumulative voting. Probably some of the opposition to cumulative voting stems from the fact that it requires a sharing of valuable information with someone not actually selected by those in control of the company.

executives in order to perform this function. The decision-making involved in these selections will be more demanding of experience and wisdom than of bookkeeping abilities.

The necessary bookkeeping becomes even more complicated when we consider the third function: determining how much "credit" particular individuals are entitled to. Again subtle, complex, and difficult questions arise. The market for valuable information is by no means a precise one in which it is easy to put a dollar figure on the information received and that disclosed. Rough and inexact approximations must constantly be made. The process is perhaps more one of artistry than of science or bookkeeping. Yet the whole complex market for inside information depends on the successful performance of this function.

Some of the factors preventing a precise distribution of valuable information may be readily imagined. Identical kinds and quality of information may occur at different stages of overall stock-market changes. What appear to be bits of information of the same value may give profits in one case and losses in another. Some information, very easily obtained or requiring little or no effort on its developer's part, may be worth considerably more than information resulting from a lifetime of hard work. The developer of the latter may often feel that he has established a considerable claim against clearinghouse balances. Furthermore, different individuals will have different financial abilities to utilize information given them. Decisions will, therefore, have to be made as to whether an "account" should be credited with the objective value of the information given or the value to the recipient of the information used. Each of these problems demands subtle computations and expert diplomacy. Clearly, the relationship of investment bankers to corporate executives must be one of great trust and confidence.[22]

22. Consider the following from *United States* v. *Morgan,* 118 Fed. Supp. 621, 817 (1953):

> But with a series of security issues, the saving in time and labor of the officers and employees of an issuer, which would have to be spent in teaching a new investment banker the intricacies of the business, and the financial setup of the company, are a matter of real consequence; and it must not be forgotten that many of the matters to be discussed are of such a character that company officials desire to have such conversations only with those whom they trust, and in whose integrity and competence they have complete confidence.

And it should not be difficult to understand why documentation and empirical data are difficult to obtain in this area.

Priority Lists

The complex process described is facilitated by two well-known devices. The first of these, the so-called *priority* or *preferred list,* is simply a list of names of individuals to be preferred in receiving specific bits of information or advice to buy certain stocks. These have been discussed for years,[23] but rarely has it been recognized that these lists may serve a function as broad as that suggested by this analysis. At one point in the 1934 Senate Hearings on Stock Exchange Practices, Ferdinand Pecora, the chief counsel of the committee, suggested that names on priority lists were those of corporate executives whose companies dealt with a particular banking house, and he suggested that the individuals listed kept the banking house informed of

23. In *Wall Street Under Oath,* Pecora explained what he considered the origins of preferred lists. After stating that J. P. Morgan & Co. entered the business of underwriting common stocks in 1929 and that they did not want any implication of speculation associated with their name, he went on:

> But they decided that it was quite all right to offer the stock *privately,* to a select list of purchasers, "People that we know intimately, that we believe have enough knowledge of business and general conditions to know exactly what they are buying. . . ."
>
> This was the origin of the famous so-called "preferred lists" whose publication stirred the nation, and opened the eyes of millions of citizens to the hidden ways of Wall Street. In each case, stock was offered by J. P. Morgan & Company to the individuals on these lists at cost, or practically at cost. In each case the offer was made with full and irrefutable knowledge that there was, or would very shortly be, a public market for the stock at a much higher figure. In effect, it was the offer of a gift of very substantial dimensions (pp. 26–27).

Pecora also pointed out that there were almost 500 persons on one or the other of these "preferred lists." They included men exceedingly prominent in both business and government (pp. 28–29).

Naturally, the *Senate Hearings on Stock Exchange Practices in 1933* were replete with many references to these lists. Discussions of the subject begin on the following pages: 138, 145, 173, 177, 396, 401, 885, 1209, and 1232. The discussions usually involved Pecora's charge that these lists were used for "reciprocity" and the bankers' heated but unconvincing denials. It is perhaps fair to say, however, that no cogent analysis of the phenomenon exists anywhere in the *Hearings* or Pecora's book.

corporate affairs.[24] The banker being questioned was indignant at the suggestion that information was being bought and sold, although he and the writers on the subject have failed to offer a plausible alternative explanation.[25] Clearly, names do not appear on these lists merely because the individuals are good friends of the banking house.

Under outdated or outlawed underwriting practices, differing numbers of bargain shares were offered to different individuals.[26] This allowed a rather precise payoff, as the exact amount being distributed could be known in advance. That technique could only be used with new issues and would have only limited utility today—if it is legal at all.[27] The modern version of the priority list contains names of people who will be told particular bits of information or advised to buy certain shares. Each of these techniques raises problems, however, as there is no way to control the further disclosure of the information. Advice to buy shares would seem to give more protection than disclosure of information, though the information itself may be considered less reliable by the recipients, because it is more difficult to confirm.

Considerable sophistication can be added to the priority list technique by the use of various lists. The most important list—or lists, if different combinations of recipients are desired—will usually contain the names of individuals who have been or are currently most instrumental in generating information. Other lists will form a descending pyramid, as the larger number of individuals with smaller claims are assigned their appropriate places on lower priority lists. Such a system could engender considerable incentive to get to the top list. But if this essentially market device is to perform the

24. *Stock Exchange Practices*, pp. 62 and 814–15.

25. George Whitney of J. P. Morgan & Co. said that persons were put on such lists "as the result of continuing relations." *Ibid.*, p. 172. We are not told what these continuing relations are, nor did Pecora follow up on the subject.

26. See footnote 22, *supra*.

27. Section 16 of Schedule A of the Securities Act of 1933 requires that a registration statement include the price at which the security will be offered to the public "and any variation therefrom at which any portion of such security is proposed to be offered to any persons or classes of persons, other than the underwriters, naming them or specifying the class. A variation in price may be proposed prior to the date of the public offering of the security, but the Commission shall immediately be notified of such variation."

function alleged for it, those spaces must be reserved for individuals whose contributions are greatest.

Discretionary Accounts

Probably more efficient than priority lists as an information-exchange control device is the so-called *discretionary account.* This is nothing more than a deposit of money with a broker who is given full discretion to buy or sell any shares for the account. Surprisingly little has been written about these accounts in the present connection. It is commonly recognized that most trust funds are at the same time discretionary accounts, and it has occasionally been complained that discretionary accounts lend themselves to "churning," or excessive trading to build up commissions.[28] Apart from these matters, neither of which concerns us here, the most common statement by brokers and bankers is that they really prefer not to have discretionary accounts and that they do not accept them as a matter of common practice.[29] Investment advisers other than brokers sell investment advice for a fee,[30] but brokers and bankers do not as a general rule handle discretionary accounts for a fee. It would appear that this service may be reserved for customers who pay in a form other than cash, because the existence of discretionary accounts with no advisory-fee charge is well known on Wall Street. The SEC's Special Study makes no mention of these accounts.

Nothing about discretionary accounts appeared in the 1933 congressional hearings either, possibly because they may not have been used then. The pool was a far more efficient device and would frequently have served the same purpose as the discretionary account. With the outlawing of pools in 1934, a tolerable substitute may have been found in the discretionary account. It would be interesting to know if their popularity is a post-1934

28. *Special Study of Securities Markets,* Part 1, p. 297.

29. See Douglas H. Bellemore, *Investments: Principals, Practices and Analysis* (New York: Simmons-Boardman Publishing Corp., 1962).

30. *Special Study of Securities Markets,* Part 1, p. 369. A few brokerage firms provide investment supervisory services, but most investment-counseling firms do not have custody of their clients' funds or securities. It is not hard to imagine a variety of business relationships between investment counselors and brokers, however. See *ibid.,* p. 370.

matter, but again the investigators seem to have been asking the wrong questions.

The discretionary account, for which the broker has broad powers to invest a specified amount of money at his discretion and to buy and sell securities, has several advantages over priority lists. These accounts are especially suitable for dealing in information whose value will be exploited rapidly in the market. The broker can enter the necessary transactions at once, without having to contact his principals. This advantage is not so important if the information can be withheld for a while, but often that cannot be done. A perfect illustration of this point is provided by *In the Matter of Cady, Roberts & Co.* There, it will be recalled, the inside information was that the company had passed a dividend. The broker, Gintel, was able to sell out his discretionary accounts in Curtiss-Wright shares very quickly and even to go short for those accounts. Had he been delayed as much as an hour, the entire operation might have been unsuccessful. If he had used priority lists to identify the same individuals and communicate with them, they would undoubtedly have gained less profits as a group, and many would have been left out altogether.

Insider trading in especially volatile information, like dividend news, has been increasingly attacked by the SEC and regulated by the New York Stock Exchange. Therefore, the popularity of discretionary accounts may be declining. But still other advantages to the discretionary account must be considered for an accurate appraisal of their usefulness. As we have seen, the priority list requires either that a particular bit of information be disclosed or that customers be advised to buy without any indication of why. If the information is disclosed—a process never required by discretionary accounts—there is no efficient way of policing the further distribution of this information by individuals on the list. Also, if only the information is disclosed, the bankers have no way of determining how skillfully the individual will evaluate the information nor how many shares he will purchase. All of these difficulties disappear if discretionary accounts are used.

With discretionary accounts the market for valuable information begins to approach an automaticity unusual in barter markets. This is not to say that the system works perfectly, or that there are no leaks in the information channels, or that mistakes will not be made—the pools were undoubtedly more efficient. But, for large-scale bartering of volatile information with the necessity of some policing, this device is probably the best available. Where policing problems do not loom large, either because the news will not be disclosed for a long time or because quick dissemination to a large number of people is desired, the priority list is the more efficient device.[31]

In comparison to the total trading in a given stock, the number of transactions based on discretionary accounts and priority lists may be quite small. Most insiders will not plan to sell out within six months, and therefore direct purchases will still be widely used—unless the courts make that illegal or the stock exchanges are successful in hampering it. Informal exchanges or gifts of valuable information may play a larger role than is commonly recognized. But, most important, as we shall see in Chapter 7, the total amount of short-swing, insider trading is itself likely to be quite small. A large fraction of this trading, however, may be accounted for by priority lists and discretionary accounts.

The important proposition of this chapter is that the market for valuable information described actually exists. Some of the evidence to establish this point is a bit dated to be sure, but recent studies indicate no fundamental changes. And, if empirical evidence is lacking, we can fall back on logical inference. Then the case for the existence of this market is very strong. It would be extraordinary if the vast riches regularly available in the form of valuable information were simply lost by astute businessmen like sand sifting through their open hands. Until convincing evidence to the contrary is available, we should assume that this market exists and is efficiently maintained by important functionaries in the financial community.

31. Two additional factors may also occasionally dictate the use of priority lists rather than discretionary accounts. The latter may, first of all, be used only by brokers, whereas anyone regularly privy to valuable information may use the priority-list method of allocation. And discretionary accounts do require relinquishment of the personal use of the funds managed in the account, a step some individuals may be either unwilling or unable to take.

6 Market Effects of Different Trading Rules

In Chapter 7 we shall observe the effect of alternative legal rules regarding insider trading upon specific individuals in the market. After that we shall consider whether a rule allowing insiders to trade in corporate securities is or is not generally beneficial to all shareholders. First, however, it is important to understand the more general market effects of different trading rules. We shall investigate three different rules. The first is the rule of completely free trading by insiders. The second is the rule of no insider trading. The third, important only for analytic purposes, is a rule that would allow insiders to trade only in puts and calls or to receive stock options from their company, but not to exploit information directly by buying and selling shares.

To aid in comparing the effects of these different rules, certain simplifying assumptions will be made. We shall assume that we can know precisely the number of points a given stock will move up or down on the disclosure of good or bad news. And, to continue with the illustration used earlier, we shall consider the case of a share selling at 50, with good news worth five points. That is, the total market value of the information is $5 times the total number of shares outstanding. Under any of the three rules we shall consider, the ultimate effect must be to cause an increase in share price from 50 to 55. And we shall assume that no external circumstances other than those relating to the inside information operate to change the price of the stock.

Practical Limits on Exploitation of Inside Information

It is important to recognize some facts about the extent to which market exploitation of information is feasible. If an individual wished to exploit the full value of a certain piece of information, it would seem that he would have to purchase every share of the company's stock. Only in this fashion could he gain that part of the value of the information that would adhere to each share of stock. Actual instances of direct purchases of all shares are quite rare in publicly traded companies, though mergers may accomplish the same thing. In these cases we can say that the purchaser has information about the company's potential under his control. His belief that he can manage the company more profitably is the valuable inside information, and, by purchasing all the shares, he may realize the full value of that information.[1]

But even if purchasing all the shares of a company's stock were practicable, it could not guarantee the realization of the full value of the information. Factors other than those known in the market will affect sellers' decisions to sell. The purchase price has to be sufficient to overcome a range of subjective individual preferences that, in our example, would make it impossible normally to buy all of the company's shares at a price of 50.[2] Clearly, a market price of 50 does not signify that all shares of the company can be bought at that price. And yet anything paid in excess of 50 for these shares reduces the market value of the information to that extent, because we are assuming that the price will rise only to 55.

The purchase of a small percentage of the outstanding shares of a company's stock will often be sufficient to raise the market price to the level indicated by the information. In a company with ten million shares outstanding, the purchase of fifty thousand shares might be sufficient to raise the quoted price of the shares from 50 to 55.[3] Here the indicated value of

1. *Speed* v. *Transamerica Corp.*, 99 Fed. Supp. 808 (D. Del., 1951) involved precisely this proposition, and the failure to disclose the intention of the stock purchaser was found to be a violation of SEC Rule 10b-5. There were independent grounds for finding a fiduciary duty, however, as the purchasers were already in control of the company. Cf. *Mills* v. *Sarjem Corp.*, 133 Fed. Supp. 753 (D.C.N.J., 1955) in which no violation of 10b-5 was found. *Speed* was distinguished, because the plan in *Mills* for purchasing control and liquidating was formulated by a complete outsider with no pre-existing fiduciary duty to the shareholders.

2. Henry G. Manne, "Some Theoretical Aspects of Share Voting," *Columbia Law Review*, 64 (1964), p. 1435. As noted in footnote 5, Chapter 5, there is usually some inelasticity in the supply curve.

3. Some explanation for the possibility of such a large leverage factor may be had by comparing the 9 billion shares listed on the New York Stock Exchange with the 1¼ billion

the information is $50 million, but, assuming an average purchase price of 52 for the insiders, the gain is only $150,000.[4] If an insider buys in excess of fifty thousand shares, he is no longer trading on his inside information but rather he is hoping for market misinterpretation of the news when it appears. As we shall see in the next chapter, this may not be illogical, but these later purchases will be made with considerably less certainty than the earlier ones. In the ensuing discussion, when we refer to an insider exploiting the full value of the information, the reference is only to his purchasing enough shares to raise the current market price of the shares to the point indicated by the value of the new information, not to his recovering the actual value of the information. In fact, however, even this kind of full exploitation is rare.

Individuals receiving valuable information about the companies whose shares are actively traded often will not be able to capture the full value of that information for themselves. Information is often more mercurial than mercury. In many instances it is impossible to prevent its rapid dissemination to others. The time period that insiders have to capture the fresh information may occasionally be as small as minutes,[5] although in some cases of really substantial news the period will be considerably longer.[6] The insiders' problem may be insufficient capital or unavailable credit within the necessary time period. Or the difficulty may take the form of their unwillingness or inability to liquidate present holdings in order to exploit the new knowledge.[7]

---

shares traded in 1964, the Exchange's most active year. See *The Exchange*, 26, No. 7 (July, 1965), p. 1. This means that an average of only 5 million of the 9 billion outstanding shares are traded daily, or slightly more than .05%. The example in the text involves .5% of outstanding shares. The ratio of average trading to outstanding shares does, of course, vary with different companies.

4. This is, of course, a fairly extreme illustration. It indicates, however, that in companies with a low ratio of traded shares to outstanding shares, insider trading presents the least problem quantitatively. Frequently these are companies in which investor confidence in management is high or companies whose securities are considered of high-investment grade.

5. Cf. *In the Matter of Cady, Roberts & Co.*, SEC Release No. 6668, *CCH Federal Securities Law Reporter* (1961), p. 81018.

6. *Texas Gulf Sulphur* might involve that kind of situation.

7. Here tax considerations will frequently loom large. If the sale of securities would occur just short of six months after acquisition, the cost of foregoing a capital gain may

The insider is also faced with a considerable amount of uncertainty. In the first place, his own knowledge will rarely be perfect, and he cannot know the extent to which others in possession of the same information have already been buying. He cannot know precisely the effect of his and other purchases on the price of the company shares since other factors may be operating to accentuate their effect or counteract it. Finally, there is no absolute certainty in the stock market even for insiders; the discovery of an important new sulphur deposit may be followed closely by a collapse of sulphur prices.

These are uncertainties with which even the most knowledgeable insider must contend. Thus many individuals are not willing to risk their entire fortune on what often appears to be a fairly sure thing.[8] Furthermore, insiders may choose not to trade at all on small bits of information that they can afford to exploit fully. The smaller the per-share value of the inside information, the larger will the effects of other market uncertainties appear. The closer the current price is to the anticipated price, the less likely are insiders to buy the stock.

Free-Trading Rule

We are now in a position to describe graphically the process of a price change under a rule of free insider trading. We shall assume that corporate insiders are free to use undisclosed information in any way they see fit. They may exploit it directly themselves, they may tell friends, or they may do both of these things. We will, however, assume that no calls will be purchased nor stock options issued.[9] As we shall see, this is a simplifying assumption that in no way detracts from the logic of the analysis.

---

be very substantial. Another common situation involves a pledge of securities physically in possession of the pledgee, with no right of substitution by the pledgor. Section 16(b) of the Securities Exchange Act of 1934 will present problems if the shares or shares of the same class had been purchased within the preceding six months.

8. This may explain why the purchases by Texas Gulf insiders were not considerably greater than they were, although it is also possible that the SEC has not identified all the transactions resulting from the inside information.

9. There are some fairly strong reasons to believe that options and calls do not play an

Beginning with the stable price of 50, we should expect the price to rise slowly as the first few insiders begin to make their purchases. But additional people now begin to buy the stock, as they believe that they are in possession of valuable information. Their number increases by some logarithmic function, and the effect can be shown by an exponential curve, or ramp function, flattening out at 55, as illustrated in Figure 1.

The shape of this curve will vary, even for one particular stock, with many different factors. We have already noted the problem of knowing the supply schedule for the stock. The kind and quality of information involved will be important. And some bits of news will travel much faster than others. Perhaps more important will be the pattern of insiders' distribution of different kinds of information. If this pattern is always the same for particular types of recurring information, such as earnings reports or new government contracts, the coefficient that will describe the exponential curve will be a constant. If this is so, and if it is possible to discover this constant, projection of some price changes of shares might be feasible. The statistical refinements necessary to prove and utilize this thesis would be extraordinarily complex. But there are some indications of this kind of price-change dependency, and these indications have not been explained in any other way.[10]

Few price changes ever result in a pure ramp-function curve. Rather, as we shall explain, the curve begins in the fashion just described, probably

---

important role in insiders' trading. The seller of a call can, if he inquires, discover the identity of the purchaser. If he were to discover, for instance, that executives of U.S. Steel were buying calls on U.S. Steel's stock, prudence would dictate that he cover quickly by buying a matching number of U.S. Steel shares. He may in fact do more than cover, as he now has reliable information about the insiders' view of the company. In addition to purchasing shares, the dealer will undoubtedly raise the call price. This last factor is sufficient by itself to explain the difficulty insiders would have in exploiting valuable information on any large scale by the purchase of calls.

There is one additional reason why calls are not efficient devices for insiders to exploit their information. Sections 3a(10) and 3a(11) of the Securities Exchange Act of 1934 define a *security* and an *equity security* in such a way as to include a call. Thus changes in holdings by insiders must be reported, and any profits made by a purchase and sale of a call within six months may be recovered by the corporation under Section 16(b). Of course, short-term trading in calls is not prohibited by 16(b) to anyone not a statutory insider.

10. See Sidney S. Alexander, "Price Movements in Speculative Markets: Trends or Random Walks, No. 2," in *The Random Character of Stock Market Prices,* ed., Paul H. Cootner (Cambridge, Mass.: M.I.T. Press, 1964), p. 338, especially the conclusion, p. 369.

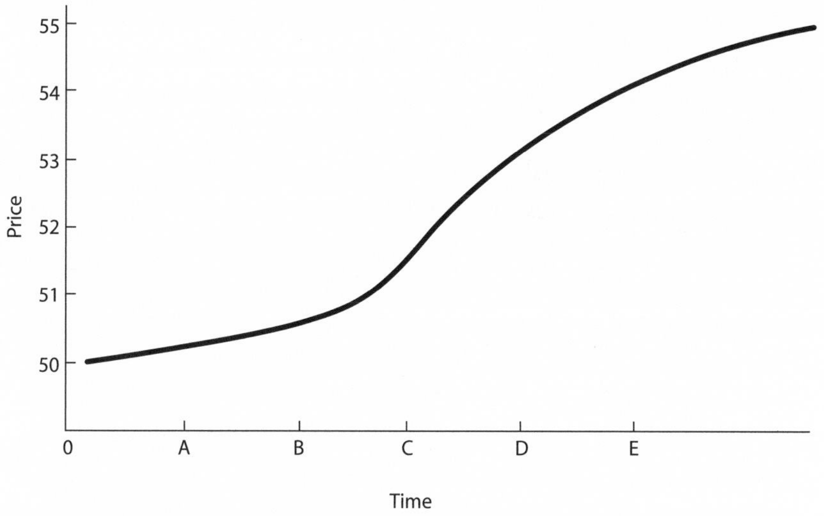

Figure 1. Simple Price Rise with Insider Trading

begins to show tremors at some point before reaching 55 but nonetheless continues above that point to, say, 58. It may then drop back to 53, go back to 56, back down to 54½, and then lose any further noticeable effect from the news. This oscillation effect can be likened to a ripple in a pond. If the pond is very still, a ripple can be followed all the way to the shore. But if several people are throwing pebbles into the same pond and creating a variety of ripples, then the oscillations from one pebble will tend to disappear or become indistinguishable from others before the first ones actually reach the shore. The effect of new information on the stock-market price in our illustration will tend to disappear while oscillating around the $55 line, but other forces may well carry the actual stock price above or below this figure. (See Figure 2.) Those changes, however, are not relevant to the present discussion.

We are now in a position to explain in more detail the entire effect of a given piece of market information under the rule of free insider trading. The curve will begin to rise in exponential fashion simply because an increasing number of people will receive the information and rely upon it over a period of time. But for reasons already examined, insiders will become

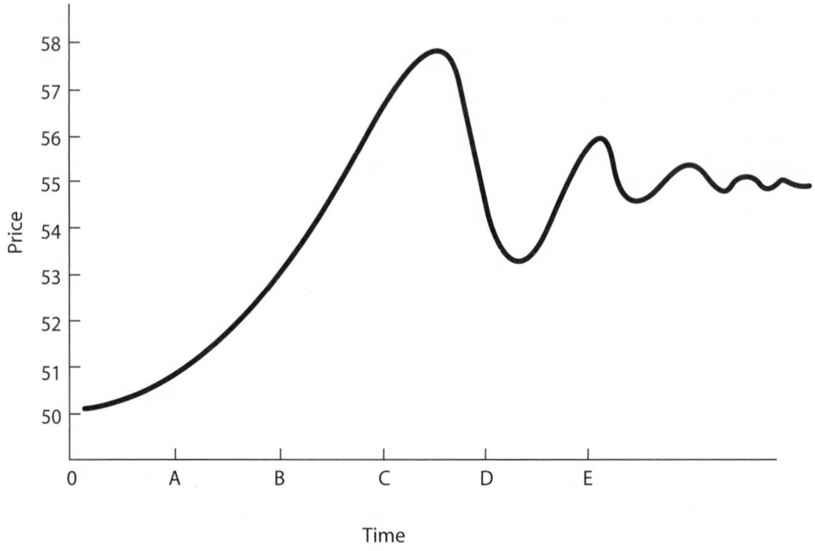

Figure 2. Price Rise with Insider Trading and Consequent Effects

less certain of profits as the price approaches that indicated by the value of the news. At some point before the stock reaches its heights, some of the original purchasers will either sell or stop their own purchasing even though the total number of purchasers may still be increasing. We have assumed that no other changes are occurring to affect the price of this share, but naturally the traders in our illustration cannot know that such changes will not occur. The effect of this may or may not be noticeable as a tremor, but at least it portends the larger oscillations that will follow.

Physical Analogies

As information originating with one or a few people is disseminated to a larger number, the effect on the market is analogous to the laws governing friction and kinetic energy. As the information moves from its original source at an exponential rate to more and more people, it will become increasingly difficult to stop it precisely at the $55 line. This might occur if the information reflects a specific, ascertainable, nonrepeating addition to value, as in the case of a tender-bid or a tax refund.

Many individuals, seeing that the stock is selling at, say, 52 and realizing that there is at least $3 of value left in the information, will put in orders to purchase. But, because there is a time lag before orders are executed[11] or because too many people had the same information at the same time, the information may actually be worth only two points. Nonetheless, the effect of the buy orders anticipating a three-point rise will be sufficient to carry the price of the share beyond the $55 point.

Time lags in the transmission of and action upon information are probably the major factors involved in the oscillation phenomenon. There are, however, other kinds of interferences operating as well, and here analogues borrowed from modern communication theory will help to explain the economics of information. Basically the three influences at work are the stock-market analogues of the concepts of *attenuation, noise,* and *distortion.*

The concept of attenuation has already been referred to. The ripple in the still pond presents a perfect analogue to the spread of information. This time, however, we must enlarge our hypothetical pool in order to understand the situation, for, no matter how still a pool, if it is large enough we will not be able to discern the wave effect at the shore. Frank Knight has stated the matter in economic terms: "When the idea becomes common property it is like any other superabundant element in production, a free good and no longer a productive factor in the effective economic sense."[12] A corollary of this statement is that the more people who have a bit of information, the less it is worth.[13]

As the price increases there is a deterioration in the "quality" of buyers, that is, there will be more buyers who cannot have a high degree of confidence in the reliability of their information, and their mode of behavior in the stock market may tend to be more erratic than that of insiders. As we have seen, the value of the original information is now approaching zero, though the market may carry the price beyond that indicated by the value

11. Except perhaps for specialists on the floor of an exchange.

12. Frank H. Knight, *Risk, Uncertainty and Profit* (Boston and New York: Houghton Mifflin Co., 1921), p. 342.

13. At least this corollary holds for the kind of information we are concerned with in this discussion. It is probably accurate as a broad generalization, but the proof would take longer than is warranted here.

of the information. Unless the insider is also willing to purchase shares based on so-called technical rather than fundamental factors, we should not ordinarily expect to find him among those buying at these higher reaches. Indeed, it is a safe assumption that few executives appear as buyers in this phase of a stock rise. It is interesting that the first group of purchasers of Texas Gulf Sulphur stock after November, 1963, purchased at prices ranging from 17 to 27,[14] although a month after their last purchase the stock sold as high as $58.

Another kind of imperfection that prevents the perfect transmission of information in the marketplace is analogous to the communications concept of noise. In a crowded room with a number of people speaking at once, it is often difficult to listen to one particular conversation. Other words, phrases, and sounds constantly intrude and blank out the sought-after conversation.[15] Similarly, in the market for valuable information, though one may be straining to hear only reliable news, one continually hears a veritable babble of rumors, hot tips, suggestions, and leads. Straining out the reliable from the unreliable is extremely difficult and in many cases, especially for smaller shareholders, literally impossible to do with any degree of confidence. The effect of this is to make one wary of all information, including that which actually is perfectly true. We must, therefore, discount the reliability of everything we hear, including what are, in fact, the true reports. At the same time we also tend to give a certain degree of credibility to other reports because we cannot know for sure that they are not among the reliable ones. The entire matter of gathering information becomes a subtle problem in statistics and probabilities.

The third kind of interference, distortion, is familiar to lawyers. The notion is similar to the policy underlying the inadmissibility of hearsay evidence. As information is transferred from one individual to another, distortions in the actual message transmitted necessarily occur. Some of these distortions result from mechanical defects in the system of communication. Others can be explained in psychological terms, as different people gain

14. Complaint, *S.E.C.* v. *Texas Gulf Sulphur Co.* Actually, aside from one defendant's purchase of 100 shares at 27 on Apr. 2, 1964, the highest price paid by this group was 25⅞.

15. See Colin Cherry, "The Cocktail Party Problem," *On Human Communication* (New York: Science Edition, Inc., 1961), pp. 277–78.

different mental images from the same external stimulus. Distortion also results from the varying degrees of sophistication with which an individual can treat a given bit of information. The accountant, upon learning that a company is shifting from FIFO to a LIFO system of inventory accounting, may quickly recognize that a smaller net-income figure will result. The layman with no accounting background may not infer anything from this disclosure. This sort of difference in reaction—and the examples could be multiplied indefinitely—will always prevent perfectly smooth transitions to new price levels.

Those who trade with least certainty will tend to predominate in number near the top of the price curve generated by the inside information. Various time lags, attenuation, noise, and distortion will all dictate that they discount the truth of their information to a larger extent than insiders do. Movements in stock prices caused by their transactions will tend to be exaggerated as they buy too late and sell too early, judged by the ideal of perfect information. Since they have some information, however, their transactions will tend to move up and down within some limits, and, because ultimately the inside information is disclosed, the movement will probably tend to oscillate around the $55 line, with the price movements generated by the $5 per share bit of news eventually becoming indistinguishable from other factors.

No-Insider-Trading Rule

The next rule we shall examine is that of no insider trading. Some preliminary refinements are necessary, as there can be many variations of the no-trading rule. The most important point is that it takes time for most disclosures of information to have a full impact upon the market, even though we exclude inside traders. That is, we cannot assume that the moment a particular piece of information is disclosed, the price will immediately jump from 50 to 55. We have already described some of the reasons for a time lag in the dissemination of information. But with full public disclosure, much of this time lag will be compensated for by the increased number of people who will be trading. The speed with which information can be disseminated on the broad tape or in the *Wall Street Journal* is very fast as compared to the word-of-mouth technique implied by our discussion of free insider trading. With a rule of full disclosure, the period required for total dissemination and market reflection of news will rarely exceed a few hours. In many cases, minutes will be adequate.

There are alternative ways to isolate the market effect of a perfect no-insider-trading rule. First we may assume that insiders will not be allowed to trade in the market until the full effect of the disclosure has occurred. That is, using our familiar illustration, even though the disclosure occurred at 50, insiders would be prevented from trading until the shares had reached a price of 55. Although such a rule would be extremely difficult to police and no one has proposed it as a practical matter, something of this sort would be necessary to insure that insiders did not continue to gain some advantage by their position. If the insider is allowed to buy at 50½ after disclosure, we have really accomplished very little over a rule allowing him to purchase at 50 before disclosure.[16] It should be clear that an effective rule against insider trading would require that insiders abstain from trading during some period after public disclosure.

Whether we exclude insiders from immediate postdisclosure trading or

16. Par. 97 of the complaint in *S.E.C.* v. *Texas Gulf Sulphur Co.* alleges that one defendant purchased or caused to be purchased 4,000 shares after information about the find was given to reporters but before it had reached the public. On the same day, Apr. 16, 1964, in perhaps the most celebrated transactions alleged in the complaint, Defendant Thomas S. Lamont advised a representative of the Morgan Guaranty Trust Co. "to 'watch the tape' for favorable news pertaining to Defendant TEXAS GULF." All of these transactions occurred in the price range of 31 to 33½. The stock closed that day at $37 and sold as high as $58 on Apr. 30, 1964.

This discussion also suggests the role played by specialists and traders on the floor of the stock exchanges. As news is flashed on the broad tape—or as they hear it from other sources—they are physically in a position to trade on this information before it has been disseminated through the whole market. Specialists are, of course, presumed to stabilize the market by buying as prices go down and selling as prices go up. But a recent investigation of their activities in the days following the assassination of President Kennedy indicates that the lure of quick profits from valuable information may have been too much to resist. See *S.E.C. Study of Specialists and Floor Trader Activities on the New York Stock Exchange on November 22 to 26, 1963*. This study, dated Jan. 21, 1964, was submitted to Representative Staggers, Chairman of the House Subcommittee on Commerce and Finance of the Committee on Interstate and Foreign Commerce. For a description of the behavior of floor traders, see SEC's *Special Study of Securities Markets,* Part 2, House Doc. No. 95, Part 2, 88th Cong., 1st Sess., 1963.

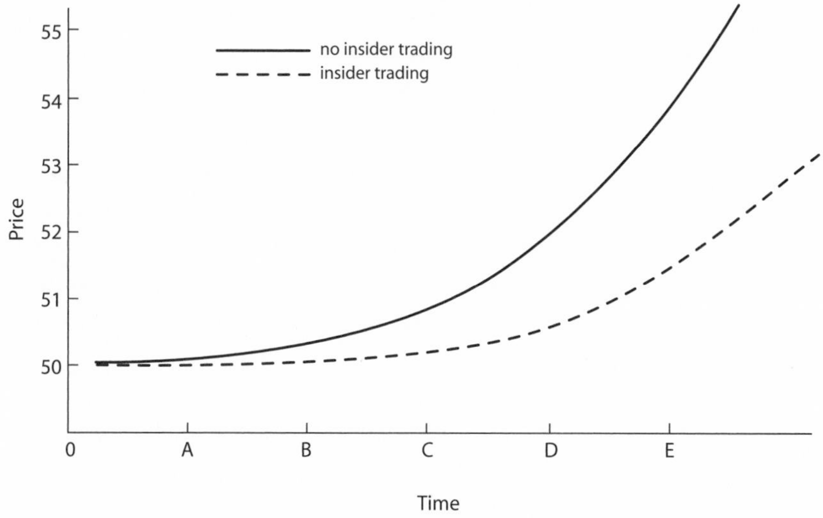

Figure 3. General Comparison of Insider-Trading and No-Insider-Trading Rules

not, the rate of increase in price will be quite steep. In fact the absence of insiders may be hardly noticeable, as they will be so few in number compared to outside traders and because the trading results of effective disclosure will generally swamp the market. In either event, as illustrated by Figure 3, the rate of price increase will generally be quite a bit steeper than would be the case when insiders can trade freely before public disclosure.

An alternative assumption letting us isolate the result of an effective rule against insider trading is more realistic than assuming a delay in insider trading after disclosure. This assumption probably gives a more accurate reflection of what would happen in the stock market if insider trading were prohibited. This time we shall assume that *all* trading in shares will be stopped just before disclosure of important information and not resumed again until the information has been disseminated and understood. With this assumption there is no problem of insider trading after public disclosure, because no one can trade during the relevant period. This technique is actually in limited use today for reasons not unrelated to our present considerations.[17]

17. See Chapter 11. Both the registered exchanges and the SEC have authority to suspend trading in a given security. The exchanges can only suspend trading through their facilities;

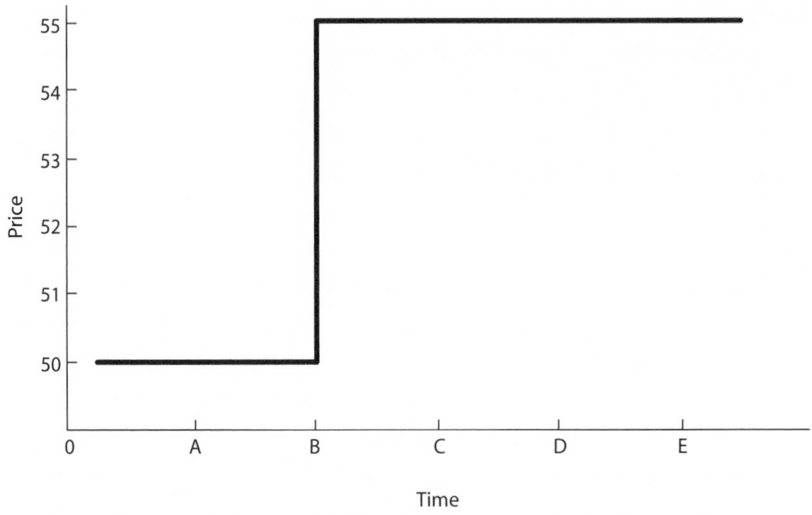

Figure 4. Trading Prevented Until Full Dissemination of Information

The effect of such a rule is dramatic. No longer will we find an exponential curve; the exponent is now infinity, and the line is absolutely vertical. That is, no transactions will occur between the price of 50, when the disclosure is made, and the final price of 55. The effect of this rule is illustrated graphically in Figure 4. If prices always change in accordance with such a step function, a graph of prices over a period of time would look like a series of plateaus of irregular width and height.

There are many practical difficulties with the assumption that all trading will be stopped for a period of time. The first problem is knowing when to stop trading. This difficulty is mitigated in theory by our assumption that no insider trading has occurred in the period before disclosure. In practice,

---

the SEC has power to suspend exchange and over-the-counter transactions. The New York Stock Exchange and the SEC have utilized this device on numerous occasions. These suspensions may result from a failure to file required information with the SEC, as well as for reasons outside of the company's control such as an involuntary bankruptcy petition. Other reasons have included the death of an important official, fraud, and errors in financial data. For a collection of the cases see Louis Loss, *Securities Regulation* (Boston and Toronto: Little, Brown and Co., 1961), pp. 851–57.

of course, it would not be so easy. The other difficulty is knowing when to resume full trading. Theoretically, a regulatory authority would sanction trading when the information had been fully disseminated and understood. Again there are practical difficulties in knowing when this moment occurs, but we shall assume for now that it can be done.

It should now be clear that any rules designed to prohibit insider trading will, on the average, generate much steeper price increases than will the free-trading rule. In fact, when the most effective device possible to prevent insider trading is utilized—the suspension of all trading—the slope of the price curve is infinitely steep, that is, vertical. In comparing the effects of these different rules on individual traders in the market, we shall deal with these two extremes, the relatively shallow exponential curve derived from the free-trading rule and the vertical, step-function result of preventing insider trading. It should be kept in mind, however, that these are theoretical abstractions, descriptive only in an average and generalized sense.

Options and Calls

The last rule we shall examine is that allowing insiders to receive stock options from their company or to buy puts or calls. The *call* is simply an option to buy shares at a stated price at a specified future time. If the insider knows bad news that will cause a downturn in the share price, then he can take a *put,* or an option to sell at a stated price at some time in the future. No one has proposed such a rule as the one we are considering, and it appears to have little independent justification. But it will aid us in properly analyzing the subject of insider trading. The purchase of a call "at the market" or the taking of an option to buy later at the present market price provides perhaps the cheapest means for an individual to realize profits from an anticipated price rise. This method is in fact used today but rarely as the sole means of exploiting inside information.

The general market effect of a rule allowing insiders to take options or calls is, ironically, almost identical in its market effect to the rule allowing no insider trading. If we assume that the cost of the option or call is borne by the insider and not by the corporation and that it is not known that insiders are taking options or calls, the fact of issuance should not cause the slightest tremor in the market price of the corporation's shares. The seller of the option may have to cover later by delivering shares, but that will occur after the news has been released and can have no effect on the earlier market price.[18]

After the information has been disclosed, the call, per share, will appreciate in value by an amount equal to the per-share value of the information. If insiders are free only to buy calls[19] and if the information is released at the same time that it would be with no insider trading, no shareholder or potential shareholder in this corporation has been affected in any way by an insider's transactions. Insiders may be enabled to gain the full value of the information, minus the cost of the call, but no shareholder has less than he would have had under the rule of no insider trading. This point may seem quite startling to some readers, as it suggests, quite properly, that insiders can fully benefit by inside information without injury to any shareholder of the corporation.

It would seem at first glance that the last statement would have to be qualified if the call seller were also a shareholder in the corporation. That is, even though the individual acted in two separate capacities, a shareholder of the corporation would be injured if he sold a call to insiders. However, to the extent that the call seller is covered by ownership of shares, he cannot lose money on his transaction with the insider, because the loss on the call will be made up by the gain in his shares. True, he will not realize the gain that other shareholders will realize, but he has not lost as much as he would have by selling the shares outright at the time he sold the call.

18. To the extent that the call seller hedges and buys long himself, the effect would be the same as if the insiders went into the market before disclosing the information. This effect should be assumed out of the present discussion in order to focus on the pure effect of the rule allowing insiders only to purchase calls or take options.

19. The more common case of stock options being granted to corporate executives will be considered in Chapter 9.

7 Effects of Different Legal Rules on Non-inside Traders

Having seen the general market effects different rules of law would produce, the ways in which information is disseminated in the market, and the interferences with smooth dissemination that exist, we can now begin to examine the effect different legal rules would have on particular individuals. Presumably the foundation of most objections to insider trading lies in the assumption of harm to outsiders. Ultimately the complaint must be that some individuals are being harmed by allowing insider trading. It is not enough simply to say that insider trading is unfair. If it is unfair, it must be unfair to somebody.

To understand whether anyone is injured—and if so, who—we might first compare the respective positions of the same individuals under the extreme rule of no insider trading and the other extreme of free trading by insiders. We will assume that the stock of our hypothetical corporation is selling at 50 and that no circumstances other than a piece of new information worth $5 will affect the price movement during the relevant time period.

The Demand Schedule for Stocks

Certain peculiarities in the demand for stocks must first be examined. The demand for a share of stock is not the simple demand for one commodity. It is rather a complex demand both for that part of the underlying security about which everything is known (and whose market price fully reflects all prior knowledge) and for the value of information that will be assimilated into the known part in the future. For the first part of this package, the known security, the underlying demand schedule is probably no different from any other commodity sold in an extremely competitive market. The demand curve is completely elastic. Assuming no uncertainty, no differences in the amount of reliable information known to all traders, and no differences in their evaluation of this information, any of the shares in our illustration offered for sale below 50 would be immediately taken, and none offered above that price would be taken at all. This is true of the entire market; no distinction can be drawn between insiders and outsiders so far as this part of the demand for shares is involved.

As we turn to the second part of the security package, we must begin to distinguish between those who have reliable, accurate information and those who do not. The truth for most traders lies between these two extremes, but for simplicity of exposition, our analysis will proceed with a "know-it-all" and a "know-nothing" group of share traders. In the first group, those who know that they have reliable information, this information will be treated simply as any other commodity in a competitive market. That is, assuming that the information is worth $5 per share, individuals will take all they can of shares reflecting an information component being sold for less than $5. And these individuals will, as we noted in the last chapter, abstain when the price exceeds what they know the value to be.

The outs, the know-nothings, must now be divided into three separate groups: those whose market decisions will be a function of time, those whose decisions will be a function of the price of the security, and those whose decisions will reflect both factors. We are interested in the reactions to changes in time and price by those who now know only that the market price of the shares is 50.

Since the only two variables are time and price, transactions during the relevant time span for any reason other than a change in price are considered as time-function transactions. The relevant time period is basically the time it will take for complete market diffusion of new information. Most time-function transactions will occur because of external events that occurred during this period, which are not related to the price of the stock. Shareholders who bought or sold because of President John F. Kennedy's assassination would illustrate this concept. Also included here are transactions resulting from changed investment needs; a desire for more or less liquidity, higher dividends, or more growth; or a desire for more or less speculative securities. A large inheritance or the need for retirement income would be examples of changed financial circumstances dictating market transactions completely independent of the price of a particular company's shares. Death of a shareowner could be included in this category, as well as changes in government policies and economic events that affect the entire equity-capital market. There is no reason to believe that the distribution of these transactions will not be perfectly random over a long period of time; that is, there is no way to predict the occurrence of events that will cause time-function stock transactions.

We turn now to those shareholders whose transactions are a function of the price of the security. Again, these are individuals who know nothing about why the price is changing. They have no inside information, either about the company or the identity of those buying the shares. Some of these individuals will take a given price change as a signal or bit of information, while others will not. Those who do see a change as the equivalent of information will still disagree on the meaning of the signal, both as to its direction and its extent. Many of these individuals are "chartists," who trade on so-called technical factors and analyze graphic depictions of previous price movements. But, with a slight exception that we shall note, available data and studies indicate that this approach is unsuccessful. As indicated by the theory of market uncertainty,[1] the distribution of their transactions will be perfectly random in any statistically significant sample.

The group who do not take individual price changes as signals, if they are included in those trading during the relevant time period, may still take the *rate* of price change as a signal. Their transactions are a function of price change over time. Some will sell and some buy, either because the price level remained stable, because it changes slowly, or because it changes quickly.

1. For the fullest treatment of this fascinating topic, see the essays collected in *The Random Character of Stock Market Prices,* ed., Paul H. Cootner (Cambridge, Mass.: M.I.T. Press, 1964), hereafter cited as "Cootner." That market uncertainty will generate randomly distributed transactions was first argued theoretically by a French mathematician in 1900. See Louis Bachelier, "Theory of Speculation" in Cootner, p. 17.

They also may be chartists, and, because they operate with total uncertainty, their transaction distribution will also tend to be random.[2]

We have now accounted for all individuals, both the know-it-alls and the know-nothings, who can be projected as traders during the time span with which we are concerned. There is no way of predicting how many transactions will occur, but it would seem normally to involve only a small fraction of the total number of outstanding shares. During the entire year 1964, with nearly nine billion shares listed on the New York Stock Exchange, only one and one-fourth billion or 14 per cent were traded.[3] On the average then only about .27 per cent of total shares are traded in a week. Many trades involve shares already counted in trades, whereas the shares not traded are only counted once. Thus the figure is actually overstated considerably.

The Brownian Effect

The effect of having no know-it-alls, or insiders, in the market for some period of time would present a situation analogous to that described by the Brownian effect in physics. This phrase is used to describe the actions of gas molecules under pressure as they collide with and bounce off one another. These collisions are thought to occur with absolutely no pattern, and it is generally believed by scientists that these collisions represent perfect indeterminacy. The stock-market analogue of this phenomenon is generally referred to as a *random walk*,[4] and it can be illustrated as in Figure 5. If the random-walk theory of stock prices were completely correct, the direction and magnitude of price changes in shares would always be uncertain.[5] There

2. The addition of *volume* as a variable in their computations would not seem to be significant for present purposes. See M. F. M. Osbourne, "Periodic Structure in the Brownian Motion of Stock Prices" in Cootner, p. 262.

3. *The Exchange*, 26, No. 6 (June, 1965) on the inside cover.

4. See Paul H. Cootner, "The Random Walk Hypothesis Reexamined," in Cootner, p. 189.

5. Cootner, *ibid.*, shows that a number of additional refinements could be added to this discussion. For the most part, these are quite technical and not immediately relevant to the theory advanced in the text. One point that should be mentioned is the existence of constraints or parameters on the area in which random movement occurs. One constraint is, of course, a bottom of zero. Stocks cannot have negative values. The other, and

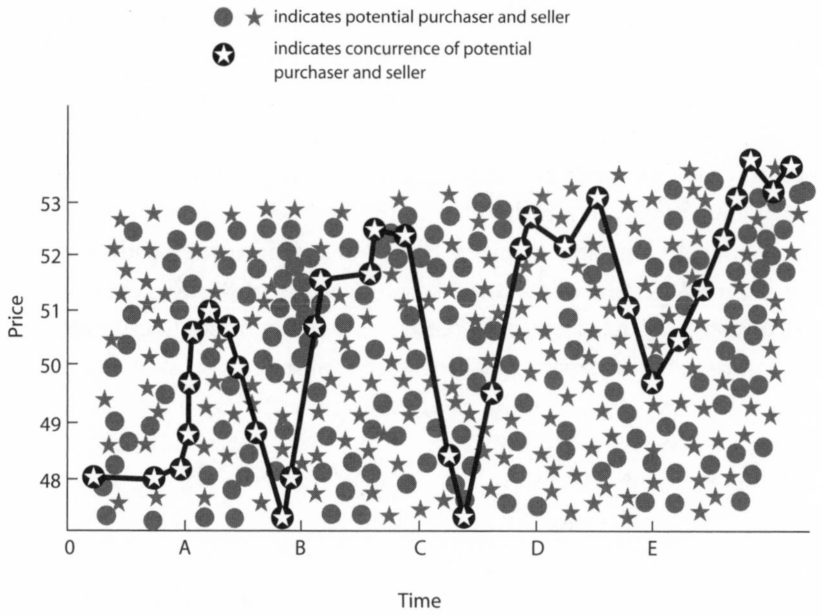

Figure 5. The Random-Walk Theory of Stock Price Changes

would be no discernible dependence of one transaction price on the immediately preceding price. Such dependency can be introduced in the stock market only by an increase in knowledge. If this information requires time for full exploitation, we should not expect price changes to be fully random in their direction or extent. We should, for reasons discussed in Chapter 5, anticipate occasional, very short periods during which the random-walk hypothesis would not be valid.

Knowledgeable transactions will occur only sporadically and even then may represent only a small fraction of transactions. Their effect will be ex-

---

more important for practical purposes, is the constraint provided by the area of actual knowledge. Because of the known aspect of any stock, even the random price changes will tend to group in an area fairly close to some base line—in our example, the price of 50. This line will exercise a kind of gravitational pull on price, but this in no way contradicts the statement that price changes occur with no dependence on previous prices within the area of constraint. It simply means that the distribution of transactions will probably be statistically normal.

tremely small and very difficult to discern statistically. However, using newer and highly complex methods of statistical analysis, some economists report slight nonrandom movements among stock prices.[6] No theoretical explanation for this phenomenon has previously been offered, but the theory expounded here could explain both the general randomness of stock prices and the occasional, slight nonrandomness.

As buyers with valuable information enter an otherwise randomly fluctuating market, their transactions will have a determinable effect on share prices.[7] Even though a few know-nothing transactions may continue to occur at varying prices, many that otherwise would have occurred at different prices will now appear on the price curve projected by the inside trader. Outside sellers will sell to the inside buyer when the price offered is more than the price outside buyers are offering. And some outside buyers and sellers, whose transactions are a function of price, will now buy from and sell to each other at a higher price. Thus many of the transactions occurring in random fashion prior to the entry into the market of insiders will now be drawn toward the insiders' transactions and tend to cluster with normal distribution around the price curve dictated by the dissemination of the new information. (See Figure 6.)

Effect of Allowing Insider Trading

We are now in a position to explore the effects that different rules of law on insider trading would have on the market. Graphically, we can illustrate these by combining an illustration of the random distribution of buyers and sellers with Figures 1 and 4 from the last chapter, showing the general market effects of different insider-trading rules. (See Figure 7.)

First we shall examine what happens to a select group of buyers and sellers of securities under the free-insider-trading rule. It will be noticed that various transactions will occur at different points along the line *OF*, which is generated by the transactions entered into when insider trading is al-

6. See Cootner, Part 3.

7. See Henry G. Manne, "Mergers and the Market for Corporate Control," *Journal of Political Economy*, 73 (1965), p. 112, fn. 10.

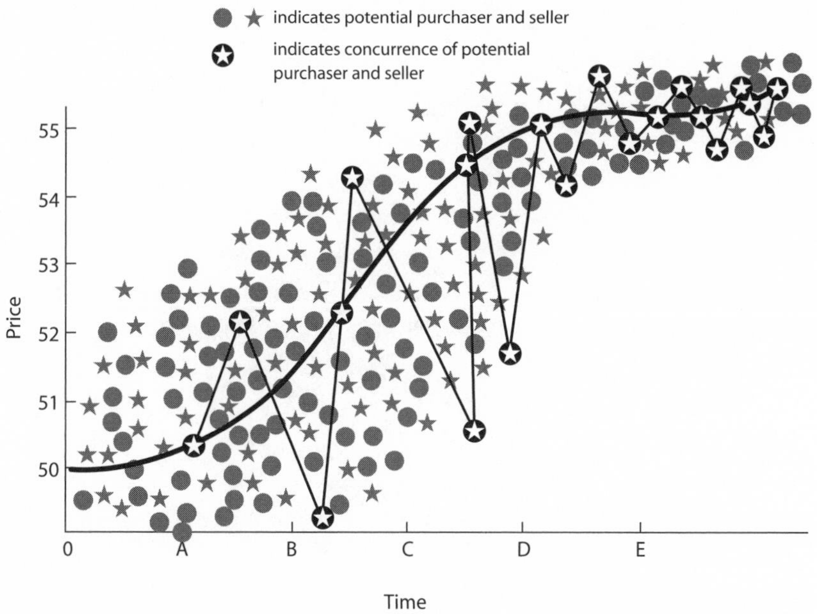

Figure 6. Effect of Insider Trading on Random Distribution of Transactions

lowed. This is not to suggest that some of the buyers, or indeed a great many of them, engaging in transactions between times *A* and *E* are not outsiders. But these transactions occur because they fall randomly at those points for reasons unrelated to the inside information. Some of the buyers may have taken the price rise as an indication that it would continue, but in no meaningful sense could they know this for a particular stock.

Undoubtedly, many of the sellers whose transactions occur on the line *OF* have sold to insiders. These sellers will have sold for reasons extraneous to the price change or because they took the price increase as a signal that it would continue no further. But, given the random distribution that will result from the ignorance of those who held stock at point *O*, some of them could be predicted in advance as potential sellers at various points along the line *OF.* However these individuals, whoever they turn out to be, are not unique or peculiar. Qualitatively they are no different from any of the other sellers, all outsiders, appearing anywhere in Figure 7. The same is true of those would-be sellers above or below the transaction line *OF* who will

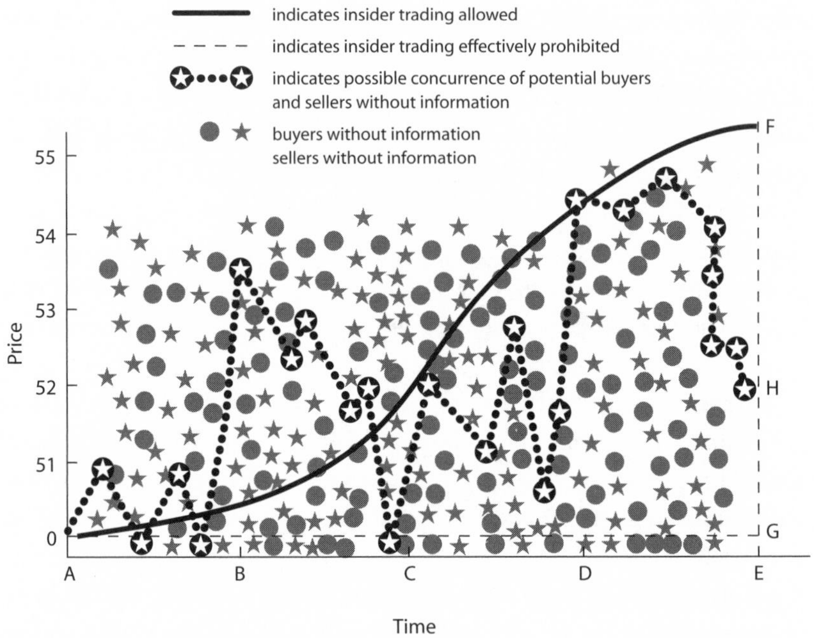

Figure 7. Comparison of Effects of Different Rules on Random Distribution of Transactions

now receive the full value of the new information. The would-be buyers, who are not on the line *OF,* suffered a loss to the same extent.

What we have done is change the market conditions for the randomly distributed buyers and sellers. All actual transactions will now fall on the line *OF* generated by insiders. Some sales would have occurred at the same point without the infusion of insider buying. Other transactions, describing the fluctuating line *OH,* that would have occurred without the price change dictated by insiders, will not now occur. Those who would have been sellers are now better off. Those who would have been buyers are worse off to the same extent.

Some critics of insider trading must assume that the sellers on the line *OF* would not have lost money (or alternatively would have made money) if their buyers had not traded with inside information. But there is simply no way of knowing whether that statement is true or not. Without the insider trading one cannot assume that the price would have progressed from 50 to 55 along the line *OF.* If the inside information had not been developed at all, manifestly each of these sellers would have been worse off, because, assuming that everything else remains constant, his shares would have remained at a price of 50. He may or may not have sold, but there can be no question that $52.50 (the assumed average price on line *OF*) is worth more than $50. To the extent that any sale was more a function of the time period involved than it was of the price, these sellers are clearly better off with insider trading, assuming that good news would otherwise be released at time *E.*

It is possible to hypothesize conditions under which outsiders as a group are injured by insider trading. Since some of the buyers along the line *OF* are insiders and none of the sellers are, it might seem that on balance existing shareholders as a group are injured by insider trading. However, we would need additional evidence to reach that conclusion. Unless these same individuals would not have sold in the time period *AE* under the rule of no insider trading, they are still better off with insider trading, because they will receive more than 50 for their shares. On the average they should receive approximately 52½. To determine accurately the extent of harm to sellers under the insider-trading rule, we would have to know what those same sellers would do under the opposite rule. If sales are more frequently a function of price than of time, with the result that there will be more transactions along the line *OF* than would otherwise have occurred in the same time span *AE* without insider trading, and if that difference is great enough to compensate for the lower price received by sellers with no insider trading, then sellers, as a group, *are* in fact worse off with insider trading on good news.

Thus, there is both a plus and a minus for outside sellers from insider trading. The plus is the higher price received by those who would otherwise have sold at the stable, lower price, and the minus is the number of sales that now occur but which otherwise would not have occurred. It would be extremely difficult to obtain accurate data on this question, though we can make one safe assumption. Those sellers who lose will tend to be those whose trades are a function of price, and those who gain will tend to be those whose trades are a function of time only. When we consider good news, we know that the less frequently one sells shares the better he will fare.[8] There are reasons to assume that good news is more important than bad news for our purposes. First the long-term trend of stock prices is upward, so that, all other things being equal, occasions of good news should exceed those of bad. Perhaps more important, substantial good news seems often to develop quickly, as with news of a new product, a favorable merger offer, or an important government contract. Bad news on the other hand may tend to unfold in more gradual fashion, or perhaps to be anticipated, as with a low earnings report or a dividend cut. Bad news may also more frequently be information affecting an entire industry and thus not be susceptible to insider trading at all.

If we limit our concern to the long-term investor rather than the short-swing share trader, there is little likelihood for injury from insider trading. The long-term investor is much less likely than the trader to sell because of price changes effected by insiders. He is more likely to become a seller because of changed financial circumstances or death. A strong argument can be made for limiting our concern to this group of shareholders, but, as we shall see, the effects will be small in any event.

The argument that insider trading may injure outsiders as a group can only hold if price changes occur more gradually with insider trading than without it. As a rule, this is probably true. But if the price curve were as steep with insider trading as without—as it is when insiders are only allowed to buy calls—no harm to outsiders could even be hypothesized. Because perfect enforcement of the full-disclosure rule does not and probably cannot exist, any possible harm to outsiders suggested by this discussion must be considerably discounted.

Effect on Outside Buyers and Sellers

But even at this point we cannot conclude that outside sellers as a group lose with the rule of no insider trading. We still do not know the answer to

8. For another analysis leading to the same conclusions, see Eugene F. Fama, "Random Walks in Stock Market Prices," *Financial Analysts Journal,* 21, No. 5 (Sept.–Oct., 1965), p. 55.

the more relevant question of how all outsiders as a group fare under one rule as against the other. We must add to the plus side of the equation the gain resulting to noninsider buyers along the line *OF*, as these individuals are benefited to the same extent as insider buyers, if they hold their shares until time *E*. This factor must in turn be countered by subtracting the $5 benefit lost by all would-be buyers during the time period *AE* if there had been a rule of no insider trading.[9] So long as there are more outsider buyers along the line *OF* than there would be buyers along the $50 transaction line *OG*, this group of outsiders will prefer a rule of insider trading. Since the outsider buyers on *OF* will tend to be individuals who have taken a signal from the price rise, it is quite possible that their number may be relatively large. We do know that there will be more transactions by outside sellers along *OF* than by outside buyers, but we cannot know *a priori* that the difference will be large.

The conditions under which all stock-market outsiders as a group will lose under a rule of insider trading can be stated generally. We need only posit substantially more price-function trading than time-function trading with good news to get that result. But even though this represents a real, though indeterminate, loss to outsiders, it is not necessarily an overall economic loss to the community. To reach that conclusion would require the absurd assumption that insiders gain less than outsiders as a group lose. Even if the loss resulting to all outsiders from a rule of insider trading did approach the amount of gain by the insiders, the question of whether insider trading should be abandoned would by no means be answered. For, as we shall see, the ultimate question of economic desirability of insider trading involves far more than these hypothetical computations.

9. A leading securities lawyer, examining the question of who might be injured by insider trading, noted that it is "plausible that an anonymous prospective buyer is the person to complain rather than one of these random sellers. To such a prospective buyer, the defendant represented competition. Were the defendant not present, a lower bid might have been accepted by one of the hypothetical sellers." Jack M. Whitney II, "Section 10b-5: From Cady, Roberts to Texas Gulf: Matters of Disclosure," *The Business Lawyer*, 21 (1965), p. 201. Whitney did not, however, examine the impact of insider trading on all outsiders in the aggregate, and consequently his otherwise astute observations are quite incomplete.

Timing of Disclosures

If insiders are allowed to exploit the value of information by purchasing calls, the time period for doing this will probably not be significantly different from the time period necessary to exploit the information under the free-trading rule. If, however, insiders are not allowed to benefit in any way from their information, it is conceivable that disclosure would occur at an earlier date. The implication from this is that if insider trading is allowed, insiders will release the information at a date more suited to their own interests. As some period of time is necessary for them to exploit their knowledge, it would seem that the information would generally be released later under the rule allowing insider trading than under the opposite rule. Only delay that actually enlarges the time period between development and disclosure should concern us. If the delay merely shifts the same time span to a later point, there will be no effect on outsiders as a group, even though a different set of individuals may be affected.

But the problem would not seem to be a serious one. Much information in a sense determines its own release date, and no alteration is feasible. A dividend declaration or the announcement of a development extraneous to the corporation, such as a tax refund, would be of this variety. In these cases it is still possible for insiders to exploit some of the value inherent in this information. There are cases in which delay will aid insiders in exploiting the value of the information. A great mining discovery, such as that of Texas Gulf Sulphur, higher earnings, or exceptional market acceptance of a new product might be examples of this sort. But these delays may also be in the interest of the corporation. Texas Gulf Sulphur's first successful sample core at Timmins was known early in November of 1963, but it was not until April, 1964, that the company had succeeded in acquiring rights to other sections of land under which the vein ran. If the announcement had been made in November, 1963, it would certainly have been more expensive to acquire mineral rights in these other properties. The same is true with new products; the faster competitors get the word of success, the faster they will begin copying. Many subtleties and complexities in business may determine the timing of public reports.

It is very difficult to estimate the extent to which insider trading would affect the length of the predisclosure period, and empirical data would be extremely untrustworthy. On the one hand, insiders may often be unable to affect disclosure dates, and in many instances they will have no incentive to do so. Many techniques are available for exploiting information quickly, and often there will be no hurry. On the other hand, where time is needed, it is possible to delay disclosure. This is to the disadvantage of anyone selling within the period of additional delay. If, however, as will be argued in Chapter 9, inside information is an appropriate form of compensation for certain corporate functionaries, some control of disclosure timing may be necessary to assure that the device is effective.

The Shareholder's Contract Argument

A somewhat different argument against insider trading focuses on the alleged expectations of particular individuals rather than on the entire group of outsiders. The argument is that the sellers who do lose under the insider-trading rule invested with the expectation of receiving particular bits of good news. Having assumed the risk of news being bad, they should benefit from any desirable developments occurring during their tenure as shareholders.

But the expectation of most investors is probably different from that implied by this argument. Investors hope that their company will be well managed, and they anticipate sharing in the benefits of this efficiency. They do not, however, anticipate that they will be told news of specific events before it has affected the market price. Rather, they anticipate merely having their shares appreciate in value as a result of these events. By holding on to his shares, the investor will ultimately realize the value of any good news developed for his company. Few shareholders would want a rule requiring them to be informed in order to realize the benefit of new developments in their corporation. Most shareholders quite sensibly rely on the market mechanism to guarantee their sharing in the value of good news.

The argument also implies that any developments in a corporation's affairs will immediately affect share prices. Only in this way can developments be related to the period in which shares are held. But there is no feasible way of relating the benefits of particular bits of information to the ownership of shares in the company at particular moments. A share would have to be owned for the full life-and-death cycle of a company for this ever to be done precisely.

If the argument under discussion were carried to its logical extreme, there would be no such thing as a stock market. Anyone who fortuitously purchased shares just before an important announcement would have to pay the gain to his seller, who may have held the shares for the ten long years of unsuccessful exploration or research.[10] These are the very uncertainties that cannot be allocated in any scientific, or precise, or even rough fashion. The market allows individuals to assume whatever risks of this sort they wish, but they receive benefits only if their investment is continued and their shares are held at the time of disclosure or exploitation by those with the information.

The Outside, Short-Term Trader

It seems appropriate to ask just what kind of trader might logically desire a rule preventing insiders from dealing in shares. Who stands to gain, financially or otherwise, by a rule barring insiders from trading? There is, of course, no recognizable or definable group who, under a full-disclosure rule, would pick up a set sum flowing to insiders under the free-trading rule. We are not dealing with a certain amount of money that can be rationally redistributed to different groups of individuals.[11]

The intelligent long-term investor, as we have seen, has substantially no interest in preventing his company's executives from trading in the company's shares. Apart from the advantage to him of this rather inexpensive form of compensation to the executives (a matter to be discussed in the chapters following), he would be indifferent as to the identity of those re-

10. In truth the shares may have been owned by a number of different individuals during the relevant time period so that the job of correlating gains and ownership would be even more difficult.

11. There would be a definite sum if we were considering corporate recovery of insiders' profits. If there were perfect enforcement of such a rule, however, insiders would have no incentive to trade. There would then be no profits for the corporation to recover. If corporate managers tried to maximize corporate income by trading for the corporation on inside information, our analysis from the point of view of outsiders would be the same as that under the rule of individual insider trading.

alizing the trading profits inherent in short-swing price movements. When the information has finally been disclosed or exploited, the long-term investor—the shareholder who holds on—receives the full value of the information developed by the executives of his corporation. Only by holding his shares does he actually guarantee the realization of this value, though at the same time he does incur the risk of suffering the effects of bad news. This, however, is precisely what the capital investor has agreed to do, and it conforms to the classical statements of the function of the capitalist. He will also be indifferent as to whether prices change gradually or fluctuate sharply, so long as the changes occur while he is a shareholder.

We have assumed that the typical investor-shareholder does not buy because he anticipates receiving specific, discrete bits of information. But another group of stock-market participants have a different interest. The individual who acts on information that he knows, or he has reason to know, is stale, unreliable, distorted, or given freely, hopes that it is true. He gambles against high odds that he can insinuate himself into the position of one who has reliable inside information. This kind of trader will ordinarily sell his shares when he has realized the assumed potential of his so-called hot tip. Thus his preference in the market is to receive the value of the good news directly rather than to participate indirectly in the ultimate market effects of the good news. In common parlance, he is a speculator and not an investor. To the extent that gambling psychology motivates his participation in the stock market, the speculator will favor a rule generating sharp fluctuations in stock prices over a rule allowing only gradual changes. Since he has gambled upon the possibility of exploiting good news, the quicker the result is known the better. He will prefer the excitement of sharp fluctuations and the possibility of winning or losing quickly. High peaks and low troughs over a short time period are precisely what stimulate and encourage him.[12]

12. In this connection it is interesting to consider part of the famous discussion of the stock market which appears in John Maynard Keynes, *The General Theory of Employment Interest and Money* (London: Macmillan Co., Ltd., 1949), p. 157.

> Moreover, life is not long enough;—human nature desires quick results, there is a peculiar zest in making money quickly, and remoter gains are discounted by the av-

As we have already seen, the prohibition of insider trading will protect the interests of this individual when there is good news. He will be injured by the same rule in the case of bad news, because he will bear the full brunt of it before he can get out of the market. But, if his psychology is the same as that of the gambler, he will be more encouraged by the possibility of gain than he will be discouraged by the same or even a higher probability of loss. As we shall see, no effective rule against insider trading is feasible, so the poor gambler may be additionally fooled into believing that the odds are better than they really are.

It is sometimes argued that the short-term traders in the market aid in maintaining liquidity. That is, their plentiful presence as ready buyers and sellers guarantees that shares may always be converted to cash and vice versa. Undoubtedly, liquidity is one of the crucial characteristics of a functioning securities market, but it undoubtedly overstates the case to credit

---

> erage man at a very high rate. The game of professional investment is intolerably boring and overexacting to anyone who is entirely exempt from the gambling instinct; whilst he who has it must pay to this propensity the appropriate toll.

Unfortunately, in his discussion of different types of traders in the stock market Keynes seems to have limited himself to short-term speculators, who are presumed to be gambling, and long-term investors. There is no discussion of the role played by the informed short-term trader or the insider. The failure to recognize the influence of the latter participants led Keynes to conclude that the influence of the speculator would in the long run predominate over that of the informed investor. The stock market became for Keynes simply a casino which could not properly perform its capital allocating function. But, to the extent that informed short-term trading does occur, it is very likely that there is an important tendency in the stock market for share prices accurately and properly to reflect underlying values. And even though there will be fads and panics in particular stocks, or in the whole market at times, it does not follow that uninformed trading will predominate in the general determination of stock prices.

> There is reason to believe that intelligence rather than ignorance ultimately determines the course of individual share prices. Stock market decisions tend to be of the one-out-of-two-alternatives variety, such as buy or not buy, hold or sell, or put or call. To the extent that decisions on these questions are made by shareholders or potential shareholders operating without reliable information, over a period of time the decisions will tend to be randomly distributed and the effect will therefore be neutral. Decisions made by those with a higher degree of certainty will to that extent not meet a canceling effect since they will not be made on a random basis. Over some period of time it would seem that the average market price of a company's shares must be the "correct" one. (Henry G. Manne, "Mergers and the Market for Corporate Control," *The Journal of Political Economy,* 73, No. 2 [April 1965], p. 112, n. 10)

this only to short-term traders. To the extent that one trader's transaction cancels another's, it is difficult to see how more than a marginal amount of liquidity is added. Furthermore, the insiders, while also performing a quasi-arbitrage function, provide additional liquidity for outsiders who wish to trade.

The Investor as a Trader

Thus far we have dealt with two extreme kinds of share purchasers, the pure speculator or trader and the pure investor or holder. At some point, however, every human investor must become a trader. Individuals cannot own shares in perpetuity, and death causes a change of ownership. At that moment, or at any other points at which ownership changes, the investor becomes a trader, and he may dispose of his shares the day before a bonanza is announced. But the investor-turned-trader may have sold and realized even less if insiders were not trading. More importantly, the longer a shareholder has held his shares, the less significant proportionately will be any gain lost to insiders the day before a piece of good news was publicly announced.

To illustrate this last point: if shares have risen over a period of five years from a price of 10 to a price of 50, the loss of two points as a result of not having inside information will not be very significant. But if the shares were bought the day before yesterday at 49 and sold today at 50, the failure to gain the two additional points seems quite important. Indeed, it means that the gain could have been tripled by holding on for a day. Thus it seems fair to conclude for a second time that the less frequently outside shareholders trade, the less they will lose as a result of the exploitation of valuable information by insiders. But the fact that the same individual may both hold and then trade stock does not justify a rule for investors when they turn into traders that we would not justify for the pure speculator.

The Rarity of Significant Inside Information

Any undeserved risk to investors resulting from insider trading must, therefore, constitute a very small fraction of the total risk assumed by long-term investors. And when we realize that the development of significant information is not a very common occurrence, the matter reaches *de minimis* proportions. The kind of information causing a flurry in Texas Gulf Sulphur stock in early 1964 may, if we are very liberal in our estimate, occur on the average of once every ten years for each listed company.[13] Because, as we have seen, the time required for full exploitation of information by insiders is generally quite short, the odds against any long-term investor's being hurt by an insider trading on undisclosed information is almost infinitesimally small.[14] It is simply not enough to say that it may on occasion happen. The truth is that for any individual with whom we are concerned, the absolute odds in favor of his losing anything as a result of insider trading are so small as to be unworthy of serious concern.

This somewhat laborious discussion of what happens in the stock market does not constitute a strong argument *against* a proposal to bar all insider trading. Indeed it is not intended for that purpose at all, but merely to point out that no strong arguments along these lines are available in *defense* of such a proposal. The implication should be put to rest, however, that someone with an important interest is being deprived of his interest when insiders are allowed to trade.

But the debate is far from over. If this were as far as we could go, the entire issue would probably not be worth the time or effort spent upon it. However, the argument developed in the following three chapters is that a rule allowing insiders to trade freely may be fundamental to the survival of our corporate system. People pressing for the rule barring insider trading may inadvertently be tampering with one of the wellsprings of American prosperity.

13. The occurrence of any such event is, of course, completely unpredictable, but it is possible, looking over a previous period, to ascertain the average rate of occurrence. The Texas Gulf development seems to have caused more than a tripling of the stock price, though other factors may have been involved in this increase. In the postwar period, if we correct for price level changes, it is doubtful that specific corporate developments causing a 50% increase in a company's stock price over a short period of time have occurred on the average of once every ten years. In the text we have used a 10% increase, from 50 to 55, to illustrate the value of inside information. The discussion in Chapter 9 will make it clear that most important instances of significant insider trading probably result from price changes in excess of 10%.

14. The Texas Gulf illustration is probably unusual in the length of the time period during which insiders traded before disclosure. Even that time period is approximately 1% of the time since the last previous important development in Texas Gulf's stock.

8 The Entrepreneur in the Large Corporation

Adam Smith was no great champion of the corporation. He felt that a corporate manager's interest in the underlying property was too attenuated for efficient management and the profit incentive too diluted for this form to be economically effective. He thought that joint-stock companies were useful only if operations were capable of being reduced to routine.[1] The Smith theory of corporations was, paradoxically, not unlike that of Berle and Means in *The Modern Corporation and Private Property*.[2] Each of them complained that a separation of ownership and control killed the incentive to profit that the sole proprietorship promoted. Smith's views in this matter were totally colored by his observations of eighteenth-century business practices. In this connection, he was undoubtedly more skilled as an observer than as an economic theoretician. For Berle and Means, however, the corrective evidence was actually close at hand.

Alfred Marshall, like Smith before him, felt that corporations or joint-stock companies were best suited for insurance, banking, and what we would call public-utility enterprises. Joint-stock companies, Marshall felt, "seldom have the enterprise, the energy, the unity of purpose and the quickness of action of a private business."[3] This made them particularly unsuited for "many branches of manufacture and of speculative commerce." Today we hardly question the efficiency of the corporate form, and in fact evidence

1. Adam Smith, *The Wealth of Nations*, ed., Edwin Cannan (New York: Modern Library, 1937), pp. 700 and 712–16.

2. (New York: The Macmillan Co., 1933), p. 343.

3. Alfred Marshall, *Principles of Economics*, 8th ed. (London: Macmillan & Co., Ltd., 1920), p. 604.

of the corporation's efficiency in competitive endeavors was available long before 1920 when the eighth edition of Marshall's great *Principles of Economics* appeared. The mystique of the corporation apparently affected the outlook of great economists and lesser ones alike.

Frank Knight, in his classic *Risk, Uncertainty and Profit,*[4] has described certain fundamental errors in Adam Smith's theory and in the classical concept of competition and profit in general.[5] Knight suggests that Smith and others had seen as the dominant form of industry men using their own capital, hiring labor, and renting land from others. It seemed natural for them then to connect the income of the business manager with the ownership of capital.[6] Smith and the early classical economists envisioned what today we would term a perfectly competitive economic system, in which innovations and *profits,* in the technical, economic sense of the term, are missing.[7] Their model contained no element of ignorance or uncertainty. It is no wonder that the classical observations on corporations and the stock market, built as they were on the construct of perfect competition, are not helpful to us today.

Risk and Uncertainty

A meaningful theory of corporate enterprise and the role played by different individuals associated with the corporation is essential to understanding the peculiarities of insider trading. Some definitions are necessary at the outset. The first of these, the distinction between *risk* and *uncertainty,* is most closely associated in the history of economic thought with the work of Frank

4. Frank H. Knight, *Risk, Uncertainty and Profit* (Boston and New York: Houghton Mifflin Co., 1921), hereinafter referred to as "Knight."

5. *Ibid.,* Chapter 2.

6. There is an interesting paradox in the classical economists' view of the corporation. As the ensuing analysis will show, Smith failed to recognize the corporation as a vehicle for specialization of functions or the division of labor, a concept closely associated with his name. Marshall makes the same error. *Principles of Economics,* p. 604.

7. Knight points out that Smith recognized profit as containing an element that was not merely interest on capital. Smith's exception differs from Knight's concept of profit resulting from uncertainty. It related more to the concept of insurable risk than of true uncertainty. Also see Marshall, *Principles of Economics,* pp. 293 and 604, where he implies an identity of the capitalist and the entrepreneur.

Knight. A slightly earlier work by Joseph Schumpeter, *The Theory of Economic Development*,[8] had already focused on this distinction for the special purpose of understanding the concept of entrepreneurship, to which we shall turn shortly.

Risk in this context refers to changes in value that may in some sense be said to be predictable. Even though we may not know the precise moment or even the quantity of gain or loss, a probability coefficient can still describe the risk of the event's occurring. To the extent that any rise or fall in value of property can be discounted by a known probability factor, its present value will in fact reflect that risk. This is most familiar to us through the concept of insurance, although the same phenomenon occurs in myriad ways in a complex market economy. Risk, for instance, is discounted in determining the present price of stocks. And though this price will also reflect the willingness or unwillingness of individuals to bear uncertainty, uncertainty as such cannot be discounted.

The assumption of risk is an economic service, and consequently it must be compensated. This compensation will be determined by familiar market forces in much the same way as any other market price. The assumption of risk does not give rise to *profit* in a competitive market system. Risk was a concept that Adam Smith did understand. He attributed to the capitalist, as his principal function, the assumption of this kind of risk. But in Adam Smith's system of pure competition, he presumed no great unforeseeable changes would occur, or at least he did not consider them to loom large in the affairs of men.

Uncertainty, as Knight describes it, relates to an entirely different phenomenon, though it is one inseparable from the affairs of men. The concept of uncertainty relates to the areas of men's ignorance, even in an approximate probability sense, of what the future holds. The invention of the internal-combustion engine reflected an unpredictable development hav-

8. Joseph A. Schumpeter, *The Theory of Economic Development,* trans., Redvers Opie (Cambridge, Mass.: Harvard University Press, 1934), hereafter referred to as "Schumpeter TED." This work was first published in German in 1911, prior to Knight's 1916 doctoral thesis on uncertainty. It was revised into a second, English edition in 1926. Some minor modifications in the theory appeared in 1939 in Schumpeter's *Business Cycles,* ed., Rendigs Fels (New York, Toronto, London: McGraw-Hill Book Co., Inc., 1964).

ing a great and unforeseeable impact on the value of men's labor, the value of existing productive facilities, and the prices of almost all commodities and services. Wars, weather, inventions, new merchandising techniques, changes in consumer preference, population shifts, and changes in birth rates may all illustrate Knight's idea of uncertainty. Any of these events may cause a rise or fall in the value of other properties whose utility depends in some fashion on this new event. If such events were merely insurable risks rather than pure uncertainties, any amount gained as a result would constitute the return for an assumption of risk but would not be profit. It is only when the rise in value results from an unpredictable event that we characterize the realized gain as profits. Anything else, including a payment for risk assumption, is either a part of the cost necessary to elicit production or supply in a competitive market or a part of monopoly rent (often referred to as *monopoly profits*).

Knight has often been criticized for pushing the distinction between risk and uncertainty too far. Clearly many of the phenomena he discusses as uncertainties can be insurable risks. The weather is perhaps the clearest example. And yet Knight's emphasis on the lack of reliable information is precisely the point needed for the present discussion. The difficulty is that Knight implied that there is an objective kind of uncertainty, an absolute lack of knowledge about the future. His concept of uncertainty is an ideal rather than a functional construct. However, our own interest is served by a purely functional definition of uncertainty. If a bit of information about the course of events can be made available only at a cost most men are unwilling to pay, we will treat this in the same way that Knight would treat pure uncertainty—although presumably Knight would not.

What may be risk from the point of view of the economy may be uncertainty for one individual. For our purposes, Knight's approach is helpful in emphasizing the fact that men do regularly act in ignorance of important variables and that there is a difference in the amount of ignorance or uncertainty with which different people operate. But the mere fact that one individual knows the risk he has assumed does not necessarily make the same matter any less uncertain for individuals without this information. Knight's distinction has considerable practical significance for our discussion.

Managers and Entrepreneurs

The introduction into economic thinking of the concepts of uncertainty and pure profits led in turn to another profound distinction, that between management and entrepreneurship. The distinction is spelled out carefully in both Knight's and Schumpeter's works. Both men recognize that managerial skill, in the abstract sense of an economic function or factor, is primarily a learnable, mechanical ability. Although the technical skills required for successful management may be very great and its market value very high, the fact remains that, within a fairly wide range, we know in advance what a manager is to do. To the extent that he is acting purely as a manager, his is not an innovating function. Because we know what the task entails, the service can be purchased like any commodity in the marketplace. A price, determined by the familiar laws of supply and demand, will be paid for the performance of this function.[9] There will still be many gradations and categories of this skill, each available at a different and commensurate price.

But the entrepreneur does not perform tasks that are in their detail predictable. Schumpeter describes the function of the entrepreneur:

> The carrying out of new combinations we call "enterprise"; the individuals whose function it is to carry them out we call "entrepreneurs." These concepts are at once broader and narrower than the usual. Broader, because in the first place we call entrepreneurs not only those "independent" businessmen in an exchange economy who are usually so designated, but all who actually fulfill the function by which we define the concept, even if they are, as is becoming the rule, "dependent" employees of a company, like managers, members of boards of directors, and so forth, or even if their actual power to perform the entrepreneurial function has any other foundations, such as the control of a majority of shares. As it is the carrying out of new combinations that constitutes the entrepreneur, it is not necessary that he should be permanently

9. There may still be some monopoly element in corporate managers' compensation. If the corporation itself is making any monopoly gain, it is quite possible that the managers are claiming part of it. Existing managers may also claim for themselves a substantial part of an amount equal to the entry costs of would-be competitors, though this is not technically a monopoly profit. See Henry G. Manne, "The 'Higher Criticism' of the Modern Corporation," *Columbia Law Review,* 62 (1962), pp. 404–06.

> connected with an individual firm; many "financiers," "promoters," and so forth are not, and still they may be entrepreneurs in our sense. On the other hand, our concept is narrower than the traditional one in that it does not include all heads of firms or managers or industrialists who merely may operate an established business, but only those who actually perform that function.[10]

For Schumpeter the entrepreneur's function is to make new combinations of productive factors, that is, to bring them together in a new way. Routine business management is a critical function in the successful operation of a corporation, but it will characterize the work of corporate executives *only after* productive factors have been successfully combined for the first time. Even then, the entrepreneurial and the management functions are not necessarily exclusive. Schumpeter suggests that an individual starting his own business is an entrepreneur, but when he settles down to running it as other people run their businesses, he is merely managing.[11] It is "just as rare for anyone always to remain an entrepreneur throughout the decades of his active life as it is for a businessman never to have a moment in which he is an entrepreneur, to however modest a degree."[12] Schumpeter later made the point even more succinctly:

> The distinction between the entrepreneur and the mere head or manager of a firm who runs it on established lines or . . . between the entrepreneurial and the managerial function, is no more difficult than the distinction between a workman and a landowner, who may also happen to form a composite economic personality called a farmer.[13]

10. Schumpeter TED, pp. 74–75.

11. *Ibid.*, p. 78. Also see Edith Penrose, *The Growth of the Firm* (New York: John Wiley & Sons, Inc., 1959), p. 31. The reader is also referred to Andreas G. Papandreou, "Some Basic Problems in the Theory of the Firm," *A Survey of Contemporary Economics,* Vol. 2, ed., Bernard F. Haley (Homewood, Ill.: Richard D. Irwin, Inc., 1952), p. 214, for a distinction between the concept of the entrepreneur as a function and as an ideal type. The distinction is not very helpful. To the extent that Papandreou's ideal type, for example, a capitalist-entrepreneur, does not function as such, *vide* the capital-poor president of a large corporation, we should have to posit a new ideal type. The confusion can be avoided by always referring to the *function* of the entrepreneur when that word is used. The problem is a minor semantic one which has obscured more than it has clarified.

12. Schumpeter TED, p. 78.

13. Schumpeter, *Business Cycles,* p. 77.

Being an entrepreneur is a functional condition relating to innovational activity and does not connote a status or class of persons. We cannot identify entrepreneurs as a separate social class, as we might landowners or capitalists or labor. Furthermore, entrepreneurial activity itself is not always easy to identify or distinguish in advance. Schumpeter would distinguish entrepreneurs from inventors,[14] although he recognizes that the entrepreneur may also be an inventor just as he may also be a capitalist. Schumpeter's hesitancy in this regard stems from the fact that inventions must actually be carried into practice before profit is possible. It was the step of putting inventions into effect that Schumpeter saw as the entrepreneurial phase of invention. It is possible that Schumpeter was unfamiliar with the extent to which the exploitation of patents has long been routinized in the United States.

Capitalists and Entrepreneurs

The third important economic distinction is that between the entrepreneur and the capitalist. This is precisely the distinction Adam Smith and Berle and Means failed to make. In the economic arena of 1776, it was not easy to discern that the provision of capital and of entrepreneurial skill were two separate, specialized functions. In fact, at that time it was extremely rare for entrepreneurial services to be marketed in any way other than in a package with capital. Even today in common parlance, the word *entrepreneur* generally signifies the individual who starts his own business.[15] It was relatively easy to apply the concept of the entrepreneur to the traditional corporate promoter who raised money to found a business, which he might or might not then manage. Undoubtedly, these promoters were performing an entrepreneurial function,[16] but this usage served to focus our attention on the

14. Schumpeter TED, at p. 88.

15. It is equally interesting that the word *management* has the much broader suggestion of considerable entrepreneurial activity.

16. Cf. the examples used by Schumpeter in TED, p. 152, and *Business Cycles*, p. 78, with those used by Knight, p. 257.

Arthur Stone Dewing in his classic, *The Financial Policy of Corporations* (New York: The Ronald Press Co., 4th ed., 1946), Vol. 1, p. 416, distinguishes the function of the in-

founding aspects of enterprise rather than on the necessity for continuing innovation.

A full understanding of the distinction between the entrepreneur and the capitalist requires detailed consideration of the characteristics of the remuneration received by the individuals in these two categories. As both Knight and Schumpeter point out, the capitalist has a function in even the most static and unprogressive kind of economy. No goods are permanent, and if the economy is to remain stable, provision must be made for replacement of depreciated facilities. The funds (or their goods counterpart) expended for this replacement purpose constitute capital, and the return on them is interest. In a stable, risk-free economy this interest would be an easily ascertainable figure determined by classically described market forces. But in that system there will be no return we can properly designate as profits to the capitalist or any other economic functionary. There can be no entrepreneur. Only the dynamic model of a competitive economy comprehends uncertainty about the future, and it is the existence of this uncertainty that gives rise to the concept of profits and the entrepreneur.

To Frank Knight we owe the origin of the concept of the entrepreneur as the "organizer of uncertainties." To Schumpeter the emphasis is more upon the entrepreneur as the creator of uncertainties, or the creator of the conditions necessary for true profit. To each of these economists and to many so-called growth economists today, it is the entrepreneur who sets progress in motion, not the capitalist.[17] The entrepreneur's relation to the capitalist is about the same as his relation to labor or the owner of land. As Schumpeter says, the entrepreneur is not the typical interest-receiver

---

ventor from that of the promoter. Dewing's emphasis is entirely on bringing different factors together to establish a new business. Thus he points out that promotion is different from "the administration of a business once it has started." *Ibid.*, p. 416. But he never noted that the continuing entrepreneurial function is quite similar to that of the promoter. His description of the characteristics of the successful promoter, *ibid.* pp. 412–15, leaves no doubt, however, that Dewing's promoter can be the same man as Schumpeter's entrepreneur.

17. Peter T. Bauer and Basil S. Yamey, *The Economics of Under-Developed Countries* (Chicago: University of Chicago Press, 1957), and Colin Clark, "Growthmanship," *Intercollegiate Review*, Vol. 1, No. 1 (Jan., 1965), p. 5.

as Adam Smith may have seen him, because he is the typical interest-payer.[18]

The capitalist may be able to wrest from the entrepreneur a contract allowing the former to share in profits, but as Schumpeter remarked, "one must distinguish the economic nature of a return from what happens to it."[19] The return to the capitalist, though the amount may be indeterminate in advance, is still interest. The capitalist may even insist that he be allowed to risk his funds against the small probability of a large gain rather than against a high probability of a smaller gain. More prosaically, this choice today is between assuming the status of a bondholder or that of a common-stockholder. But the latter, as Schumpeter pointed out, functions as a creditor who is willing to forego the normal protections accorded that category of capital, in exchange for the right to share in profits.[20]

The Entrepreneur's Reward

The entrepreneur as such, unlike the capitalist, is never the bearer of risk or uncertainty. Risk is borne only by those giving credit or otherwise extending capital. This may be the same individual as the entrepreneur, but the risk falls on him *as the capitalist* or as a possessor of goods, *not as an entrepreneur.*[21] Presumably Schumpeter would not even include the loss of time and energy as a risk to the entrepreneur as such. Knight is more explicit on this point; he assumes that the return to the entrepreneur is composed of two parts. The first is merely the ordinary wage for the labor performed,

18. Schumpeter TED, p. 180. For this entire discussion the interested reader is directed to Chapter 9 in Knight's book and Chapter 5 in Schumpeter's.

19. Schumpeter TED, p. 144. As we shall see in the next chapter, this point of Schumpeter's is slightly misleading. In the modern, large corporation the capitalist investor does not actually wrest a part of the entrepreneur's profits from him. The accretion in the value of the capitalist's holdings is analogous to the increase in the value of raw fibers after the introduction of the automatic loom. That is, the entrepreneur causes an increase in the marginal productivity of the production factors he uses. This is different from a sharing in the true profits of the entrepreneur, though this too occurs.

20. Schumpeter TED, p. 75.

21. *Ibid.*, p. 137.

that is, the competitive rate of pay. The second part is true profit and is unrelated, in any normal market sense, to the work done.[22]

What then is the nature of the return to this upsetter of stable societies, this creator of disruptive forces? To both Knight and Schumpeter the answer to this question is precisely what is meant by the word *profit.* If the entrepreneur makes an economically successful new combination of factors, a surplus will be produced over and above the amount necessary merely to pay the present cost of component productive factors. In a static system, one without innovation, these costs would just be covered and no surplus would be produced. A surplus results because the new combination or innovation allows an existing producer to operate at a lower cost than previously, or it allows him to sell a new product at a price higher than the long-term equilibrium price. The entrepreneur buys the component factors of production at the old equilibrium price. Because he uses them either in a more productive or less costly way than do others who buy these same factors in the stable system, his use will produce a surplus over and above what other uses will create.

This surplus on occasion bears a relationship to the concept of monopoly rent or profit, and there may even be a coincidental identity. If the entrepreneur has no competitors when he introduces a new product, price will be determined according to the principles of monopoly. As he sells, he will realize what is generally termed monopoly profit. There is, in a fashion Marx did not imagine, a monopoly element in capitalist profits.[23] And yet the innovation and the monopoly are two distinct economic phenomena. Only the value of the innovation at the moment of creation reflects profit and the return to the entrepreneur. Subsequent income, though its amount may be determined according to the laws of monopoly pricing, is never profit in this sense. Even assuming that the monopoly position could be made permanent and secure against a price decline brought about by new competition, there can never be an additional return to the entrepreneur as such. "Profit from founding a business and permanent return are distinguished

22. Knight, p. 277. This dichotomy is consistent with what actually happens in large corporations, where innovators also hold salaried positions.

23. Schumpeter TED, p. 152.

in practice; the former is the value of the monopoly, the latter is just the return from the monopoly condition."[24]

An illustration from the patent field will help make this point clear. An inventor who gets a patent monopoly may sell the patent or he may exploit it himself. If he sells it, all that he receives, in our sense, is entrepreneurial profit. The subsequent exploiter of the patent, though he will be charging a monopoly price for the product, will only receive a competitive return for his investment. This same division of economic functions and returns will remain, *a fortiori,* if the inventor exploits the patent himself.

Another illustration of the distinction between profits and other returns is provided by the stock market. If an individual establishes a firm that has a patent monopoly and then sells his shares, he will receive approximately the present discounted value of all future monopoly profits the company is then expected to make. The company will continue to act as a monopoly after the sale of shares, but the return to the new shareowners will not in any sense contain a monopoly element. It will generally approximate the competitive rate of return on an investment of the size and type they have made.[25]

Entrepreneurial success is like monopoly (other than those protected by patents or other government grants) in still another way. It is rare that it can be made permanent. The entrepreneur rarely triumphs for himself alone. In almost all cases he creates a model or shows a way that can be copied. Others can and do follow him, first individuals and then perhaps hordes.[26] Copiers will continue to enter the industry until a new competitive equilibrium is created, that is, until again there is no surplus over cost because production has increased and price has declined. The copiers who enter the field before the full value of entrepreneurial innovation has been

24. *Ibid.* A similar distinction between profits and permanent, nonmonopolistic returns is made by both Schumpeter and Knight. Cf. Schumpeter TED, p. 138, and Knight, p. 257.

25. Manne, "Higher Criticism," p. 403.

26. Armen A. Alchian, "Uncertainty, Evolution and Economic Theory," *Journal of Political Economy,* 58 (1950), p. 211, reprinted in American Economics Association, *Readings in Industrial Organization and Public Policy,* Vol. 8, eds., Richard B. Heflebower and George W. Stocking (Homewood, Ill.: Richard D. Irwin, Inc., 1958), p. 207; and Knight, p. 170, fn. 1.

exploited will still realize some true profit, although the existence of the surplus may be extremely ephemeral. But the greatest profit will generally be made by the firm that is first with the new combination of factors.

This surplus-over-cost plays an extraordinarily important role in the Schumpeterian theory of economic development. Without this profit there would be no accumulation of wealth, because in a stable society the "non-consumption of profit is not saving in the proper sense, for it is not an encroachment upon the customary standard of life."[27] It is the entrepreneur's action that Schumpeter sees as the only important source of new wealth.

Entrepreneurial Motivation

As the entrepreneurial return is unpredictable, the theory needs some device to account for the available supply of entrepreneurial talent. The argument is perhaps more sociological than economic, and yet it is quite cogent. As Knight expresses it:

> The income of *any particular entrepreneur* will in general tend to be larger: (1) as he himself has ability, and good luck; but (2) perhaps more important as there is in the society a scarcity of self-confidence combined with the power to make effective guarantees to employees. The abundance or scarcity of mere ability to manage business successfully exerts relatively little influence on profit; the main thing is the rashness or timidity of entrepreneurs (actual and potential) as a class in bidding up the prices of productive services. Entrepreneur income, being residual, is determined by the demand for these other services, which demand is a matter of the self-confidence of entrepreneurs as a class, rather than upon a demand for entrepreneur services in a direct sense. . . . The condition for large profits is a narrowly limited supply of high-grade ability with a low general level of initiative as well as ability.[28]

For Schumpeter a similar line of reasoning leads him to conclude that the total amount of profit actually realized by an individual entrepreneur may be much greater than necessary to call forth the entrepreneurial ser-

27. Schumpeter TED, p. 154.
28. Knight, pp. 283–84.

vices that are actually operative. He adds that the possibility of attaining the larger sum may work as a stronger incentive than would be justified by multiplying the amount by its coefficient of probability.[29] But he discounts the importance of the incentive provided by some huge gains by concluding that it is "quite clear" that the same amount of entrepreneurial service would be forthcoming if entrepreneurial profits were smaller. Thus he is able to explain why "the entrepreneur can be relatively so easily deprived of his profit and why the 'salaried' entrepreneur, for example the industrial manager who frequently plays the entrepreneurial rôle, can generally be adequately remunerated with much less than the full amount of the profit."[30]

But this point is not clear at all. In fact it portends, in a manner we shall examine shortly, Schumpeter's most famous error: his prediction that the modern large corporate system could not survive. At first, Schumpeter's point that large returns are not a necessary incentive for entrepreneurial effort seems correct. The supply would appear to be determined solely by personal, psychological forces. Entrepreneurs do appear in government and in salaried positions, and the temperament for innovation may turn up in such nonentrepreneurial professions as the clergy or teaching. But surely these are the exceptions, and, though data would be difficult to obtain, the indications are that entrepreneurial talent tends to concentrate in those industries, professions, and positions providing the greatest potential for very substantial profits.

Entrepreneurial skill may not be allocated in a free economy in the same manner that potatoes or steel are. As Knight indicates, there are sociological and psychological variables in the equation. But the allocational aspects of market theory are not irrelevant, as Schumpeter seems to suggest. There will be *some* entrepreneurs willing to accept a salary, but that fact does not lead to Schumpeter's conclusion. Entrepreneurial skill will still be attracted by the possibility of high gain. In large American corporations one must

29. Schumpeter TED, p. 155; also see Milton Friedman and L. J. Savage, "The Utility Analysis of Choices Involving Risk," *Journal of Political Economy,* 56 (1948), p. 279, reprinted in *Landmarks in Political Economy,* Vol. 2, eds., Earl J. Hamilton, Albert Rees, and Harry G. Johnson (Chicago: University of Chicago Press, 1962), p. 297.

30. Schumpeter TED, p. 155.

ordinarily perform a kind of salaried apprenticeship before entrepreneurial rewards become available. But even the most bureaucratically minded person may begin to have original ideas if the possibility of large rewards is apparent.

It is undoubtedly true that entrepreneurs may be satisfied with "less than the full amount of the profit." Clearly, imitators and fast copiers will claim some of the full profit. But this is merely one of the conditions under which most entrepreneurs must operate. It might be added, too, that we can never know what the "full amount of the profit" is, as entrepreneurial profits are peculiarly difficult to separate from other kinds of return. But none of this proves the interesting implication of Schumpeter's statement: that no greater entrepreneurial activity will be forthcoming even if the rewards are allowed to go higher. If this were true, the plight of underdeveloped countries would be sad indeed, because it would imply that their economies already receive as much entrepreneurial skill as they ever will.[31] There is much that we do not yet know about entrepreneurial motivation. One thing, however, is clear. We do not know that allowing entrepreneurs to claim higher rewards will *not* produce more of this service.

New Firms and Old

Schumpeter did not believe that entrepreneurial skills could ever be appropriately utilized within the framework of the large, publicly held corporation. This is undoubtedly why his emphasis was generally on the "new firm" aspect of innovation. Even when he dealt with the subject of innovation within an existing firm, it was in terms of establishing a new enterprise. In a slightly obscure passage, whose importance has perhaps been overlooked, Schumpeter defined *new enterprises* to comprehend innovations by existing firms. This approach has some real advantages, but for Schumpeter it probably reflects his notion that new firms are the critical form of innovation. He simply did not think in terms of ongoing innovations in large, established firms. Schumpeter stated his point as follows:

31. Bauer and Yamey, *Economics of Under-Developed*, Chapter 5.

> If the entrepreneur's strength is not exhausted on one project and yet he continues to carry on the same business, then he proceeds to *new changes which are always new enterprises according to our terminology,* [italics mine] often with means which he draws from his past profits. The process then appears to be different, but its nature is the same.[32]

But even then he went on to say that "new enterprises are mostly founded by new men and the old businesses sink into insignificance. . . . Even if an individual who previously carried on his business by annually repeating his part in the circular flow becomes an entrepreneur, no change takes place in the nature of the proceeding."[33] Thus he persisted in emphasizing the "new business firm" aspect of entrepreneurial activities.

In *The Theory of Economic Development* Schumpeter displays little familiarity with the workings of the modern company with widely diffused share ownership. His constant emphasis on the new establishment as the prime work of the entrepreneur is one aspect of this view, and his belief that entrepreneurs could be had for a salary is another. Unfortunately when the time came for him to deal explicitly with this largely American development, he shaped his theory—and his prediction—of the corporation to fit his predilections. His misleading treatment of the modern corporation leads us to a fascinating aspect of the subject of insider trading.

Schumpeter's Theory of Modern Corporate Capitalism

Schumpeter believed, along with Knight, that without recurrent entrepreneurial activity, any business would stagnate and collapse. Time and the dynamic forces of competition wait for no man. It is never sufficient for survival merely to manage a competitive business in the purely technical sense. So long as other entrepreneurs exist, Schumpeter's circular flow or Knight's static economy cannot exist. In the free-market system, one must run very fast merely to stand still. This point is most carefully articulated

32. Schumpeter TED, p. 136.
33. *Ibid.*

in Schumpeter's best-known book, *Capitalism, Socialism and Democracy*.[34] There are three steps in the analysis: the dynamics of competition, the bureaucratization of business, and the collapse.

Schumpeter's concept of competition is not that of an effete, trifling game. To him competition is robust, enormous, cataclysmic, and revolutionary. Schumpeter's statement of competitive reality makes the protestations of the Antitrust Division of the Justice Department by comparison seem pale and futile—or worse, wrong.

> In capitalist reality as distinguished from its textbook picture, it is not [price] competition which counts but the competition from the new commodity, the new technology, the new source of supply, the new type of organization (the largest-scale unit of control for instance)—competition which commands a decisive cost or quality advantage and which strikes not at the margins of the profits and the outputs of the existing firms but at their foundations and their very lives. This kind of competition is as much more effective than the other as a bombardment is in comparison with forcing a door, and so much more important that it becomes a matter of comparative indifference whether competition in the ordinary sense functions more or less promptly; the powerful lever that in the long run expands output and brings down prices is in any case made of other stuff.
>
> It is hardly necessary to point out that competition of the kind we now have in mind acts not only when in being but also when it is merely an ever-present threat. It disciplines before it attacks. The businessman feels himself to be in a competitive situation even if he is alone in his field or if, though not alone, he holds a position such that investigating government experts fail to see any effective competition between him and any other firms in the same or a neighboring field and in consequence conclude that his talk, under examination, about his competitive sorrows is all make-believe. In many cases, though not in all, this will in the long run enforce behavior very similar to the perfectly competitive pattern.[35]

At this point, however, Schumpeter's unfamiliarity with the large American corporation becomes evident. Here he seems to invent a theory to fit his preconceptions of a large corporation. Schumpeter concluded that

34. New York: Harper and Bros. Publishers, 1942.
35. *Ibid.*, pp. 84–85.

progress-destroying bureaucratization was well under way on the American corporate scene.

> This social function [entrepreneurship] is already losing importance and is bound to lose it at an accelerating rate in the future even if the economic process itself of which entrepreneurship was the prime mover went on unabated. For, on the one hand, it is much easier now than it has been in the past to do things that lie outside familiar routine—innovation itself is being reduced to routine. Technological progress is increasingly becoming the business of teams of trained specialists who turn out what is required and make it work in predictable ways. The romance of earlier commercial adventure is rapidly wearing away because so many more things can be strictly calculated that had of old to be visualized in a flash of genius.[36]

The effect of the routinization of innovation, Schumpeter believed, would be first to destroy the capitalist entrepreneurs as a class and finally, for lack of a champion, to destroy capitalism.

> The perfectly bureaucratized giant industrial unit not only ousts the small or medium-sized firm and "expropriates" its owners, but in the end it also ousts the entrepreneur and expropriates the bourgeoisie as a class which in the process stands to lose not only its income but also what is infinitely more important, its function. The true pacemakers of socialism were not the intellectuals or agitators who preached it but the Vanderbilts, Carnegies and Rockefellers.[37]

The Basis of Schumpeter's Error

This conclusion of Schumpeter's is perhaps the most criticized aspect of his entire system. Clearly the modern corporate system shows no sign of faltering. Innovation, inventions, and discovery are proceeding apace. Competitors of all sorts still feel so insecure and threatened that they beg for the government's protective wing. Companies rise and fall; industries disappear and new ones develop; personal fortunes are made, in big business and

36. *Ibid.*, p. 132.
37. *Ibid.*, p. 134.

small, and fortunes are lost. Not much has changed in these regards in our dynamic milieu.

Innovation appears to have become routine, but the difficulty is perhaps only semantic. Clearly, corporations now finance research laboratories that pour out patents. But the development of organized research is surely an entrepreneurial success of the first order. Merely because certain kinds of technological research have been routinized, in no way shows that innovation has ceased. The development of organized research laboratories should stand as one of the major innovations of our era. It is sheer wistfulness to long for the attic inventor to do the same kind of inventing that laboratories full of scientists do better. Schumpeter's "romance of earlier commercial adventure" has in more ways than one been displaced by DuPont's slogan, "The Romance of Chemistry." A new generation's romance may be only a smell in the nostrils of an older generation.

It is paradoxical that the man with whose name the concept of dynamic competition, the "perennial gale of creative destruction," is most associated should have reached these conclusions. And yet, in spite of his occasional yearnings for small, family corporations[38] and some very amateurish psychologizing about men's attitudes toward tangible property,[39] Schumpeter left us with some important clues about this "disappearing" entrepreneur.

> We have seen that, normally, the modern businessman, whether entrepreneur or mere managing administrator, is of the executive type. From the logic of his position he acquires something of the psychology of the salaried employee working in a bureaucratic organization. Whether a stockholder or not, his will to fight and to hold on is not and cannot be what it was with the man who knew ownership and its responsibilities in the full-blooded sense of those words. His system of values and his conception of duty undergo a profound change. Mere stockholders of course have ceased to count at all—quite independently of the clipping of their share by a regulating and taxing state. Thus the modern corporation, although the product of the capitalist process, socializes the bourgeois mind; it relentlessly narrows the scope of capitalist motivation; not only that, it will eventually kill its roots.[40]

38. *Ibid.*, p. 140.
39. *Ibid.*, p. 142.
40. *Ibid.*, p. 156.

In this passage, Schumpeter suggests that the very personality type characteristic of entrepreneurs will disappear. And yet his explanation for this phenomenon is unclear and unconvincing. The entrepreneur "from the logic of his position . . . acquires something of the psychology of the *salaried* [italics mine] employee. . . ."[41] Presumably "the logic of his position" refers to the bureaucratic atmosphere of a large corporation. But surely this does not infect everyone, as Schumpeter seems to suggest. The problem for the entrepreneur, the nonorganization man in the large company, is simply to rise above the levels where bureaucratic organization is a necessity. But Schumpeter was still trying to fit every large corporate employee into his anachronistic view of large companies. Thus, he implies, as he had intimated years earlier, that corporate executives should only be paid a manager's form of compensation, that is, a salary. Schumpeter must have felt uneasy about the implications of this point, for he added the following amazing footnote to the passage quoted above.

> Many people will deny this. This is due to the fact that they derive their impression from past history and from the slogans generated by past history during which the institutional change brought about by the big corporation had not yet asserted itself. Also they may think of the scope which corporate business used to give for illegal satisfactions of the capitalist motivation. But that would cut my way: the fact that *personal gain beyond salary and bonus cannot, in corporate business, be reaped by executives except by illegal or semi-illegal practices* [italics mine] shows precisely that the structural idea of the corporation is averse to it.[42]

Schumpeter believed that it was either illegal or immoral to compensate entrepreneurs within large corporations in an economically appropriate fashion. Probably the "illegal or semi-illegal" practices to which Schumpeter refers include trading on inside information. As his book was published in 1942, Schumpeter was probably familiar with Section 16(b) of the Securities Exchange Act of 1934 and with the attitude toward insider trading of various writers. If this were true, he did not examine the economic premises upon which the charges against the practice were made.

41. *Ibid.*, p. 156.
42. *Ibid.*, pp. 156–57.

Undoubtedly, if no way to reward the entrepreneur within a corporation exists, he will tend to disappear from the corporate scene. He will *seem,* as Schumpeter suggested, to have had his function routinized and his income turned into the ordinary manager's straight salary. One cannot quarrel with Schumpeter's prediction of what would happen to the large corporate system if the entrepreneur does disappear from the scene. The total bureaucratization of large private enterprises would almost necessarily ensue. The prediction for which Schumpeter has been so frequently criticized was closer to the mark than his critics realized. It follows quite logically from the compensation arrangement that Schumpeter mistakenly saw in the large corporation. His prediction might also follow in time if we abandoned our most effective system for rewarding entrepreneurs in the large corporations.

9 Inside Information: The Entrepreneur's Compensation

We have defined the economic function of the entrepreneur and shown how this function may be critical for the survival of a firm in a competitive milieu. The most important variety of competition is not that of prices or product differentiation, each of which can be handled by pure managers, but rather the dynamic, radical, destructive competition of new products, new methods, or new organizations—all the handiwork of entrepreneurs. The pioneer theorists in this field probably overemphasized the importance of business founders and promoters as entrepreneurs and seriously underestimated the enormous entrepreneurial potential of large, modern corporations. A crucial theoretical difficulty has been finding an appropriate method of compensation for these services. Compensation for entrepreneurial services is not a simple matter. It differs from the interest paid the capitalist for risk-taking and the wage paid to the manager for providing a service that can be priced in advance in the market place. The special relationship between the entrepreneurial function and inside information remains to be examined.

In a system of small corporations and family businesses, entrepreneurial compensation is inextricably bound up with return for the capitalist and managerial functions. About the only time these can be separately computed occurs when a small-business founder sells out soon after establishing a successful venture. This is not analytically dissimilar to an inventor's selling his newly patented invention. The entrepreneurial return is also easy to isolate in the promotion of publicly held corporations. The amount is the value of the shares taken by the promoters at the time of promotion. The phrase *promoters' shares* is probably the only term in our vocabulary distinguishing a specific form of compensation for entrepreneurs.

Special Conditions for Entrepreneurial Compensation

If large, publicly held corporations are to survive, our theory implies the necessity of their retaining entrepreneurs. Thus, an appropriate form of compensation must be found for the special function these individuals perform. Many peculiarities distinguish innovational activity from the capitalist or the managerial function. Therefore, the method chosen for compensating entrepreneurs must meet a number of special conditions in order to be effective.

Clearly the method chosen must allow the individuals concerned to market the value of their special contributions. This cannot be the same compensation given managers, as some of these will perform entrepreneurial services and others will not. The difficulty, as noted previously, is that innovations may spring from almost any source, whether it be from an officer, director, lawyer, investment banker, or scientist working in a laboratory. Each of these functionaries will receive the normal compensation for the job for which he was hired. Ordinarily he will not be fired for failure to introduce radical innovations. He may enjoy considerable job security and an ever-rising annual income.[1] But what incentive does he have to perform the unusual or to revolutionize a company or an industry? Without some special device, the entrepreneur cannot in any meaningful sense market his service to a large corporation.

The compensation mechanism should not require a large, long-term financial investment by the entrepreneur. There should be a guarantee that

1. Ironically this seems less true the higher the executive position. Presidents of many large companies have relatively little job security, and the lack of important innovations, when competitors are developing them, can certainly lead to early retirement. It may be that job promotions to the top are granted on the basis of actual and anticipated entrepreneurial performance and that the president is supposed to be much more than simply a co-ordinator.

anyone may sell entrepreneurial services.[2] Without such a guarantee, we should anticipate that entrepreneurial profits would be gained only by those wealthy enough to found their own businesses and exploit their own innovations. Clearly this condition is critical to the compensation of entrepreneurs in large corporations.

Perhaps the greatest peculiarity of a compensation scheme for entrepreneurs stems from the indeterminacy of results. True innovation cannot be predicted nor its value known before it has been thought of and made effective. True innovation cannot be planned and budgeted in advance. An individual cannot be hired to perform *x* amount of entrepreneurial service. He can be hired to work for a certain period of time with a title such as *entrepreneur,* but if this were regularly done, some job holders would receive handsome pay while producing no desirable results.

When functions previously considered entrepreneurial, such as inventing, are actually routinized, it is the program for routinization that constitutes the important innovation, not the anticipated discoveries. The prototype modern corporation represented a major entrepreneurial innovation. It superseded earlier, less efficient methods of organizing factors of production and has been widely copied since. But the first use of the modern corporate form was an innovation distinct from subsequent promotions of particular ventures. Subsequent promotions of publicly held companies required entrepreneurial skill, but those utilized a business form previously developed.

Salary and Bonus Modes of Compensation

Neither salary nor bonuses meet the conditions we have stated for an appropriate form of compensation for entrepreneurs. There is little need to belabor the point that salary is inadequate for the task.[3] Salary is appropriate

2. This suggests an advantage for stock options different from those usually advanced. By giving options the company may enable executives to make trading profits they might otherwise be unable to finance.

3. It must be emphasized here that we are referring to the form of compensation and not the amount. Presumably, the figure can always be made large enough to attract anyone, but to raise salaries to this level would be very wasteful if alternative means for attracting entrepreneurs are available.

only to purchase a known service in the labor market. The parties to the agreement must have a fairly clear understanding of what the job entails and what the skill of the employee is relative to others in the same market.[4] This is equally true of the lowly bookkeeper and the president of the giant company. If it is known what job either is to do in order to maintain or improve the company's earnings, no innovational activity is being contracted for. An entrepreneurial decision may have been made by whoever hired him,[5] but this must be distinguished from the work the employee does.

The bonus would seem at first glance to meet most of the conditions necessary for compensating entrepreneurs. It is paid as an addition to normal salary, and the decision to pay a bonus can often be made after a successful innovation. It is important, however, to distinguish between the simple occasional bonus, not paid as part of a profit-sharing plan, and the more popular bonus plans in which the recipients and their percentage of profits are determined in advance.[6] The *introduction* of a profit-sharing plan may constitute pure entrepreneurial compensation, but only the value of the participation at exactly the time it is granted can constitute entrepreneurial compensation. The *operation* of this or any other profit-sharing plan fails to meet our necessary conditions. The effect of such a plan is to give the recipient a proprietary stake in the business. He is then an investor and a risk-taker, and his annual return will be that of a capitalist, regardless of how it is computed. The initial, discounted value of his participation in the plan may constitute entrepreneurial profits, but subsequent withdrawals will constitute interest on his investment.

The value of a profit-sharing plan, as of the time it is granted, is like the non-profit-sharing bonus, that is, the simple bonus given as a reward for good work on an *ad hoc* basis. If the recipient chooses to invest bonus money in the stock of the company, he has clearly become a capitalist investor. If the company pays the bonus in the form of stock, that relationship is also

4. We are assuming that the parties know supply and demand conditions and are simply conforming to them by correctly classifying the job and the employee.

5. Knight, p. 342.

6. See George Thomas Washington and V. Henry Rothschild II, *Compensating the Corporate Executive*, 3d ed. (New York: The Ronald Press Co., 1962), Vol. 1, p. 84.

apparent. But there is no *economic* difference if the company gives the same individual a profit-sharing right whose value is the equivalent of the cash or stock they might have paid.[7]

The bonus scheme for compensating entrepreneurs has numerous drawbacks. Although courts do not easily overturn corporate compensation plans, the threat and the possibility of this happening always exist.[8] Furthermore, current SEC requirements require disclosure of all salaries and bonuses paid directors and certain officers in excess of $30,000, and many individuals do not want to disclose what may seem like astronomical figures. But most important, the bonus has to be decided upon unilaterally by someone other than the recipient. A certain degree of bargaining may occasionally occur, but the entrepreneur will tend to value his contribution to the company higher than others will. Furthermore, the bonus has to be determined on an annual basis, while the effects of any given innovation may be very prolonged. That makes it extremely difficult to assess accurately the value of any particular innovation.

Bonuses are not apt to be forthcoming in years when the company has actually lost money, even though the value of the innovation was substantial and without it the company might have shown greater losses. This suggests the final drawback to the use of profit-sharing bonuses to pay entrepreneurs—the extreme difficulty of determining corporate profits. Standard accounting techniques for determining profits simply cannot isolate the elements reflecting an entrepreneurial contribution. Profit-sharing plans tend to make employees emphasize current paper profits, as opposed to investments maximizing future returns.[9] Any profit-sharing plan, including bonuses, tends to give some incentive for entrepreneurial activity. But their tendency will be to induce the smaller kinds of innovations and cost-saving

7. Courts have unfortunately complicated the law on bonuses by their failure to realize that, regardless of the names used, the bonus aspect of a profit-sharing plan is the value of the right when it is acquired. Any subsequent increase is simply a capital gain or interest. The leading opinion making this error was the dissent of Judge Thomas Swan in *Rogers v. Hill*, 65 Fed. 2d 109, 113 (2d Cir., 1932), *reversed*, 289 U.S. 582 (1933).

8. Washington and Rothschild, *Compensating the Corporate Executive*, Chapter 8.

9. See Armen A. Alchian and William R. Allen, *University Economics* (Belmont, Calif.: Wadsworth Publishing Co., Inc., 1964), p. 218.

techniques rather than radical, major, dramatic developments. Unless we want to conclude that entrepreneurial activities are induced equally by a promise of large or small gains, we must look beyond bonuses and profit-sharing plans for entrepreneurial compensation.

Stock Options

One method by which the insider can gain part of the value he has produced is through stock options granted him before the valuable information has been disclosed. As we saw in Chapter 6, by exercising an option after disclosure, at the predisclosure price, the insider can claim precisely the per-share value of the information he has created. If no charge is made for the option, the gain represents pure profit.[10] The stock option appears then to be a desirable device for compensating entrepreneurial talent.

But there are serious drawbacks to using stock options as the sole or even major device for entrepreneurial compensation. Apart from the numerous conditions and restrictions on the use of stock options in the common law[11] and the Internal Revenue Code,[12] options must be granted prior to the in-

10. It should be noted that this defense of stock options offers no justification for granting an option at less than the predisclosure market price of shares.

11. Washington and Rothschild, *Compensating the Corporate Executive,* Vol. 2, pp. 572–80. The Delaware Supreme Court, in a departure from the usual judicial hands-off policy toward compensation plans, has actually created a number of specific legal tests for the validity of stock-option plans. The underlying rationale for this approach is the requirement that a corporation receive appropriate consideration for any compensation paid. Otherwise the payment will be treated as an invalid gift of corporate assets. See *Kerbs* v. *California Eastern Airways, Inc.,* 33 Del. Ch. 69, 90 Atl. 2d 652 (1952). Also see *Lieberman* v. *Becker,* 38 Del. Ch. 540, 155 Atl. 2d 596 (1954).

12. *Internal Revenue Code,* Sections 421–25 (1964). The most questionable aspect of these rules is the requirement that the stock be held for three years after exercise in order to receive capital-gains treatment. Prior to 1964, this period was six months, though it could not be less than two years after the option was granted. A reasonable feature, viewing the Internal Revenue Code as a scheme for the regulation of stock options, is the requirement that to qualify for special tax treatment the option must be granted at the market price. Options can be granted for up to five years, but they must be nontransferable.

As the *1964 House Ways and Means Committee Report* indicates, Congress viewed stock options as a device to make investors, not traders, out of employees. That report stated: "Your committee . . . decided to continue the stock option provision because it believes

novation to serve the purpose at hand. If they are granted after the information is known but before disclosure, the economic effect is precisely that of a bonus equal to the anticipated gain, and all the valuation problems inherent in the bonus scheme are again present. But if the option is granted before the innovation, there is no way of knowing whether the potential gain is appropriate or not, because it will vary with the number of shares covered. This is not to say that such options will not induce any entrepreneurial activity. Manifestly, any proprietary interest, existing or contingent, will have some incentive effect. But the incentive is precisely the same as that to be gained from share ownership of the number of shares covered by the option, as the incentive will be commensurate with the absolute gain that can be realized and not with the potential percentage gain. Stock-option plans are more likely to provide a proper incentive for managers than for entrepreneurs.

The belief that stock options are not widely used for entrepreneurial compensation is difficult to substantiate, because from 1950 until 1964 there were very substantial tax advantages in the so-called restricted stock options. Apart from tax considerations, however, options are quite expensive for the corporation issuing them. The true cost to a corporation granting an option is precisely the same as the cost of an identical option purchased in a competitive call market. Indeed, corporations are free to cover their own option grants by purchasing calls on their own stock. In effect this may be happening when corporations buy their own shares in the market to use for stock options.[13] We know that generally the cost of a call "at the market" for six months and ten days is approximately 10 percent of the current market price of the shares.[14] But corporate stock options are usually granted for periods of up to five years, and we should anticipate the price of the longer

---

that it is good for the economy for management of various businesses to have a stake in their successful operation." *CCH Federal Tax Reporter,* 1966, Vol. 3, par. 2674.03, p. 33322. This view reflects the prevailing attitude that there are only managerial and capitalist functions to be performed in corporations. It overlooks the entrepreneurial function that may have provided the original impetus for stock options for select, key employees.

13. See *The Wall Street Journal,* June 30, 1965, p. 1, col. 8.

14. Richard J. Kruizenga, "Introduction to the Option Contract," Cootner, pp. 378–79.

option to be considerably more than the price of a six-month call; it may even approach the price of the underlying share.[15]

Stock options are inefficient devices for exploiting information because they are generally not mobile or liquid assets. To gain any tax advantage, they must be nontransferable, and many companies require the executive to hold the stock for a certain period of time after exercise.[16] Stock options are also not flexible devices for insiders' quick use. Shareholders usually ratify a stock-option plan before it becomes effective, and this can be very time-consuming. Discretion may be given in advance to directors or a salary committee to issue options pursuant to the plan. But even this requires some assessment in advance of the new development as to who will be entitled to what. Stock options are probably used on occasion to exploit inside information, but the device is too cumbersome and too expensive to be used frequently for that purpose.

Insider Trading

With either bonuses or stock options, the employee is limited to a specific reward no matter how great his innovation. In the case of the options, the limit is posed by the number of shares optioned. The value of his contribution may far exceed the gain on these shares. There is no such limitation on the effectiveness of insider trading as compensation. As we have seen, even if the individual is unable to buy all the shares necessary to raise their price by the amount indicated by the value of his information, he may be able to bank his information and draw on it at a later time in the form of information about other shares.

Insider trading meets all the conditions for appropriately compensating entrepreneurs. It readily allows corporate entrepreneurs to market their innovations. As we have seen, this is not a direct marketing of the idea but

15. An estimate of the difference in call prices for different time periods might be gained by valuing long-term conversion features in bonds or preferred stocks. But this is complicated by the redemption feature commonly appearing in the same securities and tending to prevent large premiums being paid for the conversion feature.

16. See George Thomas Washington and V. Henry Rothschild II, *Compensating the Corporate Executive,* Vol. 2, Chs. 15–16.

rather a "sale" of information about an innovation. Thus, although we do not allow entrepreneurs a direct proprietary interest in their ideas, we can allow recovery for their ideas by permitting them to exploit information about the existence of the ideas in a market primarily based on information. In the next chapter we shall examine the reasons for believing that this market allocates appropriate returns to the particular individuals who have in fact performed an entrepreneurial function.

In order to exploit information, it is not essential that an individual hold any particular job or that he already have or make a large investment in the company. Only access to the new information and not status, position, or wealth will determine when an individual may be compensated by this method. He will generally have to make some investment of funds in order to exploit the information, even though the period of investment may be very short. However, assuming his willingness to disclose his information to someone else, credit should be available for this purpose, and he may at this point be introduced to financiers and bankers who will assist him in exploiting valuable information. If he already has his own funds, however, he will not have to make any disclosure to others.

There are strong similarities between the more traditional markets for entrepreneurial services and the market for inside information. Indeed an examination of these similarities should leave little doubt that the information market is merely a variant of the underlying market for entrepreneurial service. Schumpeter emphasized that the traditional entrepreneur must claim his remuneration before the forces of competition exercise their inexorable tendency to wipe out any surplus-over-costs. Now we may note the striking parallel between this point and one already examined in connection with the economics of information. As soon as information is transmitted by any of the methods described in Chapter 5, it begins to lose its value. Ultimately, as Knight has pointed out, when it "becomes common property it is like any other superabundant element in production, a free good. . . ." Thus, the modern corporate employee-entrepreneur, like his traditional counterpart, must move fast to claim the benefits of his innovation. Whether the competition be from copyists flooding into a new field or from other stock buyers pushing up the price, the entrepreneur ordinarily can cash in his special chips only if he moves quickly.

The traditional capitalist risks funds with the hope of substantial gain. Frequently this gain results because an entrepreneur has brought capital, management, and other resources together in a profitable fashion. The capitalist gains from the new combination, although, as Schumpeter points out, the nature of his return as interest is not basically changed by virtue of the fact that his investment has paid off.

When we compare the traditional relationship between the capitalist and the entrepreneur with the relationship between the inside trader and the long-term investor, another striking parallel becomes apparent. The investor gains as a result of the creation of good news, and this is reflected in the price of his shares. He participates in the new value created by an insider, just as the capitalist does vis-à-vis the traditional entrepreneur. The investor's return, unlike that of the insider who trades on his information, is compensation for the use of his funds and for his assumption of risk. The difference now is that the entrepreneur remains an employee of the company, where, hopefully, he will again produce a valuable innovation. One of the great advantages of the corporate form is that it allows a permanent employee to market the value of his entrepreneurial service alone. Because he need not have a proprietary interest in other property, he does not have to sell a separate asset in order to realize his profit.

Even if the insider simply buys shares and does not realize short-term gains by trading, he is no less like the traditional entrepreneur. The gain in the share value is his whether he realizes it immediately by a sale or holds it in the form of appreciated shares. In the latter case, he has merely opted to invest his insider profits as a capital investment. His function at that point changes, but this does not alter his prior status. He is then more like the inventor who establishes his own business in order to exploit his patent. He has changed roles, but neither of the functions he performs is changed in the process.

A major fallacy deriving from a failure to distinguish different functions is that the corporate insider should not be given any advantage over other investors in the corporation. This argument assumes that only the capitalist's kind of return is appropriate for anyone owning shares. It requires, of course, that funds already have been invested. This in turn means that funds must have been saved, borrowed, or inherited. Clearly an entrepreneur cannot guarantee his ability to participate in this way, nor is there any reason that we should demand that he combine the functions of entrepreneur and capitalist. And even if he did have sufficient funds to have made a prior investment, the egalitarian argument allows no special compensation for his entrepreneurial skill. It merely guarantees that the insider will have the same return on investment that other capitalists, who have contributed no valuable innovation, regularly enjoy as a result of the insider's successful activities. The insider is thus forced to share with all other shareholders the profit that otherwise he alone could have gained.[17]

A similar false notion is that no insider should receive compensation higher than the wage or salary expressly contracted for. This point would be well taken, as Knight has indicated, if entrepreneurial results were knowable and predictable. Compensation for this service would simply become a wage, with the same economic significance as that received by managers, technicians, and other suppliers of services in competitive markets. But no longer does the idea of a pure wage for entrepreneurs commend itself to our sense of logic. The major innovations in commercial and industrial history have not come from purely salaried employees.

Characteristics of the Entrepreneur

The ultimate difficulty in compensating the entrepreneur in large corporations may be a psychological one. He will tend to value his own potential for extraordinary gain at a higher figure than others would normally pay in advance. As Knight suggested, self-confidence is the hallmark of the entrepreneur, and his gain will be most spectacular when this quality is least available in others. He will probably not be a good organization man, satisfied with a reasonable salary and retirement benefits. We should anticipate that as business executives begin to rise above the level of the pure managers or technocrats or corporate bureaucrats, the form in which they receive their

17. A fascinating parallel is provided by Schumpeter's analysis of what happens to the value of entrepreneurial activity in a pure communist state. See TED, pp. 144–52.

income will also begin to change. In fact it may on occasion be the sole mark of the rise to a new category. More and more of their income should come in the form of profits from trading in corporate shares to exploit information they have generated. As we know almost nothing about these practices, a vast amount of empirical research needs to be done in this area.[18]

There are peculiarities other than compensation that may help identify, describe, and understand the modern American entrepreneur. Berle and Means in *The Modern Corporation and Private Property* noted a phenomenon popularized under the rubric "separation of ownership and control." As applied to the large publicly held corporation, the term implied that those who ran the company, controlled its affairs, and charted its destiny had ceased to be the same individuals who owned the property. Berle and Means' work was replete with statistics showing that the shareholdings of directors of some of the largest corporations were very frequently meager or nonexistent.[19] The authors pointed to this fact as evidence that the modern corporation does not function consistently with the principles of traditional economics. Management, Berle and Means protested, did not have a claim to legitimacy, which existed when a family or an individual owned a controlling block of shares.[20]

18. Unfortunately, even the most careful theoretical and empirical works on executive compensation have assumed that salaries, bonuses, pensions, and stock options comprise the only forms of financial compensation of corporate employees. Because they fail to consider profits resulting from stock trading as a fundamental part of executive compensation, these models and statistical results are of little use. See Robin Marris, *The Economic Theory of "Managerial" Capitalists* (New York: The Free Press, 1964), Chapter 2, and David R. Roberts, *Executive Compensation* (New York: The Free Press, 1959).

19. Adolf A. Berle and Gardiner Means, *The Modern Corporation and Private Property* (New York: The Macmillan Co., 1933), p. 51. At a more mundane level, Louis Gilbert regularly harangues the executives of large corporations for their failure to own what he considers an appropriate number of shares. Louis D. and John J. Gilbert, *Twenty-Fifth Annual Report of Stockholder Activities at Corporation Meetings During 1964* (New York: Louis D. and John J. Gilbert, n.d.), pp. 171–72.

20. Berle later modified this position and concluded that management's claim to legitimacy was established by the excellence of its performance. Adolf A. Berle, *The 20th Century Capitalist Revolution* (New York: Harcourt, Brace & Co., 1954). Cf. Henry G. Manne, "The 'Higher Criticism' of the Modern Corporation," *Columbia Law Review*, 62 (1962), pp. 414–17.

We can now see that there is nothing peculiar about the phenomenon described at all. If the key executives of large corporations are also the principal performers of the entrepreneurial function, we should not necessarily anticipate that they would be large shareholders. Share-trading, not shareholding, will be the hallmark of the entrepreneur. This does not preclude the existence of older-style family businesses or those in which an individual doubles as entrepreneur and capitalist. But it should not be surprising to find a higher degree of specialization of these functions in large corporations. We should anticipate that key individuals in large corporations, those responsible for the progress and development of a business, would earn relatively more of their wealth by trading in corporate securities than by holding large blocks of shares. The phenomenon Berle and Means described does not have the significance usually ascribed to it. If share-trading offers more inducement to profitable operation than share-holding, we should not complain because management has substituted one for the other. The absence of a substantial, permanent ownership interest by corporate executives may be a clear indication that the modern corporate system is functioning properly.

Relation Between Corporate Size and Entrepreneurship

In one respect the theory advanced in this chapter coincides with Berle's and Schumpeter's views on the nature of top management in large corporations. As a corporation grows in absolute size and number of shareholders, the effect of a given development on share price becomes less and less, in absolute terms. For example, assume that an oil company with one million shares outstanding and total assets of $50 million discovers an oil pool worth five million dollars. This should cause the price of its shares to rise from 50 to approximately 55. The same discovery by a company with assets of $1 billion and twenty million shares outstanding might be so inconsequential as to have no effect whatever on the stock price. Theoretically, each share should rise by one quarter of a point, but, as we saw earlier, other market forces may easily counteract a quarter-point gain, whereas the certainty of realizing profits from a five-point gain is quite high.

If, as we have assumed, entrepreneurs want large gains and small risks, we should anticipate the true entrepreneurial personality to be more attracted to smaller corporations. There the greatest opportunities exist to make the proverbial killing. There is no reason to believe that some entrepreneurial skill and talent will not be found in large companies, but the competitive advantage lies with smaller ones. The smaller corporations we are referring to, however, may still be large enough to be listed on the New York Stock Exchange, and they must never be so small that their shares are not publicly traded. Otherwise the competitive advantage of publicly held corporations over close corporations in securing entrepreneurial talent would be lost.

If in fact small and medium-sized publicly held companies have the advantage noted over corporate giants, the implications are far-reaching. This could explain, for instance, why there is constant shifting among the positions of the top five hundred corporations in America.[21] It would further suggest that much of the concern with corporate size shown by writers and the Antitrust Division of the Department of Justice has been misplaced. For with size comes the relative inability to attract the highest quality of entrepreneurial, as opposed to managerial, skill. Small companies will naturally attract the individuals whose performance will make them grow.

To counteract this tendency and to induce potential entrepreneurs to remain with them, large companies would be expected to offer larger salaries and more attractive retirement plans than smaller companies. This may account for the correlation that has been found between salaries and size of companies.[22] The higher salary figures represent a cost to larger companies that smaller ones will not have to bear. Therefore, unless there are compensating economies of scale, the larger company is still at a competitive disadvantage compared to smaller ones.

There are reasons other than size why entrepreneurial skills may not be attracted to certain corporations. There are business corporations to which

21. See *Fortune* (July, 1965), p. 165.

22. Roberts, *Executive Compensation,* p. 50, states that "compensation is directly and quite closely related to size and that it probably has little independent connection with profitability." To Roberts compensation includes only salary, bonuses, and pension benefits.

the very concept of the entrepreneur has no application. We have seen the importance of innovation for effective competition. But one critical aspect of the modern scheme of public-utility regulation is protection from competition. In exchange for this privilege, firms have their rates regulated. Their share prices tend to be stable, and there is little opportunity for quick trading gains. Not only is price competition impossible, but the more important creative destruction made famous by Schumpeter is also discouraged by rate regulation. Since a maximum rate of return on investment is prescribed, there is little chance for capturing in the stock market the actual value of great innovations. No rate regulation is perfect, however, and the regulatory scheme will ordinarily allow increased earnings—perhaps hidden—through small, cost-saving innovations. But the great inventive and dynamic developments associated with entrepreneurial success will rarely occur in firms that belong to efficiently regulated industries.[23]

We should therefore anticipate finding different personalities among the top executives of large and small companies and among those in regulated and nonregulated companies. The larger the company or the more regulated it is, the less likely are we to find the type of businessman commonly called a promoter, or an operator. The individual trying to boost himself socially and economically by his own bootstraps will find more opportunity to get rich quick in smaller concerns.

There is some empirical evidence that this is true. Economists have noted a higher incidence of certain minority-group members among the discernible entrepreneurial class.[24] A recent study indicates a small incidence of Jewish and Negro executives in regulated, as opposed to nonregulated, industries.[25] It is quite possible that this is true in larger, as opposed

23. This is not to say that these industries will stagnate. Innovation may simply come from without rather than from within. The diesel locomotive, the greatest advancement in modern railroading, was successfully promoted by General Motors, not the railroads.

24. Peter T. Bauer and Basil S. Yamey, *The Economics of Under-Developed Countries* (Chicago: University of Chicago Press, 1957), pp. 106–12. This section, entitled "The Foreign Entrepreneur," provides a fascinating discussion of this topic.

25. See report of study in *The New York Times* (Dec. 29, 1963), p. 1, col. 2. Vance Packard reports that utilities and heavy industries (presumably those characterized by very large corporations), including companies founded by Jews, have a low incidence of Jewish executives; see *The Pyramid Climbers* (New York: Fawcett World Library, 1962), p. 41.

to smaller, corporations as well. But this need not indicate a higher incidence of anti-Semitism or racial prejudice in those companies.[26] We may be witnessing a subtle self-selection process, or, more accurately, a self-exclusion process dictated more by economic circumstances than has generally been recognized.

26. See Armen A. Alchian and Reuben A. Kessel, "Competition, Monopoly, and the Pursuit of Money," *Aspects of Labor Economics—A Report of the National Bureau of Economic Research* (Princeton: Princeton University Press, 1962), pp. 164–70, for an alternative, though not contradictory, explanation of the same phenomenon in public utilities.

10 Objections to Information as Compensation

It has been suggested that insider trading increases the possibility of manipulation of stock prices.[1] To discuss this contention intelligently we must recognize that this manipulation may occur in several different ways. The first form of manipulation is the publication of untrue good or bad news with the intention that others in the stock market rely upon the statement. The second form of manipulation is the intentional production of bad news, again with the intention that it be relied upon in the stock market. The opposite of this, the intentional production of good news, is of course what corporate insiders are supposed to do, and it cannot be termed manipulative. The third form of manipulation is delaying the disclosure of either good or bad news (though honestly produced) for the purpose of allowing insiders more time to conduct profitable trading. A fourth form of manipulation, usually associated with pre-1934 stock-pool operations, is the buying and selling of stocks in order to create an artificial market price and an appearance of market activity.[2]

Fraudulent Manipulation

The first type of manipulation, the publication of untrue statements meant to be relied upon in the market, usually contains all the technical elements

1. Adolf A. Berle, "Publicity of Accounts and Directors' Purchases of Stock," *Michigan Law Review,* 25 (1927), pp. 830–31; and Kenneth L. Yourd, "Trading in Securities by Directors, Officers and Stockholders: Section 16 of the Securities Exchange Act," *Michigan Law Review,* 38 (1939), p. 133.

2. See James William Moore and Frank M. Wiseman, "Market Manipulation and the Exchange Act," *University of Chicago Law Review,* 2 (1934), p. 46.

of common-law fraud.[3] This does not mean that it is desirable to leave the detection and policing of every case of fraud to individual shareholders showing damage. There will be clear economic savings in administrative regulation of this problem. Criminal sanctions also seem appropriate, and the experience in New York State has proved that vigorous enforcement of criminal sanctions can be effective in dealing with fraudulent manipulation. The attorney general of New York, operating under the simplest and shortest securities law in the country, regularly vies with the SEC, operating under the most complex and detailed system, for the prosecution of fraudulent stock manipulators. There is no indication that fraudulent manipulation presents such peculiar problems of policing that radical devices are necessary to accomplish the desired end. The appropriate criminal laws will be necessary in any event to deal with non-insiders who engage in fraudulent stock practices.

If insiders could in fact be prevented from trading in their company's shares or in information about their company, they would have no incentive to manipulate stock prices for trading purposes. But we cannot conclude from this that insider trading should never be allowed. For reasons that we shall examine in the next chapter, the effective policing of insider trading is extremely difficult, if not impossible. Therefore, some incentive to manipulation might always remain. But more important, outlawing all insider trading to prevent fraud is a shotgun approach to the problem. The danger is that most of the pellets will hit the wrong targets. And, to carry the ballistic simile further, this method may also be likened to using a cannon to kill a flea.

Entrepreneurs interested in a continuing flow of information on which to trade will have little incentive to manipulate stock prices. Insiders who generate false information in effect inflate their own currency. If such occurrences ever become known (and certainly discovery by the market is only a matter of time), the value of all information from the same source, the true and the untrue, will be discounted in the marketplace. That is, as soon as it is learned that insiders have fraudulently manipulated the stock of a

3. William Prosser, *Handbook of the Law of Torts*, 3d ed. (St. Paul: West Publishing Co., 1964), p. 700; and Louis Loss, *Securities Regulation* (Boston and Toronto: Little, Brown & Co., 1961), pp. 1430ff.

particular company, all subsequent disclosures from that source will be treated with a certain degree of suspicion. True information normally worth ten points may only result in an eight-point rise upon first disclosure. The principal loser will be the insider who is compensated by short-term trading.

Most long-term investors will not be injured at all, as the market will ultimately reflect the full value of the true story. The entrepreneurs and some uninformed short-term speculators will lose the amount of the discount. When the first type of manipulation is viewed in this perspective, it seems doubtful that lying about corporate affairs for short-term trading purposes will be a popular pastime with many corporate executives. When it is further realized that sophisticated devices for detection of fraud, as well as suitable sanctions, are available to deal with this problem, its importance as an objection to insider trading almost vanishes.

It should at least be noted that insider trading may perform a valuable function that is the exact opposite of manipulation. If, for any reason, the current market price of a company's stock is known to be incorrect in terms of all available information, insiders will have an incentive to correct the market price of the stock. In time the truth will out,[4] and the price will change accordingly, whether insiders trade or not. Because this is so, anyone with information known to be correct will make money by stock-market transactions that force the price in the correct direction—in effect, by arbitrage. Given the importance of maintaining correct values on corporate securities,[5] we should perhaps be more concerned about rules preventing insiders from trading than with those raising some small possibility of artificial manipulation of prices.

The Intentional Creation of Bad News

The second form of manipulation that might constitute an objection to insider trading is that insiders may intentionally create bad news in order to make stock-market profits. The objection basically is that insiders can

4. See William J. Baumol, *The Stock Market and Economic Efficiency* (New York: Fordham University Press, 1965), Chapter 3.

5. *Ibid.*, Chap. 1.

make as much money trading on bad news as on good news and that therefore they will have as great an incentive to create bad news. But even though as much money can be made in the stock market from a specific bit of bad news as from good, there is vastly more incentive for insiders to produce good news than bad.

Most individuals in a position to make money from inside information will want to maintain that position and improve their future claims on valuable information. Nothing will succeed in that endeavor as much as the continued production of good news. There is no limit to the amount of good news the market can absorb, while bad news carries sharp constraints on its continued production. If too much bad news is created, the firm itself must inevitably fail and all trading cease. And even before that point is reached, other market forces operate to discipline creators of bad news. As the price of a corporation's shares drops relatively low, either an internal shakeup in management or a successful raid by an outsider is more likely to occur.[6] The preference for good news over bad has a very real economic basis.

There are also social and psychological pressures to produce good news rather than bad. Success is unquestionably part of the ethos of corporate executives, and bad news will be greeted with lowered esteem by the insider's colleagues, regardless of how much money is thereby made in the stock market. Success stories are repeated, not tales of failure. So while it is true that as much money can be made selling short as buying long, there can be little incentive for the intentional creation of bad news. Almost all of the vector forces operating on corporate insiders push in the direction of good news. The fact that money can be made on bad news is a neutral factor as far as incentive is concerned.

6. Henry G. Manne, "Mergers and the Market for Corporate Control," *Journal of Political Economy,* 73 (1965), p. 110. This argument would seem to have little weight, however, when applied to the trading of a trustee in bankruptcy. See Stanley A. Kaplan, "Wolf v. Weinstein: Another Chapter on Insider Trading," *The Supreme Court Review, 1963,* ed., Philip B. Kurland (Chicago and London: University of Chicago Press, 1963), pp. 280ff.

Delay in Disclosures

Delaying disclosures to allow fuller exploitation of the value of the information may be the most serious form of manipulation. It is extremely difficult to find empirical proof that such practices do or do not occur. One aspect of the story of Texas Gulf Sulphur's find in Timmins, Ontario, illustrates the difficulty. The SEC implied in its complaint that the insiders delayed disclosure in order to have more time to exploit their information. On the face of it there is nothing implausible in this supposition. If publicity had been given the discovery in November, 1963, it is quite possible that none of the insiders' transactions between that date and April 16, 1964, would have occurred. But there is an equally plausible alternative explanation of the delay, which in no way implicates the insiders. As the corporation stated in its motion to dismiss the SEC's complaint against it,[7] the delay was necessary to gain mineral rights on adjacent properties and to discover the true extent of the ore vein. Certainly this was in the interest of all shareholders. Further, the delay avoided the possibility of misleading shareholders if the vein had not proved as large as it did.

For certain kinds of information little or no delay in disclosure is feasible. The date of dividend declarations is established without reference to the speed with which the information may be exploited in the market. Government contracts, changes in market conditions, and international developments will not normally be under the control of insiders for purposes of timing disclosure. Merger negotiations normally will be under their control, while announcements of proxy fights and many tender-bids will not.

But assuming that insiders can time disclosures in order to increase their own exploitation of information, it is still questionable whether the practice is objectionable. The answer to this turns on the acceptance or rejection of the general argument that entrepreneurs in large corporations should be compensated with information. If we accept the general argument, it follows that the timing of disclosure may be necessary in many cases to allow appropriate exploitation of the information. Clearly, as would have been

7. Reported in *The Wall Street Journal,* July 9, 1965, p. 5, col. 1.

true for Texas Gulf Sulphur, premature announcements can effectively prevent insiders from realizing more than a fraction of the value inherent in news. Devices for "banking" information may not function at all, because the value of the information may have been substantially exploited before it can be exchanged.

It is difficult to be specific about the relationship between the speed with which insiders can move in the case of different kinds of information and the speed they must employ to gain a substantial return. Manifestly, the faster they buy and cause the price to increase, the shorter becomes the period they will want to delay disclosure. Here again we find a surprising identity between the interests of insiders and outside shareholders. Assuming that we allow insider trading, it will be in the interest of both parties to have it done as quickly as possible. Thus, with free and open insider trading, we may find shorter delays in disclosure of new developments than we would if the practice were ineffectively or partially policed. The matter will turn largely on the speed with which different kinds of information may be exploited, but it is not inconceivable that the shortest average periods for disclosure will occur under a rule of completely free insider trading.

Stock Pools

The final form of manipulation that might be associated with insider trading involves the artificial stimulation of the market in order to raise or lower the price of shares or merely to indicate heavy trading activity. This scheme is most commonly associated with the heyday of the stock pool in the 1920's. The Congressional Hearings on Stock Exchange Practices are replete with many instances of this occurrence,[8] and several provisions of the Act are specifically aimed at outlawing pools.[9] This form of manipulation seems comparable to the use of untrue statements. The untruths in this instance are aimed at stock traders who buy and sell on so-called *technical* factors rather than *fundamental* factors. The misleading assertion by the pool is that

8. *Hearings Before the Senate Committee on Banking and Currency*, 73d Cong., 1st Sess., 1933, pp. 3080ff. and 3245ff.; 2d Sess., 1934, pp. 6083ff.

9. Securities Exchange Act of 1934, Section 9.

there was heavy buying in the shares, rather than a false claim that the company has discovered gold.

But a careful reading of the description of pool operations in the 1933 hearings reveals an unusual fact. The formation of many pools was associated with the actual occurrence of important developments in the corporation.[10] Furthermore, most of these pools gradually disseminated true information about the company. This strongly suggests that the pool, that alleged archvillain of the pre-1933 stock market, was an efficient device for exploiting information.[11] Furthermore, manipulation geared to outsiders'

10. U.S. Senate Report No. 1455, 73d Cong., 2d Sess., 1934, p. 36.

11. Pools would have a number of advantages for this purpose. If the pool manager was a knowledgeable corporate insider, he would not have to disclose the specific news to anyone. Participants could be invited on a mutual-exchange basis, as indicated in Chapter 5. Policing problems would also be minimal. Research is needed on such questions as which pools succeeded, who managed pools, whether they disseminated true information, whether participants exchanged invitations, and whether specific bits of information were disclosed to participants.

Pools were not entirely without their defenders in the early 1930's. The position of R. W. Schabacker, *Stock Market Theory and Practice* (New York: B. C. Forbes Publishing Co., 1930), pp. 570–71, is similar to that offered in the text:

> The pool is thus a little more than an organization, on a scientific basis, of a group of "insiders." It is a group of men who are farsighted enough to see the potentiality of any stock and the logic of its eventually selling at the price and in the direction which the pool decides upon. All that the pool generally does, therefore, is to discount the future in a scientific way and hasten the market change which without organized action, might take 10 times as long to accomplish. . . .
>
> Economically the pool serves a worthy purpose of assisting the open market in evaluating correctly the true worth of the stock.

In the *1934 Senate Hearings on Stock Exchange Practices,* 73d Cong., 2d Sess., p. 6616, Richard Whitney, president of the New York Stock Exchange, offered this somewhat garbled but essentially logical defense of pools:

> I think the operation which we term now "manipulative" referred to by Mr. Pecora, where there is an endeavor to get great activity in the market by buying and selling, but through proper change of ownership, that that may well unfairly influence the market.
>
> I do think, however, that practically each and every case must rest on its own bottom. It is perfectly possible for an individual, or a joint account, or a pool, who believes that a security is selling below the level at which it should sell to buy that security in volume up to a point where they think the level is a proper one, and in doing so they are going to unquestionably influence the market, but in my opinion not unfairly.

reliance on technical factors would appear to be highly risky. It is not surprising that there were few reported cases of manipulation being used successfully for fraudulent purposes.[12]

Profits from Bad News

Another major category of objections to insider trading is that the particular individuals trading are not the ones entitled to the information. This objection may take several different forms. The first is that insiders regularly profit from bad news as well as good. That is, even if they have not intentionally produced bad news in order to sell short, bad news does occur, and to allow the insider to capitalize on it is inequitable.[13] It is not an appropriate response, as it was when we were concerned with manipulation, to say that the insider has no incentive to produce bad news. Bad news may result from reasons far removed from the insider's intent. Nationalization of foreign properties, bad weather, a change in political administration, an accidental fire or explosion, or an important development by a competitor, all may be exploited by insiders.

This argument does not have to be limited to bad news. We can deal at the same time with the argument that the insider exploiting valuable information is not necessarily responsible for a great deal of the good news to which he has access. This is not to say that certain individuals are stealing information that would not come to them in the ordinary course of business; that problem will be dealt with in the next chapter. Rather, the argument is that it is unfair to allow the use of inside information by insiders who have not performed entrepreneurial services for the corporation.

The Nature of Competition for Entrepreneurs

To answer these very important contentions, we must refine our concept of entrepreneurial compensation. Heretofore we have assumed that the mod-

12. Loss, *Securities Regulation,* pp. 1529–40. At p. 1538 Loss says that "before the mid-thirties, there was no American case of manipulation by trading alone. . . ."

13. Section 16(c) of the Securities Exchange Act of 1934 forbids the named insiders ever to sell stock in their companies short.

ern corporate innovator would exploit good news that he himself created. We have also assumed that the amount insiders could realize in the stock market because of their prior knowledge was a not-inappropriate return for innovational activity. This justification for insider trading would be sufficient if the modern, corporate insider-entrepreneur were the precise counterpart of the more traditional entrepreneur. But the older, simpler figure, classically illustrated by the corporate founder or promoter, could not make money on bad news. The founder of a business that promptly failed or the promoter of a corporation that never came into existence did not make any money functioning as an entrepreneur. This is consistent with Frank Knight's position that, on balance, America has received all of its entrepreneurial services free.[14] For the vast bulk of this service, there was simply no way to receive compensation.

With the advent of the large, publicly held corporation, however, the market for entrepreneurial services could be organized more efficiently. Now entrepreneurial services could be hired in the marketplace and not merely volunteered by corporate founders or promoters. By allowing the function of the entrepreneur to be performed by individuals exercising other jobs within the corporate structure, it became possible to hire entrepreneurial services, though valuable innovations might or might not be produced. The analogy of the hired research scientist who discovers nothing is apposite.

In the corporation individuals will be hired to perform a variety of functions at a market rate of return. Within fairly wide limits the individual will receive his compensation under the contract whether he performs his job well or not, though, if he does the job badly, he will ordinarily not be rehired when the contract expires. Advancement and security in large organizations normally do not require that the employee also be an entrepreneur. Therefore, the additional compensation provided by insider trading encourages this added activity, which also benefits the corporation.

But good or bad news can occur fortuitously or for reasons extraneous

14. Knight, p. 364. He argues that entrepreneurs have almost always also been capitalists, in effect, financing their own entrepreneurial losses. Some such explanation is necessary in a system in which entrepreneurship is not a highly specialized function. A large corporate system, however, allows this specialization and its discrete compensation.

to the operation of the corporation. Insider trading on this information would not appear to benefit the corporation. Consideration of the market for entrepreneurial services, however, leads us to the opposite conclusion. Competition for entrepreneurs does not take the usual form of offering a specific amount of money. Rather, entrepreneurs will be attracted to those positions offering the greatest opportunity for them to make large, indefinite gains. These may result from good news or bad, intentionally or unintentionally created.

There will be no important loss to shareholders if insiders do trade on this news, and it will be possible, in an inexpensive way, to give entrepreneurs within the corporation a greater opportunity for gain. Because the cost to the corporation for this form of compensation is so low, competition among corporations for entrepreneurs would quickly force all of them to allow their insider-entrepreneurs to trade in bad news as well as good. And the corporate form of business organization, with publicly traded shares, would enjoy a competitive advantage in securing entrepreneurial services over noncorporate forms, where profits from bad news are impossible.

On the other hand, some competitive advantages lie with the smaller type of enterprise. The owner of a business or one who owns all the stock of a corporation *a fortiori* gains the full value of any developments for which he is responsible. But the modern corporate insider, as we saw in Chapter 5, is rarely in a position to gain the full value of any news. Thus it is doubtful, even with the various exchange devices analyzed in Chapter 5, that insiders in large corporations ever gain the full value of their own contributions. Trading on fortuitous or extraneous good news compensates to some extent for this loss.

Profiting by Wrong Persons

The last form of the "person-is-not-entitled" objection to insider trading is that individuals making insider profits are frequently far removed from a time or place or job in which they could perform any entrepreneurial service for the company. It is, however, extremely difficult to identify individuals performing the entrepreneurial function or to know the precise moment at which an individual performs an entrepreneurial act. The selfsame act may constitute an entrepreneurial service in one company and a management function in another. Knight emphasized that the very selection of the right individuals to carry out management functions is a critical entrepreneurial job.[15] But this same activity in certain companies may constitute nothing more than a ritual or formality not requiring any fundamental exercise of discretion.

Directors, large shareholders, executives, lawyers, investment bankers, or many other individuals may, at one time or another, perform an entrepreneurial function. Most of the time, however, they will not be innovating. And for any particular development, many individuals may have made contributions. Who, among the lawyers, bankers, and executives involved, can be given full credit or the correct portions of credit for conceiving the desirability of a merger, searching out the most likely firm, and effectuating the desired plan? An entrepreneurial function has been performed, and the individuals involved will have some claim against the subsequent flow of inside information. But any attempt by an outsider to correlate the contribution and the reward on a one-for-one basis will probably fail. The contribution of an individual may be so subtle—so much a result simply of his being there—and yet so critical that we must be very cautious in concluding that no reward is deserved.

A variant of this objection is that some individuals, perhaps long retired from active participation in corporate affairs, still continue to receive the benefits of inside information. But this should occasion no surprise. In Chapter 5 we saw that insiders often find it desirable to utilize various information-exchange devices. These may also be used to postpone the time for using other information. Individuals may thus receive information later in exchange for their own earlier production that they could not or did not market directly. Many individuals, for both financial and tax reasons, will find it desirable to spread the return of information over as long a period as possible.

Individuals may also use information as gifts or payments to individuals not connected with the corporation. The most obvious example of this is the individual who gives information to his wife or children so that they

15. Knight, p. 310.

may trade in the company's shares.[16] But their profits must be imputed to the insider himself. It is immaterial to an outside observer that an individual may choose to take his gain in the form of additional wealth for his children rather than for himself, or that he may choose to make a gift of it to anyone.

Information is not a free good, and we should not assume, without more information than we now possess, that its distribution is generally capricious, arbitrary, random, or uncontrolled. Rational, self-serving individuals will not blithely and willingly allow information of tremendous value to pass freely to individuals who have no valid claim upon it. The safer assumption is that individuals with the power to control the flow of valuable information do so rationally and allocate it in a market-like system of exchange, as explained in Chapter 5. The insider-entrepreneur has more incentive than anyone else to prevent arbitrary payoffs, for he can lose more than anyone else. To find inside information in the hands of individuals with no apparent relationship to the company in question may demonstrate the effectiveness of the market in inside information rather than its ineffectiveness. But this private distribution system is not perfect, and there are leaks in the flow of valuable information. Internal policing of information is discussed in the next chapter.

16. See discussion of "beneficial" ownership under the 16(b) prohibition on insider trading in Loss, *Securities Regulation,* pp. 1100–01. Also see Stanley A. Kaplan, "Wolf v. Weinstein," p. 305.

11 The Problems of Public and Private Policing

Information is one of the most easily transmitted of all commodities. To prevent its rapid dissemination while it has exchange value is extremely difficult. Any attempt to regulate or police a market in information confronts two obstacles. The first is the extremely difficult one of knowing which transactions to prevent. The second is the actual job of policing once the undesired transactions are identified.

Outsiders with Valuable Information

Throughout this work we have assumed that the critics of insider trading wish to prevent the exploitation of information that is not equally available to all traders in the market. As indicated in Chapter 4, this involves specific bits of undisclosed information about change and not information that may be derived or deduced from published data. This distinction, though important for the policing of insider trading, is extremely difficult to maintain in practice. From published figures on earnings and other financial data, an experienced securities analyst can often predict dividend increases, stock splits, and other financial events with a very high degree of accuracy. He may forecast these events before insiders, perhaps with no higher degree of confidence, know the same thing.

Other kinds of outside specialists will also trade in the stock market with information deduced from generally available sources. The management consultant who follows personnel changes, the industry specialist who knows the effects of government policies, or the lawyer who can predict the financial implications of changes in tax laws may trade with great confidence but without any undisclosed information. Furthermore, the services of many of these outside specialists are available to anyone willing to pay for them. Their price may be high, but no charge of unfairness can be leveled against trading based on this marketed advice. Another outside specialist is the business competitor. Executives of corporations in the same industry often recognize the impact of industrial changes on firms other than their own. New developments within one company may have a predictable effect on the profits of another company. The ensuing trading can be done with the same degree of reliability that characterizes the insider using true inside information.

Competitors are not the only ones who originate information before it is known to the insiders in the company whose shares are bought. A corporate executive changing his company's source of supply may cause a downturn in one company's shares and an increase in another's. These changes may be known to him before they are known to executives of either of the other companies. Government officials know the identity of a successful bidder before the various bidding companies have received the information. And myriad government officials other than contracting officers are in comparable positions. The internal revenue or antitrust lawyers who pass on mergers, the commissioners passing on rate changes, and the regulators allocating communications channels or commercial air routes are just a few of the government functionaries privy to inside information.

Another outsider who generates and exploits valuable information is the so-called corporate raider. Whether he functions through a proxy fight, a tender-bid, or a merger offer,[1] he knows his own intentions before they are known to the corporate insiders. His intention is frequently the important piece of undisclosed information,[2] but its disclosure would in many cases prevent his operation by making it too expensive. In other cases it may be more accurate to say that the raider's undisclosed information is merely his belief that he can manage the corporation better than the incumbent man-

1. These three methods for taking over control of a corporation are compared in Henry G. Manne, "Mergers and the Market for Corporate Control," *Journal of Political Economy,* 73 (1965), p. 110.

2. For a judicial holding that an outsider does not violate Rule 10b-5 by his failure to disclose this intention, see *Mills* v. *Sarjem Corp.*, 133 Fed. Supp. 753 (D.C.N.J., 1955).

agers. In a proxy fight he will state this explicitly in an effort to convince other shareholders to believe him and vote for him. But if his strategy involves buying up shares as a prelude to a proxy fight or a merger, he will remain as silent as possible about his intentions.

A related situation involves purchases made by the corporation itself. If full disclosure were made of a corporation's intention to buy a certain number of shares, the stock price would immediately jump almost to the level indicated by the value of this news. All shares would have to be bought at this new market price, and the cost to the corporation for the same number of shares might be considerably greater than without disclosure.[3] But the action of the corporation buying without disclosure is the same—from shareholders' or traders' points of view—as an insider's buying shares when he knows undisclosed news.

The Arbitrary Approach to Enforcement

This short discussion of outsiders who may trade on reliable yet generally unknown information suggests the difficulties of identifying transactions to be proscribed. Yet, whatever arguments can be made for outlawing insider trading apply at least as strongly to these cases. Why then have the critics of "unfair" trading been almost exclusively concerned with insiders? One answer might be that the volume of trading before disclosure is greater in the case of insiders than outsiders. But we have no real evidence that this is true, and, in any event, it would still be only a partial answer because it acknowledges some "unfair" outsider trading.

Another answer has historical roots. When the first draft of the present Securities Exchange Act of 1934 was presented to Congress, Section 16 proscribed not only short-swing profits by insiders but disclosure to others and profiting by anyone to whom disclosure was made. Congress refused this broad coverage on the grounds that enforcement of such a provision was

3. See "Investing in Yourself," *The Wall Street Journal,* June 30, 1965, p. 1, col. 8. This article suggests that when publicly announced tender offers are used, the price is set about 20% above the current market price. However, this may still be cheaper than undisclosed purchasing when a large number of shares are to be bought in a short time.

not feasible.[4] Attention was thus focused on the so-called *statutory insiders*—officers, directors, and beneficial holders of 10 per cent of an equity issue.

This definitional approach is heavy-handed and frequently arbitrary in its reach. But that merely puts it on a par with Section 16(b), described by one of its authors as a "crude rule of thumb."[5] This Section makes insiders named in Section 16(a) liable to the corporation for any profits made from buying and selling their company's securities within any six-month period. We should notice just how arbitrary this provision can be in operation. First, the six-month duration bears little relation to anything connected with insider trading. Obviously the capital-gains holding-period provision of the Internal Revenue Code offers considerable inducement to hold for that period. At some point before six months have elapsed, the influence of Section 16(b) is probably superfluous.

Even more damaging to insiders is the proscription of "any" profits from short-term trading. It makes no difference that the stocks appreciated for reasons the insider knew nothing about or that he may have been forced to sell for reasons totally unrelated to inside information. There are additional inequities in the operation of Section 16 as well.[6] Yet, we may still have some sympathy for this approach. It is dictated by the need to simplify enforcement and administration in what would otherwise be a phenomenally complex area.[7] It is no wonder that a way out was found in arbitrary rules of

4. For the legal history of this subject, see *Blau* v. *Lehman*, 368 U.S. 403, at p. 412 (1962).

5. See testimony of Thomas G. Corcoran in *Stock Exchange Practices, Hearings Before Senate Committee on Banking and Currency*, 73d Cong., 2d Sess., 1934, p. 6557.

6. See Louis Loss, *Securities Regulation* (Boston and Toronto: Little, Brown & Co., 1961), pp. 1037–1132, for a detailed treatment of enforcement problems.

7. Enforcement is facilitated by a requirement that the insiders defined in the Act report monthly any changes in their holdings of their company's securities. These reports are filed in Washington and in various regional offices of the SEC. The legal proceedings required to recover these profits for the corporation are extremely simple, and other shareholders and their lawyers stand ever ready to pounce on any insider's short-swing profits, whether accidently or intentionally realized. Enforcement is undoubtedly further facilitated by the business literature of the last fifty years. Legal rules and moral preachments have not been without their effect on insiders' consciences. Enforcement, however, is still very complex. For a full discussion of the legal problem encountered in connection with enforcement of 16(b), see Donald C. Cook and Myer Feldman, "Insider Trading Under the Securities Exchange Act," *Harvard Law Review*, 66 (1953), p. 385.

thumb. And it is no less wonder that the SEC, which today is trying to make its Rule 10b-5 into a general prohibition of insider trading, has not promulgated any rules or guidelines as to how this can be done.

Section 16 has probably not been very effective in securing its stated end. Over thirty years of litigation, hearings, and SEC regulation leave no doubt that the critics of insider trading are not satisfied. The whole tenor of recent legal developments, such as *Blau* v. *Lehman* and the *Texas Gulf Sulphur* case, indicates that the SEC feels that there is much ground left uncovered. The reasons are not hard to find.

Enforcement Techniques

As a first step, the reporting requirements of Section 16(a), coupled with simple liability, seem like a step in the right direction. Criminal sanctions could be used to strengthen the effectiveness of enforcement. But if insiders find it necessary or profitable enough to do so, it is not difficult to escape detection. Shares held in street names, accounts of relatives and friends, secret accounts of all sorts, foreign brokers and bank accounts, and a host of other devices can make the job of discovering illicit inside trading extremely costly. Even the SEC, which has quite efficient discovery devices at its command, still relies largely on newspaper accounts of specific events to know when to begin a search. But there is no way of evaluating the degree of success they enjoy. As most corporate events do not receive the publicity of the Texas Gulf episode, the percentage of illicit transactions actually uncovered by police-detection methods could be very low.

But no one likes to commit even a quasi-criminal act, like a violation of Section 16(b), if he can accomplish the same end in legal fashion. Section 16(b) is strictly limited to trades in the shares of the insider's company. Other transactions and information trades are outside the scope of the Section. Some attempt might be made to broaden reporting requirements, but a reporting requirement is logical only in connection with trading in the shares of an insider's own company. Even if we required every insider of any company to report all his stock transactions—a gargantuan solution and not a very palatable one—it would still be impossible to distinguish profitable transactions properly entered into from those based on a trade of inside information. If these individuals are allowed to trade in any shares, it will be almost impossible to know when they are aided by inside information.[8]

These are the same individuals whose money is managed in discretionary accounts and whose names appear high on priority lists. They are the individuals named to the boards of directors of other corporations. They regularly follow the advice of their corporation's investment banker on what shares to buy. They may often be partners or limited partners in banking houses. Furthermore, these same executives will generally not hesitate to trade in the shares of other firms in their industry or of supplier or customer firms, even though the intelligence they bring to this trading is clearly gained by virtue of their own positions. And, finally, there are many direct methods for exchanging valuable information.

The mere listing of some of the myriad ways in which individuals can use information gained in the course of their corporate work shows how meaningless Section 16(b) is in preventing *all* insider trading. By focusing merely on one group of individuals trading in one particular company's shares, the Section becomes an open invitation to avoid its intended proscription. Many insiders, the public, and perhaps even the Securities and Exchange Commission are fooled by many of these subterfuges, but it is doubtful that determined corporate insiders have lost much money as a direct result of the Section.

Some additional techniques might improve the detection of insider trading. Each individual occupying an inside position could be paired off with individuals with whom he might be trading information. This pairing could

8. Actually any rule which does not completely prevent stock trading or ownership by insiders will be only partially effective against the use of inside information. Although it may be possible to forbid sales or purchases of shares prior to public disclosure of important information, it is not possible to forbid the nonsale or the nonpurchase of shares. Yet knowing when not to sell or buy may on occasion be as valuable as knowing when to sell or buy. As insiders would have to own shares in order to "not sell," we might expect insiders to own more shares with a partially effective rule against insider trading than if there were no rule at all. During the period between the development of valuable information and its disclosure, the insider would know not to sell his shares. In the long run this knowledge would give him some advantage over other shareholders, though certainly not as great as he would have with a free-trading rule.

be done by a detailed check of memberships in various organizations or of social engagements such as luncheon meetings, bridge games, and golf games or even by questionnaires about acquaintanceships. Special attention could be paid to individuals on interlocked boards of directors or the executives of companies who share the same investment bankers. The number of individuals to be covered would be extremely large, but computers might make the job feasible. Once these and many other pairings were programmed into a computer, it would be a relatively simple matter to detect some market transactions suggesting an exchange of information.

This kind of policing—intolerable as it must sound to anyone sensitive to gross invasions of privacy—would still not prove that any particular transaction was of the prohibited variety. It would merely raise a suspicion. Many transactions would not show up at all, as we have only programmed for pairs. The clearinghouse mechanism could easily provide, as it does, for multiparty exchanges that could not be discovered by this simple approach. Still other tools are available to the dedicated anti–inside trader. Discretionary accounts, priority lists, and interlocking boards of directors might be outlawed. The separation of investment banking and the brokerage business would also impede the smooth working of the market in information.[9] And every time any stock showed a substantial rise in price, large purchasers could be queried about their reasons for buying.

Even if all of this could be made effective, few would defend such a program. The administrative costs alone might be prohibitive. A much more important objection, however, is that such police-state tactics are simply intolerable. Spying on social meetings, computerized friendships, total disclosure of all financial affairs and decisions, the necessity to explain every profit—these are unthinkable in a civilized democracy. The costs, financially, morally, and politically, are too great, and we should never anticipate truly effective policing of insider trading by trying to ferret out every proscribed transaction as it occurs.

But this is precisely the direction in which the SEC seems to be moving. The implication of at least part of the complaint in the *Texas Gulf Sulphur*

9. This was proposed in 1933 but was not adopted. See Ralph F. De Bedts, *The New Deal's SEC* (New York and London: Columbia University Press, 1964), pp. 61, 72, and 77.

suit is that any trade known to be made before public disclosure of information violates SEC Rule 10b-5. It is one thing, however, to detect insider trading as widely publicized as that in the *Texas Gulf* case; it is another matter to administer this rule in a nondiscriminatory fashion. The SEC has ignored these dangers by relying on the courts to develop rules for it on a case-by-case basis.[10] Ultimately the enforcement difficulties remain, and they may be greater under this approach than they would be if the SEC faced up to the policing difficulties by promulgating detailed rules.

10. See Arthur Fleischer, Jr., "'Federal Corporation Law': An Assessment," *Harvard Law Review*, 78 (1965), p. 1146, and Michael Joseph, "Civil Liability Under Rule 10b-5—A Reply," *Northwestern University Law Review*, 59 (1964), p. 171, in which authors presently or formerly associated with the SEC defend this practice. It is criticized in David S. Ruder, "Pitfalls in the Development of a Federal Law of Corporations by Implication Through Rule 10b-5," *Northwestern University Law Review*, 59 (1964), p. 185. Curiously, none of these writers has defended or attacked the questionable practice of using a case-by-case approach instead of the Commission's broad rule-making powers to establish clear guidelines. Rule 10b-5 is *not* clear, and apparently was promulgated without notice and hearing for corporate insiders as affected parties. See Loss, *Securities Regulation*, p. 1427. An excellent discussion of this administrative law problem appears in Ralph F. Fuchs, "Agency Development of Policy Through Rule-Making," *Northwestern University Law Review*, 59 (1965), p. 781. See especially the cogent discussion (pp. 793–94) of legal and constitutional limitations on retroactively effective adjudicatory processes when prospectively applicable rule-making powers are available. Arguably, this issue is not raised by 10b-5, since the sought-after adjudications are interpretations of a rule. But 10b-5 is not the kind of rule which Professor Fuchs is arguing for, as the context makes clear.

It might be added that there are still serious questions about the validity of 10b-5 as applied to all insider trading. The validity of the promulgation has been discussed and affirmatively sustained in only one district court opinion, *United States* v. *Shindler*, 173 Fed. Supp. 393 (S.D.N.Y. 1959), a criminal case involving alleged manipulation of stock prices, where only the Rule's invalidity as applied to *purchases* was argued. The Supreme Court's opinion in *Blau* v. *Lehman*, 368 U.S. 403 (1962), further weakens 10b-5's claim to validity. In that case the Court refused to hold a partnership as an insider under Section 16(b) because one partner was a director of the corporation in question. After reviewing the legislative history of the Section and Congress' refusal to have it apply to "anyone," the Court stated on p. 413: "Congress can and might amend § 16(b) if the Commission would present to it the policy arguments it has presented to us, but we think that Congress is the proper agency to change an interpretation of the Act unbroken since its passage, if the change is to be made." This admonishment to the Commission should presumably have some bearing on its attempt to surmount all the restrictive qualifications in 16(b) by making 10b-5 into even a broader provision than Congress refused in 1933. The case for the validity of 10b-5, construed as a thoroughgoing rule against insider trading, may be quite shaky.

The "Stop-Trading" Approach

Ultimately, the attempt to pinpoint individual insiders and their proscribed transactions can lead to a radically different proposal. Such an attempt will not aim at preventing particular transactions or transactions by particular individuals. Rather, all trades by anyone can be stopped for some period of time before public disclosure of information. On occasion at present, the SEC and the stock exchanges, with the Commission's approval, do stop trading in a security.[11] The justifications usually offered for a trading suspension[12] could easily be extended to cover any news developments that might generate insider trading. The argument would be the same as that now used: time is needed for spectacular news to be disseminated and digested by the market to avoid wild fluctuations in price.

Implementation of this scheme in order to prevent insider trading would probably require close supervision of the affairs of every listed corporation. Trading in the company's stock could then be started and stopped as the supervisor saw the possibility of insiders' profiting by new developments. Such an approach might even seem to have an added advantage over other devices for preventing insider trading. Not only would insiders be prevented from exploiting their special knowledge, but speculation on tips by outsiders could also be prevented.

The consequences of such an extreme measure are hard to imagine. Even if the SEC displayed restraint in the exercise of such power, the operations of the capital market would undoubtedly be hampered. Public issues of new securities could not be underwritten with a high degree of confidence. The management of the entire stock market could in time pass from the hands

11. Securities Exchange Act, Section 19(a)(2) allows suspension for up to twelve months or withdrawal of a registration "if the Commission finds that an issuer of such security has failed to comply with any provision of this title or the rules and regulations thereunder." Professor Loss has termed this remedy Draconian. Loss, *Securities Regulation,* p. 845. The Commission can also suspend trading for successive periods of up to ten days under Section 19(a)(4). For cases in which this power has been used, consult Loss, pp. 852ff. Section A16 of the *New York Stock Exchange Company Manual,* p. A-291, allows suspension of trading for "any action which substantially reduces . . . the value or amount of its securities."

12. See Loss, *Securities Regulation,* p. 854.

of private investors and underwriters into the hands of government. Liquidity would be seriously lessened; and gross injustices would be done individuals wanting to sell their shares for reasons unrelated to insider trading. Most important, the market as a place for resolving differences of opinion and belief about economic values would lie shattered. Indeed, the amount of fortuitous gain and loss resulting from such a practice would be far greater than is likely under the rule of free insider trading on an open market.

Internal Policing

But if government policing of insider trading is so difficult or so undesirable, it is reasonable to ask whether insiders can effectively police the information to which they are privy. In the previous chapter we theorized that the various information-exchange devices guarantee a rational allocation of values to individuals with some claim to information. Indeed, this assumption is crucial to the entire thesis of this book. But at first glance it would seem that the same reasons offered to show that government policing cannot be effective would apply to private policing.

However, for a variety of reasons, internal policing or allocation is quite different from the enforcement of government rules proscribing trading. In the first place, the scale upon which this policing must be done is quite small. It is generally sufficient for a company to instruct particular employees not to trade in its shares or to disclose valuable information to others. It would be a rare case in which continuous, successful, clandestine trading will go unnoticed. Eventually the office boy's Cadillac will show up in the company parking lot. And even if a decision to terminate an individual's employment is based on mere rumor or surmise of prohibited trading, private employers are generally free to terminate an employment relationship that is not to their liking.

It is interesting to note that the Canons of Ethics of the American Institute of Certified Public Accountants proscribe accountants' trading in the shares of corporate clients. No comparable provision appears in the Canons of Ethics of the American Bar Association. This does not mean that lawyers are always welcomed into the inner councils of corporate clients. Lawyers are sometimes instructed not to trade in a client company's shares. And law firms often have a policy against associates or members trading in clients' stock.

Various physical arrangements are available to corporations to assure the security of valuable information. For instance, it is possible to isolate bookkeepers and others who have access to valuable information until that information has been effectively exploited by others. When the first successful drilling core was identified by the chief geologist of Texas Gulf Sulphur at Timmins, Ontario, he ordered all workers to remain in the camp while word of the find was sent back to the home office. Oil geologists are regularly instructed to communicate to one individual in the home office by a predetermined code when the results of drilling are known. The list could undoubtedly be expanded. If the employee objects to these seeming indignities, there is no great social problem. He is free to seek another job where working conditions are more to his taste. These conditions for the protection of valuable information, like those relating to trade secrets, are simply a part of the terms of employment.

Undoubtedly there are numerous leaks in any private security system. Some of this is probably accepted by corporations as a matter of desirable employment relations. In many cases it will be tolerated because it is not important. Few subordinate employees in large corporations will be in a position to exploit information in any significant fashion. Attention can be focused on the few individuals who might be privy to valuable information and in a position to exploit it significantly. Probably many individuals who receive valuable information are those who are entitled to it by reason of their entrepreneurial contributions. Placement of individuals in particular jobs may constitute an important device by which entrepreneurs are compensated.

When we remember that insiders have the most to lose from indiscriminate disclosures of information affecting the market, their incentive to design appropriate policing devices is clear.[13] These devices may become so institutionalized that few overt actions to make information secure will be

13. To the extent that insider trading by these individuals is not allowed, they have less incentive to police lower functionaries. Thus, the government's enforcement problems would probably be greater under such a rule than is indicated by the amount of insider trading presently occurring.

necessary. Strong moral strictures addressed to subordinate employees may have this effect. So may soundproof walls and doors with locks. Undoubtedly there are many more institutional arrangements to police information, even though their usefulness for that purpose may not be readily apparent.

The government's task, if it seeks to prevent insider trading, is far more difficult. The natural incentives and constraints are all against suppression of this trading, and simple institutional arrangements to prevent exploitation of information are difficult to conceive. The attempt to suppress the market in valuable information bears more resemblance to censorship and thought control than to attempts to suppress illicit transactions in drugs or whiskey. The suppression in one place of an undesired word or thought almost of necessity causes it to pop up in another place. Of all black markets, the one in ideas and knowledge is the most difficult to suppress.

12 A Postscript on Government

In our discussion of policing in the last chapter, we mentioned several types of outsiders who are frequently privy to valuable information about a corporation's shares. One class of these outsiders, government officials, is so large and so important that more detailed consideration is appropriate. Unquestionably the federal government is the largest producer of information capable of having a substantial effect on stock-market prices. And many corporate entrepreneurial developments will be known to government officials before the value has been exploited in the stock market by corporate insiders.

This last point may be illustrated by a corporation that discovers a huge new tin deposit in Bolivia. The discovery itself may represent successful entrepreneurial activity. But the ore cannot be mined unless heavy mining equipment unavailable in Bolivia is brought to the mining site, and without this equipment the discovery is worthless. The shipment of such equipment from the United States to most countries requires a permit or license from the Department of Commerce, and the application for this license requires the disclosure of considerable information.[1] It takes little imagination, given the nature of the equipment, the quantity, the consignor, and the consignee, to have some idea not only of what has been discovered but how much. Even if the government officials cannot deduce the necessary conclusions from required disclosures of this sort, it is often possible that these disclosures will serve as confirmation of other rumored events. Or they may ex-

1. 15 Code Fed. Reg., pp. 39ff (1965).

plain to an astute observer why the trading volume in this company's shares has been particularly high in recent days.

How Government Officials May Get Inside Information

But this purely hypothetical illustration does no more than illuminate one rather obscure aspect of the potential insider trading by government officials. If we look at the principal kinds of events that generally trigger large price changes in a company's stock, it is surprising how many of them either originate with the government or must be disclosed to the government. The various categories of significant events causing a change in the price of a company's shares may be broken down as follows: (1) sharply increased earnings, dividend increases, stock splits, and stock dividends; (2) a new product, an important patent, a new development in marketing, and a radical change in consumer preference; (3) public-utility rate changes and the granting of franchises for communication channels or transportation routes; (4) mergers, tender-bids, or proxy fights; and (5) large procurement contracts.

Generally, our first grouping—higher earnings, a dividend increase, stock splits, and stock dividends—requires no notice to government before the information can be fully exploited by corporate insiders. Some special situations can be included in this category, however. Frequently, higher or lower earnings may result directly from government decisions. A tax refund may be approved days before the corporate taxpayer is actually notified. A contract-renegotiation board may uphold a contractor's claim. In early 1966, after various aluminum companies announced price increases, the government decreed the sale of some of its stock-piled aluminum. If this had been offered for sale at a low enough price, the news would surely have adversely affected the price of aluminum-company stocks. Other examples of this sort could also be mentioned, but generally this first category is less important than the others.

Ordinarily information about new products does not have to be disclosed to the government, but there are some dramatic exceptions. An obvious case requiring disclosure is that of new drugs, which must receive government approval before they may be sold commercially. In this case corporate insiders may first recognize the importance of a new development, but they cannot be certain that the product can be marketed. Thus the effect is to diminish the degree of certainty with which the corporate insiders may trade, though they will not be removed from the picture entirely. However, a different person will know about the development quite early, thus possibly lessening the corporate entrepreneur's return.

In some instances, government officials or employees may be the first to know that a new drug has been approved for marketing. To the extent that a government agency, such as the Food and Drug Administration or the National Institutes of Health, is either doing the research or granting licenses for the manufacture and testing of drugs, additional possibilities appear for profitable trading in drug-company stocks by the government officials involved. It is interesting to note that security analysts specializing in drug-industry stocks are regular visitors at these two agencies.

Some new products have commercial value only if the government agrees to purchase them. This would be peculiarly true of new weapons developed privately and offered to the Department of Defense. Again, as in the case of new drugs, no matter how optimistic the developers may be, uncertainty about value remains very high prior to government approval and purchase.

Patents, though issued by the government, seldom make government officials privy to valuable information. In the nature of present patent procedures, the filing of a patent application generally will not disclose any potential stock-market information not previously exploited. If any value remained unexploited, the idea would simply be kept secret rather than disclosed in a patent application.

Strangely enough, information on changes in consumer preference may be known first by government employees. The change may originate with the government. The clearest example in recent years occurred in connection with the cigarette cancer scare. Various government reports, notably those of the Surgeon General of the United States, always had a short-run effect on tobacco-company stocks. Short selling by anyone with advance knowledge of the contents of these reports could have brought handsome returns.

Somewhat related to government reports affecting the demand for a product are those government reports that affect supply. The most notable of these is the Department of the Interior's projection of the demand for petroleum products, which in turn is used as a factor in determining how much oil can be pumped from the ground in Texas. Closely tied to this kind of information is that regarding petroleum-import quotas, which has disparate effects on different companies. Other examples can be found in regulations affecting sugar and coffee imports.

Many activities of regulatory commissions provide possibilities for inside information. Various administrative agencies in Washington regulate the rates of public-utility companies. The Federal Power Commission has jurisdiction over the rates of natural-gas producers and electric-power companies in interstate commerce. The Federal Communications Commission regulates telephone, telegraph, and other communication systems' rates, and the Interstate Commerce Commission and the Civil Aeronautics Board do the same for railroads, airlines, and truckers. Each of these agencies has important additional powers. The Federal Power Commission may, for example, determine when a particular sales transaction between two companies brings these companies within its jurisdiction. They also pass on the validity of mergers involving regulated companies, as do each of the other agencies. The Federal Communications Commission has the power to allocate radio and television frequencies and to suspend licenses and force reorganizations of operating patterns. The list could be expanded to include numerous other agencies, departments, or offices with some kind of discretionary power over some phase of business.

News of Corporate Mergers

In recent years mergers have presented important opportunities for government officials to make or know important news. At least three and often more than four agencies of the federal government may receive advance notice of a planned merger. The first of these, the Internal Revenue Service, is all-important. For some years few mergers that were not classified in advance as tax-free have been voluntarily entered. A tax-free merger merely signifies that the exchange of old securities for new will not be treated as a realization of ordinary income or capital gains. The cost to shareholders of a non-tax-free merger or reorganization is generally too high to warrant the transaction.

So important is this aspect of a corporate merger that the opinion of the Internal Revenue Service, as to whether a merger plan qualifies as tax-free, is often sought before public disclosure of a proposed merger. An IRS opinion may not be technically binding, but in practice it is usually the final word. A great variety of advance rulings on tax matters other than mergers could also be listed, although it is the merger that most frequently will affect the market price of shares.

Almost as important as tax considerations are the antitrust implications of a merger. As mentioned, specialized regulatory agencies are often involved in early stages of merger negotiations, but the Antitrust Division of the Department of Justice and the Federal Trade Commission are most frequently in the picture. Each of these has long sought premerger-notification legislation from Congress, though this legislation has never been adopted.

Occasionally companies apply for an informal clearance with these agencies. These informal approvals have no legal sanction, though they are generally relied upon. But the politics of antitrust is quite different from that of the tax field. In most cases the parties to a merger do not seek preliminary approval from the FTC or the Justice Department because to do so is to invite disapproval and accelerate the agency's legal opposition to the projected merger. Nonetheless, important stock-market information may be generated by the agency's subsequent decision to oppose a merger or, in effect, sanction it by inaction. Whether we refer to advance notification of mergers or a suit brought after a merger has occurred, a potential gain from stock trading on this information is available.

For all the lengthy and unsuccessful legislative fights by the Justice Department and the Federal Trade Commission to receive premerger notification, the Securities and Exchange Commission, under its broad rule-making authority, may gain this power with no help from Congress. A proposed amendment to the present requirements for monthly reporting of significant developments (the 8K report) will require notification of agreement on the formal terms of a merger, even though shareholder votes and other conditions have not been fulfilled.[2] It remains to be seen how this would be enforced in practice, but the potential as a source of government information is great.

It should be added that, consistent with the overall SEC philosophy of disclosure, considerable amounts of information may have to be disclosed to the Commission. But rarely does information have to be disclosed before it could be fully exploited by corporate insiders. An important exception exists, however, for control fights. The SEC requires advance notice of the intention of management or of outsiders to solicit proxies, and normally this would have to be disclosed before share purchasing begins. Under a bill presently pending in Congress, the SEC would also be given substantial powers to regulate tender-bids and other devices for taking over control of corporations.[3] All in all, however, there does not seem to be too great an opportunity for trading in information disclosed to the SEC. There may be much less than in other important agencies of the federal government, and there is certainly more surveillance of the practice in the SEC than elsewhere.

Government Procurement

Popular attention to conflicts of interest in government has, for the most part, focused on military procurement. The reason is not hard to understand: the amounts of money involved may reach gigantic proportions. The recent contract awarded to the Lockheed Corporation, to build the first military order of the C-5A transport aircraft, totalled $2 billion and will probably be increased severalfold before all C-5A's have been procured. Presumably there will be additional private procurement of this aircraft as well. It is even more common that a single government contract to a small corporation may account for a substantial portion of the company's total earnings during the period of the contract.

Public fear in these matters stems from the danger that such large contracts may be awarded because there has been a payoff or because contracting personnel hold stock in the company awarded the contract. The public

2. *CCH Federal Securities Law Reporter,* Vol. 2, par. 31001 (Proposed 8K, Item 2).
3. S. 2731, 89th Cong., 1st Sess., 1965.

seems to equate these two.[4] The danger, in either case, is that the strength and efficiency of the government are being compromised. The real force behind the abhorrence of bribery is the actual or potential harm that may be done by government officials who deliberately choose "second best" for the country in order to pad their own pockets.

It has been pointed out by many commentators, notably Dean Bayless Manning,[5] that conflicts of interest from stock ownership do not constitute a serious problem in Washington. In fact, the steps taken to overcome this danger may have done considerable disservice to the cause of good government. There can be few individuals contemplating high-ranking government positions who would think of taking the job in order to increase the value of their stock holdings. On the other hand, many have shown their willingness to make the financial sacrifice of unloading their holdings in order to take these positions.

The danger that stock ownership in large companies will consciously or unconsciously affect government officials' contract choices has undoubtedly been wildly exaggerated. And the danger that stock trading may influence choices also seems small. At first glance stock trading would not seem to present any danger at all, since it would occur only after the decision had been made to grant the contract to a particular company. The fear of buying second best for the nation does not come immediately to mind, and some individuals may even defend this method of giving greater compensation to government officials.

But this does overlook the analysis offered earlier in this book. A given

4. See Bayless Manning, "The Purity Potlatch: An Essay on Conflicts of Interest, American Government, and Moral Escalation," *Federal Bar Journal,* 24 (1964), p. 239. Dean Manning thinks that the stockholding conflict of interest has "become a modern political obsession in this country" and that it should by no means be equated with bribery.

5. *Ibid.,* and also see The Association of the Bar of the City of New York Special Committee on the Federal Conflict of Interest Laws, *Conflict of Interest and Federal Service* (Cambridge: Harvard University Press, 1960), hereafter referred to as *Conflict of Interest and Federal Service.* Dean Manning was staff director for this superb study. His article in the *Federal Bar Journal* is a colorful essay summarizing some of the findings of the special committee and presenting his own personal views on the subject. These two works must certainly stand as the cornerstone of any consideration of the classic forms of conflict of interest in government. Insider trading, unfortunately, is given rather brief consideration.

contract with a potential profit of $1 million would have no significant effect on the market price of shares of a company with annual earnings of $100 million. However, the same contract granted to a company with annual earnings of $1 million would have a dramatic impact. The direct danger of allowing government employees to trade in the shares of companies with whom they contract is that selections may be made partially or wholly on the basis of potential share-trading profits. But the potential damage to the country from this practice is probably not very great, and, if there were on balance positive advantages to be had from the practice, it could undoubtedly be tolerated. But, as we shall see below, there are other strong arguments against insider trading by government officials.

The Special Position of Congressmen

Congressmen are peculiarly in a position to *receive* valuable market news, not *create* it. They are seldom in a position to originate information as there is little a congressman can do individually to affect a particular stock's price significantly. But the receipt of information may appear quite appropriate for congressmen. For one thing, congressmen must know what is going on so that they may legislate effectively, and information needed for legislative purposes may well be the same as that needed for profitable stock-market dealings.

The idea of paying congressmen money for a favor or a vote would undoubtedly be pure anathema to the overwhelming majority of them. This would constitute bribery and, in this blatantly illegal form, probably almost never occurs. Other devices for influencing legislators, such as campaign contributions or delivering blocks of votes, undoubtedly occur more often, though these practices cannot make congressmen wealthy.

Information is a different matter. Since most of our theorists on the subject treat it as though it were a free good, it is simply not part of our thinking to see the freely given tip as a payoff or bribe. We do not ordinarily talk or think about it in those terms. There is a feeling that the share buyer still risks his own money on the investment and that no one is really giving him anything. Undoubtedly some businessmen and government officials are more clever than that, but a great many probably do not see a stock market tip as a payoff. For those who do, there are various concealment devices available, including those discussed in Chapters 5 and 6.

Congressmen on certain committees and their aides could be focal points for receiving information produced or learned in all the various executive departments and agencies. Each department, agency, or office has at least one committee, and often one committee member, critical for the continued allocation of funds to that agency. Certain committees in Congress may, therefore, carry a higher price tag than others. This price tag would relate not to the political importance of the committee, as would be true of the Senate Foreign Relations Committee or the House Rules Committee, but rather to the financial opportunities presented by the assignment. The various executive agencies are certainly not above using pressures, cajolery, and valuable information to gain their requests from these committees. It would not be surprising then that certain congressmen would be informed very early of important administrative developments.

But, if information is used as a technique for influencing congressmen, individuals in key positions may command valuable information even when the news does not relate to matters of direct concern to the recipient. Just as a President may give political support to the pet project of a senator in exchange for his critical support on a matter of political importance to the President, there are other ways, too, that a President can reward the faithful. Valuable information may not be the least of these.

In this respect the President could function in a manner similar to that suggested for investment bankers in Chapter 5. That is, he might act as a distributor of valuable information produced within the executive branch of the government. This information might be distributed in accord with past or anticipated value received from the recipients of the information. The theory of mutual advantage from exchange strongly implies that this relation, or some variant of it, is common.*

* Editor's note: In 2004, the *Wall Street Journal* reported:

> A study suggests that U.S. senators possess stock-picking skills that even the most seasoned money manager would envy. During the boom years of the 1990s, senators' stock picks beat the market by 12 percentage points a year on average, according to the study. Corporate insiders, meanwhile, beat the market by about six percentage points a year,

The Misleading Emphasis on Stock Ownership

The emphasis on the necessity for an individual to disclose his stock holdings and to divest himself of them before assuming a government position has almost totally eclipsed concern with stock trading by government officials. In presidential and vice-presidential campaigns since 1952, all leading contenders have disclosed to the press certified statements of their net worth, including a list of securities and other assets owned or held in trust.[6] In 1953 Congress conducted its celebrated investigation of Charles Wilson's finances after his nomination as Secretary of Defense. Eventually he was forced to divest himself of a large block of General Mo-

---

> while U.S. households underperformed the market by 1.4 percentage points a year on average, according to separate studies. The final details of the study will be published in the December issue of the *Journal of Financial and Quantitative Analysis*. . . .
>
> Looking at the timing of cumulative returns, the senators also appeared to know exactly when to buy or sell their holdings. Senators would buy stocks just before the shares suddenly would outperform the market by more than 25%. Conversely, senators would sell stocks that had been beating the market by about 25% for the past year just when the shares would fall back in line with the market's performance.

What explains this miraculous performance?

> The researchers say senators' uncanny ability to know when to buy or sell their shares seems to stem from having access to information that other investors wouldn't have. "I don't think you need much of an imagination to realize that they're in the know," says Alan Ziobrowski, a business professor at Georgia State University in Atlanta and one of the four authors of the study.
>
> Senators, for example, are likely to know which tax legislation is apt to pass and which companies might benefit. Or a senator who sits on a certain committee might find out that a particular company soon will be awarded a government contract or that a certain drug might get regulatory approval, says Prof. Ziobrowski. (Jane Kim, "U.S. Senators' Stock Picks Outperform the Pros'," *Wall Street Journal*, Oct. 26, 2004)—S.B.

6. It is not really clear why this information is deemed relevant or interesting to voters. Undoubtedly, some of the popular demand for financial disclosure reflects idle curiosity about the financial affairs of important figures. These disclosures have told very little. Even apart from the complex accounting and valuation problems involved, publication seems aimed at disclosing the total size of a man's estate more than anything else. Occasionally, such disclosures give rise to an implication of possible conflict of interest, in which case certain securities will be sold or various interests put in trust.

tors stock.[7] Almost regularly since then we have heard of congressional inquiries into stock holdings of presidential appointees. The mere presence of a minuscule potential for a conflict of interests seems sufficient to throw some investigators into paroxysms of moral indignation.

The point has been extremely well made by Dean Bayless Manning, that this obsession with stock ownership represents at best an exaggeration of a noble sentiment and at worst a serious hurdle for able personnel willing to serve in government in spite of a large financial sacrifice.[8] The conclusions reached in Dean Manning's studies on this subject do not seem open to serious dispute.

Insider trading, however, is a different matter. Unlike stock ownership, the dangers are not simply potential. Trading on inside information is what we may want to avoid, while it is never stock ownership per se that is deemed evil. Stock ownership is considered potentially harmful because it may warp or influence the judgment of government officials in connection with specific decisions they have to make. Very little attention has been paid, however, to the trading problem in studies of conflicts of interest among government personnel.[9] Stock ownership has been the principal concern of both academic and political investigators.

It is surprising, however, given the amount of potential profits available, that there is not a regular investigation of possible insider trading when important matters are disclosed by government officials. Stock-market price increases prior to government announcements affecting particular stocks can be easily noticed, though possibly only private individuals and not government officials account for this trading. In many instances, however, that seems highly improbable. Even though a particular government activity generates stock-market information of tremendous value, there is usually no suspicion of insider trading by government officials when disclosure of the event is made. Only rarely are we treated by a newspaper columnist or government official to the statement or even suggestion that insider trading is occurring.

7. For a detailed account of this and other congressional investigations on conflicts of interest from stockholdings, see *Conflict of Interest and Federal Service,* pp. 95–130.

8. Manning, "Purity Potlatch," pp. 248–49.

9. See *Conflict of Interest and Federal Service,* p. 238.

Aside from extremely rare intimations in the press or a cause célèbre such as the Texas Gulf affair,[10] there is no commonly voiced suspicion that trading on inside information by high government officials is endemic in Washington. Interestingly enough, when they are asked, many people in the government do not deny that it occurs. Almost everyone has heard of someone else trading with inside information or knows of someone who has done so. Yet this news, available to anyone for the asking, is usually left unexamined.

The Pros and Cons of Government Insider Trading

Two fundamental points have been made here about corporate insider trading. One is that no significant injury to corporate investors can result from the practice, and the other is that insider trading constitutes the most appropriate device for compensating entrepreneurs in large corporations. The first of these two arguments holds true whether the person trading on inside information is in government or business. Indeed, if speedy exploitation of information in the stock market is desirable, government employees' doing this would help accelerate price changes. It should be recalled from Chapter 7, however, that on balance this argument is largely neutral; it neither strongly favors nor disfavors insider trading.

10. Even with all the fanfare given Herbert Klotz's insider trading in Texas Gulf Sulphur stock and his resignation, there remain many mysteries about the entire matter. It is interesting to note that Klotz was the undersecretary in charge of patronage appointments in the Department of Commerce. At the time of his resignation he was a carryover from the Kennedy administration serving under a new secretary appointed by Johnson. Both Klotz and the SEC have claimed that a secretary in the department gave him his tip. She was reputedly a family friend of a Texas Gulf geologist in Timmins. Klotz claims that he noticed heavy buying on an upward price movement and, therefore, thought the tip was reliable.

Klotz is alleged to have made his purchases on Mar. 30 and 31, 1964, by which time rumors of the Texas Gulf discovery had already reached flood proportions in Washington. Clearly, all these rumors did not begin with a secretary in the Department of Commerce. There were undoubtedly other channels by which information about the find moved from Ontario or New York to Washington—channels reliable enough to be trusted by individuals who were not merely taking tips from secretaries.

The second part of the justification for insider trading in the corporate sector, however, has no substantial application to government. The argument can be made that government employment is frequently not financially attractive and that insider trading would encourage public service by able citizens otherwise unwilling to make the necessary financial sacrifice. The motivational aspect of this argument may be correct, and it is not unlikely that some officials have been so motivated. There would seem, however, to be overwhelming arguments, both theoretical and practical, against this justification.

The information on which government officials could trade would not ordinarily reflect entrepreneurial developments for which they are responsible. This is not to suggest that important innovations in government do not occur, nor that particular government decisions may not be of significant value to the shareholders of a given corporation. But we cannot define entrepreneurial activity in terms of any developments that will affect stock-market prices. Government innovations may injure a corporation economically as frequently as they benefit it. Very often the government official's news will have been reported to him rather than developed by him or anyone in government. And the most important innovations in government will generally have no effect on the stock market or the stock of any particular company.

We have no social, economic, or political interest in rewarding government officials simply for benefiting or injuring particular companies. Our interests are generally to the contrary and are quite the opposite of the economic interest society may have in rewarding corporate entrepreneurs. Survival of a business firm in a dynamic competitive economy demands a high degree of innovational activity. Insider trading has been justified as providing an important incentive for this desirable activity. But government officials, unless they are clearly representing private interests in their public capacities, do not play a significant role in this process of economic competition. Nor should we want activities of government officials to be aimed at the survival of any particular competing company.

Another difficulty with government insider trading relates to a point discussed in Chapter 11. There it was argued that the private allocation of valuable information will follow the dictates of market exchange and that serious leakages to the undeserving will be infrequent. However, myriad government reporting requirements may make private policing of information by corporate insiders very difficult. The net effect of requiring disclosure to unpoliced government officials may be to deprive corporate insiders of wealth they would otherwise attain and to deprive the shareholders of the benefits they would otherwise receive.

Another fundamental difficulty in allowing insider trading by government officials has already been mentioned. This is that important decisions, mainly in the area of government procurement, may be made with an eye to maximizing trading profits rather than serving the government's interest. This might occasionally be offered as an argument *for* insider trading by procurement officers. For the same contract, greater trading profits can ordinarily be made if the contract is given to the smaller of two competing companies. This does not seem, however, to be an appropriate device for dealing with problems of corporate size, and the dangers in this practice seem to outweigh any advantages.

But the principal evil inherent in government insider trading—and one that deserves much more attention than it has had—is the ease with which inside information can be utilized as a payoff device. This potential has long gone almost unnoticed, and concealment is exceptionally easy. Most of the devices mentioned in Chapter 5 can be utilized by government officials as well as private executives. Effective enforcement of rules against insider trading will never be easy. But the job in government should be begun. The very fact that cases are known of both congressional and executive-branch employees utilizing stock-market information for private gain should be sufficient to warrant a thorough investigation.

Executive Views on Insider Trading

On May 2, 1963, President Kennedy promulgated a presidential memorandum titled "Preventing Conflicts of Interest on the Part of Special Government Employees," addressed to all departments, agencies, and executive offices. His statement, though limited in application to temporary consultants or employees, is probably the first to notice officially the possibility of insider trading by government officials. It is also important for its implication that the practice occurs in significant amounts. The document states:

> *Insider Information.* The first principle of ethical behavior for the temporary or intermittent consultant or adviser is that he must refrain from any use of his public office which is motivated by, or gives the appearance of being motivated by, the desire for private gain for himself or other persons, including particularly those with whom he has family, business or financial ties. The fact that the desired gain, if it materializes, will not take place at the expense of the Government makes his action no less proper.
>
> An adviser or consultant must conduct himself in a manner devoid of the slightest suggestion that he is exploiting his Government employment for private advantage. Thus, a consultant or adviser must not, on the basis of any insider information, enter into speculation, or recommend speculation to members of his family or business associates, in commodities, land or the securities of any private company. He must obey this injunction even though his duties have no connection whatever with the Government programs or activities to avoid any appearance of acting on the basis of information obtained in the course of his Government work.[11]

There then followed in the same announcement a copy of the recently enacted, streamlined conflict-of-interest statute, pressure for which had come largely from the White House. Surprisingly, there is not one word in that statute that can be construed as applying to or disfavoring insider trading by government officials.

Very few government agencies had made any serious effort prior to 1966 to control insider trading. In 1960 careful examination showed that only three agencies had detailed any program for ferreting out insider trading by government employees and officials.[12] In one of these agencies, the Securities and Exchange Commission, specific provision in the statute creating the Commission makes unlawful the personal use of information filed with the Commission.[13] The SEC is certainly more sensitive to this question than any other agency and undoubtedly makes a continuing effort to prevent any abuse.[14] In most agencies with either detailed or simple prohibitions against

11. *Preventing Conflicts of Interest on the Part of Special Government Employees,* The President's Memorandum of May 2, 1963 (Washington: U.S. Government Printing Office, 1963), pp. 8–9.

12. *Conflict of Interest and Federal Service,* p. 85.

13. Securities Exchange Act of 1934, Section 24(c).

14. See Securities and Exchange Commission, *Regulation Regarding Conduct of Members and Employees and Former Members and Employees of the Commission* (recirculated June 29, 1962).

unauthorized use of official information, sanctions for violation of the rules almost never appear.[15] And no agency other than the SEC has regularly shown itself eager to police its rules.

In May of 1965 President Johnson promulgated an executive order revoking all earlier orders and memoranda dealing with conflicts of interest.[16] Johnson's order directed the Civil Service Commission to issue regulations consistent with the standards of conduct prescribed in his order.

Pursuant to this order, the Civil Service Commission issued rules and regulations governing conduct of government employees in connection with information, as well as other subjects.[17] These rules contain at least two provisions relating to valuable information for regular government employees[18] and one provision for special or temporary employees.[19] As might be imagined, employees were directed not to use information obtained through government employment in their own financial affairs.

The Civil Service Commission's rules directed each agency head to issue regulations for that agency's employees prescribing standards of conduct and governing the reporting of financial interests. The Civil Service regulations themselves require all employees in a grade of GS-16 or higher, with certain exceptions, to submit a statement of financial interests. And this must be kept current on a quarterly basis.

By early 1966 only the Department of Justice had issued rules pursuant to the executive order.[20] Basically this department's regulations on inside trading simply follow those stated in the rules of the Civil Service Commission. It is quite likely that most agencies and departments will model their standards accordingly.

But net-worth statements and quarterly reporting of assets are inadequate tools for ferreting out many instances of insider trading. It is doubtful that government officials who trade in their own names or give information to close relatives would ever hold securities for any length of time. Fur-

15. *Conflict of Interest and Federal Service,* pp. 93–94.
16. Executive Order 11222, *Federal Register,* May 11, 1965, p. 6469.
17. *Federal Register,* Sept. 30, 1965, p. 12529.
18. *Ibid.,* Sections 735.204 (Financial Interests) and 735.206 (Misuse of Information).
19. *Ibid.,* Section 735.303 (Use of Inside Information).
20. *Federal Register,* Dec. 31, 1965, p. 17202.

thermore, as government officials will often know the precise date on which disclosure of valuable information will be made, much of their trading could be very quick. A lot of trading can occur between points at which disclosure of holdings has to be made. And if accretions in assets between disclosure dates do not have to be explained, this form of disclosure might never turn up significant insider trading.

Of course, the mere fact that reporting is to be done quarterly does not indicate that inside traders would always have three months in which to realize their profits. On the average the maximum period for realizing profits before a new disclosure would be approximately six weeks. The rules would have been far more effective had they required immediate disclosure of any stock transactions or a statement of the source of all income.

Proposed Legislation

The various rules and regulations referred to do have the virtue of being in existence while the most far-reaching legislative proposal is and may remain at a preliminary stage. In May of 1965, a bill "To promote public confidence in the integrity of Congress and the executive branch," was introduced by Senator Clifford P. Case of New Jersey.[21] This bill covers all members of Congress, candidates for Congress, and employees of the executive or legislative branch making in excess of $17,500 a year. These individuals are directed to file with the comptroller general a statement including, among other things, "the amount and source of each item of income . . . received by him or by him and his spouse jointly during the preceding calendar year which exceeds $100 in amount or value." He must also report "all dealings in securities or commodities by him, or by him and his spouse or by any person acting on his behalf or pursuant to his direction during the preceding calendar year."

The coverage of these sections could undoubtedly be broadened to include other forms of marketing information. But the really important aspect of the bill is that it is well-designed to put teeth into disclosure provisions. Annual

21. S. 1877, 89th Cong., 1st Sess., 1965. Senators Maurine Neuberger, Joseph Clark, and Philip Hart joined Senator Case in introducing this bill.

reporting of income items will disclose even the shortest-term speculation, since the source of all items of income must be listed and not merely the amount and nature of assets as of a certain reporting date. It is possible that some of the bill's requirements are too onerous to be consistent with the goal of attracting able personnel into government positions; and there are other defects in the bill as well. But the greatest importance of this bill may lie in its recognition of the existence and nature of insider trading by government officials.

Approaches to Reform

Another unique feature of Senator Case's bill is the establishment of a Commission on Legislative Standards. This commission is directed to "conduct a thorough study of problems of conflicts of interest and of relations with executive and other agencies which confront Members of Congress with a view to devising and recommending measures and procedures to deal with such problems."[22] Such a commission, if properly directed, might be able to propose many effective devices for dealing with government insider trading. Arguably a less ambitious bill, merely to establish such an investigatory commission, would be more desirable for the present.

Certain conditions would probably have to be observed in order to develop a successful investigation of insider trading in government. The first and perhaps indispensable condition would be an agreement not to publicize particular cases uncovered. It is extremely unlikely that Congress would ever authorize an investigation that could conceivably embarrass most of its members as well as important figures in the executive branch. Second, to the extent that there have been violations of existing executive rules as well as the SEC's Rule 10b-5, a general immunity from any legal or administrative action should be declared in advance. This is consistent with the proposition that there has not been a general awareness of the evils inherent in government insider trading. More important, it is a practical necessity for accomplishing the stated goal.

Consideration should be given to treating valuable stock-market infor-

22. *Ibid.*, Section 3(d).

mation in the same way we treat information classified for security purposes. There could be gradations of clearances and a "need-to-know" standard. Realistic security measures should be instituted, and records should be maintained of the names of individuals privy to specified kinds of information. This would facilitate discovery by spot-checking of trading when there has been a substantial price change in a particular stock.

At some point techniques for discovering government-employee trading may intrude on private trading. This is one of the costs of the frequently close relationship of government and private business today, and additional study should be given to that problem. Undoubtedly policing of government trading cannot be perfect, though it should be considerably easier than government policing of private insider trading.

Undoubtedly it will be difficult for many people to comprehend a justification of corporate insider trading and a strong condemnation of the same practice by government officials. The arguments on each side are complex, but that is not a sufficient basis for concluding that both cases alike must be either condemned or condoned. The distinction between private economic activity and government administration is both real and fundamental.

List of Cases

Blau v. *Lehman,* 368 U.S. 403 (1962).

Boston & Maine R.R. Co. v. *Hillman, CCH Federal Securities Law Reporter,* par. 90,813 (S.D.N.Y., 1957).

Bosworth v. *Allen,* 168 N.Y. 157, 61 N.E. 163 (1901).

Bristol v. *Equitable Life Assurance Society of the U.S.,* 132 N.Y. 264, 30 N.E. 506 (1892).

Brophy v. *Cities Service Co.,* 31 Del. Ch. 241, 70 Atl. 2d 5 (1949).

In the Matter of Cady, Roberts & Co., SEC Release No. 6668, *CCH Federal Securities Law Reporter,* par. 76,803 (1961).

Colonial Laundries, Inc. v. *Henry,* 48 R.I. 332, 138 Atl. 47 (1927).

De Boy v. *Harris,* 207 Md. 212, 113 Atl. 2d 903 (1955).

E. I. DuPont de Nemours Powder Co. v. *Masland,* 244 U.S. 100 (1917).

Essex Universal Corp. v. *Yates,* 305 Fed. 2d 572 (2d Cir., 1962).

Goodwin v. *Agassiz,* 283 Mass. 358, 186 N.E. 659 (1933).

Gratz v. *Claughton,* 187 Fed. 2d 46 (2d Cir., 1951).

Helms v. *Duckworth,* 249 Fed. 2d 482 (D.C.C.A., 1957).

Jacquith v. *Mason,* 99 Neb. 509, 156 N.W. 1041 (1916).

J. I. Case Co. v. *Borak,* 377 U.S. 426 (1964).

Kardon v. *National Gypsum Co.,* 73 Fed. Supp. 798 (D.C.E.D.Pa., 1947).

Kerbs v. *California Eastern Airways, Inc.,* 33 Del. Ch. 69, 90 Atl. 2d 652 (1952).

Lieberman v. *Becker,* 38 Del. Ch. 540, 155 Atl. 2d 596 (1954).

Meinhard v. *Salmon,* 249 N.Y. 458, 164 N.E. 545 (1928).

Mills v. *Sarjem Corp.,* 133 Fed. Supp. 753 (D.C.N.J., 1955).

Oliver v. *Oliver,* 118 Ga. 362, 45 S.E. 232 (1903).

Rattner v. *Lehman,* 193 Fed. 2d 564 (2d Cir., 1952).

Rogers v. *Hill,* 65 Fed. 2d 109 (2d Cir., 1932), *reversed* 289 U.S. 582 (1933).

Securities & Exchange Commission v. *Capital Gains Research Bureau, Inc.,* 375 U.S. 180 (1963).

Securities & Exchange Commission v. *Chenery Corp.,* 318 U.S. 80 (1943).

Securities & Exchange Commission v. *Chenery Corp.*, 332 U.S. 194 (1947).
Sher v. *Sandler*, 325 Mass. 348, 90 N.E. 2d 536 (1950).
Smolowe v. *Delendo Corp.*, 136 Fed. 2d 231, (2d Cir., 1943), *cert. denied*, 320 U.S. 751.
Speed v. *Transamerica Corp.*, 99 Fed. Supp. 808 (D. Del., 1951).
Steele v. *Louisville & Nashville Railroad Co.*, 323 U.S. 192, (1944).
Stein v. *Morris*, 120 Va. 390, 91 S.E. 177 (1917).
Stewart v. *Harris*, 69 Kan. 498, 77 Pac. 277 (1904).
Strong v. *Repide*, 213 U.S. 419 (1909).
United States v. *Morgan*, 118 Fed. Supp. 621 (S.D.N.Y., 1953).
United States v. *Shindler*, 173 Fed. Supp. 393 (S.D.N.Y., 1959).

Appendix: Selected Cases*

BLAU v. *LEHMAN et al.*

368 U.S. 403 (1962)

Mr. Justice Black delivered the opinion of the Court.

The petitioner Blau, a stockholder in Tide Water Associated Oil Company, brought this action in a United States District Court on behalf of the company under § 16(b) of the Securities Exchange Act of 1934 to recover with interest "short swing" profits, that is, profits earned within a six months' period by the purchase and sale of securities, alleged to have been "realized" by respondents in Tide Water securities dealings. Respondents are Lehman Brothers, a partnership engaged in investment banking, securities brokerage and in securities trading for its own account, and Joseph A. Thomas, a member of Lehman Brothers and a director of Tide Water. The complaint alleged that Lehman Brothers "deputed . . . Thomas, to represent its interests as a director on the Tide Water Board of Directors," and that within a period of six months in 1954 and 1955 Thomas, while representing the interests of Lehman Brothers as a director of Tide Water and "by reason of his special and inside knowledge of the affairs of Tide Water, advised and caused the defendants, Lehman Brothers, to purchase and sell 50,000 shares of . . . stock of Tide Water, realizing profits thereon which did not inure to and [were] not recovered by Tide Water."

The case was tried before a district judge without a jury. The evidence showed that Lehman Brothers had in fact earned profits out of short-swing transactions in Tide Water securities while Thomas was a director of that company. But as to the charges of deputization and wrongful use of "inside" information by Lehman Brothers, the evidence was in conflict.

First, there was testimony that respondent Thomas had succeeded Hertz, another Lehman partner, on the board of Tide Water; that Hertz had "joined Tidewater Company thinking it was going to be in the interests of Lehman Brothers";

* All footnotes have been deleted.

and that he had suggested Thomas as his successor partly because it was in the interest of Lehman. There was also testimony, however, that Thomas, aside from having mentioned from time to time to some of his partners and other people that he thought Tide Water was "an attractive investment" and under "good" management, had never discussed the operating details of Tide Water affairs with any member of Lehman Brothers; that Lehman had bought the Tide Water securities without consulting Thomas and wholly on the basis of public announcements by Tide Water that common shareholders could thereafter convert their shares to a new cumulative preferred issue; that Thomas did not know of Lehman's intent to buy Tide Water stock until after the initial purchases had been made; that upon learning about the purchases he immediately notified Lehman that he must be excluded from "any risk of the purchase or any profit or loss from the subsequent sale"; and that this disclaimer was accepted by the firm.

From the foregoing and other testimony the District Court found that "there was no evidence that the firm of Lehman Brothers deputed Thomas to represent its interests as director on the board of Tide Water" and that there had been no actual use of inside information, Lehman Brothers having bought its Tide Water stock "solely on the basis of Tide Water's public announcements and without consulting Thomas."

On the basis of these findings the District Court refused to render a judgment, either against the partnership or against Thomas individually, for the $98,686.77 profits which it determined that Lehman Brothers had realized, holding:

> "The law is now well settled that the mere fact that a partner in Lehman Brothers was a director of Tide Water, at the time that Lehman Brothers had this short swing transaction in the stock of Tide Water, is not sufficient to make the partnership liable for the profits thereon, and that Thomas could not be held liable for the profits realized by the other partners from the firm's short swing transactions. Rattner v. Lehman, 2 Cir., 1952, 193 F.2d 564, 565, 567. This precise question was passed upon in the Rattner decision." 173 F. Supp. 590, 593.

Despite its recognition that Thomas had specifically waived his share of the Tide Water transaction profits, the trial court nevertheless held that within the meaning of § 16(b) Thomas had "realized" $3,893.41, his proportionate share of the profits of Lehman Brothers. The court consequently entered judgment against Thomas for that amount but refused to allow interest against him. On appeal, taken by both sides, the Court of Appeals for the Second Circuit adhered to the view it had taken in *Rattner* v. *Lehman,* 193 F.2d 564, and affirmed the District Court's judgment in all respects, Judge Clark dissenting. 286 F.2d 786. The Securities and Exchange Commission then sought leave from the Court of Appeals *en banc* to file an *amicus curiae* petition for rehearing urging the overruling of the *Rattner* case. The Commission's motion was denied, Judges Clark and Smith dissenting. We granted certiorari on the petition of Blau, filed on behalf of himself, other stockholders and Tide Water, and supported by the Commission. 366 U.S. 902. The questions presented by the petition are whether the courts below erred: (1) in refusing to render a judgment against the Lehman partnership for the $98,686.77 profits they were found to have "realized" from their "short-swing" transactions in Tide Water stock, (2) in refusing to render judgment against Thomas for the full $98,686.77 profits, and (3) in refusing to allow interest on the $3,893.41 recovery allowed against Thomas.

Petitioner apparently seeks to have us decide the questions presented as though he had proven the allegations of his complaint that Lehman Brothers actually deputized Thomas to represent its interests as a director of Tide Water, and that it was his advice and counsel based on his special and inside knowledge of Tide Water's affairs that caused Lehman Brothers to buy and sell Tide Water's stock. But the trial court found otherwise and the Court of Appeals affirmed these findings. Inferences could perhaps have been drawn from the evidence to support petitioner's charges, but examination of the record makes it clear to us that the findings of the two courts below were not clearly erroneous. Moreover, we cannot agree with the Commission that the courts' determinations of the disputed factual issues were conclusions of law rather than findings of fact. We must therefore decide whether Lehman Brothers, Thomas or both have an absolute liability under § 16(b) to pay over all profits made on Lehman's Tide Water stock dealings even though Thomas was not sitting on Tide Water's board to represent Lehman and even though the profits made by the partnership were on its own initiative, independently of any advice or "inside" knowledge given it by director Thomas.

First. The language of § 16 does not purport to impose its extraordinary liability on any "person," "fiduciary" or not, unless he or it is a "director," "officer" or "beneficial owner of more than 10 percentum of any class of any equity security . . . which is registered on a national securities exchange." Lehman Brothers was neither an officer nor a 10% stockholder of Tide Water, but petitioner and the Commission contend that the Lehman partnership is or should be treated as a director under § 16(b).

(a) Although admittedly not "literally designated" as one, it is contended that Lehman is a director. No doubt Lehman Brothers, though a partnership, could for purposes of § 16 be a "director" of Tide Water and function through a deputy, since § 3(a)(9) of the Act provides that "'person' means . . . partnership" and

§ 3(a)(7) that "'director' means any director of a corporation or any person performing similar functions with respect to any organization, whether incorporated or unincorporated." Consequently, Lehman Brothers would be a "director" of Tide Water, if as petitioner's complaint charged Lehman actually functioned as a director through Thomas, who had been deputized by Lehman to perform a director's duties not for himself but for Lehman. But the findings of the two courts below, which we have accepted, preclude such a holding. It was Thomas, not Lehman Brothers as an entity, that was the director of Tide Water.

(b) It is next argued that the intent of § 3(a)(9) in defining "person" as including a partnership is to treat a partnership as an inseparable entity. Because Thomas, one member of this inseparable entity, is an "insider," it is contended that the whole partnership should be considered the "insider." But the obvious intent of § 3(a)(9), as the Commission apparently realizes, is merely to make it clear that a partnership can be treated as an entity under the statute, not that it must be. This affords no reason at all for construing the word "director" in § 16(b) as though it read "partnership of which the director is a member." And the fact that Congress provided in § 3(a)(9) for a partnership to be treated as an entity in its own right likewise offers no support for the argument that Congress wanted a partnership to be subject to all the responsibilities and financial burdens of its members in carrying on their other individual business activities.

(c) Both the petitioner and the Commission contend on policy grounds that the Lehman partnership should be held liable even though it is neither a director, officer, nor a 10% stockholder. Conceding that such an interpretation is not justified by the literal language of § 16(b) which plainly limits liability to directors, officers, and 10% stockholders, it is argued that we should expand § 16(b) to cover partnerships of which a director is a member in order to carry out the congressionally declared purpose of "preventing the unfair use of information which may have been obtained by such beneficial owner, director, or officer by reason of his relationship to the issuer. . . ." Failure to do so, it is argued, will leave a large and unintended loophole in the statute—one "substantially eliminating the great Wall Street trading firms from the statute's operation." 286 F.2d, at 799. These firms it is claimed will be able to evade the Act and take advantage of the "inside" information available to their members as insiders of countless corporations merely by trading "inside" information among the various partners.

The argument of petitioner and the Commission seems to go so far as to suggest that § 16(b)'s forfeiture of profits should be extended to include all persons realizing "short swing" profits who either act on the basis of "inside" information or have the possibility of "inside" information. One may agree that petitioner and the Commission present persuasive policy arguments that the Act should be broadened in this way to prevent "the unfair use of information" more effectively than can be accomplished by leaving the Act so as to require forfeiture of profits only by those specifically designated by Congress to suffer those losses. But this very broadening of the categories of persons on whom these liabilities are imposed by the language of § 16(b) was considered and rejected by Congress when it passed the Act. Drafts of provisions that eventually became § 16(b) not only would have made it unlawful for any director, officer or 10% stockholder to disclose any confidential information regarding registered securities, but also would have made all profits received by *anyone,* "insider" or not, "to whom such unlawful disclosure" had been made recoverable by the company.

Not only did Congress refuse to give § 16(b) the content we are now urged to put into it by interpretation, but with knowledge that in 1952 the Second Circuit Court of Appeals refused, in the *Rattner* case, to apply § 16(b) to Lehman Brothers in circumstances substantially like those here, Congress has left the Act as it was. And so far as the record shows this interpretation of § 16(b) was the view of the Commission until it intervened last year in this case. Indeed in the *Rattner* case the Court of Appeals relied in part on Commission Rule X-16A-3(b) which required insider-partners to report only the amount of their own holdings and not the amount of holdings by the partnership. While the Commission has since changed this rule to require disclosure of partnership holdings too, its official release explaining the change stated that the new rule was "not intended as a modification of the principles governing liability for short-swing transactions under Section 16(b) as set forth in the case of *Rattner* v. *Lehman. . . .*" Congress can and might amend § 16(b) if the Commission would present to it the policy arguments it has presented to us, but we think that Congress is the proper agency to change an interpretation of the Act unbroken since its passage, if the change is to be made.

Second. The petitioner and the Commission contend that Thomas should be required individually to pay to Tide Water the entire $98,686.77 profit Lehman Brothers realized on the ground that under partnership law he is co-owner of the entire undivided amount and has therefore "realized" it all. "[O]nly by holding the partner-director liable for the *entire* short-swing profits realized by his firm," it is urged, can "an effective prophylactic to the stated statutory policy . . . be fully enforced." But liability under § 16(b) is to be determined neither by general partnership law nor by adding to the "prophylactic" effect Congress itself clearly prescribed in § 16(b). That section leaves no room for judicial doubt that a director is to pay to his company only "any profit realized *by him*" from short-swing transactions. (Emphasis added.) It would be nothing but a fiction to say that Thomas "realized" all the profits earned by the partnership of which he was a member. It was not error to refuse to hold Thomas liable for profits he did not make.

Third. It is contended that both courts below erred in failing to allow interest on the recovery of Thomas' share of the partnership profits. Section 16(b) says nothing about interest one way or the other. This Court has said in a kindred situation that "interest is not recovered according to a rigid theory of compensation for money withheld, but is given in response to considerations of fairness. It is denied when its exaction would be inequitable." *Board of Commissioners* v. *United States,* 308 U.S. 343, 352. Both courts below denied interest here and we cannot say that the denial was either so unfair or so inequitable as to require us to upset it.

Affirmed.

Mr. Justice Stewart took no part in the disposition of this case.

Mr. Justice Douglas, with whom The Chief Justice concurs, dissenting.

What the Court does today is substantially to eliminate "the great Wall Street trading firms" from the operation of § 16(b), as Judge Clark stated in his dissent in the Court of Appeals. 286 F.2d 786, 799. This result follows because of the wide dispersion of partners of investment banking firms among our major corporations. Lehman Bros. has partners on 100 boards. Under today's ruling that firm can make a rich harvest on the "inside information" which § 16 of the Act covers because each partner need account only for his distributive share of the firm's profits on "inside information," the other partners keeping the balance. This is a mutilation of the Act.

If a partnership can be a "director" within the meaning of § 16(a), then "any profit realized by him," as those words are used in § 16(b), includes all the profits, not merely a portion of them, which the partnership realized on the "inside information." There is no basis in reason for saying a partnership cannot be a "director" for purposes of the Act. In *Rattner* v. *Lehman,* 193 F.2d 564, 567, Judge Learned Hand said he was "not prepared to say" that a partnership could not be considered a "director," adding "for some purposes the common law does treat a firm as a jural person." In his view a partnership might be a "director" within the meaning of § 16 if it "deputed a partner" to represent its interests. Yet formal designation is no more significant than informal approval. Everyone knows that the investment banking–corporation alliances are consciously constructed so as to increase the profits of the bankers. In partnership law a debate has long raged over whether a partnership is an entity or an aggregate. Pursuit of that will-o'-

the-wisp is not profitable. For even New York with its aggregate theory recognizes that a partnership is or may be considered an entity for some purposes. It is easier to make this partnership a "director" for purposes of § 16 than to hold the opposite. Section 16(a) speaks of every "person" who is a "director." In § 3(a)(9) "person" is defined to include, *inter alia,* "a partnership." Thus, the purpose to subject a partnership to the provisions of § 16 need not turn on a strained reading of that section.

At the root of the present problem are the scope and degree of liability arising out of fiduciary relations. In modern times that liability has been strictly construed. The New York Court of Appeals, speaking through Chief Judge Cardozo in *Meinhard* v. *Salmon,* 249 N.Y. 458, 164 N.E. 545, held a joint adventurer to a higher standard than we insist upon today:

> "Many forms of conduct permissible in a workaday world for those acting at arm's length, are forbidden to those bound by fiduciary ties. A trustee is held to something stricter than the morals of the market place. Not honesty alone, but the punctilio of an honor the most sensitive, is then the standard of behavior. As to this there has developed a tradition that is unbending and inveterate. Uncompromising rigidity has been the attitude of courts of equity when petitioned to undermine the rule of undivided loyalty by the 'disintegrating erosion' of particular exceptions (*Wendt* v. *Fischer,* 243 N.Y. 439, 444). Only thus has the level of conduct for fiduciaries been kept at a level higher than that trodden by the crowd. It will not consciously be lowered by any judgment of this court." 249 N.Y., at 464, 164 N.E., at 546.

In *Mosser* v. *Darrow,* 341 U.S. 267, we allowed a reorganization trustee to be surcharged $43,447.46 for profits made by his employees through trading in securities of subsidiaries of a bankrupt company. We made this ruling even though there was "no hint or proof that he has been corrupt or that he has any interest, present or future, in the profits he has permitted these employees to make." *Id.,* at 275. We said:

> "These strict prohibitions would serve little purpose if the trustee were free to authorize others to do what he is forbidden. While there is no charge of it here, it is obvious that this would open up opportunities for devious dealings in the name of others that the trustee could not conduct in his own. The motives of man are too complex for equity to separate in the case of its trustees the motive of acquiring efficient help from motives of favoring help, for any reason at all or from anticipation of counterfavors later to come. We think that which the trustee had no right to do he had no right to authorize, and

that the transactions were as forbidden for benefit of others as they would have been on behalf of the trustee himself.

"... equity has sought to limit difficult and delicate fact-finding tasks concerning its own trustee by precluding such transactions for the reason that their effect is often difficult to trace, and the prohibition is not merely against injuring the estate—it is against profiting out of the position of trust. That this has occurred, so far as the employees are concerned, is undenied." *Id.*, at 271–273.

It is said that the failure of Congress to take action to remedy the consequences of the *Rattner* case somehow or other shows a purpose on the part of Congress to infuse § 16 with the meaning that *Rattner* gave it. We took that course in *Toolson* v. *New York Yankees*, 346 U.S. 356, and adhered to a ruling the Court made in 1922 that baseball was not within the scope of the antitrust laws, because the business had been "left for thirty years to develop, on the understanding that it was not subject to" those laws. *Id.*, p. 357. Even then we had qualms and two Justices dissented. For what we said in *Girouard* v. *United States*, 328 U.S. 61, 69, represents our usual attitude: "It is at best treacherous to find in congressional silence alone the adoption of a controlling rule of law." It is ironic to apply the *Toolson* principle here and thus sanction, as vested, a practice so notoriously unethical as profiting on inside information.

We forget much history when we give § 16 a strict and narrow construction. Brandeis in *Other People's Money* spoke of the office of "director" as "a happy hunting ground" for investment bankers. He said that "The goose that lays golden eggs has been considered a most valuable possession. But even more profitable is the privilege of taking the golden eggs laid by somebody else's goose. The investment bankers and their associates now enjoy that privilege." *Id.*, at 12.

The hearings that led to the Securities Exchange Act of 1934 are replete with episodes showing how insiders exploited for their personal gain "inside information" which came to them as fiduciaries and was therefore an asset of the entire body of security holders. The Senate Report labeled those practices as "predatory operations." S. Rep. No. 1455, 73d Cong., 2d Sess., p. 68. It said:

"Among the most vicious practices unearthed at the hearings before the subcommittee was the flagrant betrayal of their fiduciary duties by directors and officers of corporations who used their positions of trust and the confidential information which came to them in such positions, to aid them in their market activities. Closely allied to this type of abuse was the unscrupulous employment of inside information by large stockholders who, while not directors and officers, exercised sufficient control over the destinies of their companies to enable them to acquire and profit by information not available to others." *Id.*, at 55. See also S. Rep. No. 792, 73d Cong., 2d Sess., p. 9.

The theory embodied in § 16 was the one Brandeis espoused. It was stated by Sam Rayburn as follows: "Men charged with the administration of other people's money must not use inside information for their own advantage." H.R. Rep. No. 1383, 73rd Cong., 2d Sess. 13.

What we do today allows all but one partner to share in the feast which the one places on the partnership table. They in turn can offer feasts to him in 99 other companies of which they are directors. 14 Stan. L. Rev. 192, 198. This result is a dilution of the fiduciary principle that Congress wrote into § 16 of the Act. It is, with all respect, a dilution that is possible only by a strained reading of the law. Until now, the courts have given this fiduciary principle a cordial reception. We should not leave to Congress the task of restoring the edifice that it erected and that we tear down.

APPENDIX TO OPINION OF MR. JUSTICE DOUGLAS

Lehman v. *Civil Aeronautics Board, supra,* 93 U.S. App. D.C., at 85–87, 209 F.2d, at 292–294

"Petitioner Lehman is a director of Pan American; petitioner Joseph A. Thomas is a director of National Airlines, Inc., and of American Export Lines, Inc.; petitioner Frederick L. Ehrman is a director of Continental Air Lines, Inc., and Mr. John D. Hertz is a director of Consolidated Vultee Aircraft Corporation. All the companies referred to are in the aeronautic field and so must have Board approval of the kind of interlocking relationships which are made unlawful unless approved. Messrs. Lehman, Thomas, Ehrman, Hertz, and others, are also members of Lehman Brothers, a partnership which, as previously pointed out, conducts an investment banking business.

"The Board held that an individual Lehman Brothers partner who is a director of a Section 409(a) company is a representative of another partner who is a director of another such company. The relationships thus found to exist were disapproved as to those involving Pan American and National; Pan American and American Export Lines; Pan American and Consolidated Vultee; National and Pan American; National and Consolidated Vultee; and Continental Air Lines and Consolidated Vultee. . . .

"More precisely the Board concluded that a Lehman Brothers partner who is director of an air carrier has a representative 'who represents such . . . director as . . . a director' in another Section 409(a) company if another Lehman Brothers partner is a director of the latter, coupled with the circumstances that he seeks on behalf of Lehman Brothers the security underwriting and merger negotiation services used by the company of which he is director. The underwriting of security issues and the conduct of merger negotiations constitute a substantial part of the business of Lehman Brothers, who have been employed for these purposes not infrequently by Section 409(a) companies. The partners feel free to solicit this business for their firm.

". . . But we must consider the facts of the case in the light of the purpose of Congress to keep the developing aviation industry free of unhealthy interlocking relationships, though this purpose must be carried out only as the statute provides. The relevant findings which point up the problem are not in dispute. The underwriting activities of Lehman Brothers is a substantial part of its business; substantial fees are also obtained by Lehman Brothers from merger negotiations. Profits from the fees are shared by the partners. Section 409(a) companies, with Lehman Brothers partners as directors, need and use both types of services, and the partner directors seek such business for the partnership. In doing so they act as representatives of the partnership. It follows that they act as representatives of fellow partners, some of whom are directors of air carriers. Is this representation within the meaning of the statute? Does Mr. Thomas, to use his case as illustrative, who is a Lehman Brothers partner and also a director of National Airlines, represent, as director of National Airlines, Mr. Lehman, another Lehman Brothers partner and director of Pan American? We think that the affirmative answer of the Board should not be disturbed. For the situation comes to more than some community of interest and some sharing of common benefits as partners. The particular common interest and benefits are among directors of the regulated industry with respect to industry matters. The partnership link does not extend merely to a type of business remote from the aeronautical industry in which the partners are directors; it is with respect to business activities of air carriers and other aeronautical companies enumerated in Section 409(a). In these activities there is not only literal representation by one partner of another in partnership business but the particular partnership business is as well the business of aeronautical enterprises of which the partners are directors. When Mr. Thomas, again to illustrate, as director of National seeks to guide that company's underwriting business to Lehman Brothers he acts in the interest of and for the benefit of Mr. Lehman who is not only his underwriting partner but is also a director of an air carrier, Pan American. Mr. Lehman the partner is the same Mr. Lehman the director. The Board is not required to separate him into two personalities, as it were, and to say that Mr. Thomas represents him as a partner but not as a director, if, as is the case here, the representation is in regard to the carrying on of the affairs of Section 409(a) companies. The undoubted representation which grows out of the partnership we think follows into the directorships when the transactions engaged in are not only by the partners but concern companies regulated by the statute, of which the partners are directors. This is representation within not only the language but the meaning of the statute."

IN THE MATTER OF CADY, ROBERTS & Co.

Securities Exchange Act Release No. 6668
November 8, 1961

CARY, CHAIRMAN: This is a case of first impression and one of signal importance in our administration of the federal securities acts. It involves a selling broker who executes a solicited order and sells for discretionary accounts (including that of his wife) upon an exchange. The crucial question is what are the duties of such a broker after receiving non-public information as to a company's dividend action from a director who is employed by the same brokerage firm.

These proceedings were instituted to determine whether Cady, Roberts & Co. ("registrant") and Robert M. Gintel ("Gintel"), the selling broker and a partner of the registrant, willfully violated the "anti-fraud" provisions of Section 10(b) of the Securities Exchange Act of 1934 ("Exchange Act"), Rule 10b-5 issued under that Act, and Section 17(a) of the Securities Act of 1933 ("Securities Act") and, if so, whether any disciplinary action is necessary or appropriate in the public interest. The respondents have submitted an offer of settlement which essentially provides that the facts stipulated by respondents shall constitute the record in these proceedings for the purposes of determining the occurrence of a willful violation of the designated anti-fraud provisions and the entering of an appropriate order, on the condition that no sanction may be entered in excess of a suspension of Gintel for 20 days from the New York Stock Exchange.

The facts are as follows:

Early in November, 1959, Roy T. Hurley, then President and Chairman of the Board of Curtiss-Wright Corporation, invited 2,000 representatives of the press, the military and the financial and business communities to a public unveiling on November 23 of a new type of internal combustion engine being developed by the company. On November 24, 1959, press announcements concerning the new engine appeared in certain newspapers. On that day Curtiss-Wright stock was one of the most active issues on the New York Stock Exchange, closing at

35¼, up 3¼ on a volume of 88,700 shares. From November 6 through November 23, Gintel had purchased approximately 11,000 shares of Curtiss-Wright stock for about 30 discretionary accounts of customers of registrant. With the rise in the price on November 24, he began selling Curtiss-Wright shares for these accounts and sold on that day a total of 2,200 shares on the Exchange.

The activity in Curtiss-Wright stock on the Exchange continued the next morning, November 25, and the price rose to 40¾, a new high for the year. Gintel continued sales for the discretionary accounts and, between the opening of the market and about 11:00 A.M., he sold 4,300 shares.

On the morning of November 25 the Curtiss-Wright directors, including J. Cheever Cowdin ("Cowdin"), then a registered representative of registrant, met to consider, among other things, the declaration of a quarterly dividend. The company had paid a dividend, although not earned, of $.625 per share for each of the first three quarters of 1959. The Curtiss-Wright board, over the objections of Hurley, who favored declaration of a dividend at the same rate as in the prior quarters, approved a dividend for the fourth quarter at the reduced rate of $.375 per share. At approximately 11:00 A.M., the board authorized transmission of information of this action by telegram to the New York Stock Exchange. The Secretary of Curtiss-Wright immediately left the meeting room to arrange for this communication. There was a short delay in the transmission of the telegram because of a typing problem and the telegram, although transmitted to Western Union at 11:12 A.M., was not delivered to the Exchange until 12:29 P.M. It had been customary for the company also to advise the Dow Jones News Ticker of any dividend action. However, apparently through some mistake or inadvertence, the *Wall Street Journal* was not given the news until approximately 11:45 A.M. and the announcement did not appear on the Dow Jones ticker tape until 11:48 A.M.

Sometime after the dividend decision, there was a recess of the Curtiss-Wright directors' meeting, during which Cowdin telephoned registrant's office and left a message for Gintel that the dividend had been cut. Upon receiving this information, Gintel entered two sell orders for execution on the Exchange, one to sell 2,000 shares of Curtiss-Wright stock for ten accounts, and the other to sell short 5,000 shares for 11 accounts. Four hundred of the 5,000 shares were sold for three of Cowdin's customers. According to Cowdin, pursuant to directions from his clients, he had given instructions to Gintel to take profits on these 400 shares if the stock took a "run-up." These orders were executed at 11:15 and 11:18 A.M. at 40¼ and 40⅜, respectively.

When the dividend announcement appeared on the Dow Jones tape at 11:48 A.M., the Exchange was compelled to suspend trading in Curtiss-Wright because of the large number of sell orders. Trading in Curtiss-Wright stock was resumed at 1:59 P.M. at 36½, ranged during the balance of the day between 34⅛ and 37, and closed at 34⅞.

Violation of Anti-Fraud Provisions

So many times that citation is unnecessary, we have indicated that the purchase and sale of securities is a field in special need of regulation for the protection of investors. To this end one of the major purposes of the securities acts is the prevention of fraud, manipulation or deception in connection with securities transactions. Consistent with this objective, Section 17(a) of the Securities Act, Section 10(b) of the Exchange Act and Rule 10b-5, issued under that section, are broad remedial provisions aimed at reaching misleading or deceptive activities, whether or not they are precisely and technically sufficient to sustain a common law action for fraud and deceit. Indeed, despite the decline in importance of a "federal rule" in the light of *Erie R. Co.* v. *Tomkins,* the securities acts may be said to have generated a wholly new and far-reaching body of federal corporation law.

* * * * *

These anti-fraud provisions are not intended as a specification of particular acts or practices which constitute fraud, but rather are designed to encompass the infinite variety of devices by which undue advantage may be taken of investors and others.

Section 17 and Rule 10b-5 apply to securities transactions by "any person." Misrepresentations will lie within their ambit, no matter who the speaker may be. An affirmative duty to disclose material information has been traditionally imposed on corporate "insiders," particularly officers, directors, or controlling stockholders. We, and the courts, have consistently held that insiders must disclose material facts which are known to them by virtue of their position but which are not known to persons with whom they deal and which, if known, would affect their investment judgment. Failure to make disclosure in these circumstances constitutes a violation of the anti-fraud provisions. If, on the other hand, disclosure prior to effecting a purchase or sale would be improper or unrealistic under the circumstances, we believe the alternative is to forego the transaction.

The ingredients are here and we accordingly find that Gintel willfully violated Sections 17(a) and 10(b) and Rule 10b-5. We also find a similar violation by the registrant, since the actions of Gintel, a member of registrant, in the course of his employment are to be regarded as actions of registrant itself. It was obvious that a reduction in the quarterly dividend by the board of directors was a material fact which could be expected to have an adverse impact on the market price of the company's stock. The rapidity with which Gintel acted upon receipt of the information confirms his own recognition of that conclusion.

We have already noted that the anti-fraud provisions are phrased in terms of "any person" and that a special obligation has been traditionally required of corporate insiders, e.g., officers, directors and controlling stockholders. These three groups, however, do not exhaust the classes of persons upon whom there is such an obligation. Analytically, the obligation rests on two principal elements; first, the existence of a relationship giving access, directly or indirectly, to information intended to be available only for a corporate purpose and not for the personal benefit of anyone, and second, the inherent unfairness involved where a party takes advantage of such information knowing it is unavailable to those with whom he is dealing. In considering these elements under the broad language of the anti-fraud provisions we are not to be circumscribed by fine distinctions and rigid classifications. Thus our task here is to identify those persons who are in a special relationship with a company and privy to its internal affairs, and thereby suffer correlative duties in trading in its securities. Intimacy demands restraint lest the uninformed be exploited.

The facts here impose on Gintel the responsibilities of those commonly referred to as "insiders." He received the information prior to its public release from a director of Curtiss-Wright, Cowdin, who was associated with the registrant. Cowdin's relationship to the company clearly prohibited him from selling the securities affected by the information without disclosure. By logical sequence, it should prohibit Gintel, a partner of registrant. This prohibition extends not only over his own account, but to selling for discretionary accounts and soliciting and executing other orders. In somewhat analogous circumstances, we have charged a broker-dealer who effects securities transactions for an insider and who knows that the insider possesses non-public material information with the affirmative duty to make appropriate disclosures or dissociate himself from the transaction.

The three main subdivisions of Section 17 and Rule 10b-5 have been considered to be mutually supporting rather than mutually exclusive. Thus, a breach of duty of disclosure may be viewed as a device or scheme, an implied misrepresentation, and an act or practice, violative of all three subdivisions. Respondents argue that only clause (3) may be applicable here. We hold that, in these circumstances, Gintel's conduct at least violated clause (3) as a practice which operated as a fraud or deceit upon the purchasers. Therefore, we need not decide the scope of clauses (1) and (2).

We cannot accept respondents' contention that an insider's responsibility is limited to existing stockholders and that he has no special duties when sales of securities are made to non-stockholders. This approach is too narrow. It ignores the plight of the buying public—wholly unprotected from the misuse of special information.

Neither the statutes nor Rule 10b-5 establish artificial walls of responsibility. Section 17 of the Securities Act explicitly states that it shall be unlawful for any person in the offer or sale of securities to do certain prescribed acts. Although the primary function of Rule 10b-5 was to extend a remedy to a defrauded seller, the courts and this Commission have held that it is also applicable to a defrauded buyer. There is no valid reason why persons who *purchase* stock from an officer, director or other person having the responsibilities of an "insider" should not have the same protection afforded by disclosure of special information as persons who *sell* stock to them. Whatever distinctions may have existed at common law based on the view that an officer or director may stand in a fiduciary relationship to existing stockholders from whom he purchases but not to members of the public to whom he sells, it is clearly not appropriate to introduce these into the broader anti-fraud concepts embodied in the securities acts.

Respondents further assert that they made no express representations and did not in any way manipulate the market, and urge that in a transaction on an exchange, there is no further duty such as may be required in a "face-to-face" transaction. We reject this suggestion. It would be anomalous indeed if the protection afforded by the anti-fraud provisions were withdrawn from transactions effected on exchanges, primary markets for securities transactions. If purchasers on an exchange had available material information known by a selling insider, we may assume that their investment judgment would be affected and their decision whether to buy might accordingly be modified. Consequently, any sales by the insider must await disclosure of the information.

Cases cited by respondents in which relief was denied to purchasers or sellers of securities in exchange transactions are distinguishable. The action here was instituted by the Commission, not by individuals. The cited cases concern private suits brought against insiders for violation of the anti-fraud rules. They suggest that the plaintiffs may not recover because there was lacking of "semblance of privity" since it was not shown that the buyers or sellers bought from or sold to the insiders. These cases have no relevance here as they concern the remedy of the buyer or seller *vis-a-vis* the insider. The absence of a remedy of the private litigant because of lack of privity does not absolve an insider from responsibility for fraudulent conduct.

Respondents argue that any requirement that a broker-dealer in exchange transactions make disclosure of "adverse factors disclosed by his analysis" would create uncertainty and confusion as to the duties of those who are constantly acquiring and analyzing information about companies in which they or their clients are interested. Furthermore it is claimed, substantial practical difficulties would be presented as to the manner of making disclosures.

There should be no quandary on the facts here presented. While there may be a question as to the materiality and significance of some corporate facts and as to the necessity of their disclosure under particular circumstances, that is not this case. Corporate dividend action of the kind involved here is clearly recognizable as having a direct effect on the market value of securities and the judgment of investors. Moreover, knowledge of this action was not arrived at as a result of perceptive analysis of generally known facts, but was obtained from a director (and associate) during the time when respondents should have known that the board of directors of the issuer was taking steps to make the information publicly available but before it was actually announced.

Furthermore, the New York Stock Exchange has recognized that prompt disclosure of important corporate developments, including specifically dividend action, is essential for the benefit of stockholders and the investing public and has established explicit requirements and recommended procedures for the immediate public release of dividend information by issuers whose securities are listed on the Exchange. The practical problems envisaged by respondents in effecting appropriate disclosures in connection with transactions on the Exchange are easily avoided where, as here, all the registered broker-dealer need do is to keep out of the market until the established procedures for public release of the information are carried out instead of hastening to execute transactions in advance of, and in frustration of, the objectives of the release.

Finally, we do not accept respondents' contention that Gintel was merely carrying out a program of liquidating the holdings in his discretionary accounts—determined and embarked upon prior to his receipt of the dividend information. In this connection, it is further alleged that he had a fiduciary duty to these accounts to continue the sales, which overrode any obligations to unsolicited purchasers on the Exchange.

The record does not support the contention that Gintel's sales were merely a continuance of his prior schedule of liquidation. Upon receipt of the news of the dividend reduction, which Gintel knew was not public, he hastened to sell before the expected public announcement all of the Curtiss-Wright shares remaining in his discretionary accounts, contrary to his previous moderate rate of sales. In so doing, he also made short sales of securities which he then allocated to his wife's account and to the account of a customer whom he had never seen and with whom he had had no prior dealings. Moreover, while Gintel undoubtedly occupied a fiduciary relationship to his customers, this relationship could not justify any actions by him contrary to law. Even if we assume the existence of conflicting fiduciary obligations, there can be no doubt which is primary here. On these facts, clients may not expect of a broker the benefits of his inside information at the expense of the public generally. . . .

The Public Interest

All the surrounding circumstances and the state of mind of the participants may be taken into consideration in determining what sanctions should appropriately be imposed here.

It is clear that Gintel's conduct was willful in that he knew what he was doing. However, there is no evidence of a preconceived plan whereby Cowdin was to "leak" advance information of the dividend reduction so that Gintel could use it to advantage before the public announcement; on the contrary, the evidence points to the conclusion that Cowdin probably assumed, without thinking about it, that the dividend action was already a matter of public information and further that he called registrant's office to find out the effect of the dividend news upon the market. The record, moreover, indicates that Gintel's conduct was a spontaneous reaction to the dividend news, that he intended primarily to benefit existing clients of Cady, Roberts and Co. and that he acted on the spur of the moment and so quickly as to preclude the possibility of review by registrant or of his own more deliberate consideration of his responsibilities under the securities acts.

Gintel has been fined $3,000 by the New York Stock Exchange in connection with the instant transactions. The publication of this opinion, moreover, will in itself serve as a further sanction upon Gintel and registrant and will also induce a more careful observance of the requirements of the anti-fraud provisions in the area in question. Furthermore, registrant had no opportunity to prevent Gintel's spontaneous transactions and no contention has been made that its procedures for handling accounts did not meet proper standards. Under all the circumstances we conclude that the public interest and the protection of investors will be adequately and appropriately served if Gintel is suspended from the New York Stock Exchange for 20 days and if no sanction is imposed against the registrant. Accordingly, we accept respondent's offer of settlement.

An appropriate order will issue.

Commissioners Woodside and Cohen join in the above opinion. Commissioner Frear dissents in part (see below).

Frear, Commissioner Dissenting in part. I agree that the facts disclosed by the record submitted in connection with the offer of settlement show willful violations of the anti-fraud provisions of the securities acts, and I concur in the views enunciated in the part of the Commission's Findings and Opinion dealing with such violation. However, in my opinion those facts and violations require the imposition of a greater sanction than the 20-day suspension of Gintel from membership on the New York Stock Exchange which is the maximum permitted under the offer of settlement, and I would accordingly reject the offer.

SECURITIES AND EXCHANGE COMMISSION v. *CAPITAL GAINS RESEARCH BUREAU, INC.*, et al.

375 U.S. 180 (1963)

Mr. Justice Goldberg delivered the opinion of the Court.

We are called upon in this case to decide whether under the Investment Advisers Act of 1940 the Securities and Exchange Commission may obtain an injunction compelling a registered investment adviser to disclose to his clients a practice of purchasing shares of a security for his own account shortly before recommending that security for long-term investment and then immediately selling the shares at a profit upon the rise in the market price following the recommendation. The answer to this question turns on whether the practice—known in the trade as "scalping"—"operates as a fraud or deceit upon any client or prospective client" within the meaning of the Act. We hold that it does and the Commission may "enforce compliance" with the Act by obtaining an injunction requiring the adviser to make full disclosure of the practice to his clients.

The Commission brought this action against respondents in the United States District Court for the Southern District of New York. At the hearing on the application for a preliminary injunction, the following facts were established. Respondents publish two investment advisory services, one of which—"A Capital Gains Report"—is the subject of this proceeding. The Report is mailed monthly to approximately 5,000 subscribers who each pay an annual subscription price of $18. It carries the following description:

> "An Investment Service devoted exclusively to (1) The protection of investment capital. (2) The realization of a steady and attractive income there-

from. (3) The accumulation of CAPITAL GAINS thru the timely purchase of corporate equities that are proved to be undervalued."

Between March 15, 1960, and November 7, 1960, respondents, on six different occasions, purchased shares of a particular security shortly before recommending it in the Report for long-term investment. On each occasion, there was an increase in the market price and the volume of trading of the recommended security within a few days after the distribution of the Report. Immediately thereafter, respondents sold their shares of these securities at a profit. They did not disclose any aspect of these transactions to their clients or prospective clients.

On the basis of the above facts, the Commission requested a preliminary injunction as necessary to effectuate the purposes of the Investment Advisers Act of 1940. The injunction would have required respondents, in any future Report, to disclose the material facts concerning, *inter alia,* any purchase of recommended securities "within a very short period prior to the distribution of a recommendation . . . ," and "[t]he intent to sell and the sale of said securities . . . within a very short period after distribution of said recommendation. . . ."

The District Court denied the request for a preliminary injunction, holding that the words "fraud" and "deceit" are used in the Investment Advisers Act of 1940 "in their technical sense" and that the Commission had failed to show an intent to injure clients or an actual loss of money to clients. 191 F. Supp. 897. The Court of Appeals for the Second Circuit, sitting *en banc,* by a 5-to-4 vote accepted the District Court's limited construction of "fraud" and "deceit" and affirmed the denial of injunctive relief. 306 F. 2d 606. The majority concluded that no violation of the Act could be found absent proof that "any misstatements or false figures were contained in any of the bulletins"; or that "the investment advice was unsound"; or that "defendants were being bribed or paid to tout a stock contrary to their own beliefs"; or that "these bulletins were a scheme to get rid of worthless stock"; or that the recommendations were made "for the purpose of endeavoring artificially to raise the market so that [respondents] might unload [their] holdings at a profit." *Id.,* at 608–609. The four dissenting judges pointed out that "[t]he common-law doctrines of fraud and deceit grew up in a business climate very different from that involved in the sale of securities," and urged a broad remedial construction of the statute which would encompass respondents' conduct. *Id.,* at 614. We granted certiorari to consider the question of statutory construction because of its importance to the investing public and the financial community. 371 U.S. 967.

The decision in this case turns on whether Congress, in empowering the courts to enjoin any practice which operates "as a fraud or deceit upon any client or prospective client," intended to require the Commission to establish fraud and deceit "in their technical sense," including intent to injure and actual injury to clients, or whether Congress intended a broad remedial construction of the Act which would encompass nondisclosure of material facts. For resolution of this issue we consider the history and purpose of the Investment Advisers Act of 1940.

I

The Investment Advisers Act of 1940 was the last in a series of Acts designed to eliminate certain abuses in the securities industry, abuses which were found to have contributed to the stock market crash of 1929 and the depression of the 1930's. It was preceded by the Securities Act of 1933, the Securities Exchange Act of 1934, the Public Utility Holding Company Act of 1935, the Trust Indenture Act of 1939, and the Investment Company Act of 1940. A fundamental purpose, common to these statutes, was to substitute a philosophy of full disclosure for the philosophy of *caveat emptor* and thus to achieve a high standard of business ethics in the securities industry. As we recently said in a related context, "It requires but little appreciation . . . of what happened in this country during the 1920's and 1930's to realize how essential it is that the highest ethical standards prevail" in every facet of the securities industry. *Silver* v. *New York Stock Exchange*, 373 U.S. 341, 366.

The Public Utility Holding Company Act of 1935 "authorized and directed" the Securities and Exchange Commission "to make a study of the functions and activities of investment trusts and investment companies. . . ." Pursuant to this mandate, the Commission made an exhaustive study and report which included consideration of investment counsel and investment advisory services. This aspect of the study and report culminated in the Investment Advisers Act of 1940.

The report reflects the attitude—shared by investment advisers and the Commission—that investment advisers could not "completely perform their basic function—furnishing to clients on a personal basis competent, unbiased, and continuous advice regarding the sound management of their investments—unless all conflicts of interest between the investment counsel and the client were removed." The report stressed that affiliations by investment advisers with investment bankers, or corporations might be "an impediment to a disinterested, objective, or critical attitude toward an investment by clients. . . ."

This concern was not limited to deliberate or conscious impediments to objectivity. Both the advisers and the Commission were well aware that whenever advice to a client might result in financial benefit to the adviser—other than the fee for his advice—"that advice to a client might in some way be tinged with that pecuniary interest [whether consciously or] subconsciously motivated. . . ." The report quoted one leading investment adviser who said that he "would put the emphasis . . . on subconscious" motivation in such situations. It quoted a member of the Commission staff who suggested that a significant part of the problem was not the existence of a "deliberate intent" to obtain a financial advantage, but rather the existence "subconsciously [of] a prejudice" in favor of one's own financial interests. The report incorporated the Code of Ethics and Standards of Practice of one of the leading investment counsel associations, which contained the following canon:

> "[An investment adviser] should continuously occupy an impartial and disinterested position, as free as humanly possible from the *subtle* influence of prejudice, *conscious or unconscious;* he should scrupulously avoid any affiliation, or any act, which subjects his position to challenge in this respect." (Emphasis added.)

Other canons appended to the report announced the following guiding principles: that compensation for investment advice "should consist exclusively of direct charges to clients for services rendered"; that the adviser should devote his time "exclusively to the performance" of his advisory function; that he should not "share in profits" of his clients; and that he should not "directly or indirectly engage in any activity which may jeopardize [his] ability to render unbiased investment advice." These canons were adopted "to the end that the quality of services to be rendered by investment counselors may measure up to the high standards which the public has a right to expect and to demand."

One activity specifically mentioned and condemned by investment advisers who testified before the Commission was "*trading by investment counselors for their own account in securities in which their clients were interested. . . .*"

This study and report—authorized and directed by statute—culminated in the preparation and introduction by Senator Wagner of the bill which, with some changes, became the Investment Advisers Act of 1940. In its "declaration of policy" the original bill stated that

> "Upon the basis of facts disclosed by the record and report of the Securities and Exchange Commission . . . it is hereby declared that the national public interest and the interest of investors are adversely affected— . . . (4) when the business of investment advisers is so conducted as to defraud or mislead investors, or to enable such advisers to relieve themselves of their fiduciary obligations to their clients.

> "It is hereby declared that the policy and purposes of this title, in accordance with which the provisions of this title shall be interpreted, are to mitigate and, so far as is presently practicable to eliminate the abuses enumerated in this section." S. 3580, 76th Cong., 3d Sess., § 202.

Hearings were then held before Committees of both Houses of Congress. In describing their profession, leading investment advisers emphasized their relationship of "trust and confidence" with their clients and the importance of "strict limitations of [their right] to buy and sell securities in the normal way if there is any chance at all that to do so might seem to operate against the interests of clients and the public." The president of the Investment Counsel Association of America, the leading investment counsel association, testified that the

> "two fundamental principles upon which the pioneers in this new profession undertook to meet the growing need for unbiased investment information and guidance were, first, that they would limit their efforts and activities to the study of investment problems from the investor's standpoint, not engaging in any other activity, such as security selling or brokerage, which might directly or indirectly bias their investment judgment; and, second, that their remuneration for this work would consist solely of definite, professional fees fully disclosed in advance."

Although certain changes were made in the bill following the hearings, there is nothing to indicate an intent to alter the fundamental purposes of the legislation. The broad proscription against "any . . . practice . . . which operates . . . as a fraud or deceit upon any client or prospective client" remained in the bill from beginning to end. And the Committee Reports indicate a desire to preserve "the personalized character of the services of investment advisers," and to eliminate conflicts of interest between the investment adviser and the clients as safeguards both to "unsophisticated investors" and to "bona fide investment counsel." The Investment Advisers Act of 1940 thus reflects a congressional recognition "of the delicate fiduciary nature of an investment advisory relationship," as well as a congressional intent to eliminate, or at least to expose, all conflicts of interest which might incline an investment adviser—consciously or unconsciously—to render advice which was not disinterested. It would defeat the manifest purpose of the Investment Advisers Act of 1940 for us to hold, therefore, that Congress, in empowering the courts to enjoin any practice which operates "as a fraud or deceit," intended to require proof of intent to injure and actual injury to clients.

This conclusion moreover, is not in derogation of the common law of fraud, as the District Court and the majority of the Court of Appeals suggested. To the contrary, it finds support in the process by which the courts have adapted the common law of fraud to the commercial transactions of our society. It is true that at common law intent and injury have been deemed essential elements in a damage suit between parties to an arm's-length transaction. But this is not such an action. This is a suit for a preliminary injunction in which the relief sought is, as the dissenting judges below characterized it, the "mild prophylactic," 306 F. 2d, at 613, of requiring a fiduciary to disclose to his clients, not all his security holdings, but only his dealings in recommended securities just before and after the issuance of his recommendations.

The content of common-law fraud has not remained static as the courts below seem to have assumed. It has varied, for example, with the nature of the relief sought, the relationship between the parties, and the merchandise in issue. It is not necessary in a suit for equitable or prophylactic relief to establish all the elements required in a suit for monetary damages.

> "Law had come to regard fraud . . . as primarily a tort, and hedged about with stringent requirements, the chief of which was a strong moral, or rather immoral element, while equity regarded it, as it had all along regarded it, as a conveniently comprehensive word for the expression of a lapse from the high standard of conscientiousness that it exacted from any party occupying a certain contractual or fiduciary relation towards another party."

> "Fraud has a broader meaning in equity [than at law] and intention to defraud or to misrepresent is not a necessary element."

> "Fraud, indeed, in the sense of a court of equity properly includes all acts, omissions and concealments which involve a breach of legal or equitable duty, trust, or confidence, justly reposed, and are injurious to another, or by which an undue and unconscientious advantage is taken of another."

Nor is it necessary in a suit against a fiduciary, which Congress recognized the investment adviser to be, to establish all the elements required in a suit against a party to an arm's-length transaction. Courts have imposed on a fiduciary an affirmative duty of "utmost good faith, and full and fair disclosure of all material facts," as well as an affirmative obligation "to employ reasonable care to avoid misleading" his clients. There has also been a growing recognition by common-law courts that the doctrines of fraud and deceit which developed around transactions involving land and other tangible items of wealth are ill-suited to the sale of such intangibles as advice and securities, and that, accordingly, the doctrines must be adapted to the merchandise in issue. The 1909 New York case of *Ridgely v. Keene*, 134 App. Div. 647, 119 N.Y. Supp. 451, illustrates this continuing development. An investment adviser who, like respondents, published an investment advisory service, agreed, for compensation, to influence his clients to buy shares in a certain security. He did not disclose the agreement to his client but sought "to excuse his conduct by asserting that . . . he honestly believed, that his subscribers would profit by his advice. . . ." The court, holding that "his belief in the soundness of his advice is wholly immaterial," declared the act in question "a palpable fraud."

We cannot assume that Congress, in enacting legislation to prevent fraudulent practices by investment advisers, was unaware of these developments in the common law of fraud. Thus, even if we were to agree with the courts below that Congress had intended, in effect, to codify the common law of fraud in the Investment Advisers Act of 1940, it would be logical to conclude that Congress codified the common law "remedially" as the courts had adapted it to the prevention of fraudulent securities transactions by fiduciaries, not "technically" as it has traditionally been applied in damage suits between parties to arm's-length transactions involving land and ordinary chattels.

The foregoing analysis of the judicial treatment of common-law fraud reinforces our conclusion that Congress, in empowering the courts to enjoin any practice which operates "as a fraud or deceit" upon a client, did not intend to require proof of intent to injure and actual injury to the client. Congress intended the Investment Advisers Act of 1940 to be construed like other securities legislation "enacted for the purpose of avoiding frauds," not technically and restrictively, but flexibly to effectuate its remedial purposes.

II

We turn now to a consideration of whether the specific conduct here in issue was the type which Congress intended to reach in the Investment Advisers Act of 1940. It is arguable—indeed it was argued by "some investment counsel representatives" who testified before the Commission—that any "trading by investment counselors for their own account in securities in which their clients were interested . . ." creates a potential conflict of interest which must be eliminated. We need not go that far in this case, since here the Commission seeks only disclosure of a conflict of interests with significantly greater potential for abuse than in the situation described above. An adviser who, like respondents, secretly trades on the market effect of his own recommendation may be motivated—consciously or unconsciously—to recommend a given security not because of its potential for long-run price increase (which would profit the client), but because of its potential for short-run price increase in response to anticipated activity from the recommendation (which would profit the adviser). An investor seeking the advice of a registered investment adviser must, if the legislative purpose is to be served, be permitted to evaluate such overlapping motivations, through appropriate disclosure, in deciding whether an adviser is serving "two masters" or only one, "especially . . . if one of the masters happens to be economic self-interest." *United States* v. *Mississippi Valley Co.*, 364 U.S. 520, 549. Accordingly, we hold that the Investment Advisers Act of 1940 empowers the courts, upon a showing such as that made here, to require an adviser to make full and frank disclosure of his practice of trading on the effect of his recommendations.

III

Respondents offer three basic arguments against this conclusion. They argue first that Congress could have made, but did not make, failure to disclose material facts unlawful in the Investment Advisers Act of 1940, as it did in the Securities Act of 1933, and that absent specific language, it should not be assumed that Congress intended to include failure to disclose in its general proscription of any practice which operates as a fraud or deceit. But considering the history and chronology of the statutes, this omission does not seem significant. The Securities Act of 1933 was the first experiment in federal regulation of the securities industry. It was understandable, therefore, for Congress, in declaring certain practices unlawful, to include both a general proscription against fraudulent and deceptive practices and, out of an abundance of caution, a specific proscription against nondisclosure. It soon became clear, however, that the courts, aware of the previously outlined developments in the common law of fraud, were merging the proscription against nondisclosure into the general proscription against fraud, treating the former, in effect, as one variety of the latter. For example, in *Securities & Exchange Comm'n* v. *Torr*, 15 F. Supp. 315 (D.C.S.D.N.Y. 1936), rev'd on other grounds, 87 F. 2d 446, Judge Patterson held that suppression of information material to an evaluation of the disinterestedness of investment advice "operated as a deceit on purchasers," 15 F. Supp., at 317. Later cases also treated nondisclosure as one variety of fraud or deceit. In light of this, and in light of the evident purpose of the Investment Advisers Act of 1940 to substitute a philosophy of disclosure for the philosophy of *caveat emptor*, we cannot assume that the omission in the 1940 Act of a specific proscription against nondisclosure was intended to limit the application of the antifraud and antideceit provisions of the Act so as to render the Commission impotent to enjoin suppression of material facts. The more reasonable assumption, considering what had transpired between 1933 and 1940, is that Congress, in enacting the Investment Advisers Act of 1940 and proscribing any practice which operates "as a fraud or deceit," deemed a specific proscription against nondisclosure surplusage.

Respondents also argue that the 1960 amendment to the Investment Advisers Act of 1940 justifies a narrow interpretation of the original enactment. The amendment made two significant changes which are relevant here. "Manipulative" practices were added to the list of those specifically proscribed. There is nothing to suggest, however, that with respect to a requirement of disclosure, "manipulative" is any broader than fraudulent or deceptive. Nor is there any indication that by adding the new proscription Congress intended to narrow the scope of the original proscription. The new amendment also authorizes the Commission "by rules and regulations [to] define, and prescribe means reasonably designed to prevent, such acts, practices, and courses of business as are fraudulent, deceptive, or manipulative." The legislative history offers no indication, however, that Congress intended such rules to substitute for the "general and flexible" anti-fraud provisions which have long been considered necessary to control "the versatile inventions of fraud-doers." Moreover, the intent of Congress must be culled from the events surrounding the passage of the 1940 legislation. "[O]pinions attributed to a Congress twenty years after the event cannot be considered evidence of the intent of the Congress of 1940." *Securities & Exchange Comm'n* v. *Capital Gains Research Bureau, Inc.*, 306 F. 2d 606, 615 (dissenting opinion). See *United States* v. *Philadelphia Nat. Bank*, 374 U.S. 321, 348–349.

Respondents argue, finally, that their advice was "honest" in the sense that they believed it was sound and did not offer it for the purpose of furthering personal pecuniary objectives. This, of course, is but another way of putting the rejected argument that the elements of technical common-law fraud—particularly intent—must be established before an injunction requiring disclosure may be ordered. It is the practice itself, however, with its potential for abuse, which "operates as a fraud or deceit" within the meaning of the Act when relevant information is suppressed. The Investment Advisers Act of 1940 was "directed not only at dishonor, but also at conduct that tempts dishonor." *United States* v. *Mississippi Valley Co.*, 364 U.S. 520, 549. Failure to disclose material facts must be deemed fraud or deceit within its intended meaning, for, as the experience of the 1920's and 1930's amply reveals, the darkness and ignorance of commercial secrecy are the conditions upon which predatory practices best thrive. To impose upon the Securities and Exchange Commission the burden of showing deliberate dishonesty as a condition precedent to protecting investors through the prophylaxis of disclosure would effectively nullify the protective purposes of the statute. Reading the Act in light of its background we find no such requirement commanded. Neither the Commission nor the courts should be required "to separate the mental urges," *Peterson* v. *Greenville,* 373 U.S. 244, 248, of an investment adviser, for "[t]he motives of man are too complex . . . to separate. . . ." *Mosser* v. *Darrow,* 341 U.S. 267, 271. The statute, in recognition of the adviser's fiduciary relationship to his clients, requires that his advice be disinterested. To insure this it empowers the courts to require disclosure of material facts. It misconceives the purpose of the statute to confine its application to "dishonest" as opposed to "honest" motives. As Dean Shulman said in discussing the nature of securities transactions, what is required is "a picture not simply of the show window, but of the entire store . . . not simply truth in the statements volunteered, but disclosure." The high standards of business morality exacted by our laws regulating the securities industry do not permit an investment adviser to trade on the market effect of his own recommendations without fully and fairly revealing his personal interests in these recommendations to his clients.

Experience has shown that disclosure in such situations, while not onerous to the adviser, is needed to preserve the climate of fair dealing which is so essential to maintain public confidence in the securities industry and to preserve the economic health of the country.

The judgment of the Court of Appeals is reversed and the case is remanded to the District Court for proceedings consistent with this opinion.

Reversed and remanded.

Mr. Justice Douglas took no part in the consideration or decision of this case.

Mr. Justice Harlan, dissenting.

I would affirm the judgment below substantially for the reasons given by Judge Moore in his opinion for the majority of the Court of Appeals sitting *en banc,* 306 F. 2d 606, and in his earlier opinion for the panel. 300 F. 2d 745. A few additional observations are in order.

Contrary to the majority, I do not read the Court of Appeals' *en banc* opinion as holding that either § 206(1) of the Investment Advisers Act of 1940, 54 Stat. 847 (prohibiting the employment of "any device, scheme, or artifice to defraud any client or prospective client"), or § 206(2), 54 Stat. 847 (prohibiting the engaging "in any transaction, practice, or course of business which operates as a fraud or deceit upon any client or prospective client"), is confined by traditional

Appendix to Opinion of the Court

On one occasion respondents sold short some shares of a security immediately before stating in their Report that the security was overpriced. After the publication of the Report, respondents covered their short sales.

Respondents' transactions are summarized by the Commission as follows:

Stock	Purchased	Purchase price	Recommended	Sold	Sale price	Profit
Continental Insurance Co.	3/15/60	47¾–47⅞	3/18/60	3/29/60	50⅛	$ 1,125.00
United Fruit Co.	5/13, 16, 19, 20/60	21¼–22⅛	5/27/60	6/6, 7, 9, 10/60	23⅝–24½	10,725.00
Creole Petroleum Corp.	7/5, 14/60	25¼–28¾	7/15/60	7/20, 21, 22/60	27⅛–29	1,762.50
Hart, Schaffner & Marx	8/8/60	23	8/12/60	8/18, 22/60	24⅞–25¼	837.00
Union Pacific	10/28, 31/60	25⅜–25⅝	11/1/60	11/7/60	27	1,757.00
Frank G. Shattuck Co.	10/11/60 (purchased calls)	16.83 (2.53 call cost, plus 14.30 option price)	10/14/60	10/25/60 (exercised calls and sold)	19½–20⅛	695.17
Chock Full O'Nuts	10/4/60 (sold short)	68¾–69 (sale price)	10/14/60 (disparaged)	10/24/60 (covered short sale)	62–62½ (purchase price)	2,772.33

Although some of the above figures relating to profits are disputed, respondents do not substantially contest the remaining figures.

common law concepts of fraud and deceit. That court recognized that "federal securities laws are to be construed broadly to effectuate their remedial purpose." 306 F. 2d, at 608. It did not hold or intimate that proof of "intent to injure and actual injury to clients" (*ante,* p. 186) was necessary to make out a case under these sections of the statute. Rather it explicitly observed: "Nor can there be any serious dispute that a relationship of trust and confidence should exist between the advisor and the advised," *ibid.,* thus recognizing that no such proof was required. In effect the Court of Appeals simply held that the terms of the statute require, at least, some proof that an investment adviser's recommendations are not disinterested.

I think it clear that what was shown here would not make out a case of fraud or breach of fiduciary relationship under the most expansive concepts of common law or equitable principles. The nondisclosed facts indicate no more than that the respondents personally profited from the foreseeable reaction to sound and impartial investment advice.

The cases cited by the Court (*ante,* p. 198) are wide of the mark as even a skeletonized statement of them will show. In *Securities & Exchange Comm'n* v. *Torr,* 15 F. Supp. 315, reversed on other grounds, 87 F. 2d 446, defendants were in effect bribed to recommend a certain stock. Although it was not apparent that they lied in making their recommendations, it was plain that they were motivated to make them by the promise of reward. In the case before us, there is no vestige of proof that the reason for the recommendations was anything other than a belief in the soundness of the investment advice given.

Charles Hughes & Co. v. *Securities & Exchange Comm'n,* 139 F. 2d 434, involved sales of stock by customers' men to those ignorant of the market value of the stocks at 16% to 41% above the over-the-counter price. Defendant's employees must have known that the customers would have refused to buy had they been aware of the actual market price.

The defendant in *Norris & Hirshberg, Inc.,* v. *Securities & Exchange Comm'n,* 85 U.S. App. D.C. 268, 177 F. 2d 228, dealt in unlisted securities. Most of its customers believed that the firm was acting only on their behalf and that its income was derived from commissions; in fact the firm bought from and sold to its customers, and received its income from mark-ups and mark-downs. The nondisclosure of this basic relationship did not, the court stated, "necessarily establish that petitioner violated the antifraud provisions of the Securities and Securities Exchange Acts." *Id.,* at 271, 177 F. 2d, at 231. Defendant's trading practices, however, were found to establish such a violation; an example of these was the buying of shares of stock from one customer and the selling to another at a substantially higher price on the same day. The opinion explicitly distinguishes between what is necessary to prove common law fraud and the grounds under securities legislation sufficient for revocation of a broker-dealer registration. *Id.*, at 273, 177 F. 2d, at 233.

Arleen Hughes v. *Securities & Exchange Comm'n,* 85 U.S. App. D.C. 56, 174 F. 2d 969, concerned the revocation of the license of a broker-dealer who also gave investment advice but failed to disclose to customers both the best price at which the securities could be bought in the open market and the price which she had paid for them. Since the court expressly relied on language in statutes and regulations making unlawful "any omission to state a material fact," *id.*, at 63, 174 F. 2d, at 976, this case hardly stands for the proposition that the result would have been the same had such provisions been absent.

In *Speed* v. *Transamerica Corp.*, 235 F. 2d 369, the controlling stockholder of a corporation made a public offer to buy stock, concealing from the other shareholders information known to it as an insider which indicated the real value of the stock to be considerably greater than the price set by the public offer. Had shareholders been aware of the concealment, they would undoubtedly have refused to sell; as a consequence of selling they suffered ascertainable damages.

In *Archer* v. *Securities & Exchange Comm'n,* 133 F. 2d 795, defendant copartners of a company dealing in unlisted securities concealed the name of Claude Westfall, who was found to be in control of the business. Westfall was thereby enabled to defraud the customers of the brokerage firm of Harris, Upham & Co., for which he worked as a trader. Securities of the customers of the latter firm were bought by defendants' company at under the market level, and defendants' company sold securities to the clients of Harris, Upham & Co. at prices above the market.

In all of these cases but *Arleen Hughes,* which turned on explicit provisions against nondisclosure, the concealment involved clearly reflected dishonest dealing that was vital to the consummation of the relevant transactions. No such factors are revealed by the record in the present case. It is apparent that the Court is able to achieve the result reached today only by construing these provisions of the Investment Advisers Act as it might a pure conflict of interest statute, cf. *United States* v. *Mississippi Valley Co.*, 364 U.S. 520, something which this particular legislation does not purport to be.

I can find nothing in the terms of the statute or in its legislative history which lends support to the absolute rule of disclosure now established by the Court. Apart from the other factors dealt with in the two opinions of the Court of Appeals, it seems to me especially significant that Congress in enacting the Investment Advisers Act did not include the express disclosure provision found in § 17(a)(2) of the Securities Act of 1933, 48 Stat. 84, even though it did carry over to the Advisers Act the comparable fraud and deceit provisions of the Securities Act. To attribute the presence of a disclosure provision in the earlier statute to an "abundance of caution" (*ante*, p. 198) and its omission in the later statute to a congressional belief that its inclusion would be "surplusage" (*ante*, p. 199) is for me a singularly unconvincing explanation of this controlling difference between the two statutes.

However salutary may be thought the disclosure rule now fashioned by the Court, I can find no authority for it either in the statute or in any regulation duly promulgated thereunder by the S.E.C. Only two Terms ago we refused to extend certain provisions of the Securities Exchange Act of 1934 to encompass "policy" considerations at least as cogent as those urged here by the S.E.C. *Blau* v. *Lehman*, 368 U.S. 403. The Court should have exercised the same wise judicial restraint in this case. This is particularly so at this interlocutory stage of the litigation. It is conceivable that at the trial the S.E.C. would have been able to make out a case under the statute construed according to its terms.

I respectfully dissent.

ARTICLES AND ESSAYS

In Defense of Insider Trading

In April 1965, when the Securities and Exchange Commission announced its action against executives of the Texas Gulf Sulphur Company for alleged violations of rules against insider trading, there was an outcry of public indignation against the defendants. It was as though men who were highly respected members of the community had suddenly been found out in heinous crime.

But this is only one more manifestation of a long and persistent trend. The main push came with the Pecora hearings in Congress in 1933–1934, where the activities of prominent executives who conceded playing some part in insider trading were characterized as "immoral," "unscrupulous," "unfair," a "betrayal of fiduciary duties," and a "vicious practice."[1] Since that time, leading academic figures, lawyers, businessmen, and spokesmen for the SEC, with almost boring uniformity, have castigated insider trading as being costly to shareholders and giving unfair and undeserved gains to insiders. The tone of most discussions on this subject suggests that there is no doubt whatever: insider trading is a sin, and the war against it is a holy one.

From *Harvard Business Review* 113 (November–December 1966) and reprinted from "Supplementary Cases and Material for Business Associations II: Exclusively for the Use of Students at the National Law Center, George Washington University" (Washington, D.C.: Lerner Law Book, 1967), 133–142. Reproduced with permission of Harvard Business School Publishing.

Author's note: For fuller discussion and more technical details see my just-published book, *Insider Trading and the Stock Market* (New York, The Free Press, 1966).

1. *Stock Exchange Practices, Hearings Before the Committee on Banking and Currency,* U.S. Senate, 73rd Congress, 1st Session.

But, as in most holy wars, self-righteousness and hypocrisy may be the true order of the day. In the entire literature on insider trading there does not exist one careful analysis of the subject. Lawyers have been having a field day arguing about the meaning of words or the reach of the last case or any of a thousand technical and legal issues. Unfortunately, however, most lawyers do not have the skills to develop a careful economic analysis of the subject, and economists have offered no assistance. The tone of debate has remained essentially moralistic and question-begging. Logic has been totally lost to emotion.

It is very likely, however, that unless businessmen, commentators, and the courts wake up, far more than logic will be lost. For the current attack on insider trading may prove to be a fundamental attack on free capital markets and entrepreneurial capitalism. It would be a shame to lose the battle by default.

Careful analysis of insider trading requires consideration of at least three major questions:

1. Who gains and who loses from insider trading? (We cannot assume that the shareowners who should be protected are necessarily the same people who are in danger of being hurt.)

2. What are the long-run consequences of disallowing insider trading? (Even if some individuals may be hurt by it, the economy may be hurt more if we remove the incentive effect of such trading.)

3. Can insider trading be prevented, and at what financial and social cost? (There are many indirect devices for trading in information, and they can be very subtle and hard to trace.)

Full answers to these questions must await years of study and research, but we know quite a bit already and can confidently deduce quite a bit more.

This article constitutes at least a starting point for logical analysis of the subject. In particular, I shall argue that insider trading is the best, if not the only, method of adequately compensating corporate innovators, and I shall attempt to define and to answer objections to the practice of insider trading.

Gain and Loss

What, if any, advantages would flow to participants in the stock market if insider trading were effectively stopped? Here we come to one of the most astounding facts in this whole astounding business: the only stock market participants who are likely to benefit from a rule preventing insider trading are the short-term speculators and traders, not the long-term investors who are regularly stated to be the objects of the SEC's solicitude.

The initial error of most commentators is the assumption that the persons who sold to insiders before disclosure of important news would not have sold at all if the insiders were not in the market. Obviously this is absurd; the average seller has no way in the world of knowing the identity of his buyer. One of the great virtues of an organized securities market is its automaticity, which results in anonymity of traders. Publicly traded companies are quite different in this respect from small, closely held corporations, and the rules governing them should also be different.

If insiders are in the market, however, they represent additional buying power over what would prevail without them. So there must be some sellers in the market who can be said to sell only because of the insider's buying. But this is only the beginning of analysis. We need to know the identity of these additional sellers, and also we want to see if there is any benefit from the insider's trading activities that may counteract any harmful effects of this additional purchasing power.

Investors Versus Traders

To discover the identity of sellers who would not trade but for the insider's activities, we must first distinguish two types of shareholders—investors and traders. This distinction has certainly been overworked for many purposes, but it is of considerable value in the present analysis:

- Investors, the long-term shareholders, tend to select stocks based on so-called "fundamental" factors, such as earning potential, dividend history, growth prospects, or the reputation of management, to mention just a few. And they select stocks suitable for their own particular investment needs. They tend to sell either because their estimate of the fundamental factors proved wrong or because of some change in their personal circumstances or needs. They almost never buy or sell because of short-swing fluctuations in the price of a security.
- Short-swing traders, whether we call them "speculators" or not, may also trade on so-called "fundamental" factors. But many of them, unlike any of

the true investors, also buy or sell simply because of recent changes in the price of a security. That is, they assume their ability to predict future price changes from previous changes in price and volume—so-called "technical" factors. And very many of these traders simply are gambling.

This is not the place to enter the debate on whether technical strategies can ever be used successfully, though a growing academic literature is casting grave doubts on the validity of technical factors as determinants of stock price movements. The importance of this trading for our purposes is that any price change is taken as a signal by the "technicians" in the market, or by the gamblers, to buy or sell. Consequently, as insiders cause a price rise by adding their buying power to the market, the selling necessary to complete the additional transactions will ordinarily be supplied by short-term traders. It cannot and should not be denied that the stock market provides the greatest competition for Las Vegas and the racetracks we have. This is not intended as criticism. But it is seriously disturbing to find the SEC pressing hard for a rule designed either to aid this group or to encourage their gambling proclivities.

In aggregate, the gamblers in a perfectly free stock market, with no inflation, are bound to lose money. Just as the house's cut in the gambling casino guarantees the long-term gambler a loss, so stockbrokerage commissions on each transaction must injure the steady stock trader who has no valid information. Furthermore, as we noticed previously, he often supplies the stock on which insiders profit. Thus he is matching wits with an expert in a game which does not pay off for amateurs. Perhaps the analogy to gambling against someone with loaded dice or marked cards is most apt.

How Much Harm?

Though statistically this is probably not significant, the long-term investor may turn out to be the individual who in fact sells to the insider. But since he is normally selling for reasons unrelated to the insider's trading, and would be selling in any event, he should be indifferent to the identity of his buyer. Actually, he may benefit from the insider's buying on good news, as the average price received may be higher with than without insider trading. For example:

Let us assume that a stock is selling at $50, with undisclosed good news which will *ultimately* cause the stock to sell for $60, and that no factors other than the good news will affect the price.

Suppose, further, that with insider trading the price of the shares rises *gradually* to $60. The average price at which shares sell during this period is somewhere in the neighborhood of $55 (more or less depending on the shape of the time-price curve). At $60, anyone who has held his shares will have received the full benefit of the new information whether it is disclosed to him or not. This advantage to the ultimate holder remains even if we effectively prevent insider trading.

Without insider trading, however, the position of those who sell during the time required for the price to rise from $50 to $60 is radically altered. No longer do they receive an average price of $55. Assuming that the ultimate disclosure is made at the same time under either rule, they receive only $50 for their shares without insider trading. In short, they get less than they would with insider trading.

It may be argued that this overstates the direct advantages from insider trading. For, in fact, during the same relevant time period investors will be buying as well as selling, and—to take the same example—with insider trading they might buy at an average price of $55, while without it they would buy at an average price of $50. If the number of buyers among investors is the same as the number of sellers, then we are simply back where we started; the gains and losses cancel out (though not necessarily for the same individuals). It may be true, however, that a gradual price increase will cause fewer investment decisions to buy relative to decisions to sell than would be the case with an abrupt price change. (The difference, of course, is accounted for by other traders.) On balance, therefore, insider trading may still benefit investors.

Even if there is no appreciable net direct advantage or disadvantage to investors as a group from insider trading, it is likely that price fluctuations will not be so sharp, part of the excitement which attracts the gambler may be lost, and the occasionally valid "hot tip" will not pay off as much. Are not these all advantages, rather than disadvantages?

Wary Insiders

When it is further realized how rare significant insider trading must be, one wonders even more what all the shouting has been about. If insider trading does occur, insiders as a group trade in the stock market with greater certainty and success than do those not using fresh, reliable information. Accordingly, successful inside traders may tend to gamble in the stock market much less than all other traders, since they will more often have "sure things." This conservatism suggests that they have several likely attitudes toward their trading:

- The insider tends not to trade on information unless it will be very significant quantitatively. It must be of sufficient importance that the conservative trader, recognizing the natural uncertainties of the marketplace, will still trade.
- He must have some assurance that the information is not already or shortly to be in the hands of many other individuals; for if it is, he cannot expect to realize the full potential of his data.
- He will probably move very quickly to take his profit and get out of the market, since the longer he stays in, the more subject he will be to vagaries of the market which he can neither control nor know about in advance. Of course, the tax benefits for gains on assets held for six months influence him in the other direction, but an insider still has considerable incentive to buy and sell quickly.

Each of these phenomena reflects a recognition that the market is always full of uncertainties. A huge copper ore find may be followed closely by a collapse of world copper prices, and an important earnings increase may coincide with announcement of a tax hike. Thus even the most conservative insider can only deal in probabilities; and if he knows that he will regularly be privy to information, he will probably tend to trade only on that with the highest probability of allowing a gain.

Similarly, the longer stock is held, the greater becomes the risk that other factors will develop and counteract his existing paper profits. Again conservatism will dictate speed, not greed. Only rarely will all the necessary conditions for effective, regular insider trading be met. Great developments, measured in stock price impact, do not happen very often in any company.

And news of these occurrences is not always the exclusive property of a few insiders. Therefore really significant trading by insiders is probably not a very common occurrence.

Stimulus to Innovation

If this is all that could be said for or against insider trading, the matter would not be a very interesting one. But there is another and far more crucial facet to the issue, one which has not been noted in the existing literature. Basically, the argument is that profits from insider trading constitute the only effective compensation scheme for entrepreneurial services in large corporations.

Critical Distinction

I should begin this discussion with some explanation of what is meant by the "entrepreneurial function." The term is used here in a technical, economic sense, and the function differs in critical respects from that performed by managers:

Entrepreneur—An Innovator

Fundamentally the entrepreneur is a man who finds a new product or a new way to make or sell an old one. He may reorganize corporate administration, or he may be responsible for the merger of two companies. He may be a corporate promoter, or he may perform the job of selecting and guiding the managers. In short, he is the individual responsible for having or taking a new idea and causing it to be put into effect. A critical part of this definition is the "new idea," but there is no payoff unless the idea is put into effect successfully.

Since the value of an entrepreneur's contribution cannot be known until it has been made, there is rarely any way of appraising his services in advance. This is undoubtedly why early economists, including Adam Smith, did not see the entrepreneurial function as being distinct from the capitalist's function, for in the eighteenth century one was generally required to risk his own money to prove the value of his innovation. The return for successful innovation looks, superficially at least, like the return to the owner of capital.

Today, however, a sizable portion of economic literature, introduced principally by the late Joseph A. Schumpeter of Harvard University, has been built on the distinction between the entrepreneur and the capitalist, though it has not yet had a great impact on popular thinking.

Manager—A Technician

The management function is, in the pure sense, simply to administer a business along lines already determined. Though it may be extraordinarily complex and highly paid, the manager's job is basically that of a technician. As soon as he begins to reorganize the existing arrangement, then and only then is the executive performing an innovational or entrepreneurial activity, rather than a management function. Again the distinction between functions remains even though the same individual performs both. As Schumpeter commented, it is "just as rare for anyone always to remain an entrepreneur through the decades of his active life as it is for a businessman never to have a moment in which he is an entrepreneur, to however modest a degree."[2]

Reward for Performance

In return for performing its function, management receives its compensation, generally termed by economists the "wage." This wage is simply the market price for managerial skills. No one knowingly pays more or takes less. Similarly, the capitalist receives "interest," which, whatever the legal form might be called, is the economic return to him. It may be relatively certain, as in the case of bonds, or it may be very indefinite, as with speculative securities; but its economic nature remains the same. Although the degrees of risk may vary greatly, interest is the price that has to be paid for the use of money over time.

But in the sense that wages and interest are the market return for capital

2. Joseph Alois Schumpeter, *The Theory of Economic Development*, translated by Redvers Opie (Cambridge, Harvard University Press, 1934), p. 78.

and management, there is no such thing as a market price for entrepreneurial skills. In fact, almost by definition, it is impossible to value entrepreneurial activities *before they have paid off in some other form.* Economic theorists do, however, have a word for the entrepreneurial return; it is termed "profit," although that particular usage of the word has not received popular acceptance. But, aside from having a word for it, we have little knowledge about the particular form that this "profit" may take, or even whether it can redound to the benefit of entrepreneurs in large corporations.

Here it is important to turn once more to Schumpeter. Perhaps his greatest contribution to modern economic theory was the concept of dynamic competition. Schumpeter pointed out that where enterprise is allowed a free rein, no one can afford to stand still. His famous "perennial gale of creative destruction" is the process by which the most significant competition occurs. This is the competition created by the true entrepreneur, and it is a fierce thing.

Schumpeter thought that price competition, so loved by antitrusters, was effete indeed compared to the competitive effects of new products, new markets, and new ways of doing things. On this point he may well have been right. Price competition could probably be administered by pure managers, corporate bureaucrats, or today even by carefully programmed computers. But that kind of activity could never withstand the onslaught of the real entrepreneur.

Survival of Capitalism

For all his brilliance in developing the theory of entrepreneurship and dynamic competition, Schumpeter made a serious and well-known error concerning the American corporate system. This error occurred in his famous *Capitalism, Socialism and Democracy,* published in 1942.[3] Briefly, it was that the system of corporate capitalism simply could not survive. He believed that large corporations would become completely bureaucratized and management-oriented. He felt that innovation had been routinized, and the "romance of earlier commercial adventure" no longer characterized busi-

3. New York, Harper & Brothers.

ness leaders' activities. This routinization of innovation would first destroy the capitalist entrepreneurs as a class, and eventually capitalism would disappear for lack of an effective champion. "The true pacemakers of socialism," he said, "were not the intellectuals or agitators who preached it but the Vanderbilts, Carnegies, and Rockefellers."

It requires no argument to realize how wrong Schumpeter was in this prediction. For all their organization and bureaucratization, American corporations seem as dynamic, innovative, and entrepreneurial today as they have ever been. What, then, could explain such a gross misconception by one of the leading economic scholars of the century? The answer to this question seems to have eluded theoreticians up to now.

Closer examination of Schumpeter's arguments may explain his error. Schumpeter stated that any form of compensation for corporate executives other than salaries and bonuses was either "illegal or semi-illegal." Yet he realized that salary and bonuses were appropriate forms of compensation only for the pure management function. Entrepreneurs would require something much grander, though less certain. And since Schumpeter felt that this could not be made available to them in the large corporation, he assumed that they would disappear from the large corporate scene.

But he did not see the possibility of using insider information as an appropriate form of compensation for entrepreneurs in large corporations.

One cannot argue with Schumpeter's theory of what would happen to large corporations *if in fact* no entrepreneurs within them could receive an appropriate return. Government agencies and heavily regulated or protected industries are probably sufficient proof of the validity of this idea. On this basis the prediction for which Schumpeter has been frequently criticized could be closer to the mark than his critics have realized—that is, if misguided proposals to abolish our most effective system for rewarding entrepreneurs in large corporations (insider trading in one form or another) are adopted.

Compensation Not Enough

To provide an effective incentive, entrepreneurial compensation has to be available when the benefits are realized by the corporation, and it must vary with the value of the contribution. Since neither of these eventualities can ordinarily be predicted in advance, most existing compensation plans are inadequate for the task. Obviously, salary is inappropriate. The amount of salary has to be decided on in advance, it does not allow for distinguishing the manager who only manages from one who also innovates, and it is not flexible enough to reward particular contributions.

At first glance the bonus does seem to answer most of these objections. However, most bonuses today are formulated in advance and depend on total profits rather than individual contributions. Bonus plans are incentive devices, but they probably tend to generate managerial improvements, such as small cost-cutting, rather than radical innovations. The bonus plan, as opposed to the special bonus, will not serve the entrepreneur's purpose.

The special bonus can, of course, be used to reward great innovations, though there are legal restrictions if authorization is not established in advance. But the main drawback is that the true value of a particular contribution, in the form of higher profits, may not be known for many years. So there frequently are gross disparities in judgment between the bonus committee and the executive as to the latter's true worth. This misjudgment may become even more serious if the innovation has caused the price of the stock to rise but has not yet affected profits, though the stock price rise is precisely what the entrepreneur should be rewarded for.

In addition, the entrepreneurial type who is motivated by the possibility of "getting rich quick" probably does not like the idea of negotiating his reward after his contribution has been made. This distinction is like that between a patent system and a system of bonuses or government awards for inventions. Few will be found to argue that the latter system encourages as much invention as the former.

Stock options also add some incentive to efficiency for managers, but it is doubtful that they can serve the needs of the entrepreneur for massive reward for great innovations. The difficulty should be obvious. The number of shares to be optioned to various executives normally has to be determined in advance of any entrepreneurial innovation. If the options are granted after the innovation, they are the same as the special bonus, except that payment is made in the form of a free call on corporate stock rather than in the form of cash. Stock options undoubtedly add greatly to incentive, but they may still promise too little to entrepreneurial types with ambition, enthusiasm, and a large measure of self-confidence.

Incentives from Trading

On the other hand, free trading by insiders in a company's securities meets the objections mentioned for other compensation schemes and has special advantages of its own. Perhaps this can best be seen by comparing systems of compensation for patentable and nonpatentable innovations.

Basically the patent system is designed to allow inventors to receive an appropriate reward for successful innovations by preventing others from copying and participating in profits which we might say were not earned by them. The granting of a temporary monopoly to the patentee assures two goals: (1) it excludes the would-be interloper; (2) it provides the patentee with a substantial reward for his idea, although that reward will vary with the economic importance of the invention.

The patent system seems to work reasonably well, but only for patentable ideas. How can we guarantee a similar reward to inventors of nonpatentable ideas? In this area our legal system has been rather weak and ineffective; it has developed few really successful techniques for the protection of such ideas. Most businessmen recognize that secrecy and speed of marketing are the two principal devices for realizing substantial profits for their companies from nonpatentable innovations—secrecy to keep competitors away and speed because they cannot be kept away for long. But nothing in this scheme provides any protection or reward for the individual who has an important, nonpatentable idea which he personally is in no position to exploit.

For the man who has not founded his own business to exploit his idea—historically the traditional course for an entrepreneur—trading in the stock market on inside information provides a reward system, and is the only effective device available for the entrepreneur who is employed by a large corporation.

Insider trading allows any individual who works for a publicly traded corporation to play the entrepreneurial role, a very important advantage. Individuals can, in effect, sell their own ideas without the necessity of having large amounts of capital available. The increase in stock price, though not perfect, will provide as accurate a gauge of the value of the innovation as can be found, and it will leave little room for argument about an individual's worth.

Large corporations will be able to compete more effectively for entrepreneurial talent with closely owned companies, since they can now hold out the promise of very great rewards for the successful innovator. The image of corporate executives as gray bureaucrats can and should be erased. Large corporations can furnish as much romance, excitement, and opportunity for rapid economic and social advancement as any other avenues pursued today. But if corporations get hung up on foolish moralizing, such as characterizes most discussions of insider trading, they cannot hope to compete successfully or to survive the subtle attacks of government agencies.

If there really is an economic service or function that can be termed entrepreneurship, then we must have some way of compensating it. The cases are legion of new corporate managers bringing in fresh, imaginative, but often untested ideas. If these individuals were to be limited to the same compensation as their dull, unimaginative, and overly conservative predecessors, what incentive would they have to innovate? Their salaries, bonuses, and pensions are usually secure, and few large companies face imminent bankruptcy. Their stock options and bonus plans will give some motivation to improve things, but not to take very great personal risks. For the true entrepreneur, the possibility of great riches will elicit more risk-taking activities and enterprise than will the possibility of smaller though more certain gain.

It might also be added that this promise attracts a different type of personality as well, one with which successful American businessmen have traditionally been proud to identify—the self-made, rags-to-riches, "Horatio Alger" hero. There is still room for such characters in the large modern corporation.

Objections Not Significant

There are some objections that can be raised to insider trading as a compensation device, although on balance they are not very significant.

Windfall Benefits

Here the argument goes that individuals would benefit fortuitously from good news which they have not produced. This does not seem too serious an objection, since innovators rarely receive the full value of their contribution anyway. With any nonpatentable invention, competitors flock in fast to copy and to claim entrepreneurial profits for themselves. Similarly, both stockholders and other executives will ordinarily share in the corporate entrepreneur's gains. When we view insider trading as an appropriate *form* of compensation rather than a device for accurately valuing innovations and paying a precise number of dollars, the windfall argument does not seem strong at all.

Unearned Returns

It may often appear that individuals who have not contributed anything to the corporation in years, if ever, will be regularly privy to inside information. But appearances may be deceiving. Frequently these individuals may be participating in an information exchange (to be discussed shortly), or perhaps an obligation is being met with valuable information rather than money.

One individual seldom has sole possession of information and so is unable to control its dissemination both within and outside his company, although insiders will have strong incentive to police the dissemination of information efficiently. But this does not mean that it will be economical to secure perfect policing, and therefore some leakage is bound to occur.

Trading on Bad News

Nor should the fact that profits can be made in the market by selling short on bad news deter us from adopting this theory of compensation. If the appropriate incentives and constraints are built into the modern corporation system, they will generate a desire to create good news, not bad.[4] And

4. For a full discussion of this point, see my article "Mergers and the Market for Corporate Control," *Journal of Political Economy,* April 1965, p. 110.

if this is so, the fact that one may incidentally profit from bad news should be of no more significance for this discussion than the fact that one may profit from good news which he did not personally produce.

Stock "Manipulation"

Here the argument is that if insiders are allowed to trade freely, they will manipulate the affairs of the corporation so as to maximize their own trading profits rather than the company's earnings. There are many different forms to this argument, though critics of insider trading never clearly distinguish the different kinds of manipulation that are possible. Space does not allow detailed consideration of this matter, but some observations may be made:

- There are few incentives for manipulation of stock prices that conflict with the long-run interests of the corporation and its shareholders.
- Manipulation which takes the form only of changing the time at which disclosure is made is of no consequence to all outsider investors considered as a group.
- The grosser forms of manipulation can be dealt with quite effectively through less drastic techniques than preventing insider trading.

Regulatory Trends

The legal history of insider trading is one of constantly expanding regulation, by legislation, court decision, and SEC ruling.

Under Section 16(b) of the Securities Exchange Act of 1934, profits resulting from any combination of a purchase and a sale of equity securities by an insider within a six-month period inure to the benefit of the corporation and may be claimed by any shareholder on behalf of the corporation in a simplified legal action. Monthly reporting of any changes in the holdings of officers, directors, and 10% shareholders is also required. The section applies to any corporation with $1 million in assets and 750 shareholders, but next year the latter figure drops to 500 shareholders.

SEC Hampered

There is no doubt that 16(b) constitutes, in the words of one of its key draftsmen, a "crude rule of thumb." Perhaps its very arbitrariness and its harshness are a measure of Congress' emotional response to the disclosures made during the Pecora hearings in 1933–1934.

But the SEC has long found that Section 16(b) rather severely constrains any broadside attack on the practice of insider trading. For one thing, it requires both a purchase and a sale, whereas considerable gain may be had simply from knowledgeable timing of long-term investments. Furthermore, both transactions must occur within a period of six months; if the sale at a profit occurs six months and one day after purchase, the section is inapplicable.

Perhaps most important, Section 16(b) only reaches trading by insiders of the particular company whose securities are involved. It does nothing about indirect techniques, although these are probably endemic in American business. Thus two individuals, each of whom is regularly privy to valuable information, may swap their knowledge and trade with impunity as far as 16(b) is concerned.

In the celebrated case of *Blau* v. *Lehman*,[5] the Supreme Court of the United States even refused to extend 16(b) liability for insider trading to a partnership when one of the partners was on the board of directors of the company involved and the partnership was trading in the stock. Of course, the partner's individual share of the profits was recoverable, but, without a demonstration that the firm "deputed" the partner to sit on the board for it or that the partner reported information back to the firm for trading purposes, the partnership could not be held to be a director under the 1934 act.

Interestingly, the Court recounted the legislative history of Section 16(b), noting that Congress had explicitly refused to adopt a broader provision covering "anyone . . . to whom unlawful disclosure" was made. The court concluded: "Congress might amend 16(b) if the Commission would present to it the policy arguments it has presented to us, but we think that Congress

5. 368 U.S. 403 (1962).

is the proper agency to change an interpretation of the Act unbroken since its passage, if the change is to be made."

Indirect Techniques

Note that only the simplest form of insider trading is specifically restricted by Section 16(b) of the Securities Exchange Act of 1934 and by shareholders' suits based on that law. It would be an unimaginative business community which would allow perhaps billions of dollars in stock market profits to sift through its hands like sand because direct trading is outlawed. The stakes are too large, and the alternative techniques are too easy.

Since direct exploitation of valuable information is ruled out, the next step is to find an indirect method of exchanging this valuable but unusable information for valuable and usable information. This may be done by a simple exchange of information. Undoubtedly many social relationships, such as club memberships, golf foursomes, and luncheon groups, provide opportunities for these mutually beneficial exchanges. There will always be some uncertainty in advice gained this way; but when the source is reliable, it is as different from the run-of-the-mine tip or the average broker's advice as gold is from clay.

But simple barter is never a very efficient exchange mechanism compared to using a medium of exchange like money. The parties may disagree on the value of their respective contributions; one may develop considerable information of value, while nothing important happens in the other's company; and neither can effectively control the further dissemination of information once it has been given out. The last point is especially important, since businessmen with property of great value should not be assumed to toss it away carelessly as they might a cigar wrapper.

To make this barter system function effectively, some sort of bank or clearinghouse operation is required. Here valuable information can be "deposited," and the ensuing credit drawn on in the form of information about other companies when the depositor is in a legal and financial position to use it.

Clearly, the operator of the clearinghouse will have to be completely trustworthy, privy to fantastic amounts of very valuable information about many corporations and familiar with the roles played by the executives of these companies. The order may seem like a large one, but it is probably being filled regularly by familiar figures on the financial scene—the investment bankers. Some of the techniques used by investment banking houses in the operation of this information "bank" have long been evident but simply unidentified as such:

Boards of Directors

The first and most obvious of these techniques is the control of one or more seats on various boards of directors. This may be used either as a method of allowing an individual to "draw" on his credits or to secure information for the common fund, as was alleged in *Blau* v. *Lehman.* But, as the SEC's Special Study of Securities Markets[6] suggested, bankers and brokers making markets in shares can get all the information they need without "deputing" anyone to sit on the board.

Priority Lists

Another familiar device for operating an information bank is the preference or priority list. These lists simply designate certain individuals who are to be made privy to a specific bit of valuable information. This may be done either by disclosure of the information itself or simply by a recommendation to buy the stock. This method has the advantage of not requiring that the "information banker" also be the recipient's broker, but it has the disadvantage of causing a loss of control over further disclosures. It may also be too slow to be useful in some circumstances, though there are a number of variations on this technique which can improve its efficiency.

Discretionary Accounts

Perhaps the most efficient device, at least since the outlawing of stock pools, is the so-called "discretionary account." Here the information banker sim-

6. *Report of Special Study of Securities Markets of the S.E.C.,* House Document No. 95, 88th Congress, 1st Session, 1963.

ply agrees to manage an investment fund of a stated amount. He may thus carefully control the value drawn from the common information fund, and there is no problem of policing the information since no disclosure is made. This device has considerable flexibility and can be used with a high degree of speed and precision. Furthermore, in its more complicated forms, it can thwart all but the most extreme methods of government policing.

The simplest approach to policing is basically that adopted by the 1934 act: find out who is engaged in insider trading. Reporting, as required by the act, is a first step. Other methods for discovering inside traders are possible. In addition to checking the identity of individuals who traded in particular securities just before important disclosures (which the SEC has done), a system of computerized cross-references might disclose the identity of individuals engaged in simple bartering.

But unpalatable as this should be to anyone sensitive to the right of privacy and the dangers of such governmental snooping, such policing techniques could still probably be thwarted by sophisticated uses of preference lists and discretionary accounts. As yet, the SEC has not argued forcefully for outlawing these practices or for separating the investment banking and brokerage functions, though these ideas have been advanced.

Fraud Rule

In spite of the Supreme Court's admonition not to expand the coverage of 16(b), the SEC has continued to try to develop a stronger weapon against insider trading through administrative acts. In 1942 it adopted what is now known as the "SEC fraud rule," Rule 10b-5, which, among other things, makes it illegal to issue an untrue or misleading statement, or omit a material fact in a statement, or commit any act of fraud or deceit in connection with the purchase or sale of a security. It purports to follow from Section 10(b) of the Securities and Exchange Act of 1934, though its operative terms are far broader than those of the act. In fact, the important language is taken from Section 17 of the Securities Act of 1933, which applied only to sales of securities and was therefore useless in dealing with most insider trading.

Strangely enough, during the early development of 10b-5 as an insider trading provision, neither the SEC nor the most influential commentators saw it as very important. The general view was that the provision merely codified common law in the states, applied their doctrine in federal cases, and covered transactions in stocks listed on exchanges.

Whether this somewhat restrained view of 10b-5 was intended by the SEC or not, the courts began to use language strongly suggesting that the provision outlawed all forms of stock market trading with undisclosed information. The holdings themselves could be and generally were, however, justified on other grounds, so the broader references were actually *obiter dicta,* or incidental opinions. Regarding insider trading, they necessarily implied the power of the SEC to promulgate a rule to that effect, but no reported decision ever examined and sustained the broad proposition that the SEC has the power to outlaw all insider trading under its rule-making authority.

The SEC's rule-making powers are much broader in connection with stockbrokers than for others trading in the market. So there can be little question of the propriety of its holding in *In the Matter of Cady, Roberts & Co.,*[7] written by Chairman William L. Cary in 1961. That opinion penalized brokers who sold stock for their own and discretionary accounts after a dividend was passed but before public disclosure of the news. The decision could have turned solely on the clear violation of a rule of the New York Stock Exchange regarding disclosure of dividend actions. But at no point did the opinion limit itself to brokers as active parties in insider trading. Its very broad language suggests that 10b-5 has come of age as a potent weapon in the war against insider trading.

Other Weapons

The SEC is presently in the process of shaping and developing another technique, more frightening and potentially more damaging than anything yet done. Instead of trying to discover the identity of inside traders after the fact, the SEC and the New York and American Stock Exchanges have sought to prevent insider trading by stopping all trading in a company's shares. At the moment, this technique can only be used when knowledge or rumors

7. Securities Exchange Act Reference No. 6668 (1961).

of important developments, combined with heavy trading in the stock, inform the SEC or the Stock Exchange of potential insider profiting.

But the SEC has other ways of getting word of impending developments. The monthly 8-K reports required to be filed with the Commission could be made to serve this purpose. Most 8-K reports at present contain little of value in this connection, but the rules could easily be changed. For example, the SEC currently has a proposal under consideration to require advance notice in the 8-K report of certain merger negotiations. It has also been recommended by one writer that 8-K's cover any important event, with management liable for any omissions that are made with "no reasonable basis."

Concluding Note

The insider trading scheme for compensating entrepreneurs is not a neat, one-for-one exchange arrangement. It may sometimes appear highly arbitrary. But it is probably the best scheme we can devise for compensating the entrepreneurial function in large corporations. There is undoubtedly much that we need to learn about how this scheme actually works in practice, but we know enough now to have serious reservations about the prevailing attitude on the subject.

The SEC has reflected, as well as helped to develop, this attitude toward insider trading. There is strong reason to believe that this has been a real disservice to the American shareholder. The public's indignation with the defendants at the outset of the *Texas Gulf Sulphur* case may well have been directed toward the wrong party in the action.

Insider Trading and the Administrative Process

Recent years have seen a tremendous interest in the development of a federal law of corporations.[1] This development is to be distinguished from the popular topic of the 1930's and earlier periods of a federal corporation code or general incorporation law.[2] The new federal corporation law has been "discovered" to exist rather than to have sprung from the mind of a legal innovator. Its existence derives in large measure from a 1942 administrative promulgation of the Securities and Exchange Commission, Rule 10b-5.[3] The

Reprinted from *George Washington Law Review* 35 (March 1967): 473–511. Reproduced with permission of *George Washington Law Review.*

The author wishes to acknowledge the extremely helpful research assistance and stimulating suggestions of Mr. J. Gordon Arbuckle, LL.B., George Washington University, who

1. Fleischer, "'Federal Corporation Law': An Assessment," *Harv. L. Rev.* 78:1146 (1965); Friendly, "In Praise of Erie—and of the New Federal Common Law," *N.Y.U.L. Rev.* 39:383 (1964); Painter, "Inside Information—Growing Pains for the Development of Federal Corporation Law Under Rule 10b-5," *Colum. L. Rev.* 65:1361 (1965); see also Joseph, "Civil Liability Under Rule 10b-5—A Reply," *Nw. U.L. Rev.* 59:171 (1964); Ruder, "Civil Liability Under Rule 10b-5: Judicial Revision of Legislative Intent?" *Nw. U.L. Rev.* 57:627 (1963); Ruder, "Pitfalls in the Development of a Federal Law of Corporations by Implication Through Rule 10b-5," *Nw. U.L. Rev.* 59:185 (1964).

2. For a succinct history of these proposals, see Loss, *Securities Regulation* 1:107–11 (2d ed. 1961).

3. 17 C.F.R. § 240.10b-5 (1964), which states:

> It shall be unlawful for any person, directly or indirectly, by the use of any means or instrumentality of interstate commerce, or of any facility of any national securities exchange,

"official" discovery of a federal law of corporations dates from *McClure v. Borne Chemical Co.*,[4] a 1961 decision. *Borne Chemical* for the first time explicitly recognized the development[5] as an area of evolving substantive corporation law traditionally thought to be the exclusive province of the states.

Actually the appellation "federal law of corporations" seems too broad for what has occurred. It would be more accurate to refer to a federal law on insider trading, the almost exclusive subject of this new federal development.[6] The new law is significant not because it has created a novel federal cause of action, but because insider trading in stocks is a very important and complex matter which has not heretofore been effectively analyzed. The development started slowly, received a couple of almost coincidental boosts, and then began to take off. With the trial and initial decision in *SEC v. Texas Gulf Sulphur Co.*,[7] the development is certainly nearing some sort of pinnacle.

Along with this judicial evolution has come the concommitant academic, legal discourse on the limits of Rule 10b-5, the elements required for proof, the jurisdictional and procedural problems, and many other topics.[8] De-

---

(a) To employ any device, scheme, or artifice to defraud,

(b) To make any untrue statement of a material fact or to omit to state a material fact necessary in order to make the statements made, in the light of the circumstances under which they were made, not misleading or

(c) To engage in any act, practice, or course of business which operates or would operate as a fraud or deceit upon any person, in connection with the purchase or sale of any security.

4. 292 F.2d 824 (3d Cir.), *cert. denied,* 368 U.S. 939 (1961). The only earlier reference found to the phrase "federal corporation law" in this context is Baker & Cary, *Cases on Corporations* (3d ed. 1959), p. 564.

5. 292 F.2d at 834.

6. See Fleischer, "Federal Corporation Law." There have been attempts to include cases involving other areas of alleged fiduciary duty, but these have generally been unsuccessful. O'Neill v. Maytag, 339 F.2d 764 (2d Cir. 1964); Birnbaum v. Newport Steel Corp., 193 F.2d 461 (2d Cir.), *cert. denied,* 343 U.S. 956 (1952). *But see* Ruckle v. Roto Am. Corp., 339 F.2d 24 (2d Cir. 1964); Pettit v. American Stock Exch., 217 F. Supp. 21 (S.D.N.Y. 1963).

7. 258 F. Supp. 262 (S.D.N.Y. 1966).

8. See Painter, "Inside Information"; see generally Fleischer, "Securities Trading and Corporate Information Practices: The Implications of the Texas Gulf Sulphur Proceeding," *Va. L. Rev.* 51:1271 (1965); Sommer, "Rule 10b-5: Notes for Legislation," *W. Res. L. Rev.* 17:1029 (1966).

spite the great attention which the questions have received in case and commentary, it is astounding to note that perhaps the most basic and fundamental legal issue in the entire area has been ignored. Courts, litigants, and commentators alike have treated Rule 10b-5 precisely as they would have treated a statute adopted by Congress. The purpose of this paper is to argue that this is an indefensible approach to an administrative regulation.

Typically, insider trading[9] is presumed to be stock trading engaged in by officers, directors, and large (ten percent) shareholders. This popular definition of "insider" derives from section 16(b) of the Securities and Exchange Act of 1934,[10] which covers only these parties. Section 16(b), popularly known as the "insider's short swing profit rule," is the only provision in the act dealing explicitly with this subject. But, in reality, significant insider trading may involve many individuals not insiders under section 16(b),[11] and the SEC has long chafed under the rigid constraints Congress imposed in that section.[12]

In the famous *Texas Gulf Sulphur* litigation,[13] therefore, the SEC is asking for a general prohibition on stock market trading by certain insiders before general public disclosure of the new information. Heretofore, there has been no general prohibition on insider trading; either the case had to fit the

9. See generally Manne, *Insider Trading and the Stock Market* (1966).

10. 48 Stat. 896 (1934), as amended, 15 U.S.C. § 78p(b) (1964).

11. The simple expedient of "trading-off" information with others in a different company will be sufficient to avoid the reach of § 16(b). There are many versions of this practice. See Manne, *Insider Trading and the Stock Market,* pp. 59–75. The section may also be avoided by holding stock for six months and one day.

12. In 1941 the SEC sought to amend § 17(a) of the Securities Act of 1933, 48 Stat. 84, as amended, 15 U.S.C. § 77 (1964), to cover purchases as well as sales of securities, but was rebuffed by Congress. See Loss, *Securities Regulation* 3:1426. For the SEC's last effort to deal with insider trading through non-10b-5 means, see Blau v. Lehman, 368 U.S. 403 (1962), where the Court said: "Congress . . . might amend § 16(b) if the Commission would present to it the policy arguments it has presented to us, but we think that Congress is the proper agency to change an interpretation of the Act unbroken since its passage, if the change is to be made." *Id.,* p. 413.

13. See generally pre-trial memorandum for SEC, SEC v. Texas Gulf Sulphur Co., 258 F. Supp. 262 (S.D.N.Y. 1966). See also Kennedy & Wander, "Texas Gulf Sulphur, A Most Unusual Case," *Bus. Law.* 20:1057 (1965).

narrow confines of section 16(b), or some "special facts"[14] had to appear to make relief appropriate. In *Texas Gulf Sulphur,* however, the SEC is, in effect, asking for a general assumption that every pre-disclosure trade by almost anyone privy to valuable information is *ipso facto* fraudulent.[15]

As anyone familiar with the area is well aware, there are a great many legal questions at issue in *Texas Gulf Sulphur* and other Rule 10b-5 cases. These include questions of materiality,[16] privity,[17] degree of special relationship,[18] timeliness of disclosure,[19] liability for total silence,[20] sufficiency of disclosure,[21] the availability of a civil remedy,[22] the standing of the SEC

14. The so-called "special facts" or "special circumstances" doctrine began in Strong v. Repide, 213 U.S. 419 (1909). It was generally held to represent a middle ground between the "majority rule" of arm's length bargaining between insiders and shareholders and the "minority rule" of strict fiduciary relationship. The former in effect approved any transaction without fraud, and the latter required full disclosure of all relevant facts. See Ballantine, *Corporations,* pp. 212–16 (rev. ed. 1946) and Baker & Cary, *Cases on Corporations,* pp. 553–61. Unfortunately it is rarely made clear whether this represents a liberalized fraud rule (*e.g.,* silence substituting for affirmative misrepresentation) or a wider application of the fiduciary concept. For the view that these are really "fraud" cases, see Manne, *Insider Trading and the Stock Market,* pp. 22–23. Regardless, the "special facts" approach is the prevailing one today.

15. It is difficult to state concisely exactly what rule the SEC wants. There is some element of materiality, but it is less than Judge Bonsal required in his *Texas Gulf Sulphur* opinion. See Brief for Appellant, *Texas Gulf Sulphur,* No. 30882, 2d Cir., Dec. 7, 1966. It is also clear that anyone who in fact has the unexploited information is not necessarily covered. Cady, Roberts & Co., 40 S.E.C. 907 (1961) indicates that some "special relationship" with the corporation may be necessary. Nonetheless, civil suits have been filed against "tippees" outside the Texas Gulf Sulphur Co. who were named but not charged in the SEC's initial complaint. *Cf. Cady, Roberts, supra* at 911.

16. *Texas Gulf Sulphur,* 258 F. Supp. at 280–81.

17. Joseph v. Farnsworth Radio & Television Corp., 99 F. Supp. 101 (S.D.N.Y. 1951), *aff'd,* 198 F.2d 883 (2d Cir. 1952) (privity required); Miller v. Bargain City U.S.A. Inc., 229 F. Supp. 33 (E.D. Pa. 1964) (no privity required).

18. See note 15 *supra.*

19. *Texas Gulf Sulphur,* 258 F. Supp. at 288.

20. See List v. Fashion Park, Inc., 340 F.2d 457, 461 (2d Cir.), *cert. denied,* 282 U.S. 811 (1965). *But cf. Texas Gulf Sulphur,* 258 F. Supp. at 279, citing Brophy v. Cities Service Co., 31 Del. Ch. 241, 70 A.2d 5 (Ch. 1949).

21. There seem to be no 10b-5 cases explicitly raising this issue, but just as it has been a problem in connection with disclosure under the Securities Act of 1933, it would have to be so under Rule 10b-5. It may, however, be subsumed under the "materiality" question.

22. In spite of the extremely convincing argument by Professor Ruder, "Civil Liability,"

to represent an aggrieved shareholder,[23] a corporate right of action,[24] reliance,[25] and many others.[26] None of these is directly the subject of this paper. Rather, we are addressing the question of whether there is any justification for the courts to create a general rule against insider trading out of the phraseology of Rule 10b-5.

The Growth of the Rule: Judicial-Administrative Interaction

Administrative Rule Versus Legislative Enactment

For most people the development of a federal law on insider trading has seemed to be analogous to the development of a body of common-law cases interpreting the Sherman Act,[27] or perhaps a body of cases defining unfair labor practices under the Labor Management Relations Act.[28] But we must start with the proposition that Rule 10b-5 is a declaration of an administrative rule by a federal agency and that developments under such a rule must be justified in terms of administrative law, not simply the jurisprudence of statutory interpretation.

It is one thing for the judiciary to expand the meaning of the word "monopolize" by a case-by-case construction of the law in that area. This process

---

that no civil action should be found to lie for a violation of rule 10b-5, and in spite of Professor Loss's belief that such an action should probably belong only to sellers and not to buyers, Loss, *Securities Regulation* 3:1455, the issue seems resolved in favor of the civil action. This is supported by the implications of *J. I. Case Co. v. Borak*, 377 U.S. 426 (1964), which, using very broad language, allowed a civil action for a violation of the SEC's proxy rules. But the fact remains that Professor Ruder's arguments have not been squarely dealt with by the Supreme Court, and there are clear distinctions between the insider trading problem and proxy regulations.

23. *Texas Gulf Sulphur*, 258 F. Supp. at 278. See Kennedy & Wander, "Texas Gulf Sulphur."

24. This point seems well settled for the moment in favor of the corporate right of action. Ruckle v. Roto Am. Corp., 339 F.2d 24 (2d Cir. 1964).

25. Janigan v. Taylor, 344 F.2d 781 (1st Cir.), *cert. denied*, 382 U.S. 879 (1965); List v. Fashion Park, Inc., 340 F.2d 457 (2d Cir.), *cert. denied*, 382 U.S. 811 (1965). For interesting comments on the point that "causation" rather than "reliance" should be the touchstone, see Sommer, "Rule 10b-5," p. 1039.

26. See authorities cited note 8 *supra*.

27. 26 Stat. 209 (1890), as amended, 15 U.S.C. § 1 (1964).

28. 61 Stat. 136 (1947), as amended, 29 U.S.C. § 141–87 (1964).

is well understood and generally accepted.[29] But it is an entirely different and novel matter for the judiciary to significantly expand the meaning of an administrative ruling in a parallel fashion. The differences are considerable and critical. The administrative regulation must be adopted pursuant to a congressional enabling act, which is generally more specific than a constitutional provision like the Commerce Clause to which the Sherman Act must conform.[30] Even more important, there are, both in case law and legislation, a variety of procedural requirements for adopting and implementing an administrative rule. There are few comparable requirements for legislative adoption; for a court to suggest specific congressional procedures not constitutionally compelled would raise serious problems with the separation of powers.[31] Finally, there is the requirement of expertise, which in one way or another must find a place in administrative law making. Again, nothing of the sort applies to Congress; indeed, the feeling that Congress does not always have sufficient expertise in a given area was one of the fundamental reasons for the establishment of administrative agencies.[32]

Expansion of the Rule

The Adoption of Rule 10b-5

One day in 1942, a problem came to the attention of staff members in the Philadelphia regional office of the SEC.[33] The problem involved a stockholder who was intentionally disseminating false bad news about his company in an effort to buy its shares cheaply. The feeling in the office was that the SEC should be able to move against this individual, but they were sty-

29. Standard Oil Co. v. United States, 221 U.S. 1 (1910); see generally Letwin, *Law and Economic Policy in America* (1965); Rostow, *Planning for Freedom,* pp. 279–81 (1959).

30. See Levi, *An Introduction to Legal Reasoning,* pp. 5–6 (1949).

31. Crawford, *Statutory Construction,* pp. 199–200 (1940); Luce, *Legislative Procedure,* pp. 3–4 (1922). *But cf.* Deutch v. United States, 367 U.S. 456, 468–72 (1961).

32. Davis, *Administrative Law,* vol. 1, § 2.16 (1958).

33. This account is taken from remarks by Milton V. Freeman of the District of Columbia Bar, Conference on Codification of the Federal Securities Laws, sponsored by the Committee on Federal Regulation of Securities of the Section of Corporation, Banking and Business Law of the American Bar Association, Chicago, Ill., Nov. 19, 1966, copy on file at the *George Washington Law Review* (portions to be published in *Business Lawyer*).

mied by the fact that section 17(a) of the Securities Act of 1933 could not be used because it applied only to *sales* of securities—not purchases.[34] Section 10(b) of the Securities Exchange Act was of no avail since it only became operative under rules or regulations promulgated by the Commission; there were none in point. The next morning a member of the Philadelphia staff presented to the full Commission for its consideration what is now Rule 10b-5. The rule and a press release[35] were distributed to each member of the Commission. The sole response was by Commissioner Sumner T. Pike, who inquired rhetorically, "Well, we are against fraud, aren't we?" The rule was unanimously adopted.[36]

The following year the SEC discussed the rule in *Ward La France Truck Corp.*[37] The situation was similar to that which had initially generated Rule 10b-5, except that the purchaser was the corporation rather than the individual who controlled it. In fact, this individual went to some lengths to guarantee that his identity as the real buyer should not be disclosed to the sellers.[38] The SEC concluded:

34. Securities Act of 1933, § 17(a), 48 Stat. 84, as amended, 15 U.S.C. § 77(q) (1964). Securities Act of 1934, § 10(b), 48 Stat. 891, as amended, 15 U.S.C. § 78(j) (1964), provides:

> It shall be unlawful for any person, directly or indirectly, by the use of any means or instrumentality of interstate commerce or of the mails, or of any facility of any national securities exchange—
>
> (b) To use or employ, in connection with the *purchase or sale* of any security registered on a national securities exchange or any security not so registered, any manipulative or deceptive device or contrivance in contravention of such rules and regulations as the Commission may prescribe as necessary or appropriate in the public interest or for the protection of investors. (Emphasis added)

35.

> The Securities and Exchange Commission today announced the adoption of a rule prohibiting fraud by any person in connection with the purchase of securities. The previously existing rules against fraud in the purchase of securities applied only to broker dealers. The new rule closes a loophole in the protections against fraud administered by the Commission by prohibiting individuals or companies from buying securities if they engage in fraud in their purchase. (SEC, Securities Exchange Act of 1934 Release No. 3230, Philadelphia, May 21, 1942)

36. See note 33 *supra.*

37. 13 S.E.C. 373 (1943).

38. This incidentally seems to have been the very factor which most influenced the Court in Strong v. Repide, 213 U.S. 419, 430–33 (1909), to adopt its "special facts" doctrine.

> There was a clear necessity, to negate any unfair advantage over shareholders, for the issuer and those in control to make timely disclosure of the identity of the purchaser, of improved financial and operational condition of the issuer, and of the full terms of the transfer to Salta [the seller] of the Truck Corporation's business and of its liquidation.[39]

Nothing else even vaguely suggestive of analysis appears in the opinion; this constitutes the sum and substance of early SEC "interpretation" of Rule 10b-5. It is not surprising, therefore, that many commentators assumed that the SEC, borrowing the logic of the common-law "special facts" or "special circumstances" cases,[40] had simply promulgated a rule to include that common-law doctrine within the meaning of section 10(b)'s "deceptive device."[41] But the common-law special facts cases were far from a thorough-

39. 13 S.E.C. 373, 381 (1943).

40. Lattin, *Corporations,* pp. 274–75 (1959). See Loss, "The SEC and the Broker-Dealer," *Vand. L. Rev.* 1:516 (1948). Professor Loss, after citing Kardon v. National Gypsum, 69 F. Supp. 512 (E.D. Pa. 1946), and Speed v. Transamerica, 99 F. Supp. 808 (D. Del. 1951), stated, "I think it is worth stressing at the start that most of the doctrine that I am going to try to relate is neither new nor radical. In great measure it *very likely would have been developed by the courts* even if there had never been an SEC." Loss, *Securities Regulation,* p. 517 (2d ed. 1961). (Emphasis added.) In explaining *Ward La France,* the Commission said that "persons . . . have resorted to *fraud* in the purchase of securities from others. By virtue of Rule X-10b-5, such persons were guilty of violating the Securities Exchange Act." *SEC Ann. Rep.* 10:82 (1944). (Emphasis added.) See also Ruder, "Civil Liability," pp. 627, 665–71.

41. It might be argued that, even though the SEC stated explicitly that Rule 10b-5 was promulgated "pursuant to" § 10(b), it was not limited to that section for its authority. The difficulty with this argument is in finding any other sections of the 1934 act which could support the proposition. Given the strict reading of § 16(b) by the Supreme Court in Blau v. Lehman, 368 U.S. 403 (1962), it is not apparent how § 16(b) could be used for this purpose. The general rule-making power of § 23(a) surely could not mean more than that appearing in § 10(b), or there would have been no reason for the latter. See Fuchs, "Agency Development of Policy Through Rule-Making," *Nw. U.L. Rev.* 59:781, 796 (1965), suggesting that such broad grants as § 23(a) may be limited to interpretative regulations.

That leaves the intriguing possibility that the SEC in fact integrated the 1933 and 1934 acts, borrowing the substantive rule from § 17(a) of the 1933 act and the coverage from § 10(b) of the 1934 act. Actually, one case has said that "the 1933 and 1934 Acts must be read together as parts of a single statutory scheme, especially as the statute which enacted the 1934 Act also amended the 1933 Act." Fischmann v. Raytheon Mfg. Co., 188 F.2d 783, 786 (2d Cir. 1951). But this suggestion seems nowhere to have been followed, and, indeed, if it were generally believed, present thinking on the subject of integration and codification

going rule against insider trading.[42] No one suggested, at the time, that Rule 10b-5 had this much broader reach.[43]

---

of securities laws might be quite different. See Cohen, "'Truth in Securities' Revisited," *Harv. L. Rev.* 79:1340 (1966) & transcript of Conference, note 33 *supra.*

There are other problems with this integration notion as well. First, the cases dealing with § 17(a) of the 1933 act have never recognized the existence of a civil suit. See Loss, *Securities Regulation.* And § 17(a) provides nothing like the specific grant of rule-making power found in § 10(b). There is simply the general rule-making authority of § 19(a) of the 1933 act, which is only comparable to the power granted in § 23(a) of the 1934 act. Furthermore, what little evidence we have indicates that § 17(a) is actually rather narrowly conceived, see Ruder, "Civil Liability," pp. 655–57, and that the expansion of 10b-5's meaning has in no way been related to what § 17(a) was thought to mean. Finally it seems to be too late for the SEC to advance *this* argument. Surely something like estoppel or laches or legal decency should prevent it.

42. See Manne, *Insider Trading and the Stock Market,* pp. 21–24.

43. Some contemporaneous evidence is indicative of this view. For example, *SEC Ann. Rep.* 8:10 (1942) stated: "During the fiscal year the Commission adopted Rule X-10b-5 as an additional protection to investors. The new rule prohibits fraud by any person in connection with the purchase of securities, while the previously existing rules against fraud in the purchase of securities applied only to brokers and dealers." See also note 40 *supra.*

Oddly enough, we have some indirect Supreme Court authority for the proposition that in 1943 and 1947 there existed no general rule against insider trading. See SEC v. Chenery Corp., 318 U.S. 80 (1943). "Congress itself did not proscribe the respondents' purchases of preferred stock in Federal. Established judicial doctrines do not condemn these transactions. Nor has the Commission, acting under the rule-making powers delegated to it by § 11(e), promulgated new general standards of conduct." *Id.* at 93. The SEC's order had been made in 1941, before Rule 10b-5, which under the Public Utility Holding Company Act, § 21, 49 Stat. 834 (1935), 15 U.S.C. § 79(u)(1964), would otherwise have been applicable. But if Rule 10b-5 had been thought to be a general rule against insider trading, it is quite likely that it would have been mentioned here.

More significantly, however, when the case returned to the Court in 1947, we find the Court saying that

> the Commission might have promulgated a general rule dealing with this problem under its statutory rule-making powers. . . . But we do not mean to imply that the failure of the Commission to anticipate this problem and to promulgate a general rule withdrew all power from that agency to perform its statutory duty in this case. To hold that the Commission had no alternative in this proceeding but to approve the proposed transaction, while formulating any general rules it might desire for use in future cases of this nature, would be to stultify the administrative process. (SEC v. Chenery Corp., 332 U.S. 194, 201–02 [1947])

Clearly, the Court did not believe at the time of this opinion that at any time, prior to or after the 1941 order, the Commission had promulgated an applicable or related general rule.

Early Judicial Development

The next important event occurred in 1946, when a district court in *Kardon v. National Gypsum Co.*,[44] another typical special-facts case,[45] held that a civil action based on Rule 10b-5 could be maintained in any federal court under federal jurisdictional and venue rules. This case set the stage for the next very important substantive development, the famous *Speed v. Transamerica Corp.*[46] case, which could have been decided as a typical special-circumstances situation.[47] In *Speed*, Chief Judge Leahy said:

> The rule is clear. It is unlawful for an insider, such as a majority stockholder, to purchase the stock of minority stockholders without disclosing material facts affecting the value of the stock, known to the majority stockholder by virtue of his inside position but not known to the selling minority stockholders, which information would have affected the judgment of the sellers. The duty of disclosure stems from the necessity of preventing a corporate insider from utilizing his position to take unfair advantage of the uninformed minority stockholders. It is an attempt to provide some degree of equalization of bargaining position in order that the minority may exercise an informed judgment in any such transaction. Some courts have called this a fiduciary duty while others state it is a duty imposed by the "special circumstances." One of the primary purposes of the Securities and Exchange Act of 1934, 15 U.S.C.A. Sec. 78a et seq., was to outlaw the use of inside information by cor-

44. 69 F. Supp. 512 (E.D. Pa. 1946).

45. A small, four-man (two defendants and two plaintiffs) corporation was involved. The plaintiffs alleged a face-to-face transaction in which they expressly asked defendants if any negotiations were pending for the sale of the business. Defendants wrongfully denied such negotiations and purchased plaintiffs' shares. Incidentally, the judge expressly stated that he would sustain the complaint as stating a common law action for fraud. *Id.* at 514.

46. 99 F. Supp. 808 (D. Del. 1951), *aff'd*, 235 F.2d 369 (3d Cir. 1956).

47. Here the Axton-Fisher Tobacco Co. had a cigarette-tobacco inventory that had greatly appreciated in value during World War II, and this was common knowledge in tobacco and financial circles. It was not known, however, that the controlling shareholder had devised a liquidation plan whereby this appreciated value could be realized in spite of price controls on cigarettes. It was the controlling shareholder's failure to disclose to the plaintiff minority shareholders his intention to liquidate the corporation under this plan that a federal district court considered actionable.

> porate officers and principal stockholders for their own financial advantage to the detriment of uninformed public security holders.[48]

The court's language went beyond anything required by the holding in the case, or anything indicated in the history of Rule 10b-5, in that the very same facts in another suit were held to constitute actual fraud.[49] It was dictum to that extent, and could easily have been relegated to the attic of noble sentiments expressed by judges in passing. After this case, however, the feeling began to jell that Rule 10b-5 did in fact constitute a more generalized rule against insider trading than can be derived from the common-law special-facts approach,[50] although no judicial decision at that time or subsequently has encompassed a holding to that effect.[51]

Administrative Sweep

The most important subsequent development, however, was not a judicial decision. Rather, it was the administrative broker-dealer disciplinary adjudication, *In the Matter of Cady, Roberts & Co.*[52] Recognizing that it was a

48. 99 F. Supp. at 828–29.

49. Zahn v. Transamerica Corp., 162 F.2d 36 (3d Cir. 1947); Annot., 172 A.L.R. 495 (1948).

50. Perhaps the most influential writing for that point of view was a student comment, "The Prospects for Rule X-10b-5—An Emerging Remedy for Defrauded Investors," *Yale L.J.* 59:1120 (1950). See also Latty, "The Aggrieved Buyer or Seller or Holder of Shares in a Close Corporation Under the SEC Statutes," *Law & Contemp. Prob.* 18:505 (1953).

51. Daum & Phillips, "The Implications of Cady, Roberts," *Bus. Law.* 17:939, 942 (1962).

52. 40 S.E.C. 907 (1961). A registered representative of Cady, Roberts, J. Cheever Cowdin, was a director of the Curtiss-Wright Corporation. There had been a great rise in the price of that company's shares as a result of a considerable ballyhoo about a new engine under development. Shortly thereafter, the board of directors substantially cut the dividend of the company. During the period of rising prices, a broker and partner in Cady, Roberts, Robert M. Gintel, had been buying shares for approximately thirty discretionary accounts of firm customers, one of whom was his wife. The day before the dividend was cut, he began selling shares from those discretionary accounts. In the two days before the transactions in question, he had sold over half these holdings.

After the dividend decision by the board of directors, the meeting was recessed. Cowdin telephoned a message for Gintel that the dividend had been cut. Upon receiving this information, Gintel entered substantial sell orders for some of his discretionary accounts and sold a substantial block of shares short for some accounts.

The dividend action occurred at approximately 11:00 a.m., at which time the standard

"case of first impression and one of signal importance in our administration of the federal securities acts,"[53] Chairman William Cary stated that liability under Rule 10b-5 rests on two principal elements:

> [T]he existence of a relationship giving access, directly or indirectly, to information intended to be available only for a corporate purpose and not for the personal benefit of anyone, and second, the inherent unfairness involved where a party takes advantage of such information knowing it is unavailable to those with whom he is dealing.[54]

Presumably both these elements—not merely the latter—must appear to establish liability since Chairman Cary states further: "Our task here is to identify those persons who are in a special relationship with a company and privy to its internal affairs, and thereby suffer correlative duties in trading in its securities."[55] He also said:

> We, and the courts, have consistently held that insiders must disclose material facts which are known to them by virtue of their position but which are not known to persons with whom they deal and which, if known, would affect their investment judgment. Failure to make disclosure in these circumstances constitutes a violation of the anti-fraud provisions. If, on the other hand, disclosure prior to effecting a purchase or sale would be improper or unrealistic under the circumstances, we believe the alternative is to forego the transaction.[56]

---

authorization for transmission of this information to the New York Stock Exchange was given. For reasons never explained, but presumed to be inadvertent, the New York Stock Exchange did not receive this information for nearly one and one-half hours. The Dow Jones financial news service was not given the information for approximately forty-five minutes, again presumably through inadvertence.

Regardless of the reasons for these delays, the associates of Cady, Roberts & Company acted swiftly. Gintel's orders were executed in fifteen and eighteen minutes, respectively, after the dividend action. The stock, needless to say, plummeted on the later publication of the news. Gintel's actions were found to be a wilful violation of § 17(a) of the Securities Act of 1933, of § 10(b) of the Securities Exchange Act of 1934, and of Rule 10b-5.

53. 40 S.E.C. 907 (1961).

54. *Id.* at 912.

55. *Ibid.*

56. *Id.* at 911.

The Commission had no difficulty in finding the requisite "special relationship" between the issuer, one of its directors, and the latter's partner in Cady, Roberts, a brokerage house. The prohibition on trading was also extended, however, to those selling for discretionary accounts managed for third parties who did not themselves have a special relationship with the company.[57] In a discussion of this point, Chairman Cary makes it clear that the first duty of a registered broker-dealer under the act is to the investing public and not to beneficiaries of his discretionary accounts. This would seem to imply strongly that the case should be limited in its application to situations involving broker-dealers, but the language used certainly sounds applicable in any private civil action.[58] And even though the opinion requires a "special relationship" giving access to information, its general tone as an attack on all insider trading is unmistakable.[59]

The Commission expressly rejected the suggestion, made in a variety of ways by the respondents, that Rule 10b-5 was not intended to extend beyond the special-facts rule under state law. For instance, the special-facts rule is limited to shareholders selling to insiders and does not extend to purchases from insiders. Further, no special-facts decision ever found liability in a transaction over an exchange[60] and some "semblance of privity" always had to be shown.[61] The Commission replied that cases under the common-law special-facts rule were not relevant on these points, since purchasers as well as sellers over an exchange were intended to be protected by the act, and since privity was not required in an action by the Commission to discipline a broker.[62] Thus, the belief that the SEC still felt Rule 10b-5 to be circumscribed by the older special-facts approach was laid to final rest.

57. For a discussion of discretionary accounts see Manne, *Insider Trading and the Stock Market,* pp. 72–75.

58. Sommer, "Rule 10b-5: Notes for Legislation," *W. Res. L. Rev.* 17:1029, 1036 (1966).

59. See, *e.g.,* Daum & Phillips, "Implications of Cady, Roberts," p. 939.

60. See, *e.g.,* Goodwin v. Agassiz, 283 Mass. 358, 186 N.E. 659 (1933).

61. See *Cady, Roberts,* 40 S.E.C. at 914 & n. 27. Cary avoids any requirement for "semblance of privity" by distinguishing suits by the Commission from private civil actions. This suggests a feeling on his part that privity is a necessary element for a successful private action.

62. *Id.* at 914–15. The Commission was perhaps a bit disingenuous in this discussion. The "special facts" doctrine was not comprised of hard and fast technical rules. Each of

Cady, Roberts gave rise to perhaps the only criticism of the manner in which this new area of law has been developing.[63] Professor Cary subsequently stated:

> There is one criticism which was expressed to me by Professor Kenneth C. Davis (of Davis on Administrative Law) about *Cady, Roberts* that I want to bring to your attention, namely, that it was a case of rule-making by a Federal Commission without the benefit of public comment and without the possibility of judicial review (the minimal penalty having been accepted). This criticism troubled me then but it seems to me that it has been remedied now. The SEC has correctly taken the next step—to bring this issue before the courts, and to insure full due process. There has been, I believe, enough warning in the financial community; the implications of *Cady, Roberts,* I know, were being considered by counsel here.
>
> * * * * *
>
> *Texas Gulf Sulphur,* it seems to me simply dramatized the issue and, I confess, takes several more steps. . . .[64]

---

the elements developed for fairly apparent reasons, but if similar reasons appeared in a different context, the doctrine could certainly encompass them. Even *Goodwin v. Agassiz* is frequently cited because in dictum it acknowledged that in appropriate circumstances the rule could be applied to exchange transactions. And it would have been very simple to extend the rule's protection to buyers as well as sellers if other circumstances indicated a need for protection. The fact that the Commission went so far out of its way to deny the special-facts approach suggests strongly that they were aware that they were engaging in rule-making rather than adjudication. See text *infra.*

63. *Cady, Roberts,* to be sure, only represents a way station on the road to the far more disturbing problems of administrative law raised by *Texas Gulf Sulphur.* But it is instructive to note Professor Davis's criticism of what occurred in *Cady, Roberts.* In answer to a defense of administrative adjudications, Cohen & Rabin, "Broker-Dealer Selling Practice Standards: The Importance of Administrative Adjudication in Their Development," *Law & Contemp. Prob.* 29:691 (1964), Davis contended that rule-making is generally superior to adjudication. Davis, *Administrative Law,* vol. 1 (Supp. 1965 § 6.13, pp. 146–57).

Davis also stated, in a reference to the NLRB applicable to the SEC as well: "When the rule-making element in an adjudication becomes the dominant element, . . . the Board may be in a very deep sense . . . violating both § 3 and § 4 of the Administrative Procedure Act, because the result then involves procedural injustice." *Id.,* p. 149.

64. "Symposium, Insider Trading in Stocks," *Bus. Law.* 21:1009, 1011 (1966). In his just-published book, *Politics and the Regulatory Agencies* (1967), Professor Cary elaborates his disagreement with the strong anti-adjudication position of Professor Davis, and further

It is quite possible that this cure entails far more legal difficulties than did the evil at which Professor Cary aimed.

The Texas Gulf Sulphur Case

SEC v. Texas Gulf Sulphur marks the culmination of the judicial-administrative drift toward a thorough-going rule against insider trading. At the time of this writing a federal district court has written a somewhat mixed opinion,[65] and appeals have been taken both by the SEC and the two defendants found guilty of violating Rule 10b-5. Judge Bonsal seemed to agree with the Commission's formulation of the meaning of Rule 10b-5 to some extent, but he added important qualifications. In stating the fundamental basis on which the case is to be decided, he quoted from *Cady, Roberts* to explain the obligation to disclose material information.[66]

At numerous points substantive contentions are answered by reference to *Cady, Roberts.* Overwhelming reliance is placed on that opinion for settling questions of law. Indeed, Judge Bonsal found very little basis for distinguishing *Cady, Roberts* from *Texas Gulf Sulphur,* although in an important caveat he did conclude that an absolute rule against all insider trading should not yet be pronounced:

---

explains *Cady, Roberts.* He may also have made the legal justification of *Cady, Roberts* and *Texas Gulf Sulphur* more difficult than it was already. After indicating his agreement with Manuel Cohen's defense of adjudication in the anti-fraud area (paradoxically for the reason of "flexibility" Davis uses to defend rule-making), Cary states that "that case, stated broadly, concerned the duties of all persons possessing nonpublic information as a result of a special relationship with an issue of securities, but specifically dealt with the duties of a broker-dealer." *Id.*, pp. 82–83. Clearly, Cary admits that *Cady, Roberts* made a significant *new rule.* He does not come to grips with the question of when the agencies should be required to use rule-making rather than adjudication. See text *infra.*

65. The court seems to have granted the basic legal argument the SEC wanted to have answered, that is, that Rule 10b-5 did stand for a general prohibition on insider trading. The court found, however, that prior to April 9, 1964, no information deemed "material" had been developed. *Id.* at 284. The Commission has stated in its appeal brief that "the lax application by the trial court of the requirement of disclosure under Rule 10b-5, if upheld by this court, would seriously restrict the efficacy of that rule." Brief of the Appellant, p. 24, *Texas Gulf Sulphur,* No. 30882, 2d Cir., Dec. 7, 1966.

66. *Cady, Roberts,* 40 S.E.C. at 912.

> But even were the Court prepared to accept the proposition that all insider trading is unfair, a proposition of doubtful validity at best, it would be deterred by the admonition of Judge Learned Hand that it is not "desirable for a lower court to embrace the exhilarating opportunity of anticipating a doctrine which may be in the womb of time, but whose birth is distant. . . ."[67]

His limitation was exclusively in terms of a "materiality" test, however, certainly a very elastic and flexible barrier to a general prohibition on all insider trading.[68]

Judge Bonsal is probably quite correct when he stated that section 10(b) and Rule 10b-5 "go at least as far as the federal common law rule." He cited the case which originated the special-facts doctrine, *Strong v. Repide,*[69] but then confusingly added:[70] "Applying this 'special facts' doctrine to section 10(b) and Rule 10b-5, trading by an insider on the basis of material undisclosed information constitutes a deceptive practice in violation of the statute and rule."[71] No attempt whatever is made to distinguish either a special-facts situation or *Cady, Roberts* from *Texas Gulf Sulphur;* but there is no explanation why they should be treated identically. Moreover, we are not told how the special-facts doctrine is to be "applied to" section 10(b) and

67. *Texas Gulf Sulphur,* 258 F. Supp. at 278.

68. *Cf.* Brief for Appellant, *Texas Gulf Sulphur.*

69. 213 U.S. 419 (1909).

70. *Texas Gulf Sulphur,* 258 F. Supp. at 278.

71. To support this contention the court cites Loss, *Securities Regulation,* pp. 1445–73 (2d ed. 1961). But this heaps ambiguity upon ambiguity. Is Judge Bonsal making 10b-5 exactly commensurate with the common-law rule? The actual holdings of the case could certainly be interpreted that way. But Loss refers to Rule 10b-5 as hastening the process of developing a "trusteeship" notion he finds in the common law. *Id.,* p. 1448. But, as we have seen, every common-law case involved some "special facts" in addition to the mere practice of insider trading, and transactions over an exchange have always been rightfully distinguished. See Manne, *Insider Trading and the Stock Market,* pp. 21–24 (1966). *Cady, Roberts,* of course, explicitly stated that 10b-5 was *not* bound by the elements of common-law special-facts cases, 40 S.E.C. at 913–15. But we cannot have it both ways. Either the courts must now adopt the dictum of *Cady, Roberts* as the law, or they must hold Rule 10b-5 to its probably intended reach, a "special facts" rule which also covers transactions over an exchange. The latter cases would probably require intentional misstatements or some actually manipulative devices.

Rule 10b-5. The court's citation of a 1903 Georgia case[72] adopting the so-called minority or strict fiduciary duty approach[73] is perhaps even more questionable, since there was never any suggestion in the pre-*Erie* days that any federal court had ever adopted this rule. Indeed, the special-facts rule was originally widely known as the "federal rule" to distinguish it from the two more extreme positions of the states.[74]

But most unsettling is the court's seeming reliance on *SEC v. Capital Gains Research Bureau, Inc.*,[75] which dealt with the practice of "scalping" by investment advisers and was prosecuted by the SEC under section 206 of the Investment Advisers Act of 1940,[76] identical in its wording to Rule 10b-5. The Supreme Court held that the words implied a strict application of fiduciary duty notions to investment advisers.[77] Judge Bonsal said, "Since there is a direct parallel between the language of Rule 10b-5(3) and Section 206 of the Investment Advisers Act of 1940, both in wording and in intent, the use of 'fraud' in Rule 10b-5(3) cannot be interpreted in its narrow common law sense."[78]

In *Capital Gains,* however, the Supreme Court was construing an *act of Congress—not a rule of the Commission.* Had this distinction been emphasized to the court in *Texas Gulf Sulphur,*[79] it is difficult to see how it could

72. Oliver v. Oliver, 118 Ga. 362, 45 S.E. 232 (1903). Judge Bonsal also cites Brophy v. Cities Service Co., 31 Del. Ch. 241, 70 A.2d 5 (Ch. 1949), perhaps the most academically overrated case on record. See Manne, *Insider Trading and the Stock Market,* pp. 24–26, for an explanation of this case. This is actually the first time *Brophy* has ever been judicially cited on the merits. A close reading might make it the last.

73. See Ballantine, *Corporations,* p. 213. Ballantine indicates that only Georgia, Iowa, Kansas, and Nebraska had adopted this rule.

74. Ballantine, *Corporations,* pp. 213–16.

75. 375 U.S. 180 (1963).

76. 54 Stat. 847, 15 U.S.C. § 80b-6 (1964).

77. See Manne, *Insider Trading and the Stock Market,* pp. 50–54.

78. *Texas Gulf Sulphur,* 258 F. Supp. at 278.

79. This same confusion of the legislative provision of the Investment Advisers Act with an identically worded *rule* promulgated under a differently worded section of the Securities Exchange Act of 1934, occurs in the Post-Trial Memorandum for SEC, *Texas Gulf Sulphur,* 258 F. Supp. 262, pp. 35, 37–38. Even the defendants' brief implies the same confusion. Brief for Appellants, *Texas Gulf Sulphur,* p. 13, No. 308882, 2d Cir. Their argument is that SEC v. Capital Gains Research Bureau, Inc., 375 U.S. 180 (1963), involved a "quite different statute," thus suggesting statutory status for Rule 10b-5, while denying

have assumed that each is deserving of identical treatment by a court. Clearly, there is no problem of administrative authority in *Capital Gains* and the court there could feel free to engage in "creative interpretation"[80] of congressional general phraseology. But Congress did not adopt Rule 10b-5 and there are certain conditions which must be met before a court can deal with an agency regulation as if it were expressly authorized by Congress.

The General Requirements of Administrative Law

There are several generally accepted methods by which administrative processes may lead to a judicially enforceable final result. An agency may simply adopt the desired rule.[81] In its clearest form, this method raises only two common legal issues: whether or not the rule is consistent with and authorized by the underlying statutory provision[82] and whether or not the agency complied with the judicial and statutory procedures required for effectuating its rule.[83]

This process of rule-making to reach a particular result must be distin-

---

that the same words have to be given the same meaning in each place. There is some suggestion of this confusion in Justice Goldberg's Supreme Court opinion, since he cites *Speed v. Transamerica* and other 10b-5 cases in a related context. *Id.* at 198. But no one has suggested, or could suggest, that the Supreme Court in this fashion was making a finding of the validity of Rule 10b-5 as the SEC wants it applied.

80. Davis, *Administrative Law,* vol. 1, § 5.09, p. 349.

81. See Davis, *Administrative Law,* vol. 1, § 5.01, p. 349. The definition in § 2(c) of the Administrative Procedure Act of 1946, 60 Stat. 237, 5 U.S.C. § 1001–11 (1964), is instructive:

> "Rule" means the whole or any part of any agency statement of general or particular applicability and future effect designed to implement, interpret, or prescribe law or policy or to describe the organization, procedure, or practice requirements of any agency and includes the approval or prescription for the future of rates, wages, corporate or financial structures or reorganizations thereof, prices, facilities, appliances, services or allowances therefor or of valuations, costs, or accounting, or practices bearing upon any of the foregoing. "Rule making" means agency process for the formulation, amendment, or repeal of a rule.

82. See, *e.g.,* Stark v. Wickard, 321 U.S. 288 (1944).

83. See generally Davis, *Administrative Law,* vol. 1, §§ 5.01–.11. Section 4 of the APA is helpful for setting out, as Professor Davis says, "minimum standards for party participation." *Id.* § 6.01, p. 360.

guished from the process of interpretation of an existing rule or statute.[84] The principal legal question, if it is clear that interpretation of an existing rule and not the promulgation of a new rule is involved, is whether the interpretation is in fact consistent with the rule allegedly being interpreted.[85] With certain limitations, there are no specific procedural requirements for

84. Davis, *Administrative Law,* vol. 1, § 5.05. There are other kinds of interpretative rules than those interpreting a legislative rule. *Id.,* p. 304. But in the present context the "interpretation" we are primarily concerned with is that of Rule 10b-5. Section 10(b) does not authorize the Commission to promulgate rules "interpreting" the statute, the violation of which may be the basis for Commission action under § 21(e) of the act. Only legislative rules may furnish the basis for an injunction such as the SEC is seeking in the *Texas Gulf Sulphur* case. Section 10(b) is not self-executing, though the grant of legislative power is a broad one. See Hooper v. Mountain States Securities Corp., 282 F.2d 195, 201 (5th Cir. 1960), *cert. denied,* 365 U.S. 814 (1961).

85. Unfortunately, Professor Davis's principal discussion is of little help in the present context as it is limited almost entirely to interpretations of statutory provisions and that is at most only incidentally involved in the *Texas Gulf Sulphur* administrative law problem. See also Lee, "Legislative and Interpretative Regulations," *Geo. L.J.* 29:1 (1940). In Davis, *Administrative Law,* vol. 1, § 5.04 (Supp. 1965, p. 122), however, we are treated to a helpful discussion of regulation interpretation in Garelick Mfg. Co. v. Dillon, 313 F.2d 899 (D.C. Cir. 1963):

> A manufacturer of boating accessories, including plastic identification numerals and letters, sought a declaratory judgment against the Secretary of the Treasury that a regulation was invalid. The statute required numbers to be attached to boats "as may be prescribed by the Secretary." A 1958 regulation, issued after notice and hearing, required "block characters." A 1961 regulation, issued without party participation, interpreted block characters to mean that the numerals must be vertical and not slanted. The company had on hand a large supply of slanted numerals. The court held that the 1961 regulation was "interpretive" and therefore exempt from the procedural requirements of § 4 of the Administrative Procedure Act. It upheld the regulation because it was neither arbitrary nor capricious; the 1958 regulation was legislative, the test of its validity was whether it was arbitrary or capricious. But since the 1961 regulation was interpretative, the court was free to make its own interpretation of the 1958 regulation which it interpreted. The court's statement that the regulation was not arbitrary or capricious can be interpreted to mean that the court made a discretionary choice not to substitute judgment. (*Ibid.*)

He could surely have added that the 1961 regulation not only *purported* to interpret the earlier one, it did not logically involve an extension of the 1958 regulation. It also appears that only one firm was seriously affected by the regulation. Nothing of the sort can be said about the SEC's converting Rule 10b-5 into a general prohibition of all insider trading. See also Gibson Wine Co. v. Snyder, 194 F.2d 329 (D.C. Cir. 1952).

an agency's interpreting[86] its own rules and the courts will defer in large measure to the agency's conclusion.[87] A most troublesome question, however, is whether a specific result involves simple interpretation of a rule or an extension or amendment of the rule. If a new finding constitutes an extension, in effect it is a new rule, and consequently all procedural and substantive requirements for rule-making must be complied with for the extension to be sustained.[88]

There is still another dimension to the problem—the fundamental distinction between rule-making (here in the sense of a process, not a result) and adjudication. A new rule may require particular procedures,[89] as will the extension of an old rule. But interpretation is always possible whether by the legislative rule-making process or in an adjudicatory proceeding.[90]

86. See Davis, *Administrative Law,* vol. 1, §§ 5.01–.03. Section 4(a) of the APA, 5 U.S.C.A. § 554(b) (Special pamph. 1966) expressly exempts "interpretative rules" from its requirements, but it does not define the term.

87. *E.g.,* Bowles v. Seminole Rock & Sand Co., 325 U.S. 410 (1945). See Davis, *Administrative Law,* vol. 1, § 5.05, p. 322. It is nonetheless clear that when an interpretation, as opposed to a rule, is involved the courts are free to review it for legal validity. See *id.* at § 5.03 and cases cited.

88. Newman, "How Courts Interpret Regulations," *Calif. L. Rev.* 35:509 (1947). Especially relevant are Professor Newman's following remarks:

> Deliberative rulings approved by top officials are sometimes phrased as interpretations in order to avoid amendment procedures. These procedures are usually planned to insure public participation in rule-making, or to guarantee administrative review. Since an interpretation issued without regard to their requirements has not been exposed to the kind of participation or review deemed advisable for amendments, it should not be given amendatory effect. (*Id.*, p. 533)

89. The rules are rarely hard and fast, but in general it is safe to say that the courts are highly sensitive to the policies underlying the procedural requirements and apply the rules most strictly when it seems consonant with those policies. Davis, *Administrative Law,* vol. 1, §§ 6.01–7.20.

90. SEC v. Chenery Corp., 332 U.S. 194 (1947). Davis discusses Yellow Transit Freight Lines v. United States, 221 F. Supp. 465 (N.D. Tex. 1963) as follows:

> If the rule was a legislative rule, as it probably was, then the Commission had no authority to violate it in an adjudication, because in legal contemplation a legislative rule is as binding on the Commission as a statute. But the Commission did have the authority to interpret the regulation in the adjudication. Interpretations which make textual words mean the opposite of what they say are not uncommon in our legal system, even though uneasiness about such interpretations may be rather common.

But it is not generally believed today that a new legislative rule which is both significant and generally applicable, can or should be promulgated through a single adjudication.[91] Indeed, this is precisely the basis for Professor Davis's objection to *Cady, Roberts.*[92]

This is not precisely the fundamental problem raised by the development of a federal rule barring all insider trading, however, since the SEC has not explicitly claimed that *Cady, Roberts* constitutes such a rule.[93] It appears that a fourth method for reaching a particular substantive result is developing: the agency adopts a legislative rule intended for one purpose and it then

---

> But was the Commission interpreting its rule or was it amending the rule? The Commission did not say. Yet the procedure it was following was inconsistent with amending; the presumption of regularity (see 2 Davis *op. cit supra* note 83, § 11.06) can be invoked for saying that the Commission was neither amending nor violating; therefore, it was interpreting.
>
> The reviewing court was free to hold that the Commission had misinterpreted its rule, for the proper interpretation of the rule was a question of law. Indeed, the court was free to substitute judgment as to the meaning of the legislative rule, just as it could substitute judgment as to the meaning of a statute. But none of the three judges considered the question whether the interpretation was a permissible one.
>
> Altogether, the case brings out some unsatisfactory features of our conceptualism about legislative rules, interpretive rules, law making through adjudication, and law making through what is supposed to be interpretation. (Davis, *Administrative Law,* vol. 1, § 5.01 [Supp. 1965, pp. 114–15])

91. Davis, *Administrative Law,* vol. 1, § 6.13 (Supp. 1965); Fuchs, "Agency Development of Policy Through Rule-Making," *Nw. U.L. Rev.* 59:781 (1965). See SEC v. Chenery Corp., 332 U.S. 194, 202 (1947).

92. Davis, *Administrative Law,* vol. 1, § 6.13 (Supp. 1965).

93. *Cf.* Deluxe Metal Furniture Co., 121 N.L.R.B. 995 (1958); General Cable Corp., 139 N.L.R.B. 1123 (1962). For comments on those two cases, see Davis, *Administrative Law,* vol. 1 (Supp. 1965, § 6.13, pp. 148–49):

> The Board in these two cases was doing something more than adjudicating particular cases. Although the line between adjudication and rule-making is hard to locate, the Board was more concerned with the general rules than it was with the particular cases before it, and the reasons for saying that the Board was engaging in rule-making are strong. Those reasons are not merely the conceptual ones having to do with applicability of a legal concept as defined, but those reasons have to do with essential fairness. Even though thousands of parties were affected, the Board published no notice in the Federal Register. It did not allow comments on proposed rules. And it did not publish the final sets of rules in the Federal Register. Yet all of these steps were procedurally desirable.

asks *the courts* to extend that rule to cover situations not considered at the time of promulgation or in new rule-making proceedings subsequent to the original promulgation. In *Texas Gulf Sulphur* the SEC contends that Rule 10b-5 actually can be made to prohibit all insider trading, even though the Commission, the duly authorized expert body, has never exercised its expertise or discretion in the manner required for the promulgation of a rule to that effect.

At this point it is necessary to analyze each of the methods by which the SEC might establish a general prohibition on insider trading. We will then examine more closely the impact of the legislative-adjudicative dichotomy and the new mode of law creation implicit in the *Texas Gulf Sulphur* complaint.

Legislative Rule-Making

Pre-APA Standards

It is probably too late seriously to question whether the procedures involved in the adoption of Rule 10b-5 were sufficient even under the relatively liberal standards dictated by judicial tests prior to the Administrative Procedure Act (APA).[94] There is something important to be learned, however.

It is sometimes assumed that no formalities whatever were required for the promulgation of an administrative rule prior to 1946. But the fact that the courts did not formulate specific procedural rules of general application before 1946 does not mean they would accept any agency method of rule-making. As one authority familiar with the pre-APA approach has put it:

> The courts have found it expedient to exercise their control over the commissions by keeping rather flexible and even vague the principles which they apply in cases involving the commissions. Instead of hard and fast precepts the courts seem to judge each case on its individual merits; if they gain an impression of good faith and scrupulous adherence to procedural rules they

94. Section 12 of the APA, 5 U.S.C.A. § 559 (Special pamph. 1966), states that "no procedural requirement shall be mandatory as to any agency proceeding initiated prior to the effective date of such requirement."

maintain an attitude of aloofness confining their review to strictly constitutional or statutory questions.[95]

The Validity of 10b-5 as a Special-Facts Rule

The history of the adoption of Rule 10b-5 leads to the fascinating question—if there were any standards, even flexible and fairly liberal ones, by which arbitrarily adopted rules could be successfully attacked, why did Rule 10b-5 never come under judicial scrutiny? One strong possibility is that this question did not arise because no one was seriously bothered by the rule. The early cases or matters, such as *Kardon*, were sufficiently serious violations under common-law standards that an argument raising the invalidity of Rule 10b-5 as a rule against insider trading might have been strategically unwise. Thus it appears that the observers of Rule 10b-5 in its early years did not view it as going much beyond the substantive tests for the quasi-fraud condemned in common-law special-facts cases.

Perhaps more significant, however, is the view that Rule 10b-5 was not attacked because there really was nothing wrong with it—at least not as it was understood in 1942. An objection based on the case law before the APA would require a showing of either procedural unfairness or a failure to exercise expertise in the adoption of the rule.[96] Unfairness is not even hinted at in Rule 10b-5's history, so the question is primarily whether or not expertise was appropriately exercised. If a fairly circumscribed meaning is attributed to the rule, then it seems clear that there would be no problem of expertise. The rule can be taken as intended to serve as a new procedural or enforcement device by which the Commission might deal more effectively with a familiar substantive problem; that is, the SEC could thereby base actions against certain stock buyers or sellers on familiar common-law principles. No showing of expertise about the substance of the rule would

95. Forman, "The Role of the Courts in Effecting Administrative Responsibility," *Temp. L. Rev.* 22:300, 306–07 (1949). For a review of case law establishing standards of procedural fairness prior to the APA, see Vanderbilt, "Administrative Law," *Ann. Survey Am. L.* 1943:101 (1945) & *Ann. Survey Am. L.* 1946:187, 206 (1947).

96. Republic Aviation Corp. v. NLRB, 324 U.S. 793, 800 (1945). See Fuchs, "Fairness and Effectiveness in Administrative Agency Organization and Procedures," *Ind. L.J.* 36:11 (1960).

be required. Indeed, only minimal Commission consideration of such a proposal would be indicated for such a charge, since the expertise on how to proceed under or how to enforce familiar rules can be assumed in anything the Commission does. A rule allowing the agency to develop a new enforcement technique does not require the same kind of showing of expertise that would be required for a significant change in the substantive law.[97] The agency's power to adopt such a procedural rule by informal means seems quite clear.[98] It is a very different matter, however, to make a significant new law for an important and highly complex area like insider trading. If this had really been intended and announced in 1942, there is little doubt that Rule 10b-5 would have quickly come under close judicial scrutiny.

As the cases began to build up, especially in *Speed,* where the broadening of 10b-5 seemed so completely gratuitous, it is quite possible that lawyers simply overlooked the problem of the origins of the rule.[99] Indeed, only one case, a criminal case involving a broker-dealer over whom the SEC has far-reaching powers, even discusses the legislative authority of Rule 10b-5.[100] After the APA's promulgation, fair procedures became the norm in administrative developments and undoubtedly many attorneys simply lost interest in what could only be an occasional problem arising for rules adopted prior to 1946. For some reason, nevertheless, the question has simply not yet been

97. Davis, *Administrative Law,* vol. 1, § 5.03, pp. 299–300.

98. *Ibid.*

99. Both Fischmann v. Raytheon Mfg. Co., 188 F.2d 783, 786 (2d Cir. 1951) and Speed v. Transamerica Corp., 99 F. Supp. 808, 831–32 (D. Del. 1951), assume without discussion that the rule was validly promulgated.

100. United States v. Shindler, 173 F. Supp. 393 (S.D.N.Y. 1959). The discussion is entirely about the defendant's somewhat peculiar argument that 10b-5 is invalid because it extends § 17(a) of the 1933 act to purchases as well as sales. The court replied:

> The Rule clearly implements § 10(b) in accordance with the design of that section, and that is the primary issue. Since the Rule in no way impinges upon or is in conflict with § 17(a) it does not matter that it incidentally may have the effect of extending that section, so long as it is a valid exercise of the quasi-legislative function of the Commission within the scope of the authority delegated to it by § 10(b). (*Id.* at 394–95, citing Joseph v. Farnsworth Radio and Television Corp., 198 F.2d 883 [2d Cir. 1952] and Fischmann v. Raytheon Mfg. Co., 188 F.2d 783, 786 [2d Cir. 1951])

dealt with in a relevant case.[101] In summary, the facts seem to be damning from the SEC's point of view. A few minutes of juggling statutory provisions and unanimous adoption by the full Commission within less than twenty-four hours would not seem to meet those standards of exercise of discretion and expertise demanded by pre-APA cases for an important substantive change. The notions of real fraud and the quasi-fraud of the special facts cases were well understood long before the SEC came into existence; Rule 10b-5, which has come to be known as the SEC fraud rule,[102] was a significant new departure. It should have had careful and rigorous analysis, investigation, and discussion by expert individuals capable of recognizing the economic and financial ramifications of a broadly-based fiduciary concept. Such treatment is nowhere apparent in the history of Rule 10b-5.[103]

Interpretation

The second method for reaching a particular desired result in administrative law is that of "interpretation." This word suggests two possibilities: interpretation of the statute (section 10(b)) and interpretation of the rule (10b-5). Clearly, if the *statute* cannot be interpreted to allow the prohibition of all insider trading, then the rule promulgated thereunder cannot be so interpreted.

The Scope of Section 10(b)

The argument that a general rule against insider trading is implicit in section 10(b) seems weak at best. Aside from the fact that nothing purporting to be an interpretation of the section by the Commission has appeared,[104] the

101. At this late stage, the courts would probably not be inclined to review the procedures giving rise to Rule 10b-5. That is not the objection raised by this paper, however, since the farthest back we can go to find a "rule" against all insider trading is *Cady, Roberts* in 1961.

102. Loss, *Securities Regulation* 3:1474–1481 (2d ed. 1961).

103. Manne, *Insider Trading and the Stock Market,* pp. 10–15 (1966).

104. *Cady, Roberts* and *Texas Gulf Sulphur* are both alleged by the SEC to be actions brought under § 10(b), among others. *Cady, Roberts* contains no reference to the words

substantive difficulties are tremendous. In the first place, section 10(b) refers to "any manipulative or deceptive device or contrivance." None of these words is expressly defined in the act, but the background and legislative history make it fairly evident that Congress never intended these words to cover all insider trading.[105] Not to belabor the obvious, there *is* section 16(b), dealing explicitly with insider trading; and there is no suggestion anywhere in the legislative history of the 1934 act that Congress intended any other provision to deal with the subject.[106] Additionally, there is the crucial statement of the Supreme Court in *Blau v. Lehman*,[107] in which the Commission had argued for an expansion of statutory rules against insider trading by interpretation: "Congress . . . might amend Section 16(b) if the Commission would present to it the policy arguments it has presented to us, but we think that Congress is the proper agency to change an interpretation of the Act unbroken since its passage, if the change is to be made."[108] The court further noted that Congress had considered and rejected draft provisions extending the section's liability to anyone, statutory insider or not, "to whom such unlawful disclosure was made."[109]

What is now section 10(b) appeared, in an earlier draft of the bill, as section 9(c).[110] Reference in Committee hearings to this provision[111] clearly

---

of 10(b), although the district court opinion in *Texas Gulf Sulphur* does, but only to show that it has a different reach (*e.g.*, buyers as well as sellers) than § 16(b). 258 F. Supp. at 278. There is no discussion of the meaning of the words "manipulative or deceptive device or contrivance" from § 10(b), only a reference to the words "course of business" and "fraud or deceit . . . in connection with the purchase or sale of any security" from Rule 10b-5. *Ibid.*

105. The best discussion of the legislative history of § 10(b) will be found in Ruder, "Civil Liability Under Rule 10b-5: Judicial Revision of Legislative Intent?" *Nw. U.L. Rev.* 57:627, 654 (1962).

106. *Id.*, pp. 652–54.

107. 368 U.S. 403 (1962).

108. *Id.* at 413. This is not to say, however, that this is necessarily controlling for purposes of determining the reach of the SEC's rule-making authority under § 10(b). The latter section, unlike 16(b), does contain a liberal grant of rule-making power, and this may be sufficient to distinguish *Blau v. Lehman.*

109. *Id.* at 412.

110. S. 2693; H.R. 7852, 73d Cong., 2d Sess. (1934).

111. *Hearings on Stock Exchange Regulations Before the House Committee on Interstate and Foreign Commerce*, 73d Cong. 2d Sess. 115 (testimony of Thomas C. Corcoran) (1934).

shows that it was designed as a catch-all to insure that no actual manipulation or fraud not specifically prohibited by the express provisions of section 9 would later be invented.[112] Consequently, it must be taken as an *eiusdem generis* provision. At no point was it argued that the shift of this provision to section 10(b) was meant to make a substantive change in its meaning. Interpretation should thus be limited to finding forms of manipulation and deception, other than those specifically described in section 9, which could be said to have either the same elements or the same consequences as those listed. It is difficult to imagine how *all* insider trading, including that in no way related to generating an artificial price, could possibly be comprehended within the term "manipulation."[113] Even if insider trading could be called a "device or contrivance," it can scarcely be termed "deceptive" to a seller already in the market who would not have received the information any sooner if there were a flat prohibition against insider trading.[114]

Congress quite clearly assumed that insider trading was distinguishable from the general problem of manipulation and fraud,[115] although insider trading might sometimes constitute the form by which manipulation or deception occurs.[116] Thus, a rule which declared illegal insider trading of the sort involved in common-law special-facts cases, as occurred in *Ward La France* and *Kardon,* might clearly be a valid interpretation of section 10(b). Indeed, there is considerable authority predating *Cady, Roberts* to

112. Loss, *Securities Regulation* 3:1424; Ruder, "Civil Liability," p. 658.

113. See the discussion of the various types of manipulation in Manne, *Insider Trading and the Stock Market,* pp. 148–53.

114. *Id.,* pp. 93–110.

115. See Ruder, "Civil Liability," p. 657, and sources cited therein; Smolowe v. Delendo Corp., 136 F.2d 231 (2d Cir. 1943).

116. Clearly, an individual intentionally disseminating false information about a company can only capitalize on the effect of his misstatement by buying or selling shares or options. Thus he would be engaged in insider trading and in manipulation. It would be within the congressional grant of power to the SEC to deal with this form of manipulation. It should be noticed, however, that this would not carry the rule beyond the common-law special-facts rule except for its application to transactions over an exchange. This precise form of manipulation is proscribed by § 9(a)(4) and is very likely the kind of manipulation Congress had in mind when it adopted an *eiusdem generis* provision relating to other forms of manipulation.

indicate that this is what 10b-5 was intended to do.[117] It should be noted that there is no suggestion in this interpretation that section 10(b) was in any way concerned with the general subject of fiduciary duties[118] or even with the general philosophy of disclosure.

The Scope of Rule 10b-5 as Adopted Under Section 10(b)

Even assuming that section 10(b) could be interpreted by the Commission to comprehend all insider trading, two problems still remain. The section can be implemented only through rules and regulations prescribed by the Commission. Thus, courts are not free, as might otherwise be the case, simply to interpret the section to determine its substantive reach. They may only interpret rules and regulations promulgated by the Commission pursuant to the statutory section. Interpretation of the section, therefore, is only relevant to discover whether it authorizes a particular rule; it cannot of itself broaden the meaning of a rule adopted under the section although it may expand the legislative constraints within which the rule must fit. Thus, although the argument that insider trading proscriptions were not intended for section 10(b) may not be too strong, it is also not very important. The real problem of interpretation relates to Rule 10b-5: can it be interpreted as broadly as the SEC has requested in *Texas Gulf Sulphur*? If so have the procedures followed in reaching that result been appropriate?

The Scope of Rule 10b-5 as Presented in Texas Gulf Sulphur

There is considerable jurisprudence on the power of an administrative agency to interpret its own rules.[119] The general thrust of this literature is quite clear: courts will defer, in a proper matter for interpretation, to the

117. See note 40 *supra*.

118. *Cf.* SEC v. Capital Gains Research Bureau, Inc., 375 U.S. 180 (1963), where precisely this concern was found for § 20(c) of the Investment Advisers Act of 1940, 54 Stat. 847, as amended, 15 U.S.C. §§ 80(b)(1)–80(b)(21) (1964).

119. See Newman, "How Courts Interpret Regulations," *Calif. L. Rev.* 35:509 (1947).

substantive conclusion that the agency prescribes.[120] Manifestly this is a sound approach. We are simply seeking to know the meaning intended for a regulation by the agency which promulgated it. There is no simpler, more direct, and more accurate method of determining that issue than allowing the agency itself almost complete discretion in interpreting its own words. There is a distinct administrative advantage to this approach. Interpretation is almost necessarily involved in any effort to make a specific application of a general provision. Even a decision to hold a hearing or investigate a matter may in itself require interpretation of a rule, no matter how simple that task may be. Thus it is recognized that the interpretative function does not necessarily require formalities or particular procedures for implementation.[121] Interpretation may take the form of administrative adjudication, quasi-legislative rule-making, publication of interpretative rulings, or the taking of a position in litigation, either as a party or as amicus curiae.[122]

In at least two widely publicized matters, *Cady, Roberts* and *Texas Gulf Sulphur,* it can be inferred that the SEC takes the position that it has interpreted Rule 10b-5 to prohibit all insider trading.[123] We have already seen the dictum in *Cady, Roberts,* which clearly represents a statement by the Commission of what it would like Rule 10b-5 to cover. Similarly, the complaint and briefs in *Texas Gulf Sulphur* make it clear that the aim of the SEC is the prohibition of all significant insider trading. The procedures followed in

120. *Id.,* pp. 520–22; see Udall v. Tallman, 380 U.S. 1 (1965).

121. Davis, *Administrative Law,* vol. 1, § 5.01, p. 289.

122. The participation of the SEC as amicus curiae in private actions has been severely criticized as unauthorized. Shipley, "The SEC's Amicus Curiae Aid to Plaintiffs in Mutual Fund Litigation," *A.B.A.J.* 52:337 (1966); *contra,* Loomis & Eisenberg, "The SEC as Amicus Curiae in Shareholder Litigation—A Reply," *A.B.A.J.* 52:749 (1966). Strangely, the General Counsel and Assistant General Counsel of the SEC did not meet head-on Shipley's complaint that this practice is unauthorized. They pointed out that the courts have welcomed the SEC's amicus help and found their position was supported by judicial acquiescence in private actions. *Id.,* pp. 752–53. They do not argue, as it certainly seems they could have, that this is merely the form the agency's interpretation is taking, and no special authorization is needed for any method by which an agency exercises its interpretive function. See Blair-Smith, "Forms of Administrative Interpretations Under the Securities Laws," *Iowa L. Rev.* 26:241 (1941).

123. The contention that Rule 10b-5 prohibits all insider trading was rejected by Judge Bonsal in *Texas Gulf Sulphur,* 258 F. Supp. at 284.

bringing an adjudicatory action such as *Cady, Roberts* or in filing a complaint and appeal as in *Texas Gulf Sulphur* are quite ordinary; there is no basis for suggesting that these ordinary procedures cannot be used as a method for an agency to present an interpretation of its own regulation. But this does not mean that such procedure is an acceptable mode for reaching the ultimate legal conclusion that insider trading is forbidden.

Interpretation or New Rule

This brings us to another crucial question: can Rule 10b-5 be made into a general prohibition of insider trading through the procedure known as interpretation?[124] If not, it can be readily seen that a great oversight has occurred which should be corrected without further ado.[125] By definition, a new substantive rule is not an interpretation; whether it be honestly entitled a new rule or called an extension of an old rule, if it occurs after 1946, the provisions of the APA must be met. How then are we to determine whether or not a general rule against insider trading can logically be deduced *as an interpretation* of Rule 10b-5?

We can simply look at the words of the regulation and in some instances it will be clear that the problem only involves the resolution of semantic ambiguities. This would be consistent with the dictionary definition of "interpret" as "to explain or tell the meaning of; to translate into intelligible or familiar language or terms; to expand; elucidate."[126] It should be noted from the dictionary definition that the connotation is that the true meaning must be implicit though it is unclear or abstruse and that the interpretation is merely the setting forth of that meaning or making it more clear.

We might also look at the contemporaneous understanding of the provision as an aid to discovering the Commission's intention at the time the

124. Unfortunately this precise question has never been considered in any reported litigation.

125. Professor Davis has answered this query in a nutshell: "Of course the way to solve problems of classifying activities which analytically fall into more than one category or into no category is to keep an eye on producing a good practical result in the particular case." Davis, *Administrative Law,* vol. 1, § 5.03, p. 298 (1958).

126. *Webster's New International Dictionary,* vol. 2 (2d ed. 1953).

rule was promulgated.[127] If their intention was to prohibit all insider trading, then it is easier to conclude that such a rule can logically follow from 10b-5 as a matter of interpretation. If, on the other hand, no evidence of this intention can be found, then it is more reasonable to characterize such a prohibition as constituting a new rule rather than an interpretation. For this purpose we are only interested in the agency's interpretation *at the time of promulgation.* The concept of "interpretation" necessarily signifies an existing, objective, substantive provision which has to be interpreted; this underlying substance is unvarying from its inception. It is the meaning of this substance that we seek in order to determine whether the change suggested by *Texas Gulf Sulphur* constitutes merely an interpretation or a new rule. The Commission's subsequent intention to have Rule 10b-5 cover all insider trading is irrelevant to the underlying question of whether this new approach would constitute an interpretation or a new rule. The question, however, raises one of the most fundamental and important questions that courts can deal with in administrative law,[128] since it is central to the issue of when procedural safeguards against administrative abuse must be used. The responsibility for resolving this issue is peculiarly judicial and no deference to the SEC's view is required from the courts.

The Words of Rule 10b-5

The words of Rule 10b-5 are ambiguous at best. Clearly, subsection 1 of the rule requires fraud and subsection 2 requires that some statement be made from which there is an omission of "a material fact necessary in order to make the statements made, *in the light of the circumstances,* not misleading. . . ."[129] The requirement that some statement be made suggests that complete silence, the basic problem in insider trading, cannot be covered

127. Davis, *Administrative Law,* vol. 1, § 5.03, p. 298.

128. The courts show no hesitation about making this determination. *See, e.g.,* Garelick Mfg. Co. v. Dillon, 313 F.2d 899 (D.C. Cir. 1963); Gibson Wine Co. v. Snyder, 194 F.2d 329 (D.C. Cir. 1952); Boller Beverages, Inc. v. Davis, 38 N.J. 138, 183 A.2d 64 (1962); People v. Cull, 10 N.Y.2d 123, 176 N.E.2d 495, 218 N.Y.S.2d 38 (1961); State v. Freeman, 370 P.2d 307 (Okla. 1962).

129. See text of Rule 10b-5, note 3 *supra.* (Emphasis added.)

by subsection 2.[130] The italicized words also imply that something very close to the special facts or special circumstances rule was intended.

The main weapon against insider trading, therefore, would have to be subsection 3. This requires an "act, practice, or course of business." It is difficult to see how the failure to make full disclosure of inside information constitutes any of these, although conceivably a purchase of stock is an "act" within the meaning of the rule.[131] One case has said that "it is the *use of the insider information* that gives rise to a violation of Rule 10b-5."[132] But this *act* must operate as a "fraud or deceit." Again, it is difficult to see how, simply as a matter of interpretation, insider trading can be conceived as generally constituting fraud or deceit under the most liberal meaning of those words. Many writers and the SEC seem to assume that all insider trading is of itself fraudulent. But this is the purest supposition or question begging; it has been demonstrated elsewhere that this generalization cannot logically be maintained.[133]

Original Administrative Intent

It seems clear that nothing like a general rule against insider trading was comprehended or intended by the Commission when Rule 10b-5 was promulgated in 1942. The preamble to the rule itself refers only to fraud and manipulation—never to insider trading. The very case suggesting the need for a rule, *Ward La France,* could have been comprehended under the developing common law of fraud as a special-facts case. Additionally, the only statement made by a member of the Commission implied that the provision was designed only to reach new modes of fraud. The Commission's earliest consideration of the rule in *Ward La France* relates only to a quasi-fraud

130. See Ruder, "Civil Liability," p. 667. This suggests the validity of the result reached by Judge Bonsal, since the two defendants found in violations of the Rule purchased their shares after the arguably misleading press release of April 12, 1964. See *Texas Gulf Sulphur,* 258 F. Supp. at 275, 286–87.

131. The SEC's position seems to be that any insider occupies a fiduciary relationship to potential buyers or sellers of stock, not that the precise wording of the rule must be complied with. See Ruder, "Civil Liability," p. 668.

132. Cochran v. Channing Corp., 211 F. Supp. 239, 243 (1962), citing *Cady, Roberts.*

133. Manne, *Insider Trading and the Stock Market.*

matter of the sort traditionally comprehended within the common-law special-circumstances rule. Louis Loss, undoubtedly the foremost interpreter of SEC law, as late as 1948, still thought that Rule 10b-5 was a codification of the special-facts rule, making it applicable to transactions across an exchange as well as in face-to-face dealings.[134] Indeed, it was not until Judge Leahy's opinion in the *Speed* case that we received the first inkling[135] that Rule 10b-5 had any potential for dealing with the subject previously thought to be the exclusive domain of section 16(b). The evidence, therefore, overwhelmingly favors the proposition that Rule 10b-5 was not meant to be a general rule against insider trading.

Thus, it can be seen that the SEC is seeking to gain by interpretation a provision far more significant than the underlying rule was ever thought to be. It would be absurd to conclude that a rule as earth-shattering, or at least as precedent-shattering, as that requested in *Texas Gulf Sulphur* could grow out of mere interpretation of a provision which had never previously created any concern for the business community or even been brought to their general attention. If there are no inherent or intrinsic bases for distinguishing an interpretation from a new rule, this apathy is at least significant and relevant extrinsic evidence. Fairness in the administrative process demands some respect for the reactions the affected community reasonably displays.[136]

Rule-Making Procedures

A look at the policies underlying the fairly strict procedural requirements for substantive or legislative rule-making and a comparison with the policies underlying the rule of informality in interpretive rule-making, provide

134. Loss, "The SEC and the Broker-Dealer," *Vand. L. Rev.* 1:516 (1948).

135. Even here there is a problem. The SEC participated as amicus curiae in that litigation. Possibly their briefs contained statements suggesting, as did Judge Leahy's opinion, that Rule 10b-5 reached all insider trading. But that brief has never been published and is certainly not generally familiar to litigants or their lawyers, if it is available at all.

136. See Davis, discussion, *Administrative Law,* vol. 1, § 5.01, p. 285, for helpful examples of rule-making called interpretation.

a helpful approach to the instant problem.[137] By and large, the procedural requirements of the APA are designed to guarantee that parties who will be affected by a significant impending change in the rules will be given sufficient notice and opportunity to be heard.[138] Rule-making by experts in our system of law does not allow rule dictation by experts. As the field of administrative law has developed, the idea has become firmly ingrained that the process of rule change requires two elements, expertise and due process.[139] Neither is sufficient standing alone but in combination they provide the outline for a workable system of delegation of legislative powers from Congress to administrative agencies.

The Requirement of Due Process

The two principal aspects of due process protections with which we are concerned are the right to a timely hearing and the right not to have interests determined by retroactive rules. Arguably, the latter point is not too important, since, if the SEC wins its point in *Texas Gulf Sulphur,* there will be few people in the financial community who will not have notice. Thus, only a few individuals might have relied to their detriment on the opposite rule. But the second aspect of due process, the hearing, is crucial, and it is extremely important to notice that hearings were never held on the subject of insider trading. Until recently, there was almost no analysis of the subject[140] in the literature, although there was a good deal of emoting. And there is still a need for a considerable amount of research[141] which the SEC is qual-

137. For a scholarly discussion of the various considerations of rule-making versus adjudication, see Shapiro, "The Choice of Rulemaking or Adjudication in the Development of Administrative Policy," *Harv. L. Rev.* 78:921 (1965), Professor Shapiro's article is relevant in some particulars to the balance of this article, although he does not discuss the instant problem specifically.

138. See generally H.R. Rep. No. 1980, 79th Cong., 2d Sess. (1946).

139. Fuchs, "Fairness and Effectiveness in Administrative Organization and Procedures," *Ind. L.J.* 36:1 (1960).

140. The two exceptions found were Brudney, "Insider Securities Dealings During Corporate Crises," *Mich. L. Rev.* 61:1 (1962), and Conant, "Duties of Disclosure of Corporate Insiders Who Purchase Shares," *Cornell L.Q.* 46:53 (1960).

141. See Manne, *Insider Trading and the Stock Market,* pp. 142, 151, 162, 163.

ified to perform and which should occur as part of a broad SEC consideration of the whole insider trading question.

A general rule against insider trading is precisely the kind of quasi-legislation for which the due process rules were designed. Clearly, vast numbers of participants in the business community can be affected by such a prohibition. If this result can be accomplished simply by informal interpretation or by a single administrative adjudication, none of those protections normally associated with the development of general provisions can be provided. The courts should eschew such an approach which by implication allows a very important rule to become effective simply as a matter of informal interpretation.

Judicial Recognition of the Need for Due Process

Judge Bonsal, in *Texas Gulf Sulphur,* was sensitive to this problem in a different connection. When requested to specify a time period during which insiders, under the circumstances of that case, should refrain from trading, he replied that this would require the court to perform the very function for which the agency was established. In a highly appropriate slap on the wrist, he in effect remanded that question back to the agency for consideration:

> A decision in one case would not control another case with different facts. No insider would know whether he waited long enough after an announcement had been made. He would be subject to suit by the Commission (and to private suits brought by others riding on the Commission's coattails).
>
> * * * * *
>
> The Commission has not supplied, nor has the Court found, decisions specifying a waiting period after a corporate announcement is made. After this action was instituted, Cary, the former chairman of the Commission, and Fleischer, his former executive assistant, discussed a waiting period in policy terms. If a waiting period is to be fixed, this could be most appropriately done by the Commission, which was established by Congress with broad rule-making powers. Should the Commission determine that it lacks authority to fix a waiting period, authority should come from Congress rather than from the courts.[142]

142. *Texas Gulf Sulphur,* 258 F. Supp. at 289 (1966).

Presumably the agency could accomplish this by rule-making[143]—though Judge Bonsal seems to have some reservation about this—or, *in an individual adjudication,* it could set limits for *that case.* The latter approach would not, of course, have the quasi-legislative impact of the former. Unfortunately, Judge Bonsal did not recognize that precisely this same issue was involved in the underlying SEC assumption that Rule 10b-5 dealt generally with insider trading[144] and that the SEC was requesting the court to approve this radical and highly debatable conclusion as an interpretation of an old rule which was thought to be neither radical nor highly debatable.[145]

Assuming that Rule 10b-5 as a general prohibition on insider trading does constitute a rule rather than an interpretation, a question still remains: can such a rule be said to have been validly promulgated? *Cady, Roberts* is the earliest case in which such a rule can be said to have been laid down. Thus, APA legal standards for substantive, quasi-legislative rule-making must be applied and they clearly have not been complied with.[146] It is probably safe to say that strict compliance with the APA has never been required,[147] although it is also true that strict compliance never got a rule into trouble with the courts. Here, however, there has clearly been no notice, no hearing,

143. It is possible that the SEC has failed to utilize strict rule-making procedures to outlaw insider trading for fear that they would bog down on details of just this sort. But surely that would have not stopped their considering a single basic rule prohibiting trading on material, unpublicized information. The details could easily be fixed either by interpretative rule-making or by adjudication on an *ad hoc* basis. That is not what Judge Bonsal is decrying in the first quoted paragraph. Rather, quite properly, he is criticizing using the courts for this peculiarly administrative kind of problem.

144. *Cf. Texas Gulf Sulphur,* 258 F. Supp. at 276–77.

145. This is simply the effect of what the SEC is doing, but it is not stated in this fashion in the agency's briefs.

146. These include notice, § 4(a), 5 U.S.C.A. § 553(b) (Special pamph. 1966), opportunity for interested persons to participate in the rule-making and incorporation in its rule of a general statement of its basis and purpose, § 4(b), 5 U.S.C.A. § 553(c) (Special pamph. 1966), publication in the Federal Register of substantive rules, § 3(a), 5 U.S.C.A. § 552(b) (Special pamph. 1966), and the taking of evidence, § 7(c), 5 U.S.C.A. § 556(d).

147. The principal reasons for this are inherent in the original act which exempted "interpretive rules, general statements of policy, rules of agency organization, procedure or practice, or in any situation in which the agency for good cause finds . . . that notice and public procedure thereon are impracticable, unnecessary or contrary to the public interest." 60 Stat. 239, 5 U.S.C. § 1003(a) (1964).

and no publication. If a valid rule is to be found, some justification other than compliance with the APA must be found.[148]

Adjudicative Rule-Making

It would probably be the SEC's position that substantive law can be made by the Commission through procedures other than those provided in section 4 of the APA for quasi-legislative rule-making.[149] The first argument might be that the existence of Rule 10b-5, plus an adjudication complying with section 5 of the APA, could effectively substitute for direct rule-making.[150] The basic requirements of expertise and due process would arguably be present. The Commission has already implied its belief in *Texas Gulf Sulphur* that *Cady, Roberts* served this purpose. Indeed, considerable reliance was placed in the SEC's post-trial memorandum in the *Texas Gulf Sulphur* litigation on that matter:[151]

> We wish to emphasize here that the basic proposition upon which the Commission relies is that corporate insiders who have been entrusted with knowledge of material undisclosed facts are obligated to refrain from trading in the Company's securities or inducing others to trade until disclosure of the facts can be, and is made.
>
> * * * * *

148. If, as the SEC contends, a general rule against insider trading has developed through *Cady, Roberts* and private litigation, it would seem to fit none of the exceptions appearing in § 4 of the unamended APA, since it is too broad to be encompassed within the meaning of an "interpretative rule." But this is not to say that the SEC would accept the underlying premise of the discussion at this point, *i.e.,* that Rule 10b-5 did not constitute a rule outlawing all insider trading *at its inception.* Indeed, in their appellate brief in *Texas Gulf Sulphur,* the Commission seems to be taking the position that 10b-5 has always had the meaning suggested.

149. Their argument will have to be either that the rule actually predates the APA or that the newer development against all insider trading is merely an interpretative rule. See note 148 *supra.*

150. The argument here is not simply that *Cady, Roberts* constitutes merely interpretation of Rule 10b-5, but that the method used, adjudication, could be used for that purpose.

151. Post-Trial Memorandum of SEC, *Texas Gulf Sulphur,* 258 F. Supp. 262, p. 32.

> The Commission explained the basis for this proposition in *Cady, Roberts & Co.* . . .[152]

Furthermore, Professor Cary has stated that *Cady, Roberts* is one example of the growth of federal corporation law.[153] Neither of these statements seems to imply that the agency is standing on *Cady, Roberts* as simply an *ad hoc* interpretation of Rule 10b-5.

Agency Discretion

The administrative adjudicatory process cannot bear the weight this argument places on it. While an administrative agency is given very broad discretion in determining whether, as a matter of policy in administering the underlying act, it will proceed in a given matter by adjudication or rule-making, this does not mean that the agency may use the adjudicatory process when rule-making for a specific substantive proposal is to be accomplished in effect.[154] It is entirely within the agency's discretion—and indeed is a necessary part of efficient internal administration—to adjudicate any case which is proper for adjudication or to use the quasi-legislative rule-making procedures for the same purpose. But this does not mean that an agency always enjoys *carte blanche* on whether to adjudicate or make a rule. It merely means that there are two categories of cases: first, those in which the strict standards for legislative rule-making must be complied with; and second, those in which the agency has a choice of proceeding under the more strict legislative standards or under the less strict rules for adjudication. But it is only within the latter category that the agency is given full discretion.

152. It should be noted, however, that *Cady, Roberts* did not "explain the basis" for the proposition. Instead it established that proposition as an agency rule *for the first time*. See text *supra*.

153. "Symposium, Insider Trading in Stocks," *Bus. Law.* 21:1009, 1010 (1966).

154. *Cf.* Elof Hannson, Inc. v. United States, 178 F. Supp. 922, 928 (3d. Div Ct. Cust. 1959). See also Davis, *Administrative Law,* vol. 1 (Supp. 1965, § 6.13, p. 144). Fuchs, "Agency Development of Policy Through Rule-Making," *Nw. U.L. Rev.* 59:781, 800–01 (1965).

The Second Chenery Case

The second *Chenery* case,[155] although it is not generally realized, makes precisely this point. Basically, second *Chenery* involved the agency's choice to proceed with adjudication rather than rule-making in a case requiring an interpretation of an act of Congress. The court in *Chenery* did not address itself to the question of whether the particular legal result had to assume the form of a quasi-legislative rule.[156] Rather, the opinion means only that the particular result in question fell within the category of cases in which the agency has a choice.[157] It certainly did not say that there was no other category of cases for which the agency is denied this discretion and in which only quasi-legislative rule-making procedures can be allowed.

When the question is an interpretation of a congressional statute, as in *Chenery,* adjudication cannot be said to be intrinsically inappropriate apart from a specific directive, as in section 10(b), to proceed *only* with rules or regulations. This does not mean that in such a case the agency may not use the rule-making procedure if it wishes. But when rule-making is specially required, either because of an explicit statutory demand or because of the nature of the result sought, then, with one exception to be noted, this option is foreclosed. This point is made clear by the language of second *Chenery:*

> Since the Commission, unlike a court, does have the ability to make new law prospectively through the exercise of its rule-making powers, it has less reason to rely upon *ad hoc* adjudication to formulate new standards of conduct. . . . The function of filling in the interstices of the Act should be performed, as much as possible, through this quasi-legislative promulgation of rules to be applied in the future. But any rigid requirement to that effect would make the administrative process inflexible and incapable of dealing with many

155. *Chenery,* 332 U.S. 194 (1947).

156. Nor, for that matter, had first *Chenery* addressed that question either. *Chenery,* 318 U.S. 80. That case merely held that the standards for decision announced by the agency had not been conformed to. See Dodd, "The Chenery Corporation Case: A New Landmark in the Law of Administrative Procedure," *Harv. L. Rev.* 56:1002, 1005 (1943).

157. "The function of filling in the interstices of the Act should be performed, as much as possible, through this quasi-legislative promulgation of rules to be applied in the future." *Chenery,* 332 U.S. 194, 202. This clearly implies a category in which rule-making is imperative. See also note 161 *infra.*

> of the specialized problems which arise. . . . Not every principle essential to the effective administration of a statute can or should be cast, immediately into the mold of a general rule. Some principles must await their own development, while others must be adjusted to meet particular, unforeseeable situations. In performing its important functions in these respects, therefore, an administrative agency must be equipped to act either by general rule or by individual order. To insist on one form of action to the exclusion of the other is to exalt form over necessity.
>
> In other words, problems may arise in a case which the administrative agency could not reasonably foresee, problems which must be solved despite the absence of a relevant general rule. Or the agency may not have had sufficient experience with a particular problem to warrant rigidifying its tentative judgment into a hard and fast rule. Or the problem may be so specialized and varying in nature as to be impossible of capture within the boundaries of a general rule. In those situations, the agency must retain power to deal with the problems on a case-to-case basis if the administrative process is to be effective. There is thus a very definite place for case-by-case evolution of statutory standards. And the choice made between proceeding by general rule or by individual, *ad hoc* litigation is one that lies primarily in the informed discretion of the administrative agency.[158]

Justice Murphy was primarily concerned here with the efficiency of the administrative process. He is not asserting that in any case an agency has *carte blanche* to develop what constitutes a rule purely by the process of adjudication. Instead he spelled out those particular instances in which, in the interest of developing a successful administrative process, adjudication may be required. Only to meet the demands of administrative necessity—the need for experimentation and flexibility, unpredictability of result, or unforeseeability of the problem—should the prospective rule-making device be sacrificed to retrospective adjudication.[159]

158. 332 U.S. 194, 202–03 (1947).

159. In applying this balancing test to the development of Rule 10b-5, it should be noted that the question is not rule-making versus adjudication as in *Chenery,* but rule-making procedure versus rule-making by a single adjudicative case. It would appear that this latter procedure has none of the advantages of flexibility that led the court to permit case-by-case adjudication in *Chenery.* See Peck, "The Atrophied Rule-Making Powers of the National Labor Relations Board," *Yale L.J.* 70:729, 758 (1961). For an agreement with this analysis of what *Chenery* requires, see Cohen & Rabin, "Broker-Dealer Selling Practice

The Chenery Balancing Test—Administrative Necessity or Individual Due Process

But even with this, there is no suggestion in second *Chenery* that an adjudicated result, allowed for reasons of administrative efficiency, should be accepted forthwith as constituting a rule of general applicability. When Justice Murphy says the agency must have discretion in certain instances to proceed through adjudication, he does not say that the adjudication will have the effect of promulgating a rule of general applicability. Indeed, apart from the reference to a case-by-case development, there is no suggestion that rules can be made in this fashion.[160]

The whole point of Justice Murphy's discussion is the protection of the particular litigants in the adjudicatory proceeding. It would be a complete contradiction of the underlying meaning of second *Chenery* to say that it allowed agencies full discretion to proceed in *any* case by adjudication or by rule-making. To do so would multiply the very danger with which Justice Murphy was most concerned—a lack of fairness to the parties involved in the particular proceeding. There is no suggestion that he would condone, even under the balancing test that he prescribes, extending this little bit of unfairness, tolerable in one adjudicatory proceeding, to vast numbers of individuals who might, at some future time, be covered by a general rule. The question today seems to be whether or not the interest in protecting *one individual's* justified reliance and his right to fair procedure outweighs

---

Standards: The Importance of Administrative Adjudication in Their Development," *Law & Contemp. Prob.* 29:691, 696 (1964).

160. This is not to say that the agency is not free to follow that adjudication in a subsequent adjudication, but that as far as courts are concerned this cannot be accepted as a rule, certainly not a rule or regulation within the meaning of § 10(b) of the Securities and Exchange Act of 1934, 48 Stat. 891, 15 U.S.C. 78(j) (1964).

What makes the problem of some moment in *Chenery* and in *Texas Gulf Sulphur* is that a *judicial precedent* is being set. If nothing but administrative adjudication were involved, there would be little cause for comment or concern, since the doctrine of stare decisis has little meaning there. See Fuchs, "Fairness and Effectiveness," p. 46. The SEC is not usually quick to overturn its own interpretation as are some governmental agencies, but it is still the court adjudication which makes the matter important. And it must not be forgotten, in this connection, that civil suits will be the principal mode of enforcement for the rule.

or is outweighed by some matter of administrative necessity dictating the use of an *ad hoc* adjudication.[161]

In addition, the Supreme Court in second *Chenery* did not condone rule-making by one adjudication, but rather a "case-by-case evolution of statutory standards." *One* administrative adjudication does not a case-by-case evolution make![162] That was, of course, of little moment in *Chenery* itself, as that case simply represented the inception of such a development. The case necessarily began as an SEC adjudicatory proceeding, since the SEC had to review a plan of reorganization under the Public Utility Holding Company Act.[163] The Commission could either stop the proceeding altogether and hold hearings to formulate a rule for the new problem which had arisen, or make an *ad hoc* finding; it did the latter.[164] Certainly under

161. NLRB v. A.P.W. Prod. Co., 316 F.2d 899, 906 (2d Cir. 1966), is significant:

> There has been increasing expression of regret over the Board's failure to react more positively to the Supreme Court's rather pointed hint, SEC v. Chenery Corp., 332 U.S. 194, 202 (1947), that since an administrative agency has "the ability to make new law prospectively through the exercise of its rule-making powers, it has less reason than a court to rely upon ad hoc adjudication to formulate new standards of conduct," and that the "function of filling in the interstices," of regulatory statutes "should be performed, as much as possible, through this quasi-legislative promulgation of rules to be applied in the future." . . . Although courts have not generally balked at allowing administrative agencies to apply a rule newly fashioned in an adjudicative proceeding to past conduct, a decision branding as "unfair" conduct stamped "fair" at the time a party acted, raises judicial hackles considerably more than a determination that merely brings within the agency's jurisdiction an employer previously left without, . . . or imposes a more severe remedy for conduct already prohibited. . . . And the hackles bristle still more when a financial penalty is assessed for action that might well have been avoided if the agency's changed disposition had been earlier made known, or might even have been taken in express reliance on the standard previously established. (*Id.* at 860)

162. This is a very different proposition than filling in the details after a general rule has been promulgated. Presumably the latter is what Professor Cary has made reference to when he says that the questions left open by *Cady, Roberts* "can be gradually developed through succeeding opinions." Cary, *Politics and the Regulatory Agencies*, p. 84 (1967).

163. 49 Stat. 803 (1934), 15 U.S.C. 79(k)(b) (1964).

164. Justice Murphy goes even further, suggesting this was the *only* way the Commission could proceed:

> The Commission was asked to grant or deny effectiveness to a proposed amendment to Federal's reorganization plan whereby the management would be accorded parity

these circumstances the finding of administrative necessity was justified. That is not so, however, with *Texas Gulf Sulphur.* Nothing has ever prevented the SEC from holding full-scale hearings on the question of insider trading, and no reason has been adduced as to why they should now ask the courts to enforce their position as a rule.[165] One prior adjudication, *Cady, Roberts,* certainly cannot make up the deficiency.

Using this balancing test to determine the propriety of giving *Cady, Roberts* the effect of rule-making rather than adjudication, no strong reason presents itself to tip the scales in favor of administrative necessity. In the first place, *Cady, Roberts* was a broker-dealer disciplinary action.[166] Apart from the dictum relating it to all persons bearing a special relationship to a corporation and the innuendo that this has always been the rule,[167] there is nothing about the proceeding to suggest that it represents a firm declaration of a legislative rule generally prohibiting insider trading. We need not examine whether it has that effect for all broker-dealers, since no broker-dealer is a defendant in *Texas Gulf Sulphur.* Furthermore, the SEC's powers over broker-dealers is far broader and more plenary than that with regard to general regulation of stock market transactions.[168]

Yet, in retrospect, the Commission's reliance on *Cady, Roberts* in *Texas Gulf Sulphur* would seem to have the effect of making all corporate directors, executives, and employees (and "tippees"?) "interested parties" in the *Cady, Roberts* proceeding within the meaning of section 4 of the APA. But no publicity was given in advance to this fact, and the adjudication provided no opportunity for anyone who might wish to question the Commission's policy to appear and argue. Even assuming that the insiders in a particular

---

> treatment on its holdings. It could do that *only in the form of an order,* entered after due consideration of the peculiar facts in light of the relevant and proper standards. (Chenery Corp., 332 U.S. at 201 [1947]; emphasis added)

165. *Cf.* California v. Lo-Vaca Gathering Co., 379 U.S. 366, 376 (1965) (Harlan J., dissenting).

166. Sections 15(b), 15A(1)(2), and 19(a)(3) of the 1934 act were cited.

167. *Cady, Roberts,* 40 S.E.C. at 910–11.

168. Broker-dealers are regulated by the Securities Act of 1934, §§ 5, 6, 8, 11, 12, 15, 17, 19, 48 Stat. 385, 888, 892, 895, 897, 898, 15 U.S.C. §§ 78(e), 78(f), 78(h), 78(k), 78(o), 78(s) (1964).

company had kept close watch on the *Cady, Roberts* proceedings, it would still have been impossible for anyone to realize that the opinion might affect their interests until after it was announced. Consequently, even if insiders would have been allowed to submit amicus briefs in *Cady, Roberts,* the right would have been meaningless,[169] since they would not have known the grounds on which to argue their position. If the possibility of various insiders appearing as amici in the *Cady, Roberts* proceeding sounds absurd, then the point is made. It *is* absurd, for it makes no sense whatever to allow important rules of general applicability in subsequent judicial actions to be made in this type proceeding.[170] What remains is for the courts to notice that, intentionally or not, this is the box into which the SEC has pushed them.

Another important consideration appears regarding second *Chenery's* balancing test. In *Chenery* it was administrative necessity, flexibility, or efficiency which was to be weighed against the evils of agency rule-making by adjudication. Some *special administrative reason* had to be shown in order to avoid the necessity for rule-making procedures. But no showing of *agency* need can be made if the agency is, in effect, asking the *courts* to formulate a rule for them. Clearly, second *Chenery* was aimed at liberalizing the options open to the Commissions for doing their own job. But going to court to have the rule declared is an abdication of the very responsibility Justice Murphy gave the agency scope to meet. *Chenery* recognized that a hard and fast rule presented difficulties of application and applicability. It decided, therefore, that rule-making should not always be required, even if the substantive matter was significant.

But this argument cannot be made for what the SEC seeks in *Texas Gulf Sulphur.* Clearly, it wants a rule and not an *ad hoc* adjudication, though no arguments of administrative necessity have been advanced. Therefore, none of the reasons of *Chenery,* which explain when an agency may proceed with-

169. See Peck, "Atrophied Rule-Making Powers," pp. 730–31.

170. See Air Line Pilots Ass'n. v. Quesada, 276 F.2d 892 (2d Cir. 1960), pointing out the absurdity of adjudicative hearings to determine if each of possibly 18,000 affected pilots could be subjected to a maximum age rule for flying. *Cf.* Air Line Pilots Ass'n. v. CAB, 215 F.2d 122 (2d Cir. 1954).

out otherwise required rule-making, can apply to a situation in which the agency asks the court to adopt a rule for it.[171]

The Requirement of Publication

As a more minor matter, it should also be noted that since the opinion in *Cady, Roberts* is arguably being treated by the SEC as a rule, it should have been published in the Federal Register as required by section 3(a) of the APA[172] and the provisions of the Federal Register Act.[173] Section 10(e) of the APA provides that a reviewing court, which the *Texas Gulf Sulphur* court may be for the proposition advanced in the SEC's complaint, shall "hold unlawful and set aside agency action . . . found to be without observance of procedure required by law."[174]

This argument, that the *Texas Gulf Sulphur* defendants should not be punished for violation of a rule not published in the Federal Register as required by section 3(a)[175] derives additional strength from the provision in section 23(a) of the Securities Exchange Act of 1934 that ". . . No provision of this title imposing any liability shall apply to any act done or omitted in good faith in conformity with any rule or regulation of the Commission. . . ."[176] In this context, the statute indicates that Congress placed high priority on the value of certainty and reliability in securities law. The device of making law by dicta in adjudicative proceedings flies in the face of this policy both in its unavoidable retroactive effect and because, like judicial dictum, it establishes uncertainty about whether it will be followed in subsequent cases.

171. This position should be contrasted with a more appropriate one stated by SEC Chairman Cohen in another context. See Cohen & Rabin, "Broker-Dealer Selling Practice Standards," p. 713, where the point is made that judicial review serves the function of forcing the "agency to focus on the issues more clearly and to define the issues more sharply." The SEC should not ask the courts to do more than this for it.

172. 60 Stat. 238 (1946).

173. 49 Stat. 501 (1935).

174. 60 Stat. 243 (1946).

175. See Davis, *Administrative Law,* vol. 1, §§ 6.09, 6.10.

176. 48 Stat. 901 (1934), as amended 15 U.S.C. § 78(w)(a) (1964).

The Requirement of Expertise

The discussion thus far relates to the due process part of the dual rule-making requirements of expertise and due process. But the first of these requirements also poses considerable difficulties for anyone taking the position that *Cady, Roberts* constitutes a rule.

A reading of *Cady, Roberts* makes it quite clear that insider trading by a broker on dividend news not yet publicized is considered "unfair" to individuals trading in the market without this information. But unless a simple allegation of unfairness is to be allowed as a substitute for research and analysis, *Cady, Roberts* does not meet the standards which are required for the exercise of administrative expertise. And it should be noted, "unfairness" is not required here as a jurisdictional fact. It represents the Commission's "reasoning" on the subject. None of the complex analytical questions of impact on the overall market,[177] impact on particular kinds of traders,[178] the effect in terms of executive compensation,[179] or the problems involved in policing such a rule[180] were shown to have been considered by the Commission. It is quite evident that the agency had never carefully considered any of these questions at the time the *Texas Gulf Sulphur* litigation was begun.[181]

The language in *Cady, Roberts* goes far beyond what was needed to decide the case before the Commission.[182] While an adjudicatory decision may or may not require extensive expertise to insure that the result is in harmony with the purpose of a regulation, going beyond the issues in the case or reaching out to settle non-essential questions of law may indicate that the Commission is exercising rule-making powers without conforming to basic protections required for that result;[183] the require-

177. Manne, *Insider Trading and the Stock Market*, pp. 77–91 (1966).
178. *Id.*, pp. 93–110.
179. *Id.*, pp. 111–45.
180. *Id.*, pp. 159–69.
181. *Id.*, pp. 1–15.
182. See text accompanying notes 52–64 *supra.*
183. *Chenery*, 318 U.S. 80.

ment of a showing of expert consideration should accordingly be strictly enforced.[184]

Section 10(b) Limitations on Agency Discretion

There is one other important reason why *Cady, Roberts* should not be accepted as formulating a rule for the later purposes of *Texas Gulf Sulphur.* Section 10(b) requires that the development of new substantive policies be accomplished only by means of "rules and regulations." It is certainly arguable that in this context "rules and regulations" refers only to those promulgated in the proper fashion. The standards of agency care should be correlative to the responsibility which Congress has placed on the agency in a particular delegation. It would have been a simple matter for Congress otherwise to have omitted this provision and simply given the SEC direct enforcement powers, thereby extending *carte blanche* to the agency to proceed in any fashion, whether by rule-making or adjudication, to effectuate the policies of the section. Clearly, Congress was asking for something more.

SEC Amicus Appearances as an Exercise of Expertise

The SEC could make a slightly different defense of the route it has taken to its complaint in *Texas Gulf Sulphur.* It could argue that it has considered not merely the problem raised in *Cady, Roberts* but also those raised in the many cases in which it has appeared as amicus curiae,[185] the cases brought by the Commission involving insider trading,[186] and the many civil actions

184. *Cf.* Chief Justice Warren, dissenting, in Communist Party v. Subversive Activities Control Board, 367 U.S. 1, 135 (1960): "[I]t will not do for the Court of Appeals or this court to conclude that the Board would have reached the same conclusion without relying upon the unsupported findings. Congress has placed the responsibility for making that determination in the Board and not in the courts" (citing *Chenery,* 318 U.S. at 88).

185. Unfortunately, the annual report of the Securities and Exchange Commission does not break down the number of amicus briefs filed by the Commission in terms of subject matter. Since the Commission's use of amicus appearances in private actions has become such a significant part of the agency's enforcement pattern it would be highly desirable if the SEC would disclose this information in its annual report.

186. This is limited to two cases before *Texas Gulf Sulphur* (*Chenery* and *Capital Gains*

under 10b-5[187] that it has studied. The subject of insider trading was also mentioned in the SEC's Special Study of the Securities Market,[188] and in the recent Mutual Funds Study.[189] But none of these actions displays any affirmative exercise of Commission expertise to analyze the problem of insider training.

It is not clear who makes the decision to appear as amicus. If the decision to appear is made by the office of the General Counsel, the argument becomes even weaker. This almost random consideration of insider trading could not constitute the case-by-case evolution of standards, as allowed by second *Chenery,* since only *Cady, Roberts* purports to be agency action attempting to formulate standards at all, and it is the *first matter even to deal with exchange transactions.* No interested parties were invited to participate in this entire process, and, of course, there has been no publication in the Federal Register. And perhaps most important, this scheme precludes any intelligent or effective judicial review of the process, or the results established, prior to the *Texas Gulf Sulphur* litigation.[190] Looking at all the oc-

---

Research Bureau) and neither involved Rule 10b-5 or a problem comparable to that in the *Texas Gulf Sulphur* litigation.

187. The cases decided up to early 1963 are collected in Ruder, "Civil Liability Under Rule 10b-5: Judicial Revision of Legislative Intent?" *Nw. U.L. Rev.* 57:627, 687–90 (1962). The number of cases may have doubled in the ensuing four years.

188. House Comm. on Interstate and Foreign Commerce, *Report of Special Study of Securities Markets of the Securities and Exchange Commission,* H.R. Doc. No. 95, 88th Cong., 1st Sess. (1963).

189. House Comm. on Interstate and Foreign Commerce, *Report of the Securities and Exchange Commission on the Public Policy Implications of Investment Company Growth,* H.R. Rep. No. 2337, 89th Cong., 2d Sess. (1966).

190. *Cf. Chenery,* 318 U.S. at 94 where the Court said:

> For the courts cannot exercise their duty of review unless they are advised of the considerations underlying the action under review. If the action rests upon an administrative determination—an exercise of judgment in an area which Congress has entrusted to the agency—of course it must not be set aside because the reviewing court might have made a different determination were it empowered to do so. But if the action is based upon a determination of law as to which the reviewing authority of the courts does come into play, an order may not stand if the agency has misconceived the law. In either event the orderly functioning of the process of review requires that the grounds upon which the administrative agency acted be clearly disclosed and adequately sustained.

casions on which insider trading has been considered simply multiplies the problems the Commission would have in relying solely on *Cady, Roberts.* There is nothing in the jurisprudence of administrative law which would justify or condone such an approach. For a court to adopt it now would be an unfortunate abdication of judicial responsibility for the orderly development of administrative procedures. It would constitute an open invitation to agencies to circumvent the duties of careful scholarship and apolitical expert regulation which are their very *raison d'etre.*

Correction of Administrative Omissions Through Litigation

Professor Cary's Approach: Texas Gulf Sulphur Supplies Required Due Process

A more refined argument for solving the due process problem has been advanced by Professor William L. Cary.[191] Indeed it is specifically this theory which should be called into question by *Texas Gulf Sulphur.* We have already noted that Professor Cary said:

> There is one criticism which was expressed to me by Professor Kenneth C. Davis (of "Davis on Administrative Law") about *Cady, Roberts,* that I want to bring to your attention, namely, that it was a case of rule-making by a Federal Commission without the benefit of public comment and without the possibility of judicial review (the minimal penalty having been accepted). This criticism troubled me then but it seems to me that it has been remedied now. The SEC has correctly taken the next step—to bring this issue before the courts, and to insure full due process. There has been, I believe, enough warning in the financial community; the implications of *Cady, Roberts,* I know, were being considered by counsel here.
>
> *Texas Gulf Sulphur,* it seems to me simply dramatized the issue and, I confess, takes several more steps. . . .[192]

He seems to agree that the *Cady, Roberts* proceeding standing alone would not be sufficient to constitute a rule. He implies that the only thing

191. "Symposium, Insider Trading in Stocks," *Bus. Law.* 21:1009, 1011 (1966).
192. *Ibid.* See also Cary, *Politics and the Regulatory Agencies,* p. 84.

lacking for *Cady, Roberts* to be made into a rule applicable in *Texas Gulf Sulphur,* however, is the due process part of the dual requirements of expertise and due process. (The matter of notice is taken care of because there has been "enough warning in the financial community.") And there can then be no problem of due process for the defendants in the *Texas Gulf Sulphur* litigation because they are guaranteed the full panoply of procedural protections guaranteed any litigant in the federal courts.

Even aside from Professor Cary's concession that *Texas Gulf Sulphur* "takes several more steps," the logic of his argument seems seriously inadequate. The basis for the dual requirement of expertise and due process in administrative law does not allow the two to be advanced separately.[193] They are inextricably interwoven. It is due process in the exercise and review of expertise that is required, not a dash of expertise and a later dash of due process. And no matter how much due process the defendants in *Texas Gulf Sulphur* may receive as defendants in a suit, they are still entitled to have the substantive requirements of administrative law complied with. The due process they receive in court can give them none of the protection required by the APA in the course of promulgation of a general rule. If some due process was lacking for Texas Gulf Sulphur officials at the time of *Cady, Roberts,* it cannot be remedied by trying a later suit against these officials.

The "Expert" Decision to Litigate

On the other hand, Professor Cary may be arguing that publicity plus an "expert" decision to bring a case is sufficient to meet the dual requirements of expertise and due process. Under this analysis, the problems are compounded. If he is suggesting that the agency exercised its expertise in deciding to bring this case, presumably that decision, which directly affects

193. Perhaps the most obvious reason for this is found in the notion of judicial review, certainly a crucial part of due process in administrative law. Estep v. United States, 327 U.S. 114 (1946). Cary's two-step process for rule development prevents this from occurring. In the first action, *Cady, Roberts,* no review was available, and in the second, *Texas Gulf Sulphur,* there is nothing to review, since the court and not the agency is making the new rule. So the defendants in *Texas Gulf Sulphur* could never have judicial review of the rule-creating action which is now alleged to bind them. And, as we have seen, they could not even participate in that action.

the *Texas Gulf Sulphur* litigants, should have been open to them. Indeed, in many administrative agencies, as a matter of informal practice, parties to be indicted or charged in a complaint are regularly consulted in advance.[194] Apparently only the SEC among all the agencies regularly follows the practice of first informing defendants that they are being sued by the service of the complaint.[195] Clearly, there was insufficient due process mingled with that exercise of expertise. This is not to say that there is something wrong with *ex parte* decisions by an agency to bring a suit. It is to suggest, rather, that such a decision standing alone cannot be relied upon to fill the administrative law gaps in the substantive development of a rule against insider trading, even if that decision was made with the concurrence of the entire Commission.

Agency Discretion to Substitute the Court as Expert

There is one further explanation for what the SEC has done in developing a rule against insider trading. In many ways it is the least palatable of all the arguments, though it is consistent with the SEC's actions and Chairman Cary's statement. And it probably best explains what the new federal law of corporations is really all about. The argument seems to be that the judicial procedures involved in deciding the *Texas Gulf Sulphur* case can be substituted, *at the discretion of the agency*, for the exercise of its administrative responsibilities. In the first place, the requirement of section 10(b) that it be implemented only by rules and regulations of the Commission would thereby be violated. More important, this would seem to substitute the court for the administrative agency as the expert in the quasi-legislative pro-

194. The new APA codification provides for informal consultation in connection with rule-making. 5 U.S.C.A. § 553(b) (Special pamph. 1966). There would seem to be no bar to doing the same in connection with the agency or court adjudications—especially when they would have the effect of rule-making.

195. See remarks of Milton V. Freeman, *supra* note 33. This same point would seem to hold for the SEC's amicus appearances. If those decisions to appear represent any significant substantive thinking on the subject, at least this minimal, informal opportunity for the defendant to discuss his position with the SEC should be granted.

cesses, a suggestion bristling with constitutional difficulties[196] and one making especially little sense in an area like insider trading where empirical data and rigorous economic analysis would be so desirable. This is not an area where we can condone the courts making policy because they are comparatively as well qualified as the agency.[197] The basic requirement is that the agency show that it has functioned as an expert; yet nothing in this theory would meet that requirement.

Constitutional questions may also be raised by the appearance of the SEC as a party litigant in an action which is not to enforce the agency's own adjudication, but in which it also poses as the administrative expert. Here we have the bizarre occurrence that the SEC sues as a civil litigant but, in effect, asks that its position on the law be given special consideration because it is the expert on this subject. If this is a valid course of action, it must be because the law on the subject already exists and the Commission is simply seeking enforcement of it. But with that logic it cannot be argued that the agency may, at the same time, ask the court to formulate rules for it. Under traditional administrative law attitudes, we often do not allow the prosecutor also to be the judge in an agency's adjudication.[198] We should perhaps recognize the existence of a comparable barrier when an agency

196. Board of Trade v. United States, 314 U.S. 534 (1942); Moog Indus. v. FTC, 355 U.S. 411 (1958). See also *Texas Gulf Sulphur,* 258 F. Supp. at 289: "If a waiting period is to be fixed, this could be most appropriately done by the Commission, which was established by Congress with broad rule-making powers. Should the Commission determine that it lacks authority to fix a waiting period, authority should come from Congress rather than from the courts."

197. This doctrine is limited to questions of constitutional law, common law, ethics, overall philosophy of law and government, judge-made law developed through statutory interpretation, legislative history, and problems transcending the particular field of the agency. Davis, *Administrative Law,* vol. 4, § 30.09.

198. See Wong Yong Sung v. McGrath, 339 U.S. 33 (1950), interpreting § 5(c) of the APA, 60 Stat. 240 (1946), which provided: "No officer, employee, or agent engaged in the performance of investigative or prosecuting functions for any agency in any case shall, in that or a factually related case, participate or advise in the decision, recommended decision, or agency review." Although this section has had its principal application in intra-agency proceedings, no reason appears that the statute should not apply in a case like *Texas Gulf Sulphur.* See Davis, *Administrative Law,* vol. 2, § 13.01, p. 171, for a very helpful discussion of this problem and review of the cases.

seeks to function in the same case, without prior hearing, both as the expert and as the prosecutor.

When the SEC comes into court in the posture assumed in the *Texas Gulf Sulphur* litigation, two questions must necessarily be asked by the court. The first of these, the obvious one of substantive law, would regularly be noticed by any lawyer: does Rule 10b-5 outlaw all insider trading? This was the question answered with a qualified "yes" by Judge Bonsal. He did insist that a degree of materiality, higher than the SEC liked, be retained to measure when the information was of the sort covered by the rule. But he failed to ask the second question which seems to have been ignored by everyone: has the SEC engaged in those procedures necessary for the promulgation of a rule having the effect of his holding? The SEC is in substance asking the court to declare a rule for it. Assuming that the court has some authority to do this, that authority must still be limited by the procedural requirements surrounding Commission activity. Since the rule requested in *Texas Gulf Sulphur* must have been devised after 1946, the court should, with each application, extension, or modification of a rule, respect a defendant's demand that the Commission show that it has complied with the requirements of the APA or their equivalent. This should be a minimum condition for any further development of a federal law of corporations.[199]

199. On March 16, 1967, when this article was in page proofs, the author first saw the reply brief for defendants in the case of SEC v. David M. Crawford and Richard H. Clayton, No. 30882, 2d Cir. Because of similarities of positions in that brief and in this article and a possible inference of lack of disinterest on the author's part, the author wishes to state that he does not have, nor has he ever had, any legal or financial interest or connection with that litigation, the Texas Gulf Sulphur Co., or any of its employees or past employees.

Insider Trading and the Law Professors

I. Introduction

When *Insider Trading and the Stock Market*[1] appeared in November, 1966, I was fully prepared for a goodly amount of disagreement. I was not prepared however for the emotional, almost hostile response my book received from some members of the academic community.[2] This is not to say that all the reviews by law professors were unsympathetic and emotional in tone. Indeed the majority of them were not, and while critical reviews outnumbered favorable ones, most were in some degree mixed, and the tone was generally scholarly, impersonal, and in many cases con-

Reprinted from *Vanderbilt Law Review* 23 (April 1970): 547–90, by permission of *Vanderbilt Law Review.*

1. H. Manne, *Insider Trading and the Stock Market* (1966) [hereinafter cited as ITSM].

2. *See* Hetherington, "Insider Trading and the Logic of the Law," *Wis. L. Rev.* 1967, 720; Schotland, "Unsafe at Any Price: A Reply to Manne, *Insider Trading and the Stock Market,*" *Va. L. Rev.* 53:1425 (1967). For other reviews by law professors, see Baum, Book Review, *Duke L.J.* 1967, 456; Jennings, Book Review, *Calif. L. Rev.* 55:1229 (1967); Kripke, Book Review, *N.Y.U.L. Rev.* 42:212 (1967); Marsh, Book Review, *Mich. L. Rev.* 66:1317 (1968); Painter, Book Review, *Geo. Wash. L. Rev.* 35:146 (1966). For reviews in law journals by nonlaw professors, see Garrett, Book Review, *Notre Dame Law.* 43:465 (1968); Poser, Book Review, *Va. L. Rev.* 53:753 (1967); Sommer, Book Review, *A.B.A.J.* 54:692 (1968); Tunks, Book Review, *S. Tex. L.J.* 10:179 (1968); Vogt, Book Review, *Buffalo L. Rev.* 16:520 (1967); Weston, Book Review, *Geo. Wash. L. Rev.* 35:140 (1966); Wright, Book Review, *Sw. L.J.* 21:405 (1967). *See also* Cary, *Cases and Materials on Corporations,* pp. 714–15 (4th ed. 1969). The present article will also consider Mendelson, "The Economics of Insider Trading Reconsidered," *U. Pa. L. Rev.* 117:470 (1969) (an article review of my book by a professor of finance).

structive.[3] But the response to my book in the academic community outside of law schools has been more gratifying personally. Unfortunately this response cannot be objectively measured in terms of the number of pro and con book reviews, but with a number of economists of high academic standing my book is taken as an original contribution to the analysis of an important but heretofore almost unexamined area.[4]

Some disparity of reaction between economists and lawyers is not too surprising. The book was written largely as an exegesis into economics, although the subject was of primary interest to lawyers. I claim only amateur expertise in economics, but no more than that is needed to let one conclude that the reviews of my book by certain law professors displayed an abysmal ignorance of the principles of market economics, principles which are of utmost importance if the complex subject of stock market information is to be understood and appropriately treated in the law. Many reviewers assumed the matter to be one simply of political doctrine or one to be resolved solely as an ethical or normative matter. But this is not the case. The debatable aspects of insider trading are capable of resolution through tools of economic analysis. The "discovery" of ethical and moral issues and a recurrent insistence on this approach strike me more as an outgrowth of frustration than of cogent analysis.

Another aspect of my critics' work is far more disturbing than their lack of sophistication about economic concepts. Many professors teaching securities law today have worked within the Securities and Exchange Commission. With these, and with others perhaps trained in the same point of view, there regularly appears a firm and unwavering conviction that what the SEC says is right. The desirability of securities regulation is assumed almost as a matter of faith. For 35 years hardly a law professor in the United States wrote a piece really critical of the SEC, nor had anyone ever carefully

3. I would mention specifically Professors Baum, Cary, Hetherington, and Painter for doing me the courtesy, not always displayed by others, of carefully reading and trying to understand my book and for appreciating the spirit in which it was offered.

4. *See, e.g.*, Demsetz, "Perfect Competition, Regulation, and the Stock Market," in *Economic Policy and the Regulation of Corporate Securities*, p. 1 (H. Manne ed. 1969); Benston, "The Effectiveness and the Effects of the SEC's Accounting Disclosure Requirements," *id.*, p. 23; Williamson, "Corporate Control and the Theory of the Firm," *id.*, p. 281.

analyzed the fundamental economic premises on which the Commission operates.[5] That is what I attempted to do, and what was uncovered was a fierce loyalty to a Government agency and its totally unexamined "philosophy."

This is unseemly behavior for academics. If they have a single great responsibility beyond teaching it is to be loyal, competent, and objective critics of the establishment. Political partisanship is more destructive of honest academic endeavor than is anything else. This problem, of course, goes much deeper than the narrow specialty of SEC regulation. It is at the base of much of the ambiguity surrounding the position of a law school as part of a university.[6] Forty years of legal realism and neo-realism have not been sufficient to make law professors as comfortable with other academians as they are with other lawyers.

With that introduction, or spleen-venting, as the case may be, I should like to turn to what I consider the major errors in my critics' reviews. I have selected only what I consider the more important and basic of these ideas. In the course of these various discussions, I shall also offer some new arguments which did not appear in my book, and I will discuss evidence which has appeared since my book, all of which seems strongly to substantiate my thesis. If I were writing the book now for the first time, I should certainly emphasize different points than I did initially. But the basic thesis has weathered the storm of complaint with considerably more vigor and utility than

5. There were naturally hundreds of lawyer-like pieces praising the cases or splitting legislative hairs with great skill and intelligence, even though the general tone of the great mass of legal literature in this field has been of the "how-to-do-it" variety. *See* ABA Section of Corporation, Banking and Business Law, *Selected Articles on Federal Securities Law* (1968). The first truly critical analysis was Stigler, "Public Regulation of the Securities Markets," *J. Bus.* 37:117 (1964). This piece, by an eminent economist, critical of the SEC, *Report of the Special Study of Securities Markets,* H.R. Doc. No. 95, 88th Cong., 1st Sess. (1963), occasioned cries of anguish from a somewhat coddled bureaucracy not used to criticism. Subsequent to the special study and the debate spawned thereby, only "law reform" type materials have been significant. *See* Cohen, "'Truth in Securities' Revisited," *Harv. L. Rev.* 79:1340 (1966). For an indication that future reform is in the hands of the old guard, see Loss, "The American Law Institute's Federal Securities Code Project," *Bus. Law.* 25:27 (1969).

6. *Cf.* Goldstein, "The Unfulfilled Promise of Legal Education," in *Law in a Changing America,* p. 157 (G. Hazard ed. 1968).

I anticipated for such a complex and fundamental new model of our securities markets.

II. Morals, Morals, Morals

Morals, someone once said, are a private luxury. Carried into the arena of serious debate on public policy, moral arguments are frequently either sham or a refuge for the intellectually bankrupt. Just because the phrase "insider trading" raises a specter of dishonesty, fraud, exploitation, and greed is not sufficient basis for assuming that the fact must be so or that the practice must, ipso facto, be outlawed. Yet one of the leading academic figures in the field of securities regulation stated to me personally, "We didn't need any book on insider trading. I know it's wrong, and that's all there is to it." As far as I know, however, no one has adduced actual evidence that this person is God.

For some writers the moral argument seemed to be substantiated simply by changing the terminology. To this group, insider trading must be outlawed because the information is the "property" of the shareholders.[7] These victims of acute formalism establish themselves one rung below the divinity of the last paragraph. They are content merely to conclude that they are law givers. For them the ukase that the information does not belong to the insider but rather is the property of the shareholders seems to satisfy all demands of logic.[8]

One is certainly tempted to suggest that by now intelligent lawyers would realize the emptiness of that position. They should recognize that the concept of property is no more nor less than the rights and obligations recognized by law[9] and that the statement above neither proves nor disproves a thing. But the statement was not only vacuous; as a legal matter, it was

7. Professor Jennings, for instance, clearly illustrates this fallacy when he states that inside information is not the property of the insiders, "but fairly belongs to all of the shareholders." Jennings, Book Review, p. 1234.

8. It should be clear, moreover, that the lawyers making this argument were not merely offering it as a statement of law but, perhaps more important, as a reason why insider trading should not be allowed. The circularity of this approach should be readily apparent.

9. *See* Reich, "The New Property," *Yale L.J.* 73:733, 739 (1964).

also erroneous. As I stated numerous times in my book, the question at issue was how the law should develop after the date of writing.[10] At that time the *Texas Gulf Sulphur* case[11] had not been decided in the district court, and it just could not be said with the serene confidence evinced in a number of reviews, that the information "belonged" to the shareholders. And why the *shareholders?* How about an insider selling to an outsider when the insider has knowledge of an earnings decline? Is that knowledge to be considered the "property" of the outsider? The argument is not worthy of serious attention, and first year law students should always be taught to be on guard against this fallacy.

To demonstrate just how artificial the morality and the property arguments are, one need only consider other situations in which information is used in a transaction to the benefit of the person who has it. For instance a large corporation plans to establish an extensive production facility in a new location. Typically, with all the secrecy of the CIA planning an assassination, the company will send its agents out to purchase land as discreetly as possible. The case law is clear that unless the seller has been deceived, as for instance by being told that there is no undisclosed principal,[12] the transaction is a perfectly valid one.[13] And I do not know of any commentator who has ever classified this as immoral conduct.

So notice the irony: TGS officials buying stock with knowledge of a new ore vein have somehow done something immoral, but the company itself buying surrounding land, *utilizing precisely the same information,* has merely performed in a business-like fashion.[14] Nor will it do, as one high official of the SEC tried, to distinguish these two cases on the not-so-obviously pertinent ground that "after all, one case involved land and the other securi-

10. ITSM, pp. 33–46.

11. SEC v. Texas Gulf Sulphur Co., 258 F. Supp. 262 (S.D.N.Y. 1966), *rev'd,* 401 F.2d 833 (2d Cir. 1968).

12. *Restatement (Second) of Agency* § 302 (1957).

13. *Id.* § 304.

14. This behavior was expressly condoned by the court of appeals in the *Texas Gulf Sulphur* litigation and presumably by the SEC. *See* SEC v. Texas Gulf Sulphur Co., 401 F.2d 833, 850 n. 12 ("valuable corporate purpose was served by delaying the publication of the K-55-1 discovery").

ties."[15] Lawyers especially, it would seem, should be very circumspect about characterizing the utilization of superior information as immoral. That is, after all, their stock in trade.

III. Harm to Outsiders

A. Tricks with Time

Repeatedly, academic lawyers made one fundamental error in economic analysis. The frequency of its appearance and the intensity with which it is presented suggest that this view may play an important psychological role in my critics' view of insider trading. The error, like so many in economics, has a superficial plausibility which most people never seem to get beyond. Almost at random one finds statements like, "[I]f [the shareholder] should decide to sell, he sells at a lower price than he would *if the facts were known.* . . . When the facts are known, he cannot but regret having sold."[16] Of course an individual with knowledge of forthcoming good news does not sell his shares; and manifestly he would be better off if he had the information than if he did not. Could anyone seriously think that I ever disagreed with that proposition? The fundamental premise of the entire book is that infor-

15. This remark was made by David Ferber, Solicitor of the SEC in a panel discussion during a symposium on federal and state securities regulation. Part of the panel discussion, not including this remark, is reported in "The Emergence of 'Federal Corporation Law' and Federal Control of Inside Information," *U. Mo. K.C.L. Rev.* 34:228 (1966).

16. Painter, Book Review, p. 149. *See also* Jennings, Book Review, p. 1232; Mendelson, "Economics of Insider Trading Reconsidered," p. 482; and Poser, Book Review, p. 754. Professor Schotland tried to delve deeply into this subject, but his discussion of the impact of insider trading on outsiders is incomprehensible to me. His principal error seems to result from his confusing the familiar "long-term investor" with my "time-function trader." ITSM, *supra* note 1, p. 95. In specific instances, however, he turns around and confuses the long-term investor with the price-function trader. In fact neither price nor time-function trading has anything necessarily to do with how long shares have been held.

Schotland, "Unsafe at Any Price," p. 1434, refers to trades being made "on the basis of time" and "on the basis of price." But time-function trading is not trading which occurs because the shares have been held for a certain period of time. They are trades that occur at a specific time independent of any change in the price of shares. *See* note 43, *infra.* It is difficult to understand how anyone who read the book carefully could make this error, which incidentally is also made by Mendelson, "Economics of Insider Trading Reconsidered," p. 483.

mation is a valuable good which will be sought after by human beings who prefer more rather than less of anything good.[17] It is gratifying to note that my critics at least understand that shareholders want valuable information, but they also seem to equate this simple human wish for more with some legal or moral claim and to assume that a denial of that wish constitutes an injury to those individuals.

The error, however, is not difficult to track down. To say that the shareholder would not have sold if he had had the information, in effect, switches the time of disclosure under the two rules. The critics assume a situation, without insider trading, in which the news is disclosed earlier than it is under the insider trading rule. That is, their position assumes that without insider trading the time of public disclosure will be the time at which the first insider would otherwise have traded, while a rule permitting insider trading will result in public disclosure after the insider has traded.[18] I believe that writers reached this conclusion because of what Professor Demsetz has called the "grass is always greener" fallacy derived from the "nirvana" approach to economics.[19] They are comparing the real, imperfect world of insider trading to a never-never land of perfect solutions to all problems, especially enforcement. They assume that a rule against insider trading is

17. This statement holds, of course, only if all other conditions remain the same. For a series of related economic postulates, see A. Alchian & W. Allen, *University Economics,* pp. 14–19 (2d ed. 1967).

18. Mendelson is quite insistent on making this error. He says we can only compare the case without insider trading in which "the information had been made public from the beginning." Mendelson, "Economics of Insider Trading Reconsidered," p. 482. He does not explain why this is so.

19. Demsetz, "Information and Efficiency: Another Viewpoint," *J. Law & Econ.* 12:1, 2 (1969). This is a critique of Arrow, "Economic Welfare and the Allocation of Resources for Invention," in National Bureau of Economic Research, *The Rate and Direction of Inventive Activity,* p. 609 (1962). "Given the nirvana view of the problem, a deduced discrepancy between the ideal and the real is sufficient to call forth perfection by incantation, that is, by committing the grass is always greener fallacy." Demsetz, *supra,* p. 3.

Mendelson also tries to argue that while my logic might hold for traders with absolutely no knowledge, it is faulty for those with partial knowledge, such as mutual funds. *But cf.* Jensen, "The Performance of Mutual Funds in the Period 1945–1964," *J. Fin.* 22:389 (1968); Sharpe, "Mutual Fund Performance," *J. Bus.* 39:119 (1966) (both indicating, as have other studies, including some by Professor Mendelson's colleagues, that the knowledge Mendelson posits does not exist in mutual funds).

the equivalent of a full and timely disclosure rule perfectly enforced. Unfortunately, that would not be the case. Enforcement will be imperfect at best, and there is certainly no guarantee of early disclosure even with the complete absence of insider trading. The only reasonable approach is to compare the financial status of the average outsider under the two different trading rules with disclosure occurring at the same time in each case.

After that issue is settled, then one can turn logically to the question of whether the trading rule affects the time of disclosure. If indeed a rule against insider trading could be perfectly enforced, then, with good news as indicated above, there would be no profit to the insiders and there would be a saving to those who would otherwise have sold at a subsequent time. Again, nothing inconsistent with this proposition appears in my book. But I naturally spent more time on the more important and complex comparison of the situations with disclosure occurring at the same time.

B. The Economics of Partial Enforcement

Some authors explicitly argue that allowing insider trading delays public disclosure.[20] The superficially plausible explanation is that insiders will need time to transmit knowledge to friends, assemble needed financing, or otherwise arrange a large purchase of securities. That such a propensity may exist cannot be denied, though there is little reason to believe that this would normally take much time. Contrariwise, it should be noted that insiders will usually be in a very great hurry to use their information before others get it or before it becomes worthless for unforeseen reasons. Thus they may have a tremendous incentive to use it fast. And this is only a beginning, since we cannot properly assess this issue in terms of the ideal of perfect enforcement of a rule against insider trading.[21] We live in a real world, and unfor-

20. *See* Mendelson, "Economics of Insider Trading Reconsidered," pp. 473, 489; Schotland, "Unsafe at Any Price," p. 1448. If this period were anything near as long as Mendelson implies (though his time-period implications vary throughout his article), it is very doubtful that we could see a random walk in the stock market. *See* notes 40–43 *infra* and accompanying text.

21. For further discussion of the economics of partial enforcement, see note 28 *infra* and accompanying text.

tunately enforcement of a rule like that in the *Texas Gulf Sulphur* decision is going to be partial at best. The matter has been well argued by Professor Demsetz.

> [I]t is not clear that attempts to discourage insider trading will shorten the time between the acquisition of valuable market knowledge by the firm and its revelation to shareholders and the general public. By increasing the cost of using the direct and obvious methods of capturing some of the value of this information, the SEC will encourage insiders to rely in greater degree on the less direct and more time-consuming methods. The possible or probable result will be to lengthen the time period during which insiders attempt to keep really valuable information secret. Inside information that can be used profitably only if direct trading methods are used may become available sooner or later depending on whether managers decide to reveal the knowledge or confine it to the next quarterly or annual report.[22]

Interestingly a number of aspects of the insider trading debate turn on the efficiency with which a rule against such trading can be enforced. This is a point which I discussed at length in my book[23] and have developed further in subsequent writing.[24] But with a sanguinity worthy of safer bets, my critics assure their readers that the SEC "good guys" always catch the "bad uns."[25] Professor Kripke thinks that the facts of cases like *Cady, Roberts*[26] are rare and that when they occur they are apprehended.[27] Perhaps no one whom Professor Kripke knows is guilty of a violation of Rule 10b-5; nearly everyone I know is. But the significant thing for present purposes is the failure of the opponents of insider trading to comprehend the economic and political effects of partial enforcement.

Enforcement of the rules, as well as the punishments to be meted out,

22. Demsetz, "Perfect Competition," p. 14.

23. ITSM, pp. 159–69.

24. Manne, "Prohibition on Wall Street?" *Barron's*, Dec. 16, 1968, p. 5.

25. Jennings, Book Review, p. 1232; Schotland, "Unsafe at Any Price," pp. 1456–57. While Schotland says enforcement is easy, he realizes that something that looks like insider trading regularly occurs and that the SEC does nothing about it. This is blamed on a shortage of funds! *Id.*, pp. 1474–75.

26. *In re* Cady, Roberts & Co., 40 S.E.C. 907 (1961).

27. Kripke, Book Review, p. 214. I wonder if Professor Kripke would really care to defend this proposition.

will of necessity be discretionary and discriminatory. There is no way to avoid this. Decisions will have to be made about where the limited enforcement resources can be spent; they will inevitably be spent to oppose those least in favor with the Commission.

If we look at the great failures of liberal governments to maintain their principles, it will readily be seen that a significant danger has been laws which could not be or were not readily enforced against all violators. The most obvious example from modern history is the American experiment with prohibition. The breakdown of law began because the potential payoff from illicit activities was extremely high relative to the risk of apprehension and punishment. Effective enforcement on a broad scale would have required unacceptable police measures. Only partial enforcement was feasible. As a result a cancerous corruption of law enforcement officials resulted from the undoubtedly well-intended prohibition.

Political discretion in such government areas as zoning and occupational licensing have likewise lent themselves to corruption of governments and demoralization of communities. And the blackmail and corruption potential of partially enforced rules against prostitution, gambling, and narcotics are too well known to need discussion.

The more decent, law abiding, and risk-averse members of the financial community will not knowingly engage in insider trading if it is a prohibited activity. They have the most to lose from apprehension and are thus the most vulnerable to charges by the SEC. But the scoundrels and those with little to lose—or perhaps just the very sharp and clever operators—will quickly fill any gap. Thus the absence of the more high-minded participants from a segment of the securities field makes it that much more lucrative and attractive for those we least want to encourage.

This phenomenon has been nicely described by Herbert Packer as a "crime tariff."[28] A tariff, of course, puts imported goods at a competitive disadvantage compared to domestic goods and to that extent protects the domestic producer. Partial law enforcement, similarly, gives a completely unwarranted competitive advantage to those against whom the law is not enforced.

28. Packer, "The Crime Tariff," *Am. Scholar* 33:551 (1964).

Historically, it seems that this created a vicious cycle. Those who became richer by the illicit activity found it profitable to expend some of their resources to corrupt government officials in order to preserve their monopoly positions. That is, they try to guarantee enforcement against competitors while preserving their own sanctuary. The Volstead Act again affords the best-known illustration, though many more exist. Selective and partial enforcement by the SEC of the whole gamut of 10b-5 and related rules will in all likelihood result in some new group of insiders growing wealthier and eventually constituting a vested interest with strong influence over the very government regulatory agency created to protect the public. There is no reason to believe that individuals who can profit by partial enforcement of SEC rules against insider trading will not try to do so.

C. Distributive Effects of Legal Rules

There would be real harm to outsiders if they were being deprived of something that we could normally characterize as their "property." That is, if there were an existing rule of law stating that all information belongs to shareholders or would-be shareholders, then to change that rule would be to deprive existing outsiders of something they had some right to continue to enjoy. It is extremely doubtful that any significant part of the stock trading public assumed that any such rule existed. No one has actually claimed so. And no matter how loudly the contrary is shouted, at the time of the writing of my book there was no rule to this effect.[29] There were practices

29. I certainly made it clear in my book that I was not referring to § 16(b) of the Securities Exchange Act of 1934, 15 U.S.C. § 78p(b) (1964). I was at some pains to explain that I had no great quarrel with that provision, since I did not believe that it was effective to counter the most significant form of insider trading, trading in a company's shares by an individual who has reliable information from an inside source but who is not, within the meaning of § 16(b), 15 U.S.C. § 78p(b) (1964), an insider himself. This is what Louis Loss has referred to as "tippees." I chose to use the more descriptive term for a trader with reliable information of "advisee." I bow now to a superior word popularizer. At any rate it is inconceivable that any careful reader of my book would not be aware that it was addressed to the problem posed by the pending interpretation of Rule 10b-5, 17 C.F.R. § 240.10b-5 (1969).

I did say about § 16(b), 15 U.S.C. § 78p(b) (1964), that it might possibly serve to prevent

and warnings, to be sure[30] (many people have noticed the pushy ways of federal regulatory agencies), but no rule existed whose change I was advocating. While my critics may claim that I am "seldom inclined to let facts interfere with theory,"[31] the thing that emerges much more clearly is their total unwillingness to allow either facts or theory to interfere with their wishes. Moral fervor, whether held by fundamentalist ministers or by law professors, is not easily shaken by rational argument. So much then for the

---

some manipulation in stocks by statutory insiders. Indeed this was the only real justification that I could find for it since its official justification has almost no persuasive force, even among its supporters. *See* L. Loss, *Securities Regulation,* pp. 1042–43 (2d ed. 1961). As I stated, "Section 16(b) can be rationalized as an antimanipulation device but not as an effective prohibition of insider trading. . . .

"[N]either legislative history nor the subsequent literature on the Section has viewed Section 16 as another of the antimanipulation devices Congress included in the 1934 Act." ITSM, p. 30. Nonetheless Professor Jennings concluded that I claimed § 16(b), 15 U.S.C. § 78p(b) (1964), was "mainly aimed" at preventing manipulation. Jennings, Book Review, pp. 1230–31 n. 3.

30. *See* Fleischer, "Securities Trading and Corporate Information Practices: The Implications of the Texas Gulf Sulphur Proceedings," *Va. L. Rev.* 51:1271 (1965).

31. Jennings, Book Review, p. 1232. Professor Jennings has also erroneously alleged that I would shrink from allowing insiders to sell information for cash. Jennings, Book Review, p. 1231. This is simply incorrect. What I said was that "[a]lthough there are no cases directly on the point, it is very likely that a court would hold the direct sale of insider information by an insider to be a breach of fiduciary duty." ITSM, p. 60. I then mentioned two legal analogies that could be made and stated that I thought neither of them was analytically the same as a direct sale of information. The point I was making was about the obtuseness of legalists, not about the undesirability of selling information in an open market. Certainly if this right could be found as an implicit or explicit part of a contract between an insider and his corporation, I would not shrink from enforcing it.

In the same vein Professor Jennings, Book Review, p. 1233, wrongly asserts that I would also fault the holding in Meinhard v. Salmon, 249 N.Y. 458, 164 N.E. 545 (1928). But I would view this case exclusively as a matter of defining an implicit contractual term. Had the matter been explicitly provided for in the agreement, it should have been enforced as written. Clearly I could not possibly have the same objection to that case that I have to *Texas Gulf Sulphur.*

While I am at it, I might just point out that Professor Jennings displays gross lack of familiarity with economic concepts when he states that neither is the question of allocation of resources pertinent—we don't allow stealing even though the thief may have a better economic use for the money. Jennings, Book Review, p. 1223. See the index of any good micro-economic text to gain some feeling for my sense of frustration with this and similar views. *See* Mendelson, "Economics of Insider Trading Reconsidered," p. 470.

argument that shareholders are injured by insider trading because they are losing a legal interest they have been led to believe was theirs.

The real analytical point at issue is the distributive effect of a rule allowing insider trading as compared to the effect of a rule effectively preventing it. There is of course some immediate distributive effect to changing any legal rule on which persons have relied. But that is a separate issue (and much less significant quantitatively) from that of how a rule will affect different categories of persons forever in the future. I spent at least two chapters in my book on this subject.[32] Unfortunately, I must have confused several reviewers of the book. Indeed, one confessed that, "[t]he reviewer (no economist or mathematician he) could not cope with the purported mathematical demonstration."[33] This confusion, however, did not deter him from concluding that it was "apparent on the face of things that the author's description of the stock market behavior of a stock uninfluenced by insider trading conformed to nothing existing on earth."[34] This sentence displays only his inability to comprehend a straightforward abstract model of a market situation, and his little amusement of having an anonymous mathematician look at the diagrams[35] certainly tells us far more about him than it does about my work. Why a mathematician? Why not an artist to criticize the aesthetic value of my drawings? The latter might have had more to offer.

32. ITSM, pp. 77–110.

33. Kripke, Book Review, p. 213.

34. *Id.* This may take the prize as the most disingenuous statement in any of the reviews. I somehow have the feeling that Professor Kripke joined a coterie of critics who tried to see who could laugh the loudest at my work. He may or may not have realized that this was more a matter of strategy than of serious critique. Professor Schotland reports that the former Chairman of the SEC, Manuel F. Cohen, had agreed to review the book and then "understandably" changed his mind. Schotland, "Unsafe at Any Price," p. 1425 n. 2. SEC insiders, after an initial outburst of high-level fury, apparently concluded that either silence or laughter would be the most effective device for countering the effects of my insidious book. They were correct and, furthermore, this strategy has not been unsuccessful. But, while I cannot say that I have enjoyed being chided in public as a modern version of the village idiot, I believe there is evidence that my work is beginning to have significant influence on thinking in this field. Why, even Professor Jennings has referred to it as "the beginning of a counterrevolutionary effort." Henkel, "Codification—Civil Liberty Under the Federal Securities Law, Conference on Codification of the Federal Securities Laws," *Bus. Law.* 22:793, 882 (1967) (remarks of Richard W. Jennings).

35. Kripke, Book Review, p. 213.

Several legal writers failed to comprehend that an economic discussion may (indeed, often must) be offered in terms of the performance of functions rather than in terms of real, identifiable human beings.[36] This, as we have seen, leads Schotland and others to confuse my "time-function trader" with the "long-term investor" of popular financial parlance.[37] Interestingly, Professor Schotland fails to mention once, a matter that I, as opposed to he, consider basic to my thesis. The crucial omission from this and other reviews is any mention of the so-called random walk hypothesis of stock market price movements, which is crucial to an understanding of this subject.[38] I referred the reader of my book to all the literature on the random

36. For a definition of functional analysis in economics, see A. Alchian & W. Allen, *University Economics,* pp. 21–22.

37. *See* note 16 *supra.* The elaborations of this error in Schotland's article are too extensive even to summarize. But I should like to repeat the point made in my book that the period of time for which shares are held has absolutely no necessary relevance to the question of whether a particular transaction is either a time-function or a price-function transaction. To repeat, the price-function trader is one who buys or sells securities exclusively on the assumption that he has received significant information from an observed price change, and time-function traders are everyone else. Manifestly one may be a price-function seller of shares he has owned for 50 years, and just as clearly one may be a time-function seller of shares he acquired yesterday. The error was constantly made of relating my time-function trader to the familiar long-term investor. This confusion completely skews the analysis since the price-function trader is making an assumption that he has new information about the company, while the time-function trader makes no assumption about having new corporate information. He trades for reasons exogenous to the market price of the shares.

38. Having missed a truly basic point, but sure that there is one, Schotland's error about functions leads him to conclude that "the prevalence of such an 'induced effect' is one of the basic assumptions of the Manne thesis." Schotland, "Unsafe at Any Price," p. 1444. The reference is presumably to the existence of price-function traders, that is, those who base buy or sell decisions on changes in share prices caused by insiders' trading. I do not understand how Professor Schotland concludes that the "prevalance" of this trading is one of the "basic assumptions" of my thesis. The only reason such traders have any relevance for the discussion was to see whether anyone was injured as a result of insider trading, and that analysis would not be changed in any particular if no one traded on this basis since it would then be impossible to find a group injured by this kind of trading. Indeed, the very significance of the discussion of the "random walk" was that these traders do not have any real information. Consequently, their trades merely supplement the random movement of stock prices.

This is one of so many misstatements of my thesis as to have left me completely bewildered as to how to deal with this particular review. Time and temperament prevent my responding to every error. I hope that independent persons may in the future study both works carefully in an effort to straighten out my disagreements with Professor Schotland. Several economists to whom I have shown his work find it so uninformed and error-ridden as not to warrant serious attention. Less surprisingly perhaps, a Commissioner of the SEC has stated publicly that Professor Schotland has destroyed my thesis.

Professor Schotland's article was presumably prepared during the summer of 1967 when he enjoyed some sort of close and friendly relationship with the Securities and Exchange Commission in Washington. There is internal evidence of this relationship during the time of writing. *See* Schotland, "Unsafe at Any Price," pp. 1456–57 n. 88. Professor Schotland quotes my statement that "rumors of the Texas Gulf discovery had already reached flood proportions in Washington." "In fact," says Schotland, "the 'flood' was not even a good flow, but a mere trickle." *Id.* He then cites a "reliable authority" to the effect that my statement was not true since "fewer than a dozen people in Washington *bought* Texas Gulf shares in the period in question." *Id.* But I had stated nothing about how many people in Washington actually bought shares, only what I had heard about the TGS rumors. Also, what is the "period in question"? Did it start in November 1963 or March 1964 or some other time?

Professor Schotland, presumably according to the same reliable authority, goes on to state that "[t]he SEC traced all the round-lot buying which originated in Washington, and even the buying done in New York by New York residents *known to have been phoned* by relatives or friends in Washington. Almost all of these purchases were traceable directly, or at one remove, to tips from the site geologist." *Id.* (emphasis added). When Professor Schotland says that the SEC traced all round-lot buying which originated in Washington, I presume that this means the SEC traced all round-lot buying placed by brokers in Washington. But unless every transaction in the stock were traced, the SEC could not know that Washingtonians were not utilizing non-Washington brokers for this purpose. Indeed there is strong independent evidence that many Washingtonians do their trading in that fashion. *See* "Leaky Capital: Washington Attracts Many Seeking to Profit from Inside Information," *Wall Street Journal,* Mar. 14, 1968, p. 1, col. 1.

But the most disturbing thing about Schotland's disclosure is the apparent claim that the SEC knows which New York residents purchasing Texas Gulf stock phoned or were phoned by relatives or friends in Washington. Alternatively Schotland could be saying that the SEC traced New York purchases they were told about by Washington sources. Then, of course, the statement would be of no significance whatever. It seems more likely that the former interpretation is correct. But if that is so, how could the SEC have this information? They may have means of which I am unaware, but it would seem necessary for them first to have the list of all individuals in New York ordering Texas Gulf stock. That might be a fairly sizable job and still not reveal the true beneficiaries of every transaction, but I will presume that the SEC did this. Then I presume that it would be within their frightening power to check telephone company records of Washington calls to and from these individuals. Of course, they might also find other interesting information in this way, such as that certain officials in Washington were holding telephone conversations with racketeers or that persons under investigation were in clandestine communication with judges or with the White House, congressmen, or other public officials. In other

walk idea existing up until that time, and I tried to explain it in fairly simplified terms to readers who might be unfamiliar with the concept.[39]

---

words, the SEC, through Professor Schotland, now appears to admit the utilization of an extraordinarily dangerous police state tactic in the interest of what at best is a minor moral obsession. We hear regularly of the dangers of invasion of privacy from computer banks of information and other technological methods. Well, the danger is here, and the worst may be happening daily. Is it not ironic that my critics call me a conservative?

39. My attempt to introduce this material and explain its importance was evidently overlooked by Professor Schotland when he stated that my book does not "cite or draw upon any empirical studies to support its thesis, nor itself offer any new data." Schotland, "Unsafe at Any Price," p. 1443 n. 59. It is, of course, a favorite gambit of reviewers to criticize an author for not writing the book they would like but also have not written. I must respectfully decline the gambit. I had no intention of preparing a statistical study of insider trading, nor would I be qualified to do so.

The clear implication of Professor Schotland's reference to my failure to cite empirical data is that I was hiding evidence contrary to my thesis. *See* Schotland, "Unsafe at Any Price," p. 1443 nn. 59 & 60. I do not apologize for not finding unpublished theses, but one of the works cited by Professor Schotland, that of Professor Wu, "Corporate Insider Trading in the Stock Market, 1957–1961," *Nat'l Bank Rev.* 2:373 (1965), came to my attention when my book was in galley proof. I concluded then that since Professor Wu had devoted himself exclusively to instances of insider transactions reported under § 16(a) of the Securities Exchange Act of 1934, 15 U.S.C. § 78p(a) (1964), his work was not actually relevant enough to my thesis to warrant the expense of changes at that point. I had heard of the book by E. Smith, *Management Trading: Stock Market Prices and Profits* (1941), and that the same thing was true there, but I was unable to locate that book in any library in Washington, D.C., including the Library of Congress. I did not try to use the library at the SEC.

But none of the works cited by Schotland contained data of the sort that I "repeatedly deplore the lack of." The data I requested, ITSM, p. 63, easily within the power of the SEC to ascertain, would almost conclusively settle much of the controversy, since it would have shown the amount of *indirect* insider trading. *See* note 44 *infra*. The second thing to note about Professor Schotland's remarks is that he apparently read Professor Wu's findings quite the opposite of what they are. *Compare* Schotland, "Unsafe at Any Price," p. 1445, *with* Mendelson, "Economics of Insider Trading Reconsidered," p. 479.

The truth is that I was wrong about the propriety of Wu's and Smith's approach. I assumed that indirect insider trading was so tremendously important that no statistically significant amount of direct trading by insiders in the stock of their companies would show up. Since the publication of my book, the most scholarly and exacting study yet on the subject of direct insider trading has appeared. *See* Lorie & Niederhoffer, "Predictive and Statistical Properties of Insider Trading," *J. Law & Econ.* 11:35 (1968). Their conclusion is unmistakable and convincing. "Insiders tend to buy more often than usual before large price increases and sell more than usual before price decreases." *Id.*, p. 52. This study is actually a devastating blow to anyone who wants to proclaim that insider trading has not regularly been occurring or that it does not continue even now.

Without going into great detail, readers should understand that the existence of random walk in stock market pricing is generally taken by economists as an indication that the market is functioning very efficiently,[40] that is, that the market assimilates new information quickly and accurately. Significant time lags in the assimilation of new information would presumably show up as nonrandom movements. If every outside purchaser or seller of securities confronts a random walk—and it must be remembered that if the hypothesis is correct, this condition will exist for every trader other than one who actually has inside information—then for any given transaction he cannot know whether he would benefit or be harmed by either of the rules on insider trading. That is, he cannot know at point X whether he will be benefited or harmed at point $X + Y$ by a rule allowing insider trading or by a rule forbidding it. By hypothesis, he has no basis for predicting in advance (without information, as he is) what his ex post position would be. Since he cannot know what these two positions would be in advance, he has no way of comparing one to the other.[41]

There are various other works as well which support this and other aspects of my total thesis, though not quite so directly. *See* Mendelson, "Economics of Insider Trading Reconsidered," p. 479 nn. 21–23. *See also* note 43 *infra.* But one of the more ironic must be mentioned now. Professor Wu, the very one Schotland most relies upon, has, in a subsequent work, made the strongest plea since the appearance of my book for allowing insider trading because it is economically beneficial. He concludes that "the arbitrary short-term trading restrictions provided by Section 16(b) and the recent vigorous attempt of the SEC to apply Rule 10b-5 to insider trading may be harmful to the economy." Wu, "An Economist Looks at Section 16 of the Securities Exchange Act of 1934," *Colum. L. Rev.* 68:260, 269 (1968).

40. *E.g.*, Samuelson, "Proof That Properly Anticipated Prices Fluctuate Randomly," *Indus. Mgt. Rev.* 6:41 (2d pt. 1965). *See also* Mandelbrot, "Forecasts of Future Prices, Unbiased Markets, and 'Martingale' Models," *J. Bus.* 39:242 (1966).

41. Consider a bettor at the race track who looks over the odds and sees Romper Roy at 10 to 1. We can assume that those are correct odds in the sense of accurately measuring the probability of Romper Roy's winning. If this is the case, it makes no difference to the bettor that someone else actually *knows* that Romper Roy ran his early morning test mile in record time and has a better than usual chance of winning today, even though the odds are correct at 10 to 1. Presumably the odds, like the stock price, will at race time reflect all information known about the horse. If the morning workout had been skipped, the odds might or might not be 10 to 1 now, but we cannot say that a casual bettor is better or worse off because someone else in fact knows the information. Rossett, "Gambling and Ration-

My critics should realize, however, that the existence of a random walk does not necessarily militate against the view that no insider trading is occurring. Indeed, if there were instantaneous recognition of new information by all participants in the market, as would be the effect of perfect enforcement of a rule requiring timely disclosure and no insider trading, a random walk would still appear.[42]

I take the random walk as support for my proposition because I cannot conceive of information being disclosed and assimilated that perfectly by a broad spectrum of investors in the market. I believe that the random walk is better explained by the existence of large scale insider trading than it is by the general absence of this practice.[43]

---

ality," *J. Pol. Econ.* 73:595 (1965) (an important article with perhaps more significance for the insider trading question than would appear at first glance).

Part of the confusion probably results from the different frames of reference of the economist and the lawyer. When I say that no individual trader faced with the random walk can predict his future position under the different insider trading rules, I refer to one individual taken as representative of the entire class of all traders. It would not be fair for instance to pick out the single individual who by happenstance would be the one selling to an insider with undisclosed good news. *Accord,* Loss, "The American Law Institute Federal Securities Law Project," *Bus. Law.* 25:27, 35 (1969); Painter, "Inside Information: Growing Pains for the Development of Federal Corporation Law Under Rule 10b-5," *Colum. L. Rev.* 65:1361, 1377 (1965). Now it is true that one individual or more must occupy that position, but in advance no one can know who that is, and an individual would certainly be foolish to stay out of the market because insider trading was allowed, or to enter it because it was forbidden.

42. *See* note 40 *supra.*

43. *See* Fama, Fisher, Jensen & Roll, "The Adjustment of Stock Prices to New Information," *Int'l Econ. Rev.* 10:1, 20 (1969), where the authors conclude that the stock market is so efficient in reflecting new information that no one without inside information could benefit from almost immediate purchases of stock upon announcement of a stock split (which is followed by higher subsequent dividends per share). We can choose one of two explanations for this efficiency. Either the market, through public disclosure (or magic), instantaneously reflects the new value, or insiders are causing the price change. Which explanation would you choose? Other studies are equally convincing on this matter of the stock market's phenomenal efficiency in reflecting new information. Since it is very doubtful that much of this is caused by direct insider trading, my hypothesis about a market for information and indirect insider trading seems strongly substantiated. The best current summary will be found in Fama, "Efficient Capital Markets: A Review of Theory and Empirical Work," Jan., 1970 (unpublished manuscript, University of Chicago). *See also* Scholes, "A Test of the Competitive Market Hypothesis: The Market for New Issues and Secondary Offerings" (1969) (unpublished Ph.D. thesis, University of

IV. Existential Mysteries of Insider Trading

When I wrote *Insider Trading and the Stock Market,* I believed that the SEC was probably fairly efficient in preventing any direct insider trading. Certainly the requirement that direct trading in his own company's shares by an officer, director, or ten percent shareholder be reported under 16(a), plus the sanction of 16(b), would effectively discourage most of this obvious kind of insider trading. And yet, the first significant study of this phenomenon indicates beyond any doubt that a significant amount of *direct* insider trading continues to the very present, though presumably without a purchase and sale occurring within six months of each other.[44]

At this point I should like to deal with another common error in my critics' reviews. Repeatedly, they become confused about how I was using the word "insiders." I tried to make it clear that I was referring to *any trading* by any individual based on information which had not yet been publicly disclosed or completely exploited by other traders.[45] I did not intend to qualify the term in the usual ways that lawyers might think of. I certainly did not limit my definition to officers, directors, and ten percent shareholders,[46] nor did it make any difference in my view whether the individual who ultimately traded knew what the facts were or merely traded on the basis of informed advice which he trusted.[47] I spent an entire chapter dis-

Chicago) (strongly suggesting insider "knowledge" by pointing out that secondary offerings by control persons are more profitable to sellers than secondaries sold by anyone else); Jensen & Benington, "Random Walks and Technical Theories: Some Additional Evidence," Dec., 1969 (unpublished paper presented at American Finance Association Meetings, New York).

44. Lorie & Niederhoffer, "Predictive and Statistical." The astounding thing is that so much insider trading shows up even though stock must be held for a minimum of 6 months after it is purchased, since the insiders reporting in the study by Lorie and Niederhoffer would have been liable for any gains made by a purchase and sale within 6 months under § 16(b) of the Securities Exchange Act of 1934, 15 U.S.C. § 78p(b) (1964). I would still believe that the vastly greater source of knowledgeable trading is done by those at least once removed from statutory insiders.

45. *See* ITSM, chs. 4, 5.

46. Not too surprisingly, it was an economist who seemed most to have confused § 16(b), 15 U.S.C. § 78p(b) (1964) and Rule 10b-5, 17 C.F.R. § 240.10b-5 (1969). *See* Weston, Book Review, *Geo. Wash. L. Rev.* 35:140 (1966).

47. ITSM, p. 63.

cussing various methods by which the value of information could be transferred without an actual transfer of the information itself.[48] Discretionary accounts and straight recommendations to buy (without further explanation) are two of the more obvious. Since writing the book, I have come to understand that I should have included limited partnerships in investment banking houses and a variety of mutual funds as well.[49]

It would be relatively easy for the SEC to perform the statistical test necessary to answer the question of how much indirect trading occurs. They need only get an appropriate set of tax returns showing stock market trading profits for individuals who could be identified as likely to have access to information about companies. The results of the trading of these individuals would then be compared to that of a control group such as security analysts or professors of finance, who certainly have considerable sophistication but who do not necessarily have access to new information.[50]

If the results of such a test showed the former group to be doing significantly better in the stock market than the latter group, we might then have confirmation of my thesis of how new information gets transmuted into the proper stock market price. But, as I have said before, until such a test is performed, it should not be assumed that people with access to tremendous wealth would let it slip through their fingers like sand. The opposite assumption is vastly more in keeping with our knowledge of human nature and business institutions.[51]

48. *Id.*, ch. 5.

49. Text accompanying notes 108–12 *infra.*

50. Somehow Mendelson, "Economics of Insider Trading Reconsidered," p. 473, assumes that security analysts will have inside information because they have thoroughly familiarized themselves with the company. Apparently he and I have a different kind of information in mind.

51. I made the precise point of this last sentence in a concluding paragraph of Chapter 5 of my book. I began that paragraph with the following sentence: "The important proposition of this chapter is that the market for valuable information described actually exists." ITSM, p. 75. I then mentioned that the chapter had examined the evidence to substantiate this proposition and concluded as I have in the text above. This paragraph sent Professor Schotland gyrating to dizzying literary heights: "I find this paragraph astonishing. The leap from the *opening assertion that the case has been proved* to the very different conclusion that at least its opposite has not been proved is dazzling—the blur of fact, allegation and assumption, dizzying." Schotland, "Unsafe at Any Price," p. 1432 n. 22 (em-

I am neither a statistician nor a mathematician, but I urge any reader to try the following simple test that I and students of mine have conducted on several occasions: write down for some period of time every story appearing in *The Wall Street Journal* which could be expected to have a truly significant impact on a company's stock price; then go through the price reports well before and after that disclosure to find when the correlating price change seemed actually to occur.[52] My somewhat unscientific evidence to date suggests that in a very large percentage of cases the stock price reaction occurs before the news appears in print. And this is at least consistent with every statistical study relevant to the same question.[53]

---

phasis added). This is followed by a characteristically "cute" quote from Lewis Carroll, the characteristic being Schotland's, not Carroll's.

I found this footnote of Schotland's not astonishing, but puzzling, mainly because I could not understand the italicized phrase. Finally it dawned upon me that Professor Schotland did not know the meaning of the word "proposition." For his edification I quote from *Webster's Third New International Dictionary* (1961): "something proposed or offered for consideration, acceptance, or adoption . . . , the point to be discussed or maintained in argument usually stated in sentence form near the outset. . . ." *Id.*, p. 1819.

No wonder Professor Schotland has such difficulty understanding insider transactions; he doesn't know a proposition when he sees one.

52. This is not a rigorous test; at best the results should be termed impressionistic. There are very great difficulties in trying to correlate new developments with stock price changes, since prices are changing for a variety of reasons at all times and one cannot be certain that the information which seems to be desirable will actually be taken that way. As Lorie and Niederhoffer state, "[u]nfortunately, analysis of insider trading around such events in isolation from the price movements of the company can never reveal whether insiders profited from their information. For example, the price of the stock frequently increases consistently before and after the announcement of a divided reduction and a decrease in earnings." Lorie & Niederhoffer, "Predictive and Statistical," p. 46.

53. Again, the best thing on the subject is Lorie & Niederhoffer, "Predictive and Statistical." They analyzed insider trading before large price changes in a stock (defined as changes of 8% or more) and found insiders to be considerably superior forecasters of large changes. In fact, such a difference between insiders and non-insiders could occur incidentally only in 1 out of 10,000 cases. Their other tests gave similar results. *Id.*, pp. 46, 47, 49. Indeed, anyone interested in the subject of insider trading must study this article carefully. This is also consistent with the interesting study of Bellemore & Blucher, "A Study of Stock Splits in the Postwar Years," *Financial Analysts J.* 15:19 (1956). They report findings that from 8 weeks before to the day after the announcement of a desirable stock split, 86 out of 100 stocks registered percentage price increases greater than those of the Standard and Poor's Stock Price Index for the relevant industry group. From the day after to 8 weeks after the announcement date, however, only 43 stocks registered percentage

We should not be fooled by the scarcity of SEC enforcement actions[54] into believing that there is not much insider trading and that the SEC apprehends that little bit when it occurs—though that is what we are told the facts are.[55] That is like pleas to New York City cab drivers to treat Harlem like any other section of the city since the police do not make any more arrests for muggings there than elsewhere.

There is no reason to believe that the use of valuable information, albeit perhaps in the indirect fashion which I discussed in my book, has changed in any significant degree in the years since *Texas Gulf Sulphur.* The truth of the matter is that the much touted, highly sophisticated, computerized detection techniques used by the SEC to ferret out insider trading do not work very well. This may explain why they have not publicized these techniques, though it is said that their machines pick up any dramatic shift in price or volume in trading in a particular stock.[56] This must be a long, long way from proving, or perhaps even suspecting, which individuals are exploiting new information. The peculiar thing is that the SEC has announced so few cases. While I do not believe their enforcement techniques are nearly as good as they say, I find it difficult to believe that they could be as bad as their track record would indicate. Perhaps the Commission does not fully investigate every insider trading case. It could be that already this extremely potent device is being used arbitrarily or politically.[57]

---

price increases greater than the relevant industry index. There must be some reason for this disparity, and the most likely is certainly insider trading. *See also* S. Pratt & De Vere, "Relationship Between Insider Trading and Rates of Return for NYSE Common Stocks, 1960–1966" (1968) (unpublished manuscript available from Professor Shannon P. Pratt, Portland State College, Portland, Oregon).

54. Since the much heralded *Texas Gulf* litigation began, there have been only 2 announced matters involving indirect insider trading. SEC v. Golconda Mining Co., *CCH Fed. Sec. L. Rep.*, ¶ 92, 504 (S.D.N.Y. Oct. 30, 1969) and the Merrill Lynch matter involving Douglas Aircraft stock, SEC Securities Act Release No. 8459 (Nov. 25, 1968).

55. *See, e.g.*, Kripke, Book Review, p. 214. *See also* note 106 *infra.*

56. Jennings, Book Review, p. 1232. *See also* 1966 *SEC Ann. Rep.* 8–9.

57. *Cf.* M. Shulman, *The Billion Dollar Windfall*, p. 219 (1969) (reporting the whispered suggestion that this explains the appearance of the *Texas Gulf* case in the first place).

V. Stock Market Efficiency

There are still at least two good reasons for defending insider trading aside from the point that ultimately there is no loss to outsiders from the practice. The more controversial of the two arguments is that insider trading provides an appropriate form of compensation for entrepreneurial activity in large corporations. The other argument, that insider trading makes the stock market function more efficiently, is probably the more obvious economic argument.

The efficient functioning of the stock market is actually one of the strongest arguments for unfettered insider trading, though at first blush it may appear to have little relationship to the issue at hand. I must confess that the significance of this point escaped me at the time I wrote my book, even though the point itself was recognized.[58] For this reason I cannot take my critics to task for not realizing that there was a very significant additional argument for insider trading. Of course, they were not exactly looking for arguments in its favor.

Efficiency in the stock market refers to both the speed and accuracy with which the market integrates new information into the market price of a security.[59] All other things being equal, the more efficiently the stock market functions, the better off everyone is for many reasons. An efficient market is one in which capital will be allocated to its highest-return uses, thus ensuring that capital goes into those uses with the greatest individual and social utility. This significance of the stock market as an allocator of capital has long been recognized.[60] More recently recognized, however, is that stock market prices may also serve to allocate management and the control of

58. *See, e.g.,* ITSM, p. 88. *See also* Manne, "Our Two Corporation Systems: Law and Economics," *Va. L. Rev.* 53:259, 266 (1967). For a slightly different version of this thesis, see Wu, "An Economist Looks at Section 16 of the Securities Exchange Act of 1934," *Colum. L. Rev.* 68:260 (1968).

59. *See* Benston, "The Effectiveness and Effects of the SEC's Accounting Disclosure Requirements," in *Economic Policy and the Regulation of Corporate Securities,* p. 26 (H. Manne ed. 1969).

60. A. Berle & G. Means, *The Modern Corporation and Private Property,* p. 280 (1932).

corporations.[61] The price of a company's stock is the best indicator of the performance record of existing management and the potential profitability of a takeover. Thus to the extent that the stock market is functioning efficiently, both the capital markets and the market for corporate control function more effectively.

The ultimate social significance of market efficiency is somewhat difficult to assess. It is, of course, an oft-stated goal of the SEC, though that alone does little to establish its significance. Ultimately, the desirability of efficiency in a market relates to individual goals. If we assume that individuals can maximize their own trading positions or diversify investment portfolios more accurately with information than without, then it follows that the most rapid and correct reflection of new information in quoted prices will allow each individual the maximum opportunity to help himself. Delays in the reflection of new information, or the inaccurate reflection of information, must increase uncertainty in the market and thereby make beneficial trading more costly and less likely than would otherwise be the case. But it is the nature of the case that at any one moment, no individual knows whether the market is operating efficiently or not for the security he contemplates buying or selling. The gains from efficiency are diffuse and often specifically unidentifiable. If it were otherwise, commentators would probably not treat the SEC so nicely when it lessens that efficiency.

A. Market Speed

Quite clearly there is a time lag between the development of new information and its ultimate publication to outsiders, even if we could assume perfect compliance with a rule against insider trading. But, as discussed earlier, perfect enforcement is not possible, and therefore subterfuges and devices to circumvent the rule against insider trading will be discovered and utilized. Of necessity these devices will consume time, and to the extent that

61. Manne, "Our Two Corporation Systems," p. 265; Manne, "Mergers and the Market for Corporate Control," *J. Pol. Econ.* 73:110 (1965). *See also* Bromberg, "The Securities Law of Tender Offers," *N.Y.L.F.* 15:459 (1969); Schwartz, "The Effect of the 1934 Act on Sales of Control," *N.Y.L.F.* 15:674 (1969).

time is expended in order to avoid compliance with the SEC rule, all other individuals who benefit from an efficient stock market are injured.

Nonetheless, we have it on the affidavit of Professor Schotland that

> *[a]llowing any* trading on undisclosed material information makes improper delay of disclosure more likely. . . . To ensure timely disclosure—an end to which the SEC and the self-regulatory bodies are equally dedicated—it is obvious that we must avoid encouraging motivations for improper delay, however subconscious they may be. If we abandon restraints on insider trading, we tempt insiders to delay disclosures so that they can buy more shares or arrange financing for more buying; we also invite the timing of disclosure to get maximum market response.[62]

Perhaps this need not detain us, however, for in the very next sentence, just in passing, Professor Schotland contradicts himself: "[O]n occasion the concern for insider trading profits might cause disclosure to be made earlier than it would be without insider trading; but they may not be in the best interests of the corporation. . . ."

There are several errors in the principal quote that should be exposed, since Schotland is not the only one who makes them. First of all he implies, without any supporting evidence, that present restraints on insider trading are completely effective. Obviously, if they are not completely effective then Professor Schotland cannot know that the time spent in circumventing rules would not be greater than the time spent in "arranging financing" or whatever else needs to be done to capitalize legally on information. The presumption would seem to be the opposite, but Schotland never notices the impact of partial enforcement, and consequently his position is unrealistic.

He did, however, take note of the obvious proposition that the disclosure time for a great deal of news cannot be controlled and therefore is not delayed by allowing insider trading. But then, in what seems like a fretful non sequitur, he responds that it is no "answer to allow unfettered inside trading by personnel who have no role in deciding upon the timing of disclosure. . . ."[63]

62. Schotland, "Unsafe at Any Price," pp. 1448–49 (emphasis added).

63. *Id.* p. 1449. Professor Schotland has in this response apparently shifted the ground

Another thing that Professor Schotland fails to realize in his conclusion is that any insider trading must cause an improper delay in disclosure. People with accurate and reliable information will generally be well advised not to risk their almost certain profit by delaying the exploitation of that information. That is, their incentive will be to move very quickly, with whatever resources are at their command, to profit from their information. Even if news were 100 percent reliable and correct, with each additional minute, hour, or day the probability of a new event occurring to cause a decline in the same stock's price rises rapidly. It will generally be a poorer but wiser insider who fails to take immediate advantage of reliable information. It should be noted that disclosure must in any event occur fairly shortly after insider trading if the insider is to make any profit. While his own trading and that of other traders may drive the price up, it would ordinarily be extremely expensive to maintain such a high price unless new information justifying it is disclosed. In the short run, then, insider trading may have the same effect as disclosure, but in the longer run, unless there is very substantial money supporting the market, disclosure will have to occur very quickly.[64]

Possibly Professor Schotland and the SEC could adduce individual cases in which some form of delay in disclosure occurred while insider trading was or might be occurring. But once again, perhaps with a need for more

---

away from the point at issue, the timing of disclosure, back to the propriety of insider trading.

64. This point, I believe, explains the rough going Professor Mendelson has in trying to establish outsider injury. His "long run," where he posits some injury, probably *never* occurs. Mendelson, "Economics of Insider Trading Reconsidered," pp. 476–77. His argument is as follows: Since all shares of stock are readily substitutable and investors plan their portfolios based on diversification of anticipated rates of return (discounted by risk), insider purchasing of securities on undisclosed information would seem to have an undesirable effect. As insiders purchased without disclosing reasons why, other investors would continue to evaluate the shares as they previously had, and thus would want fewer of those shares at the new higher price causing a decrease in the price of the stock. Q.E.D. Insider trading on good news causes lower prices for shares. Mendelson's error, apart from the fact that it is blatantly contradicted by every empirical study ever made on the subject, derives from his failure to realize that insiders will disclose the information long before the secondary effect he describes can take place. Schotland makes exactly the same mistake, "Unsafe at Any Price," p. 1448.

patience than I have, one is constrained to point out that social policy should not be made on the basis of episodic vignettes taken from the annals of SEC enforcement actions. We must either utilize hard, accurate data or we should proceed on the assumptions dictated by the most logical economic doctrines. Lawyers simply must get over their bad habit of assuming that because they can conjure up one horrible case, it must reflect the general behavior of humanity; otherwise, someone eventually will be tempted to say that social policy is too important to be left to the lawyers.

B. Market Accuracy

1. Feasibility of Disclosure

The second functional relationship between insider trading and an efficient stock market might be termed accuracy. The point most simply stated is that insiders are generally in the best position to weigh new information accurately and assess its future impact on market price. To some degree, however, speed and accuracy become intermingled, for ultimately the proper weight to be attributed to any information becomes evident to others in the market. One may indeed have to wait months or even years until the true value of the information shows up in the form of changed earnings, but ultimately the truth will come out. The most important question is who is in the best position to do this weighing at the time the information actually develops.

The answer to this question has far reaching significance. It calls into doubt not simply the rule about insider trading, but the entire "philosophy of full disclosure." This so-called philosophy has captivated many observers of government regulation. The popularity of the notion accounts in large measure for the almost religious fervor with which politicians, bureaucrats, and professors adore the SEC. After all, who can be against full disclosure? The very suggestion smacks of condoning fraud, lying, and deceit. Nor need one join the radicals to favor a regulatory philosophy of full disclosure since it is simply designed to make free markets function better.[65] Thus, propo-

65. It also allows such nonsense statements as that "any friend of the free market . . .

nents of this idea can appear at one and the same time to be practical hard-headed men of affairs and yet idealists concerned with the commonweal.

Historically, the idea traces back to the early part of this century,[66] but it was just a bit of academic rhetoric until the advent of the Securities Act of 1933, the "Truth in Securities" law. At that point a great innovation was proclaimed, an administrative system designed, not to regulate, but to make promoters and underwriters tell the full truth about new securities. Even today the idea of direct securities regulation makes a dedicated SEC partisan frown. He knows that direct regulation—unless it happens to be of investment advisors, stock brokers, stock exchanges, holding companies, or mutual funds—is futile or even harmful, and he prefers not to be involved with petty administration that is better left to state Blue Sky administrators.

Over the years, adherents of the disclosure religion have had it very easy, psychologically speaking. No one has seriously questioned their belief. Indeed, whole new generations of lawyers have been brought up to appreciate the beauty of the disclosure arrangement. But "full disclosure" should no longer enjoy this sanctuary. In the Age of Aquarius, some troubling questions simply must be raised. For instance, what is the cost of administering a full disclosure system *as compared to the benefits actually gained;* what private interests are actually benefited, and at what cost to others; what is the effect of the present system of disclosure on the production of valuable information; and to what extent is the service provided by the SEC merely a subsidy to a financial group who would otherwise have to pay their own way?

For now, however, we must limit ourselves to another very fundamental question, so fundamental indeed that one is almost embarrassed for his profession to report that prior to the publication of *Insider Trading and the Stock Market,* no one had ever raised it. The issue is whether full disclosure is in any meaningful sense feasible! Can it even be done?[67]

We start by recognizing that there are two kinds of information in the

---

almost certainly should urge additional regulatory steps." Schotland, "Unsafe at Any Price," p. 1468. The problem becomes the solution.

66. W. Ripley, *Main Street and Wall Street* (1927) is the best-known work on the subject.

67. The discussion following is not intended to be an exhaustive catalog of all disclosure feasibility problems. The effort is merely to note some of the highlights.

world: (1) information which has been previously disclosed or evaluated in the market, and (2) information which represents a move to a new objective circumstance, that is, change. I denoted these as first and second category information. I apologize for such prosaic titles, and if that is why the reviewers have ignored the point, perhaps they were justified.

First category information has no market value as such, since the present market price fully reflects all the past events leading to the present position. It is a free good[68] and is of no direct interest to this discussion, though it is of some derivative interest, as we shall note shortly.

New information relevant to a security's price, second category information, may be of many different sorts. Although some of this information does not lend itself to full disclosure in the usual sense at all, it is the only kind of information relevant to individual stock price changes. We may organize interesting bits of information about change into several broad categories. First, we might look at the familiar kinds of financial information. The financial news most commonly affecting share price is a significant change in annual earnings. Yet, even the least sophisticated market habitues are familiar with cases where apparently excellent earnings are met by a neutral or even negative market response. Conversely lower earnings may not cause what would seem to be a sufficient decline in price. Simply having the new earnings figure might not be sufficient to allow informed trading.

There are numerous possible explanations for this phenomenon. The most likely is that the information has already been anticipated in the market. That is, the new earnings report is not actually news at all, and only those with blind confidence in the SEC's disclosure philosophy could be misled into losing money by following such a disclosure. More important for immediate purposes, however, is the possibility that the current earnings, while not previously discounted, are still insufficient to change the market's estimate of the present value of potential future earnings. Sometimes this may be evident to a good securities analyst, but there must be a significant number of instances in which the best guess about the company's present worth is based not on current earnings but on information that has

68. A free good has been defined as one for which nothing at all need be sacrificed to acquire as much as one wishes. *See* A. Alchian & W. Allen, *University Economics.*

not been or indeed could not be legally divulged in any SEC-regulated financial statement.[69]

There is another kind of information which the SEC seems absolutely determined to hide from the world. This is the true value of the capital assets used in a business. The familiar rule, rigidly enforced by the SEC, is that assets must be carried by the company at the lower of cost or market, minus depreciation.[70] No matter how much inflation has occurred and no matter how much a particular asset may have appreciated, the SEC generally forbids publication of the true value.[71] Asset values would seem to be first category information and therefore not of great interest. However, in some specialized instances they may become extremely relevant. If for instance the useful life of a particular asset is about to expire, analysts may be very interested to know the replacement cost. More important is the possibility that always exists for an asset to be sold at a high profit.[72]

This is not the appropriate place to enter a lengthy discussion of problems of asset value accounting.[73] But it is proper to make one simple observation: insiders in a company or an industry are frequently the only people who can possibly make realistic valuation assessments. Of necessity, they will generally be able to do this more accurately and efficiently than anyone else, and there may be no accurate or efficient way of passing this information along to the public.[74] Consequently, allowing those individuals to trade on this information would necessarily improve the efficiency with

69. *E.g.*, Rule 14a-9, 17 C.F.R. § 240.14a-9 (1969) (forbidding predictions as to "specific future market values, earnings or dividends" in proxy solicitation materials).

70. *See generally Business Organizations—Securities Regulation,* vol. 11, H. Sowards, Federal Securities Act § 8.01[3] (1965).

71. I say "generally" because apparently when it suits their purpose the SEC will change rules in midstream. *See* Manne, "Some Accounting and Administrative Law Aspects of *Gerstle v. Gamble-Skogmo, Inc.,*" *N.Y.L.F.* 15:304 (1969).

72. The SEC in Gerstle v. Gamble-Skogmo, 298 F. Supp. 66 (E.D.N.Y. 1969), tries to make a classification of assets for which "a ready market exists." *See* Manne, "Some Accounting," p. 320. But since that likelihood, at least in the real world, is always a function of the price offered in the market for the asset, the test will probably not yield helpful results.

73. *Id.*, pp. 314–27.

74. Consider, for instance, whether one should use replacement value or liquidation value, and how to compute these? *See generally* R. Chambers, *Accounting, Evaluation and Economic Behavior,* chs. 9, 10 (1966).

which the stock market assimilates new information into stock prices. *A fortiori,* the same analysis holds for the SEC's other big bugaboo, earnings estimates.[75]

There are many other accounting issues about which the same point can be made. For instance, there are all those accounting questions on which there is more than one generally accepted accounting standard. One need only wander lightly over issues such as inventory accounting, treatment of tax credits, allocation of overhead costs, merger accounting, and accounting for economic risk (e.g., leases or stock options) to realize that a science of accounting is still an idle dream. Basing a regulatory system on the idea that such an ethereal concept is scientific guarantees either that the public will be deceived or that the market cannot function efficiently, or both.

Frequently, new developments in a firm or industry cannot be the subject of full disclosure. The development may be a new product, a new mineral discovery, an important government or private contract, a finding of a health hazard in a product—or any of these things happening to a competitor. For a variety of reasons it may be impossible to make a straightforward, useful disclosure to the public. Obviously this need not be true in every case, but there will be a significant number of such cases, and we know almost nothing about the magnitudes involved. Not surprisingly, nothing is ever said about these instances by proponents of the full disclosure philosophy.[76]

For example, a new defense contract may inevitably lead to an actual loss for a company, even though the unsophisticated public's reaction to the news would be to bid up the price of the stock. New product announcements have frequently occasioned this sort of difficulty.[77] Who can know how much start-up costs will be, or what the market might be for a new

75. Rule 14a-9, 17 C.F.R. § 240.14a-9 (1969).

76. Presumably a few lawyers who practice actively in the area are sophisticated about these problems when they arise. But their knowledge relates more to techniques for dealing with the SEC on the matter than to the policy or quantitative questions left hanging in this area. In the camaraderie of intra-professional conversation most lawyers admit that many of the most significant facts relating to the value of a company stock never pass through the SEC's disclosure mill. *But see* Mendelson, "Economics of Insider Trading Reconsidered," p. 476.

77. *See, e.g., In re* Cady, Roberts & Co., 40 S.E.C. 907, 908 (1961).

product, or what the competition has up its sleeve? It would be far better to allow those insiders who understand these matters in detail to "make the market" for these companies' shares. True, a good securities analyst may discover much of this information, but equally true, he will rarely be in the same position as insiders to assess all of the relevant factors. Furthermore, information can be processed and acted upon much more quickly by an insider than by the public, and, of course, the insider can hire outside expertise as well as the next man. The list of problem disclosure areas could be enlarged indefinitely, yet all one hears about are developments which *in retrospect* the SEC argues were appropriate for full public disclosure.[78]

The final type of information which does not lend itself to full disclosure might be termed management news. In this category occur some of the most significant events ever affecting business. High on the list would be the problem of personal animosities developing within a corporation which threaten to tear apart a smoothly functioning organization. Certainly no one seriously proposes public disclosure of such sensitive, and often private, information. The benefit to competitors would far outweigh any benefits others might receive from the information. But the effect of a full disclosure rule in these circumstances is necessarily to maintain an artificial price until the disruption in management has caused severe deterioration in the earnings of the company or some other dramatic event has occurred. During that entire period of time the market price of that company's securities could be wrong. Can anyone seriously suggest that the harm to the public from this is somehow less than it would be from allowing insiders to assure an informed current price for the company's shares?

Other managerial developments might have the same effect. The most common is probably the case of failing health of a key executive. The problem of failing mental faculties could never be objectively reported, though they might be clearly observed by others around the executive. Again, how much smoother and more efficient it would be to allow insiders to register this news in the market, even though actual disclosure would not be possible.

78. The two signal cases in this regard are Texas Gulf Sulphur, 401 F.2d 833 (2d Cir. 1968), and Gerstle v. Gamble-Skogmo, Inc., 298 F. Supp. 66 (E.D.N.Y. 1969).

The point should now be clear. Asset valuation problems, accounting issues, competitive positions, potential earnings, and managerial developments are examples of news items that will always prevent the philosophy of full disclosure, no matter what its theoretical merit, from existing in the real world. The time is past for assuming on faith that the amount of disclosure which does actually occur as a result of SEC rules is either significant or by itself helpful.

2. The Market-Smoothing Effect of Insider Trading

The suggestion that insider trading gives us a more efficient stock market leads to still another advantage which I did not discuss in my book.[79] There I was concerned exclusively with the exploitation of news about significant events.[80] In fact, however, it is desirable to have all ups and downs smoothed out to the extent possible by an efficient market mechanism that reacts sensitively to even small inappropriate movements. This suggests the desirability of allowing insiders in corporations to do something on the order of "making a market" in their company's shares. As indicated above, they are in the best position to do that job effectively, and, in spite of some expressed fears that they would spend all their time trading in the market, there is really no reason to believe that this practice would have undesirable effects on their managerial skills. It would remain true that good management would bring the greatest profits to the managers. The time necessary to exploit information, or correct misconceptions as they appear in the market, would in all likelihood be considerably shorter than the time required to circumvent rules against insider trading.

In over-the-counter stocks, where market makers may still occupy positions on boards of directors, this is almost exactly what occurs, and it is

79. *See* note 58 *supra.*

80. I took these to be events causing a 10% or greater change in the stock's price. For a while, perhaps under the influence of *Texas Gulf Sulphur,* I felt that I had been too optimistic and that I should have considered changes in the range of 20% to 30%. Lorie & Niederhoffer, "Predictive and Statistical," however, used changes of 8% to indicate significant price movement. The point in the text is that the figure really makes no difference, since if it is large enough to motivate insiders to trade, that is the trading we are talking about.

difficult to see the market maker as anything other than a privileged insider.[81] Would it not at least be a good idea for the SEC to know whether underwriters make or lose money in their market making function? Does anyone seriously believe that market makers have no more information than public investors, or less than the chief executive of the company? And how are we "nuts"[82] supposed to think they get it—through research?

C. Market Manipulation

To complete the discussion of whether or not allowing insider trading would give a more efficient market than do post–*Texas Gulf Sulphur* legal rules, we must still look at one additional factor that may vary with the rule. That additional factor is market manipulation. No one defends this, and there is general agreement that manipulation does add a high cost to the functioning of the market. It causes the market to function less efficiently, that is, to reflect objective values less accurately. Moreover, individuals are directly injured by manipulative activity, as with any fraudulent behavior.

Manipulation differs dramatically from insider trading, just as a reliable tip on a winning horse differs from having the race "fixed." If all insider trading could be effectively prevented, there would probably be no fraudulent manipulation of stock prices, since no one could gain from it. But that does not decide the underlying issue about insider trading, for clearly there may be policing costs which are too high for anyone to accept. After all, outlawing horse racing is the surest method of preventing fixed races.

No evidence has been adduced by the SEC or its spokesmen that allowing insider trading actually encourages manipulation. Professor Schotland[83] is hard pressed to say anything meaningful about manipulation. He conjures up one single situation in which insiders have bought shares well in advance of disclosure of the information and then manipulated the market to keep

81. He is, however, exempt from the usual short-swing insiders' profit rule. 1934 Act § 16(d), 15 U.S.C. § 78p(d) (1964). *See also* SEC Securities Act Release No. 7905 (June 16, 1966); L. Loss, *Securities Regulation* 5:3084, 3089 (1969).

82. This term, as applied to me, originates with the SEC official quoted in Schotland, "Unsafe at Any Price," p. 1425.

83. *Id.*, p. 1449.

the price high over a lengthy period so that they would not lose on their purchase. Among other things, he does not explain to us why insiders in these circumstances would buy at all when they did. Perhaps more important, he does not tell us how they will perform the particular manipulation involved, or why they would not make the disclosure earlier. If in fact they are able to perform this task without detection, they have every interest in doing so *regardless of the rule against insider trading*. For that matter, people who are not insiders would have just as much interest in doing so. Therefore, even if such activity really does go on, which is highly doubtful, its relationship to the rule regarding insider trading is not proved.

Even more mystifying is Professor Schotland's second and concluding reason why insider trading makes manipulation more likely: "As seen earlier, insider buying in itself does not have any significant impact on share price. But the contrary may well be the case, if a group of insiders intentionally time their buying so as to affect the price. It is an old tactic of manipulation to intentionally time orders to have such effect. . . ."[84] It is an old tactic of polemical debate to use obfuscation as a conscious means of argument, and we have here a perfect example. Even apart from the volte-face on the price impact question, this statement as an argument against insider trading is meaningless. At best, it only says that manipulation of stock market prices is possible. To give it one more bit of credit, it also says that this may be done by insiders. It certainly does not say that it may not as well be done by others or even that such action is not more likely to be done by outsiders. The case used to illustrate the point, *SEC v. Georgia-Pacific Corp.*,[85] is actually inapposite since it does not even deal with an insider's utilizing undisclosed information to gain an edge in stock trading. It is a case of stock price manipulation to which the insider aspect is purely incidental.[86]

84. *Id.*

85. [1964–1966 Transfer Binder] *CCH Fed. Sec. L. Rep.* ¶ 91,692 (S.D. N.Y. 1966).

86. *See* SEC v. Golconda Mining Co., *CCH Fed. Sec. L. Rep.* ¶ 92,504 (S.D.N.Y. Oct. 30, 1969) (while not providing reliable evidence of the impact of insider trading rules on manipulation, this case at least illustrates the point Professor Schotland had in mind).

D. The SEC's Confidence Game

Supporters of the SEC have voiced one further argument against insider trading. It is an all-purpose argument which undoubtedly originated in the earliest days of federal securities legislation. In its general form it seems to say that unless the public knows that the market is being regulated by the government, they will be afraid to invest in the public securities market. The specialized variant for insider trading purposes says that if the public believed that insider trading was occurring regularly, they would lose all confidence in the stock market and cease investing funds there.[87]

There are several things wrong with this line of argument. The first and most obvious is that the public has never shown any signs of losing confidence in the stock market because of the existence of insider trading. No one cognizant of the history of the twenties could claim otherwise. In 1929 there were over twenty million shareholders on the books of American companies,[88] though the actual number of individual investors was, of course, much smaller. Nonetheless, it is doubtful that direct shareholders during the bull markets of 1962 or 1968 actually were a larger percentage of the total population than those of 1929.[89] Moreover, all of this occurred with the widest publicity and notoriety imaginable being given to bull pools and other insider trading devices. In fact, stories of these activities were the normal daily fare of the pre-crash financial press. The loss of public confidence in the stock market is not visible. The public, it would seem, is less gullible than spokesmen for the SEC.

The next problem with the confidence argument is the implicit proposition that insider trading is not occurring today. As we have already seen,[90] there is little evidence to warrant that assumption. But publicizing such an idea may have troublesome consequences. Some unsophisticated members

87. Marsh, Book Review, p. 1320; Poser, Book Review, p. 754; Schotland, "Unsafe at Any Price," p. 1475; Sommer, Book Review, p. 692.

88. R. Sobel, *The Great Bull Market,* p. 73 (1968).

89. New York Stock Exchange, *Economic Effects of Negotiated Commission Rates on the Brokerage Industry—The Market for Corporate Securities and the Investing Public,* p. 13 (1968).

90. *See* notes 39 & 43 *supra.*

of the investing public must believe that the SEC has removed all risk of loss from the securities market, or at least lessened it in some meaningful sense by stopping insider trading. That, of course, is not the case. The risk to an outsider is unchanged in any significant degree by the insider trading rule adopted. Therefore, some investors are lured into the stock market by an SEC-instigated notion that the risk is less than is actually the case.

I doubt that a great many people have been sandbagged by the government in this way, though a reliable informant at the Commission tells me that a substantial amount of mail is received by the Commission and Congress from individuals complaining that they have lost money in the stock market even though the SEC was supposed to prevent this.

There is undoubtedly some problem of public confidence in the integrity of the participants in the stock market. The disclosures of fraud and manipulation by the Pecora Hearings[91] in 1933 were by no means without foundation. But the actual fraud and manipulation publicized by the hearings never involved just trading on inside information, and in numerous instances there was no insider participation whatever. The public does have a real interest in knowing whether fraudulent types of criminal behavior are being effectively policed. Unfortunately, it is impossible to assess how good or bad a job the SEC does on this, as they do not publish adequate data from which a reliable conclusion could be drawn. Probably their detection and prevention of truly harmful behavior could be improved upon. Certainly if they would devote more of their resources to such clearly justifiable activities, everyone would be better off.[92]

There is one other aspect of the confidence argument which should be examined. It is the questionable assumption that there is some clear social interest in having people channel their savings into investments in the stock market. Of course, stock exchanges, brokers, and underwriters are benefited by any encouragement a government agency can give their particular efforts, but that is not necessarily true for the public. Any savings will even-

91. *Hearings on Stock Exchange Practices Before the Senate Comm. on Banking and Currency,* 73d Cong., 1st Sess. (1933).

92. Actually the SEC seems to be bucking a trend, since elsewhere the direction of criminal law is away from enforcing purely moral codes such as those involved in the prohibition of pornography, marijuana, prostitution, and insider trading.

tually become invested, and the money does not have to be channeled through the stock market to effect this. Commercial banks or any number of other intermediaries might serve as well.

This is not to suggest that the stock market is not a highly efficient and desirable means for channeling investment. It is to say, however, that it is unseemly for a government agency to gear its regulatory activities to encouraging business for the industry it is supposed to regulate. In principle, at least, the SEC should be indifferent to whether the public prefers stocks to savings accounts or mutual funds to brokers. It is well recognized, however, that agencies do come to "represent" their industries—usually to the public's detriment,[93] and they do this typically under the guise of keeping the industry "healthy," so that the public will not lose confidence in it.

VI. Entrepreneurial Reward

My principal affirmative argument for insider trading was that it provided a meaningful form of compensation in large corporations for the entrepreneurial function. This occasioned the greatest and most vociferous opposition of any point in the book. In a way, this was quite surprising, since the principles I drew upon constitute the most fundamental and basic postulates known to economic theory; people would rather have more of a good thing than less, and normally there is a point at which a person will give up some amount of one good to gain an amount of another which he values more highly.[94] That is, human wants are infinite, and all demand curves have negative slopes. As a corollary, the amount of the goods offered goes up as the price offered increases.

In terms of the thesis of the book, one need note only, as Professor Schotland said, some "simple economics." If any service presently being purchased by the corporation is compensated more highly, more of that service

93. For an excellent inside story on regulatory agencies, see "The Regulators Can't Go On This Way." *Business Week*, Feb. 28, 1970, p. 60. Incidentally, Ralph Nader is quoted therein as saying that stock tips are used to pay off agency staff members in Washington. *Id.*, p. 65.

94. A. Alchian & W. Allen, *University Economics*, p. 16.

will be offered. Valuable information is an economic good that can be substituted for other media in which the higher compensation can be paid. If the service performed is or can be one which gives access to valuable information, less of other forms of compensation must be paid in order to secure the same amount of the service.

This is true regardless of the nature of the employment. It is true of clerks, accountants, lawyers, or someone performing an entrepreneurial service. Clearly, if some entrepreneurship is being performed for publicly held corporations, more of it will occur if the potential pay-off is greater. One may argue about identifying the performers of this function or controlling access to information. But the basic point stated above simply cannot be denied or disparaged. There are economic laws, and they are not repealed by anyone's ignorance of them, whether participants or observers.

The news may not impress my critics, but I for one still cannot understand why anyone finds it to be unfair, unjust, or immoral to allow a voluntary arrangement in which individuals are given an additional incentive to produce more of a valuable commodity by sharing in the new value they produce. Lawyers familiar with the contingent fee should scarcely be surprised. But law professors apparently are not comfortable with abstract ideas of economic functions, like entrepreneurship.

A. The Moral Imperative

In some ways the most disconcerting thing about many of the reviews of my book was the strange belief that we *must* decide whether everyone will act in one way or the other; either every corporation must allow insider trading, or none may. Why the note of compulsion? Why the moral imperative? Why not the liberty of choice?

It is difficult to understand the origins of this particular attitude. Perhaps it derives from a notion that the express contractual terms of an employment relationship must describe all aspects of that relationship. Thus, if an individual enters into a contract providing a straight salary and no other form of compensation, then it is argued that he is entitled only to that salary and nothing else. Any additional income is, as various proponents of the

Texas Gulf rule have declared, "covert," "unjust enrichment," or "unnecessary to secure performance." As Professor Hetherington in his generally logical and insightful piece states:

> [T]here is a strong argument that the innovations produced by these persons have already been bought and paid for. Their employer gives them salaries, bonuses, stock options, retirement plans and freedom from the distracting worries of running a business, worries that beset the small inventor attempting to exploit his idea.[95]

While more calmly stated than most, this is typical of the underlying notion that the terms of an employment relationship in a corporation must be set either by regulatory authorities or explicitly in a fully integrated contract of employment.

Manifestly there is no such doctrine of contract law, and yet none of the usual legal approaches to the question of intent or implied rights are discussed.[96] No effort is made to show that the parties either by their actions or their ambiguous words intended salaries, bonuses, and other benefits to be the total means of compensation. Silence does not usually have that effect.

Why then is everyone so quick to insist what the implied provision in an insider's employment contract must be? Why do they assume that the implied provision is so different today than it per force was before the development of Rule 10b-5? And why finally do they assume that anyone advocating no government rule against insider trading is necessarily saying that it may not be banned in a private contract? All the evidence seems to lean in the other direction—or at least it did before *Texas Gulf Sulphur.*

I think that part of the answer goes to a set of attitudes characteristic of many academics and their students. We live, as Professor Hetherington eloquently points out, in a period of "moral escalation."[97] But what Professor Hetherington fails to note about this condition is how often moral indignation is used as a cover for unanalyzed conclusions. While it is certainly the province of professors to identify and explain such developments as

95. Hetherington, "Insider Trading," p. 727.
96. *See* A. Corbin, *Contracts,* vol. 3, § 561 (1960).
97. Hetherington, "Insider Trading," p. 734.

moral escalation, it is their ultimate responsibility to seek rational, logical answers to social problems. As much as they might like to don the mantle of high priests of moral theology, this is neither their assignment nor their skill. Theirs is a difficult job, but it will not long be respected unless the academic profession stands foursquare behind the idea of rational inquiry.

At no point in my entire book do I express the belief that corporations should be *required* to tolerate insider trading.[98] As an economist or objective analyst, I do not care what any corporation may do in this regard. I personally would prefer to invest in the shares of corporations which did allow insider trading. But if through legal means a corporation properly indicates that its rule is no insider trading, that should be the business of that corporation and its shareholders and the courts if a violation is alleged. I wish that I had said this earlier, but all I am pleading for is a *rule of full disclosure.* If the SEC were faithful to its stated philosophy, it would simply require every corporation to state whether or not insiders will be allowed to use information in the stock market or under what conditions this will be allowed. No more need be done.

Government regulators, however, do not like to take the risk of having the regulated sector and the free market sector so easily compared by the public. With regulatory philosophies as vacuous as those which have been offered by friends of the SEC, it is no wonder that they seek refuge in moral laws. And moral laws, unlike the rules of government in a free society, can admit of no choice contrary to their dictates. If one is to be moral, HE SHALL NOT ENGAGE IN INSIDER TRADING. Deviant behavior, whether condoned by the board of directors, the shareholders, or anyone else, remains immoral and unjust. The main trouble with moral escalation is that it is so frequently fatuous.

98. Manifestly that would be contrary to my whole economic philosophy. The only point of my book was to defend individuals and corporations from the coercive mandate of a government agency. Not one single reviewer noticed that while I am *allowing,* they would all *forbid absolutely.* Ironically Professor Schotland states "that the Manne thesis miscasts the issue by stating the question in terms of black and white: Shall insider trading be free, absolutely, or banned absolutely?" Schotland, "Unsafe at Any Price," p. 1439. The rest of the discussion on the same page bears reading by anyone interested in the logical quality of this work, but I will not trouble the reader with it further.

B. Enough Is Enough

Professor Schotland says that there is "no reason to believe that available forms of compensation are inadequate to stimulate [entrepreneurial activity]."[99] I believe that he reads into my work attitudes and thoughts that are foreign to it. I never talk about adequacy or inadequacy in a vacuum. I do not know the distinction between an adequate and an inadequate amount of entrepreneurial activity. Like the economists, I can only say that if a larger amount of compensation is offered for the performance of a function, more of it will be forthcoming. I will stand by that statement until some evidence is shown to the contrary. I might add that that proposition has stood the test of time as well as anything known to the social sciences.

A related point, which piqued nearly all the reviewers, was that the individuals who will exploit the news may not truly be entrepreneurs.[100] I discussed this point at length in my book and explained many reasons why non-entrepreneurs would have access to new information.[101] The treatment of this material in the reviews was highly selective and frequently inaccurate, and I see nothing to be gained by rehashing the same points. Rather, I should like to try a different tack and suggest to my critics that it really does not make any difference who gets unexploited information or whether we can pin the tag of "entrepreneur" on him. To reach the general conclusion of my thesis, it will be sufficient merely to posit that the flow of information to individuals without legal constraint is *not random*. About this, there should be no argument, for if the flow is random, everyone has an equal chance to benefit from it, and there would be no significant "insider" problem. Thus, presumably everyone agrees that in an unregulated or partially regulated information market, the flow of new information will to some extent be directed.

If the allocation of information is in fact purposive, individuals can make behavioral decisions based on the expectations created thereby. The ad-

99. Schotland, "Unsafe at Any Price," p. 1457.

100. Brudney, "A Note on Chilling Tender Solicitations," *Rutgers L. Rev.* 21:609, 625 (1967); Hetherington, "Insider Trading," p. 727; Jennings, Book Review, p. 1233; Kripke, Book Review, p. 213; Marsh, Book Review, p. 1319; Painter, Book Review, p. 151.

101. *See, e.g.*, ITSM, pp. 65, 66, 69, 70, 153, 156–58, 160, 161, 171–89.

ditional wealth (or some positive probability of achieving this wealth) will still be viewed as additional compensation by those to whom it will be directed or allowed to flow. If other compensation remains the same, more of their function will be offered by them or by others and their incentive to produce new information or to cause more to be produced will be greater.

Since they have the most to gain thereby, the individuals receiving information will already have or will eventually gain some power to encourage new developments. This, I take it, is the quintessential function of the entrepreneur in classical theory,[102] and it is what I had in mind in my book. But it should have been clear to any reader that I did not wish to suggest that all recipients of information would necessarily be this kind of entrepreneur. I was at great pains to point out[103] that leakage of confidential information is quite common and that normally it would not pay insiders to invest in perfect policing. I also pointed out that information might be used to pay off a variety of debts, thus making it appear that the information was being used by individuals with no important connection whatever to the corporation. It is somewhat astounding to see some of these very points turned around and used as criticisms of the thesis in which they appear.[104]

Much of this dispute relates to the question of whether one can assume a detectable, controllable, nonrandom flow of information within a corporation. By implication the critics seem to be saying that while it is not random, it *always* goes to the wrong people. Schotland, for instance, states that it is an "ineluctable fact . . . that the use of confidential information, if permitted at all, cannot be kept from running rampant."[105] This, incidentally, is followed by the ineluctable proposition that it is "comparatively easy for the SEC and the self-regulatory bodies to detect insider trading on undisclosed material information."[106] Why it is so much easier for the SEC

102. *Id.*, pp. 115–19.

103. *Id.*, p. 169.

104. *See, e.g.*, Schotland, "Unsafe at Any Price," p. 1456.

105. *Id.*

106. *Id.* Professor Schotland is not alone in this claim. *See* Jennings, Book Review, p. 1232; Kripke, Book Review, p. 214. *See also* Poser, Book Review, p. 754. Professor Schotland tells us at some length about the SEC's "stock watch" program which has "no problem"

than for people who have a real economic interest in detecting this loss is not made clear.

My prediction of SEC ineffectiveness in policing insider trading would have been even more accurate had all participants in the stock market realized how poorly the SEC enforces its rule. But Wall Street is terrified of the SEC, and this definitely changes some individuals' behavior.

There is, however, one thing on Wall Street which will overcome even terror—money. The potential for profits in the utilization of previously undisclosed information is enormous. I do not know of anyone who has ever totaled up the full value of all the new developments in a year for listed companies, but it must be in the tens or even hundreds of billions of dollars, every single cent of it adding to the incentive to find a way to avoid the terrible plight of the *Texas Gulf Sulphur* insiders. With odds like that it is not surprising that they have been fairly successful. Their very success may have created whole new institutions in the financial community and had international repercussions and countless personal effects. But succeed they undoubtedly have, for if they had not, there would not be, as Professor

---

in tracing buyers and sellers whenever there is suspicion of insider trading. Schotland, "Unsafe at Any Price," p. 1456.

Professor Schotland proceeds then, as he does on several other occasions in his article, substantially to contradict himself. On the very next page he concedes that tracing may be made impossible by the use of "straws" or Swiss bank accounts. I presume by "straws" he means literally everyone that I include in my discussion of indirect trading on undisclosed information. But this doesn't worry him since "there are not likely to be many such people. Compared with most activity that must be made unlawful, enforcement here is as easy as it is for a young family to figure out who ate the cookies." Let's see how easy it is to figure out who has to eat crow.

Schotland fails to recognize that the amount of violation of any law is a function of the benefit to be gained by the violation. He then calmly proceeds to contradict himself by citing a point with which I could not agree more, "the frequency with which significant corporate news is preceeded by a notable rise in share price and then is followed by 'selling on the news.'" Schotland, "Unsafe at Any Price," p. 1474. And as topping for the dessert, just a few pages later we have confirmation of this very point from none other than former SEC Chairman Manuel F. Cohen: "We have recently received indications that premature disclosure of corporate information to limited groups of people who are in a position to act on it may be more prevalent than we had supposed." Schotland, "Unsafe at Any Price," p. 1478. So my critics no longer have to take my word (and that of the economists cited in footnotes 39 and 43 *supra*) for the existence of a substantial amount of insider trading. They also have it on the authority of Professor Schotland and Mr. Cohen.

Schotland reminds us, such a high "frequency with which significant corporate news is preceded by a notable rise in share price . . . followed by 'selling on the news.' "[107]

C. Adjustments to the New Rules—
The Interesting Case of Mutual Funds

Interestingly, it is possible to find in the mutual fund industry examples of personal, institutional, and international adjustments to rules about insider trading. It is well known, of course, that this industry has had an enormous growth in the past fifteen to twenty years, and in the last five years we have seen the rapid expansion of the hedge funds and in the last year or two, a veritable mushrooming of "off-shore funds." Perhaps there is some link between each of these developments and the need to find acceptable modes for marketing new information.

Even though the value of new information in American companies every year is enormous, it is obviously difficult for a small number of insiders to exploit all this news. Some mechanism is needed which will allow this information to be marketed profitably to masses of people. It could be sold directly in the form of investment advice, and it could be added to the value received from brokers who charge more than a competitive price for their service. Finally, it could be marketed on a truly grand scale through investment companies. It is this last hypothesis which we examine here.

If mutual fund management companies are in some sense "selling" new information to mutual fund shareholders, we might look for compensation arrangements which would reflect this fact. Since the value of a specific bit of information remains constant regardless of the size of the mutual fund, any given bit is worth less to each mutual fund shareholder as the total fund is larger. Thus, a given piece of information, worth say one million dollars, results in a net improvement of ten percent in a ten million dollar fund and of one percent in a hundred million dollar fund. But as the new information is used by a smaller fund, that fund naturally grows larger. The ideal arrangement, therefore, would allow fund managers to be compensated on

107. Schotland, "Unsafe at Any Price," p. 1474.

the basis of growth of the fund up to a certain point and then to switch over to compensation on the basis of total asset size. At that point it would pay the fund managers to manage the enlarged fund conservatively so as to give investors adequate diversification of risk but no growth from actual new information. Any new information would then be channeled into a new small fund, and the entire process would be repeated time and again.

If this hypothesis is true, we should anticipate that smaller funds generally would tend to be less conservative than large ones and figure more prominently in the annual list of high performance funds. But we should not anticipate many years' repetition of high performance by any one fund.

Every aspect of this hypothesis seems to conform to what we know about the recent history of mutual funds.[108] The only problem with the thesis is that it would hold true equally for fund managers who either "guessed" correctly about which stocks to buy or ferreted out their solutions by so-called technical analysis. The latter hypothesis actually seems easy to rule out since every study indicates the near impossibility of succeeding in the stock market with this approach.[109] The guess hypothesis is a little more difficult, since obviously the moves of guessers will be pretty much random—some will go in one direction and others in another. Since there will be a successful and an unsuccessful direction, some will win and some will lose. The winning guessers will look just like the managers hypothesized to be using inside information rationally. But there will still be ways of distinguishing the two. A fruitful approach to this question, for instance, might be to examine the performance records of new funds established by successful managers of funds which have already become large. If a pattern appears, and the same individuals consistently turn in a better performance than others and tend to establish new funds over and over, the indications would be very strong that the inside information hypothesis is correct.

Success of mutual funds as a channeling device for information may account for an even more specialized version of the same thing. The so-called hedge funds began life, as their name implies, with power to do more than

108. *See* Manne, "Offshore and On—The SEC's Reach Threatens to Exceed Its Grasp," *Barron's*, Nov. 3, 1969, p. 1; Glenn, "'Heads We Win . . .': Performance-Fee Mutual Funds Have Had Their Ups and Downs," *Barron's*, March 2, 1970, p. 5.

109. *See* note 19 *supra*.

simply buy and sell securities in the market. Although hedging is normally thought of as a conservative, risk covering operation, it came to stand for the actively trading, high risk, go-go funds of the late 1960's. With only an insignificant exception or two, all hedge funds have one important characteristic: they are all exempt from SEC regulations under the Investment Company Act of 1940 and the Securities Act of 1933. Typically, the exemption from the 1940 Act resulted from their having fewer than one hundred participants. But one hundred offerees might still be sufficient to require a registration under the Securities Act of 1933.[110] Consequently, to avoid that result the participants in these funds are typically important businessmen, frequently the very individuals who might typically have access to valuable information. It is quite possible that the hedge funds of the sixties are very similar in their economic impact and operation to the famous—now infamous—bull pools of the late twenties.[111] That is, hedge funds may be nothing more nor less than efficient devices for exploiting information and exchanging its values among a select group.

In my book I argued that devices like discretionary accounts and priority lists had become the post-SEC version of the bull pools outlawed by the Securities Exchange Act of 1934. I also suggested that the pools were actually a far more efficient device for exploiting new information than were the other devices. Incidentally, I certainly should have included in the list of devices limited partnerships in investment banking houses, since frequently these were really invitations to share in trading profits. There was, after all, a time when people thought that reliance on *Blau v. Lehman*[112] was still safe.

But all of these practices are suspect today, mayhap because I pointed out the possibility that discretionary accounts and related devices had obvious implications for insider trading. My hypothesis about hedge funds would appear very strong if a simple survey (even by the SEC) turned up the information that the increased participation in hedge funds in recent years correlates with a steady decline in invitations to invest in discretionary accounts or to become a limited partner or in the use of priority lists by

110. L. Loss, *Securities Regulation* 1:653–65 (2d ed. 1961); 4:2621–47 (Supp. 1969).
111. *See* ITSM, p. 73.
112. 368 U.S. 403 (1962).

investment banking houses. One caveat: I am not saying that every hedge fund was established for the sole purpose of trading on inside information. Undoubtedly many of them have been formed for other purposes. But it should be realized that an occurrence, to be statistically significant, does not have to appear in every possible case. Each cigarette does not produce lung cancer.

A final and most interesting possible relationship between mutual funds and insider trading occurs in connection with the rapid expansion of so-called off-shore funds. The phrase actually has no hard and fast technical meaning. It refers generally to mutual funds established outside of United States territory, largely investing in American securities, operated by American managers but selling their fund shares to foreign nationals only. These funds are outside the jurisdictional ambit of the Securities and Exchange Commission. They are technically corporations established under and domiciled in countries other than the United States, and the mere fact that foreign corporations may buy shares in American markets is generally not considered sufficient to bring them under our regulatory jurisdiction.

My hypothesis is that the tremendous increase in the number of such funds reflects efforts of fund managers to escape the American law of insider trading. If the United States declares valuable information a kind of contraband goods, it would seem most natural to export it to countries where it is not illegal. Even during prohibition, American whiskey barreled in bond was legally exported.

The growth in the number of off-shore funds can be explained very simply by the increased popularity of such investments with foreign nationals. But it would still seem peculiar, if that were the case, that American managers would take such extreme precautions to avoid any jurisdictional tie to the United States. Careful study of the identity of the individuals actually managing these off-shore funds might reveal interesting data. Until some evidence to the contrary is adduced, it is at least a logical supposition that some of the movement off-shore has simply been a device to export inside information in a fashion that allowed American banking houses, through their brokerage operations and the management of the funds, to profit by this device. The odd thing, if this hypothesis is true, is that investors in foreign mutual funds will be able to profit by information which American mutual fund shareholders are prevented from enjoying. The irony is perhaps even further compounded when it is realized that any strenuous effort by the SEC to police this flow of information by curtailing off-shore investment in American securities would probably meet with strong objection on balance-of-payments grounds from the Treasury Department.

VII. Should We Go Back to the Twenty-first Century?

One of the *least* irritating digs that I found in the various reviews is that I want to turn the clock back, that I want to return to a period of jungle warfare in the stock market, and that I want to erase the moral gains which have been made in dealing with the financial enemies of the public. I must demur and point out to my friends that, for whatever reason, they have misstated my position. At no time did I advocate a change in the law that existed as of the time my book was written. The *Texas Gulf Sulphur* case had not been decided, even in the district court, at the time I wrote, though it was decided approximately three months before the actual publication date of the book. At that point I did begin to advocate a change in the law. But up until that point there was no rule against insider trading of the sort with which I was dealing. Certainly it was not known that there was any liability for someone who did not have a "special relationship"[113] to the corporation, nor was it known that there did not have to be "special circumstances" creating some duty.[114]

Certainly there were commentators who proposed that courts should decide the matter this way, but even they recognized that this was not then existing doctrine.[115] Nor did I advocate repeal of Section 16(b). On the contrary, I offered for the first time a reasoned argument for that provision. I concede that I was not too concerned about it, however, for the obvious reason that I did not and do not think that the provision is effective in dealing with insider trading as I defined it. I was extremely careful to state that

113. *In re* Cady, Roberts & Co., 40 S.E.C. 907 (1961).

114. *Id.*

115. *E.g.*, Fleischer, "Securities Trading and Corporate Information Practices: The Implications of the Texas Gulf Sulphur Proceeding," *Va. L. Rev.* 51:1271 (1965).

I was not dealing only with statutory insiders, that is, officers, directors, or ten percent shareholders. That would have been contrary to the very foundation of my argument that there is a functioning market for information and that unexploited information may get into the hands of anyone for a variety of reasons before it is actually used in the market.

The real trouble, as I have said before, is that my critics are confusing their ethical preferences with the law. What they mean when they say that I was advocating a change in the law is that I was advocating a rule (no mandatory prohibition on insider trading) which violated their moral precepts of what deferal law ought to be on the subject.

Of course, they probably meant that my position was contrary to the direction in which the law seemed to be moving. In this sense I had proposed a change in what Adolf Berle has called the "inchoate" law.[116] To this, of course, I must plead guilty. Had I not believed that the law was heading in that direction, it would have seemed useless to write such a troublesome book.

But I do not feel that my responsibility ends with predicting how the courts will move. Nor do I feel obliged to flow along with the tide of opinion. My effort was to give a rigorous analysis of a field that had been treated in a most superficial, moralizing fashion. I still maintain that such an approach violates the responsibility of serious academics, to say nothing of the love feast so apparent between certain law professors and a government agency. I find it very troubling to hear a professor of law argue that "the SEC in its suit against Texas Gulf Sulphur is entitled to escape the wise impatience with administrative expertise which has appeared recently in the Supreme Court and which suggests a new mood there."[117] Such special pleading on behalf of an agency which has never shown sincere interest in utilizing economic expertise to analyze its own regulatory area is as unseemly as it is incorrect. It is frustrating to be a minority of one on any issue in the legal academic community. But it certainly would be worse to be in the majority for the reasons that some members seem to be there now.

116. Berle, "Corporate Decision-Making and Social Control," *Bus. Law.* 24:149 (1968).
117. Schotland, "Unsafe at Any Price," p. 1478.

A Rejoinder to Mr. Ferber

A fundamental difference between my approach to this problem and Mr. Ferber's is shown by his intimation that for him and the SEC Congress ordains what is moral and what is not. That, however, is not the appropriate posture for scholars seeking objective resolution of a complex issue. I for one am not willing to have Congress decree my attitudes on what is moral. But frankly I find unconvincing Mr. Ferber's suggestion that notions of morality and honesty as indicated by Congress have had anything to do with the development of Rule 10b-5. After all that is the same Congress that refused to adopt an express provision outlawing all insider trading.

No one questions that Congress wanted securities markets honestly conducted when they adopted the federal securities laws. But that hardly explains the creation of the Securities and Exchange Commission. Congress certainly did not say to an unknown commission, "Here is 'the word.' Go forth and do good!" What Congress indicated was that this area was too complicated and too dynamic for specific legislation on every issue that might arise. Therefore they created a commission which, through its staff of experts, was supposed to learn and then do what was in the interest of the public.

Furthermore I should surmise—and I would be very curious to know whether the Commissioners themselves agree with Mr. Ferber or me on this—that most of Congress wanted the securities markets of the country regulated in the *economic* interest of the public. Indeed one could say that

Reprinted from *Vanderbilt Law Review* 23 (April 1970): 627–30, by permission of *Vanderbilt Law Review.*

there is a moral obligation on the SEC to know that its regulations are not causing more harm than good to the public's financial interests.

And yet, we find the Solicitor of the SEC making the almost unbelievable statement that "economic effect is largely irrelevant." This is a terrible confession that the SEC and spokesmen for it do not comprehend the significance of what they are doing nor do they personally concern themselves about the impact of their regulation on millions of investors who do indeed think that they are receiving *economic, not moral, benefits* from the agency. No congressman would tell his constituents, "You may be losing money by SEC regulation, but that is irrelevant, since the men down there are serving a higher moral order."

The truth of the matter is that there need be no conflict between good economics and good morality. The confusion arises when the attempt is made to substitute superficial ideas of morality for fundamental economic doctrine. Clearly every decision has an economic impact just as it has moral implications. But how can one judge the moral content or desirability of an act of economic regulation without knowing the effects of it?

But this is all a charade, or some form of high comedy. The SEC does not consult theologians or philosophers in its policy making any more than it consults economists. The Commission plays a serious game of law and politics, though the real winners are not always announced. Securities regulation has probably been of greatest economic benefit to members of the securities industry and to the lawyers who practice in and before the SEC. The rest of the country, whose influence is not so easily felt, have to accept disingenuous palaver about the morality of government and the irrelevance of their own wealth position.

I shall comment on a few of Mr. Ferber's more egregious errors. In my article I never credited the SEC with making the argument that information is the property of shareholders. I addressed myself only to the academic critics of my book. As a matter of fact the SEC itself has said so little about the policy underlying their interpretation of Rule 10b-5 that they have never given me much to respond to. Of course that way they are free to dissociate themselves from positions of their supporters as they see fit.

Mr. Ferber finds "a natural tendency for insiders to prolong the period prior to disclosure" if insider trading is allowed. This statement is certainly contrary to the economic analysis and studies made on the same subject.

Mr. Ferber simply does not understand my discussion of the economics of partial enforcement of certain kinds of laws. The reason that prostitution, marijuana, pornography, and insider trading are of one kind is because an organized market in the illicit goods will develop. But that is not true generally of fraud, murder, or many other forms of crimes against which enforcement is also only partial. As illicit businesses organize, grow, and prosper, so does the danger of their corrupting government officials.

Mr. Ferber is absolutely correct when he says there are potential conflicts of interest from insider trading by a trustee of a corporation in reorganization. Since he did not read my book, however, he could not know that I made precisely and exactly that point. But Mr. Ferber goes on to say that the same possible conflict "may exist to some extent whenever there is trading by corporate officials." Unfortunately he does not supply us with the minor premise in this syllogism, the one equating all companies with insolvent ones. And, unfortunately for his logic, the position of trustees in reorganization is vastly different from that of corporate officials generally. His suggestion that this analogy explains the Commission's position in *Texas Gulf* will certainly come as a surprise to many people.

Lawyers interested in anticipating new directions by the SEC should notice what may be the most important single sentence in Mr. Ferber's reply. He states that "the Commission has objected [to insider trading] only where the person taking advantage of information owes a duty of loyalty to the person he is trading with and is breaching that duty or where some type of aiding and abetting in such a breach of trust occurs." This sentence sounds suspiciously more like *Cady, Roberts* than it does like *Texas Gulf.* It is difficult to conclude that the Commission in *Texas Gulf* was saying that the defendants had some special duty of loyalty to the individuals with whom they were trading, though that is perfectly consistent with the standards stated in the *Cady, Roberts* opinion. Does this represent backtracking by the SEC on the frighteningly broad holding of *Texas Gulf?* Does this statement mean that "tippees" are excluded from liability under Rule 10b-5, or are they aiders and abettors? What are the standards for establishing whether a duty of loyalty is owed? Or is this statement merely another question-begging explanation of why we have a rule against insider trading?

Many readers will be somewhat confused by the juxtaposition of the paragraph on accounting procedures in the midst of a discussion of insider trading. I do not understand that either, though I think I know what he is unhappy about. Mr. Ferber is actually complaining because in another article (Manne, "Accounting and Administrative Law Aspects of *Gerstle v. Gamble-Skogmo, Inc.*," 15 N.Y.L.F. 304 [1969]) I had not praised the Commission for what I consider a grotesque example of regulatory misbehavior. The reference is to the case of *Gerstle v. Gamble-Skogmo.* I hope that my readers will realize that in that case the SEC took an amicus position flatly contrary to a stern warning they earlier gave the defendants on the same point. Thus, in a civil suit for damages, which could go as high as five million dollars, the SEC announced its new approach *for this case.* The accounting rule in question dealt with evaluations of appreciated assets, and I can only say that it took a long time for the SEC, in Mr. Ferber's words, to "learn from its experience." The old rule had been (and may still be) blindly followed by the SEC almost from its inception, despite widespread criticism. They certainly picked an odd place, time, and way to display their new found learning. I find it incredible that Mr. Ferber would even mention so shameful a travesty on justice and morality as the SEC perpetrated in the *Gerstle* litigation. But I am glad he mentioned the case, and I strongly recommend an examination of the SEC behavior therein to anyone interested in morals in government.

If I understand it correctly, Mr. Ferber's footnote number 21 says that no private interest groups have gained strong influence with the Commission in its thirty-six years. How about the New York Stock Exchange as opposed to small regionals, Mr. Ferber, or the larger member firms of the New York Stock Exchange, or the NASD, or old line mutual funds, or entrenched corporate managers who pushed for the Williams Bill? This sounds like a claim that bootleggers had no influence with the Chicago police during prohibition, or that the railroads were never closer than a counsel's arm's length to the ICC.

Only one last point needs to be clarified. Did Professor Schotland know what he was talking about or not when he claimed that the SEC traced all New York City trades in Texas Gulf stock based on information originating in Washington, D.C.? Obviously if he meant no more than that a few Washingtonians were asked whom they had contacted in New York, he did not say anything of significance, and the SEC stands accused, as I stated in my main article, of not discovering all the insider trading it claims to detect—or of hiding what it knew. On the contrary, if Schotland was correct, then the SEC should tell exactly how they do get the information. I have not accused the SEC of wiretapping. I have said that information which Schotland claims to have gotten from the Commission strongly suggests government investigation into records probably better kept private. This raises a serious civil liberties question and it should not be shrugged off, obfuscated, or denied without explanation. Mr. Ferber's comments are too unresponsive to be significant or satisfying. And someone in the Commission should certainly explain carefully what procedures the Commission uses in its policing activities. There is no reason that SEC policemen should be freer of public surveillance than any other police force.

Definition of "Insider Trading"

"Insider trading" generally refers to the practice of corporate agents buying or selling their corporation's securities without disclosing to the public significant information which is known to them but which has not yet affected the price of the security. Although this same issue can arise in face-to-face transactions with unlisted securities, most discussions of the subject assume trades across anonymous, organized exchanges or otherwise through brokers. Prior to 1961 this practice was not illegal anywhere in the world.

In that year the United States Securities and Exchange Commission published an opinion (Cady Roberts & Co.) suggesting for the first time that an insider with undisclosed information must either disclose the information or refrain from trading. Insider trading was there held to violate the Commission's Rule 10b-5, a very general statement making illegal any practice that "would operate as a fraud . . ." in connection with the purchase or sale of a security. US courts upheld the SEC's interpretation of Rule 10b-5 in the celebrated case of Texas Gulf Sulphur (1968), and the financial world has not been the same since.

Any discussion of this topic must begin with a disclaimer about matters not included, since there is much confusion between insider trading and various other kinds of traditionally illegal behaviour. For example, the topic at issue does not include failures to make disclosures of information required by the terms of an employment contract, another agreement, or

Reprinted from *The Palgrave Dictionary of Money and Finance,* vol. 2, edited by Peter Newman, Murray Milgate, and John Eatwell (London and Basingstoke: Macmillan Press Limited, 1992), 16–19. Reproduced with permission of Palgrave Macmillan.

some independent legal rule. Thus advocates of insider trading are only justifying cases in which the practice has been properly authorized and publicly disclosed by the corporation (Manne 1970). Insider trading, as used here, also does not include any form of common law fraud or breach of an independent fiduciary duty, although often the underlying economic welfare issue is begged (especially in the legal literature) simply by assuming that insider trading is *ipso facto* a breach of a fiduciary duty. Normally the discussion would also preclude someone who was not an officer or other official of the issuing corporation, but recent US Supreme Court holdings and SEC rules have cast some doubt on that exclusion.

Another matter often confused with insider trading prohibitions is SEC Rule 16b. This rule requires that any profits made by an officer, director, or ten percent shareholder as a result of buying and selling the company's securities within a six month period be paid to the company. Thus stock purchased and held for more than six months is not covered by Rule 16b even though the purchase was clearly made to exploit undisclosed information. The legislative history and judicial interpretations of this provision make it clear that it was not intended as an insider trading rule as such, and it has played no significant role in the modern discussion of insider trading.

At the outset we might inquire why the SEC has been so insistent on a broad rule against insider trading while most countries of the world have shown little if any interest in the subject. In spite of intense international lobbying for such rules by the SEC, even those countries that have adopted insider trading rules have shown almost no interest in enforcing them. It should be noted, however, that SEC enforcement powers, especially powers of extradition and discovery, may be enhanced merely by foreign adoption of such rules. Also any competitive advantage that foreign markets may have over US markets because of costly US regulations will be diminished to the extent that other countries adopt the same rules.

It is possible that the SEC's original interest in a rule against insider trading arose in part from its vigorous enforcement of the fixed commission rate structure for brokers on the New York Stock Exchange. Information, as a valuable commodity, could easily be used to make rebates to favoured customers, thus upsetting the "cartel" arrangement and the rules of the New York Stock Exchange, which are subject to SEC enforcement. The ruling, therefore, served a dual purpose. It sent a clear signal that the use of "inside information" to lower costs for favoured brokerage customers was forbidden, which certainly the brokerage community wanted. And at the same time, it allowed the Commission to formulate a general rule against all insider trading, which alone the brokers may have resisted.

Even after fixed commission rates were abandoned in the United States in 1975, strong interests long supported by the SEC found other reasons for wanting to prevent corporate insiders from trading on undisclosed information. In spite of the SEC's professed interest in making new information equally available to all traders, market professionals, particularly investment bankers, would obviously be able to obtain new information and trade on it faster than the general public (Haddock and Macey 1987). And specialists on the floor of the exchanges would also benefit from restricting informed trading by insiders, since they would buy from or sell to insiders as part of their duty to deal with all comers. These market professionals strongly support the SEC's efforts to curtail insider trading, and it is likely that their counterparts in other countries have the same interests.

Subsequently the SEC developed another constituency with a strong interest in rules against insider trading. As successful hostile takeovers increased rapidly in the early 1980s, it became apparent that "tipping" information about proposed tender offers to the so-called "risk arbitrageurs" ("arbs") greatly facilitated takeovers. But the US Supreme Court in the Chiarella case (1980) had already held that Rule 10b-5 did not cover a trader with no special relationship to the issuer (in that case a printer working on takeover documents). This rule would have protected the arbs, so the SEC promulgated a special insider trading rule, Rule 14e-3, pursuant to Congressional legislation on takeovers, in order to prevent risk arbitrageurs from using takeover information that was not yet public. Incumbent managers of large corporations subject to the threat of a takeover obviously had the most to gain from such a rule and had pressed vigorously for it. In fact without such a rule their earlier success in securing Congressional adoption of an anti-takeover law (the Williams Act) would have been subverted by risk arbitrage. The SEC has been very successful in convincing the public that insider trading, already a popular bugaboo, was the chief evil of the takeover period, while in fact the major economic significance of that episode had little to do with insider trading.

Early in the public debate on insider trading the SEC and its supporters regularly stated that the individuals selling to or buying from insiders were injured because "they would not have sold if they had had the information." This clearly confuses *ex ante* and *ex post* considerations. A seller of stock would of course like more information about the future, just as he would prefer more wealth to less. But if a sale at a particular moment represents a rational portfolio decision, the fact that the buyer in the particular case, or for that matter any buyer, may have more information than the seller should be a matter of complete indifference to the seller (Manne 1966). The *ex ante* rule to be followed cannot be judged by the *ex post* results in particular situations. Happily this argument has largely disappeared from serious discussions of this topic.

Alternatively defenders of the SEC position may have been confusing another matter. They may have been assuming that if there were no insider trading, disclosure of the new information would have occurred at an earlier time so that this particular seller would have profited by the higher price. But this confounds the question of the impact of the insider's trade with that of the timing of corporate disclosures. There may be some general relation between the two, but for a specific trader to have lost anything, the delay in the announcement must have been caused by the requirements of the insider (see discussion below). And even if insider trading systematically encouraged delays in the time of disclosures, this would still only cause a shift of wealth from one group of uninformed outsiders to another. It would not have an effect *ex ante* on the average rate of return of outside investors. It would appear then that insider trading is a victimless crime, certainly so far as the trading partners of insiders are concerned. Yet in 1988 Congress increased criminal penalties and the civil liability of anyone trading "contemporaneously" with an insider who had undisclosed information.

In the years since exposure of the fallacy of assuming that insider trading injured the outside trading partner, the more serious economic arguments against insider trading have shifted ground. Today the SEC's principal argument—sometimes supported and sometimes opposed by highly mathematical, often narrowly focused, and generally inconclusive econometric work (see Dennert 1991)—is that insider trading destroys investor confidence in the market and therefore reduces liquidity and investment. This argument has been repeated so frequently that it has gained a certain currency, thus perhaps making it something of a self-fulfilling prophecy. But this is not likely to be significant. We have no direct empirical measure of investor confidence in what the SEC terms the "integrity of the market," but the most relevant evidence on the subject (Benston) shows that investor participation in the stock market is exclusively a function of the recent performance of stock prices. If prices have risen, the public comes into the market, and if prices have tumbled, they depart. There is no evidence that revelations of particular "insider trading scandals" affect the public's willingness to invest.

It has also been argued that insiders would delay corporate disclosure of new information so that they could maximize their own return on new information, thus making the market less efficient informationally (Schotland 1967). This is an empirical question on which, like most questions about insider trading, we are not apt to secure reliable data. The argument might be plausible (though certainly not determinative of the policy question) if we could assume that top executives would experience considerable delays in financing their stock transactions and that no one else would discover the information and use it while these financing arrangements were being made. It is far more likely that executives with volatile information would take their positions as quickly as possible and then speed up disclosure of the information in order to register their trading gains (Demsetz 1969). After all, the faster they can move in and out of the stock, the higher will be the rate of return on any given investment.

But managers will have more reason than their own investment returns to speed up disclosure. All the vectors operating on managerial incentive (salary, job tenure, reputation, threats of takeovers, corporate profits, etc.) will also motivate managers to desire fast and accurate disclosure of new information about the company. Efficient stock pricing is a desirable attribute for corporations, and the stock of a company (and therefore the managers) will be worth more if the market believes that the stock is being priced accurately. Aside from a not very serious end-period problem, positive incentive forces should overwhelm any negative impact on disclosure timing, assuming that the insiders can even control it. Insider trading should have little impact on the timing of corporate announcements, but what it does have would seem to be beneficial.

A final argument against insider trading is that it will change the managers' taste for risk and cause them to take more risk than shareholders would prefer (Easterbrook 1981). This would be so since greater variability in the company's stock price would provide more insider trading opportunities and because the riskier, higher-payoff investments would provide more opportunities for insider transactions without jeopardizing the fixed compensation of the executives. But managers are primarily compensated in the form of salary, and this in itself creates substantial risk aversion on their part. Thus insider trading may be just as likely to help right the risk imbalance resulting from salary compensation as it is to create one on its own.

But there are still additional arguments for allowing corporations to decide for themselves whether to permit insider trading by their managers, an option the SEC will not countenance even with full disclosure by the company. Perhaps the central economic argument in favour of allowing insider trading is that such trading always pushes the price of the stock in the "correct" direction. That is, insiders' purchases will only be made when good news has developed and sales made only when there is bad news. To the extent that the insider's transaction has any effect on the share price, it will always push the price towards its correct equilibrium level. And the insider will only buy or sell up to that equilibrium point. Thus insider trading always contributes to the efficiency of the stock market (Manne 1966).

This argument, like the argument that no outside trader is injured by insider trading, is generally accepted by all serious commentators today. But its significance has often been underestimated. Stock market efficiency, in the sense of prices quickly and accurately reflecting all news that could affect the value of shares, is essential to all of the stock market's major functions: the efficient allocation of capital by corporations and by outside investors, the correct compensation of managers, and the efficient operation of the market for corporate control. If there were effective enforcement of laws against insider trading, all corrections of price would have to come from individuals who received the information more slowly than insiders and who generally could not evaluate new developments as expertly. Certainly the stock market would be less efficient than it is with no insider trading.

The next substantial advantage that can be claimed for insider trading relates to its role in appropriately compensating managers. Clearly a right to exploit new information before it is impounded into a stock's price is valuable, and in a competitive market for managers the value of this "property right" will be taken into account in determining total real compensation (Carlton and Fischel 1983). But the incentives afforded an insider by the right to trade and by straight salary may be quite different. Salary will always make managers more risk-averse than will compensation that makes them residual claimants. Both bonuses and stock option plans have been adopted in an effort to deal with this problem, but neither of them can completely capture the incentive characteristics of allowing trading on new information (Manne 1966).

Insider trading, unlike a bonus, does not require an accounting calculation which is often based on numbers irrelevant to the purpose at hand and which may even relate "profits" to an inappropriate time period. The benefits from insider trading on the other hand will be based on actual increases in share price, a highly accurate estimate of the discounted present value of all anticipated future returns.

Stock options too have drawbacks not shared with insider trading. They may be exercised after a price run-up the option holder did not influence, and the proper number of shares to be optioned will always be difficult to establish. Stock options are as likely to be compensation for past performance as an inducement for future behaviour. Furthermore the right to trade on undisclosed information makes managers holders of residual claims without the necessity of their also being subject to general market risk, as are shareholders and option holders. But perhaps the most significant feature of all these advantages for insider trading is that they are obtained without its costing the shareholders anything. The extra reward to the managers simply does not come out of the residual amount available for shareholders.

The principal argument against this use of insider trading is that it may bias managers' decisions in a wrong direction because it allows gains to be made on bad news as well as good. But this argument, though plausible, is probably not significant. All other managerial incentives, as we saw in connection with the discussion of disclosure timing, impel efforts to produce good news. Aside from an easily monitored end-period problem, these forces would overwhelm any tendency for insider trading to induce managers to produce bad news. Further, the amount of good news that the market can take is infinite, while the amount of bad news will be sharply restricted by natural market forces.

The last important economic issue in connection with insider trading has nothing to do with the intrinsic merits of the practice. Rather it has to do with the possibility of effectively enforcing the law. No one suggests that any particular rule against insider trading (short of a draconian halt to all trading any time that material information develops) could result in truly equal shareholder access to new information (Dooley 1980). Some traders, particularly the professionals in the field, will always be quicker and smarter than the others. Thus insider trading laws, to the extent that they can be enforced, will in all likelihood merely shift wealth from one group, corporate managers, to another group, mostly market professionals (Carlton and Fischel 1983). However, in this wealth transfer process the shareholders will lose the benefit of costlessly compensating their corporation's managers through this device and, of course, they would suffer any harm inherent in any insider trading.

There are obviously many straightforward problems with trying to police rules against insider trading. Detection will always be very difficult, and new forms of deception and subterfuge, though costly, will be invented constantly. This may in turn encourage regulators to use extreme measures of detection and enforcement, the economic and social costs of which can also be very high. It is clear today that vastly more insider trading occurs than the SEC acknowledges. Casual observation of stock prices reveals many cases where large price changes are followed some time later by news explaining the change. It is not likely that this phenomenon is always or even generally caused by the diligent research of financial analysts.

But the strongest reason that rules against insider trading can never be very effective lies in the fact that inside information can be exploited without the beneficiaries' engaging in a securities transaction at all. As much money can be made by knowing when not to sell or not to buy as can be made from knowing when to buy or to sell. All that is required is that the object shares be held in the portfolio (in the case of good news) rather than sold, as would have occurred in the absence of inside information. (And *vice versa* with bad news.) The price of a security will rise just as much because of an increase in a seller's reservation price as through actual purchases in the market. And yet when a trader decides not to buy or not to sell, there has been no securities transaction, and it is doubtful that this could ever be made illegal (Manne 1974). This mode of exploiting new information may in fact represent a principal method by which stock prices change. This would explain, among other things, why stock prices often change with little or no activity in the stock.

At a minimum, then, only partial enforcement of insider trading laws is feasible, and that can only be accomplished at very high compliance and avoidance costs. To the extent that the law is enforced, shareholders lose the opportunity to gain an important compensation device costlessly, and the pricing of corporate stocks becomes much less efficient than it would otherwise be. While no stockholder interest is injured by insider trading, effective laws against it result in a large and unjustifiable wealth transfer from corporate insiders to various market professionals.

Bibliography

Carlton, D. W., and Fischel, D. R. 1983. "The Regulation of Insider Trading." *Stanford Law Review* 35:857–95.

Demsetz, H. 1969. "Perfect Competition, Regulation and the Stock Market." In *Economic Policy and the Regulation of Corporate Securities,* ed. H. G. Manne, Washington, D.C.: American Enterprise Institute.

Dennert, J. 1991. "Insider Trading." *Kyklos* 44:181–202.

Dooley, M. 1980. "Enforcement of Insider Trading Restrictions." *Virginia Law Review* 66:1–83.

Easterbrook, F. H. 1981. "Insider Trading, Secret Agents, Evidentiary Privileges, and the Production of Information." *Supreme Court Review* 11:309–65.

Glosten, L., and Milgrom, P. 1985. "Bid, Ask and Transaction Prices in a Specialist Market with Heterogeneously Informed Traders." *Journal of Financial Economics* 14:71–100.

Haddock, D. D., and Macey, J. R. 1987. "Regulation on Demand: A Private Interest Model, with an Application to Insider Trading." *Journal of Law and Economics* 30:311–52.

Jaffe, J. F. 1974. "The Effect of Regulation Changes on Insider Trading." *Bell Journal of Economics & Management Science* 5(1):93–121.

Manne, H. G. 1966. *Insider Trading and the Stock Market.* New York: Free Press.

Manne, H. G. 1970. "Insider Trading and the Law Professors." *Vanderbilt Law Review* 23:547–627.

Manne, H. G. 1974. "Economic Aspects of Required Disclosure Under Federal Securities Laws." In *Wall Street in Transition,* ed. H. G. Manne and E. Solomon, New York: New York University Press.

Schotland, R. 1967. "Unsafe at Any Price: A Reply to Manne." *Virginia Law Review* 53:1478.

Bring Back the Hostile Takeover

Since Enron, there has been an outbreak of regulatory fever in Washington: A tide of "solutions" has sluiced from the pens of journalists and the mouths of politicians. Apparently forgotten is how Enron and other recent scandals were the direct result of regulatory and judicial efforts to stem abuses in the takeover arena 20 and more years ago. They still haven't learned just how high the cost of interfering with salutary market forces can be.

Among current proposed guardians of executive morality are auditors, lawyers, analysts, financial intermediaries, independent directors, and government officials. But no proposal involving these actors addresses the real problem. New scandals will continue until we bring back the most powerful market mechanism for displacing bad managers: hostile takeovers.

The principle is simple: If a corporation is badly enough managed, its share price will decline relative to other companies in the industry. At that point it can be profitable for a new group to make a tender offer, bringing in more efficient leadership. Just the threat of a takeover provides incentive for managers to run companies in the interest of the shareholders.

In 1932, a book called *The Modern Corporation and Private Property* by Adolf Berle and Gardiner Means popularized the concept of the "separation of ownership and control." The book argued that the managers of large, publicly held corporations could cheat, manipulate, and steal blind the shareholders, since they were not subject to effective monitoring. Not least among the evils attributable to this separation were extravagant salaries, self-perpetuating boards of directors, insider trading, and various perqui-

Reprinted from *Wall Street Journal* (June 26, 2002), by permission of Henry G. Manne.

sites for the top executives. For Berle and Means, the solution lay in the realm of political theory. If corporations could be made more democratic, shareholders could "vote the rascals out," and the effects of the separation could be averted.

By 1965 however, when I introduced the concept of a market for corporate control, economists and others began explicitly to recognize that the corporation was not a political institution but a creation and function of the marketplace. The separation of ownership and control problem, tidily renamed in modern corporate governance literature as the problem of "agency costs," was seen as largely amenable to the forces of a market for corporate control.

For a brief period in the late '50s, until the mid-'60s, when modern hostile takeover techniques were perfected, we had a pretty much unregulated market for corporate control. Shareholders received on average 40% over the pre-bid price for their shares. But the chorus of screams by threatened executives and their lawyers became politically excruciating enough that Congress, in 1968, passed the Williams Act, which made it vastly more expensive for outsiders to mount successful tender offers. The highly profitable element of surprise was removed entirely.

The even stronger inhibition on takeovers resulted from actions taken by state legislatures and state courts in the '80s. The number of hostile tender offers dropped precipitously and with it the most effective device for policing top managers of large, publicly held companies.

There continue to be changes of control in publicly held corporations even if hostile tender offers are discouraged. But now, with the legal power to shift control in the hands of the incumbents, they, rather than shareholders, will receive any premium paid for control. Ironically, this is the same premium that has been made larger by their own poor management.

This transfer of control may take the form of a merger, or simply a series of agreed-upon high-level resignations after a new board has been put in place. The compensation paid the managers for their assent to such a change may take the form of a lucrative consulting arrangement, stock or stock options in the acquiring company, a generous severance package, or some other bonus. But the salient fact in each of these situations is that the managers and not the shareholders receive the premium being paid for control.

It should come as no surprise then that, as hostile takeovers declined to 4% from 14% of all mergers, executive compensation started a steep climb, eventually ending for some companies with bankruptcy and management scandal. The largely mythical abuses alleged to result from an unfettered takeover system were less costly to investors than what has occurred since.

Every statute, adjudication, or regulation that in any way inhibited the free functioning of the market for corporate control simply raised the real cost of ousting inappropriate managers. Dollar for dollar, every increase in those costs could be claimed by incumbent managers, either in greater rewards to themselves or in inefficient management policies. Until the real cost of wastefulness equals the cost of a successful takeover fight, they remain secure behind a legal barrier to their ouster, at least until the whole house of cards collapses. Enron is a predictable consequence of rules that inhibit the efficient functioning of the market for corporate control.

The solution is straightforward but by no means simple: repeal and reverse all the many statutes, rules, and case holdings that interfere with tender offers. American corporations would have to restructure themselves, as they did in the '70s and '80s, to live in a more deregulated market. There would be heavy human costs in the ensuing dislocations, and we could expect a screeching replay of the spurious arguments that won the day in the late '60s and mid-'80s.

But with such a reversal of policy, however unlikely, executive compensation would begin to plummet, there would be less pressure on accountants to cook the books, and American corporations would probably enter another period of innovation, efficiency, and profitability.

Options? Nah, Try Insider Trading

When insider trading was first outlawed in the 1960s, the Securities and Exchange Commission and many academics were certain that stock-option plans provided all the incentive necessary for appropriately aligning the interests of managers and shareholders. The argument was convenient since at the time it was something less than de rigueur to defend insider trading.

Now, however, as we are seeing the problems of stock-option plans, insider trading is beginning to look like an interesting alternative.

Many large corporations, especially the high-tech companies whose survival depends on new ideas and inventions, need to properly compensate for innovation. Without incentives for growth, the people who run publicly-held corporations will behave like salaried bureaucrats, averse to anything new and risky. Their interests will be peculiarly aligned with those of debt holders, not shareholders.

This point at least has been dimly understood in the various debates over the past 40 years or so about stock options. The problem was—and is—that no one could suggest an alternative to stock options for encouraging management to behave in the interests of shareholders. A few academics have joined me in suggesting that insider trading was nearly ideal for that purpose. But politicians won't come near it, and the SEC gags at the suggestion.

Now look where we are. The problems with stock options I identified in my 1966 book, *Insider Trading and the Stock Market,* are now apparent to

Reprinted from *Wall Street Journal* (August 2, 2002), by permission of Henry G. Manne.

everyone. But, crow not being the preferred diet of Washington officials, it still seems unlikely that the damage caused by the ban on insider trading will get a fair hearing inside the Beltway.

Stock options have always been inefficient at best. As compensation, they have incentive effects in two different ways. When the option is granted, it has a present value equal to the market price for a call on that number of shares. The incentive effect of this kind of compensation, which is more often granted as a reward than as an incentive, will generally be no greater than a bonus paid in shares would be.

After the option is exercised, the executive becomes a larger shareholder. Stock ownership pushes management to maximize share price, especially if the shares represent a substantial part of an employee's undiversified portfolio. But as the employee's shares represent only a tiny fraction of all shares outstanding, the induced incentive for risky choices may still fall short of what would be dictated by the interest of shareholders. In other words, stock options offer no greater incentive than would a similar number of shares held by the manager, however acquired.

Insider trading, on the other hand, allows the insiders to meticulously craft their own reward for innovations almost as soon as they occur and to trade without harm to any investors. The incentive is immediate and precise and is never confounded with stock-price changes that are not of the managers' making. The effect of this trading will always be to move the stock price in the correct direction quickly and accurately, irrespective of what accounting entries are made for the underlying event. Stock prices will, for example, reflect the present value of anticipated future gains from new developments, something accounting cannot and should not provide for.

Look at the alternative, as we have seen in recent months: When stock options are used to encourage risky decisions and insider trading is outlawed, the financial focus of corporate officials necessarily will be on accounting information. When real-world events underlying those entries cannot be traded on directly, the books become their crude proxies. The legal flow of information to the market will be via the formal release of SEC-sanctioned disclosures, such as quarterly reports and 10-Ks.

Since future expected profits cannot be shown on the books and trading on the underlying information is not allowed, the urge to make the accounting picture look better in order to have it conform to management's view of the company's prospects may become irresistible. Arguably this is what occurred at Enron and WorldCom.

Currently, the SEC sees its job as regulating the entire market for information. This is madness. It starts at the supply side with accounting rules that began life as managerial tools and tries to make them into a valuation scheme. It finishes on the demand side by restricting insider trading, which merely shifts the identity of the people who may trade first on undisclosed information.

If insider trading were legal and used to replace or supplement stock options, there would be no "tragedies" of employees being left high and dry with options way out of the money. There would be no loss of reward when an innovation merely resulted in a reduction of an expected loss. There would be no unearned gain because a company's stock appreciated in line with a market or industry rise. And there would be no peculiar problems of accounting since such trading would be entirely extraneous to the company's accounts.

There are plenty of ways companies could regulate their own insider trading to best fit their needs. Some might limit trading to buying on good news and prohibit selling on bad news. Some could limit the amount of stock an employee could purchase, or outlaw insider trading altogether. We would certainly see some innovation in enforcement techniques and perhaps in the publicity given to insider transactions.

There is no reason to believe that U.S. corporations are incapable of designing workable and safe programs of insider trading. All we have to do is make the present laws optional. Just one thing: I would require companies to disclose details when they had adopted an insider trading system. That way I could go load up on the company's shares.

The Case for Insider Trading

Insider-trading regulation had its primordial introduction in the muck of New Deal securities regulation, which was itself justified on the trumped-up theory that full disclosure was the best way to deal with corporate fraud and deception. Over the years, the benign-sounding idea of passive regulation in the form of full disclosure has morphed into a morass of active regulation. Full disclosure now wraps around—and regulates—corporate governance, accounting, takeovers, investment banking, financial analysts, corporate counsel, and, not least, insider trading.

Some history of insider-trading regulation is instructive in this regard. In 1934 Congress refused an early draft of the Securities and Exchange Act that contained a provision outlawing insider trading, perhaps because it would have covered members of Congress. But in 1961 the SEC, not to be denied, invented a new theory to force insiders either to "disclose or abstain from trading." In 1968 this unorthodox bit of lawmaking received judicial sanction, and subsequently Congress itself recognized fait accompli in what the SEC had ordained.

Prior to 1968, insider trading was very common, well-known, and generally accepted when it was thought about at all. When the time came, the corporate world was neither able nor inclined to mount a defense of the practice, while those who demanded its regulation were strident and successful in its demonization. The business community was as hoodwinked by these frightening arguments as was the public generally.

Reprinted from *Wall Street Journal* (March 17, 2003), by permission of Henry G. Manne.

Since then, however, insider trading has been strongly, if by no means universally, defended in scholarly journals. There have been three primary economic arguments (not counting the show-stopper that the present law simply cannot be effectively enforced). The first and generally undisputed argument is that insider trading does little or no direct harm to any individual trading in the market, even when an insider is on the other side of the trades.

The second argument in favor of allowing insider trading is that it always (fraud aside) helps move the price of a corporation's shares to its "correct" level. Thus insider trading is one of the most important reasons we have an "efficient" stock market. While there have been arguments about the relative weight to be attributed to insider trading and to other devices also performing this function, the basic idea that insider trading pushes stock prices in the right direction is largely unquestioned today.

The third economic defense of insider trading has been that it is an efficient and highly desirable form of incentive compensation, especially for corporations dependent on innovation and new developments. This argument has come to the fore recently with the spate of scandals involving stock options. These are the closest substitute for insider trading in managerial compensation, but they suffer many disadvantages not found with insider trading. The strongest argument against insider trading as compensation is the difficulty of calibrating entitlement and rewards.

Critics of insider trading have responded to these arguments principally with two aggregate-harm theories, one psychological and the other economic. The first, the faraway favorite of the SEC, is the "market confidence" argument: If investors in the stock market know that insider trading is common, they will refuse to invest in such an "unfair" market. Thus investment and liquidity will be seriously diminished. But there is no evidence that publicity about insider trading ever caused a significant reduction in aggregate stock market activity. It is merely one of many scare arguments that the SEC and others have used over the years as a substitute for sound economics.

The more responsible aggregate-harm argument is the "adverse selection" theory. This argument is that specialists and other market makers, when faced with insider trading, will broaden their bid-ask spreads to cover the losses implicit in dealing with insiders. The larger spread in effect becomes a "tax" on all traders, thus impacting investment and liquidity. This is a plausible scenario, but it is of very questionable applicability and significance. Such an effect, while there is some confirming data, is certainly not large enough in aggregate to justify outlawing insider trading.

But there is still another justification for insider trading, and this one may explain why corporations did not regulate the practice themselves before the SEC got into the act. Management and the shareholders of large, publicly-held corporations have a strong common interest in the accurate pricing of the company's shares. If pricing is not reliable, investors will demand a higher return in order to be compensated for assuming this added risk. Thus, all other things being equal, the shares of a company with reliable pricing of its shares will sell for more than otherwise identical shares.

Lack of confidence in the reliability of a share's price, reflected in a higher risk premium, will have several negative effects. The company will have to pay more for new capital, boards of directors and the managers themselves will have less reliable feedback on managerial performance, managers' professional reputations will suffer, and the managers will be at greater risk of displacement either through a takeover or action of their own board of directors.

Like many well-functioning markets, the market for valuable information requires little attention or comprehension. The fact that insiders, who may not even be in managerial positions, profit from the system certainly does not mean that they necessarily understand or care about the economic importance of reliable pricing, or that their gain detracts from the benefits others receive from the system. The system would not work unless they profited, but there is no need for them to understand the larger picture.

No other device can approach knowledgeable trading by insiders for efficiently and accurately pricing endogenous developments in a company. Insiders, driven by self-interest and competition among themselves, will trade until the correct price is reached. This will be true even when the new information involves trading on bad news. You do not need whistleblowers if you have insider trading.

If such trading is allowed, there are no delays or uncertainties about what has to be disclosed. There are no issues about when information must be published, or in what form. There is no need to regulate investment bankers, auditors, or stock analysts. The evaluation of new information will be done efficiently through a pure market process. Investors receive "virtual" full disclosure in the form of immediate and correct price adjustments.

This also helps us understand why stock exchanges, even before the SEC, required periodic financial disclosures to shareholders. Insider and other knowledgeable trading might keep the price of a company's shares at the right level, but the investing public would need confirmation of this. Periodic disclosure of financial statements confirmed to the investing public that the price level of shares, reached by trading, was reliable. Both exchanges and companies had an interest in this.

In time even the SEC noticed that periodic financial disclosures were not having much effect on stock prices. Their reaction was merely to require more frequent and more detailed disclosures. But the SEC never realized that insider trading was already the form of "disclosing" that maintained the efficiency of stock pricing. Instead, they outlawed it. Happily for us all, enforcement has not been too successful. Now it is time to reconsider the whole matter.

Citizen Donaldson

A recent report from the Securities and Exchange Commission's Division of Corporate Finance proposes allowing small shareholders to nominate directors for company boards directly. There's a terrible idea.

The report, enthusiastically endorsed by Chairman William Donaldson, would allow a holder of perhaps as little as 3% of the company's shares, who has held the shares for at least a year, to make a "limited number" of nominations after the occurrence of certain "trigger events." Among them may be financial scandals and certainly the failure of a corporation to comply with a shareholder proxy resolution. (Shouldn't that already be a part of the SEC's enforcement job?) Yet neither Mr. Donaldson, nor the SEC staff who prepared the report, seems to know or care that the theory of corporate democracy, from which the nomination idea is derived, has long been a standing joke among sophisticated finance economists. The report was written in an intellectual time warp.

Seventy years ago it was fashionable among intellectuals to talk about large, publicly held corporations as if they were little republics. Directors should stand for periodic contested elections after some form of shareholder nomination of candidates; shareholders should have rights comparable to the referendum and recall in politics; and, of course, corporate affairs should be conducted in the sunshine. Many of these notions were realized in provisions of our federal securities laws, and the new plan is certainly of a piece with much of what has gone before.

Reprinted from *Wall Street Journal* (August 7, 2003), by permission of Henry G. Manne.

But the idea of corporate democracy never made any sense. A corporation is not a small republic. It has no governmental powers over its shareholders or anyone else. Shareholders have entered a perfectly well understood risk-assumption contract and can exit their corporate "citizenship" for the cost of a stock broker's sales commission. The board of directors of a corporation is not a legislature. Management and the board are constituent parts of a team that runs a corporation. Each monitors the other, and reciprocity in their selection is precisely what we should expect in a well run company.

Aside from the tiny fraction of corporate activists who have undoubtedly been very costly to the rest of us, shareholders want only one thing from their corporate involvement, the highest possible value for their shares. This near unanimity of preference makes ludicrous the idea of the board as a debating society or a place for political compromises.

The vote attached to a share in a modern, large corporation is totally different from a political vote. It is not intended to facilitate personal involvement by shareholders in a corporate version of a New England town meeting or an American presidential election. The management and control of a large enterprise will either be in the hands of a single controlling shareholder or group, in which case the votes of minorities are usually superfluous, or 50% or more of the shares will be publicly held, in which case the vote becomes valuable when there is a fight for control.

Getting rid of bad corporate managers is nothing like the cumbersome and expensive political device of a political election either. It starts (and ends) with the assembling of a controlling number of voting shares, or, when there are large institutional holdings, often with just a quiet suggestion for change. The system works because unhappy shareholders sell or threaten to sell their shares and thus eventually make the change of control a profitable exercise. The essence of individual shareholder participation is "exit," not "voice."

The traditional mainstays of SEC involvement with corporate democracy, apart from the idea of full disclosure, are the proxy rules and the shareholder proposal rule. Studies have shown these to be almost totally irrelevant in promoting the real interest of corporate investors either in higher share prices or more efficient corporate governance. Few if any battles for control have been resolved mainly through a proxy fight (i.e., without a lot of voting shares changing hands first). And the shareholder proposal rule has mainly been the playground of activists seeking publicity but generally uninterested in the hard job of serious corporate management.

The report pays great deference to the 690 commentators who accepted the commission's invitation to ruminate on this idea. The vast majority of the recognizable respondents are clearly special pleaders with no real stake in a properly functioning corporate system, and few have any demonstrable sophistication about corporate economics. The SEC could probably get this many affirmative responses to a proposal to abolish the New York Stock Exchange.

The 28 lawyers and corporations responding, as well as the Business Roundtable, all expressed serious reservations about the new proposal, some on reasonable, substantive grounds of cost, inconvenience, divisiveness or unworkability. Mainly, however, they objected that the new directive follows too closely on Sarbanes-Oxley, which has not yet been digested or implemented. (It may yet prove indigestible.) They wanted more time. But Chairman Donaldson, with what seems to be unseemly urgency, wants a formal rule proposal completed by next month.

Shareholder activists have been ecstatic about the SEC's recent report. And well they might be, since their primary interest in the corporate governance process is to facilitate publicity for their own special-interest programs. This nomination scheme is perfectly crafted to do just that. Maybe this is what the SEC staff had in mind when they called this "the cost-effective way (for shareholders to) exercise their rights and responsibilities as owners of their companies."

It is revealing that no corporations have ever opted into such a scheme on their own, even though they would be free to do so under the laws of many states. On the other hand, the new SEC rule will in all likelihood be mandatory, and companies will not be allowed to opt out of the system. Here we have both another preemption of state corporation laws by the SEC and another example of the SEC's one-size-fits-all kind of regulation.

Modern activists do not want the responsibility of running large corporations. If they did, they would turn their efforts toward amassing control blocks of shares. They really want to interfere with the property and contractual rights of others in order to achieve their own ends without paying the market price. It is terribly discouraging that the SEC and its chairman should still be condoning this form of corporate fraud.

What Mutual-Fund Scandal?

For months now, New York Attorney General Eliot Spitzer has terrified the investing public with lurid charges of mutual-fund high jinks. Vast sums of money are alleged to have been lost by long-term investors because some funds allowed a favored few to engage in late trading (using new information to trade in funds at the "stale" price after the legal 4 p.m. closing time) or market timing (basically arbitraging stale-priced funds within fund families). But there is much more innocent behavior and more public welfare in this mutual-fund story than has appeared in the press, and vastly less damage than Mr. Spitzer would have us believe.

The economic justification for much of Mr. Spitzer's claims rests squarely on a recent, widely cited academic paper, "Who Cares About Shareholders? Arbitrage-Proofing Mutual Funds," by Prof. Eric Zitzewitz of the Stanford Graduate School of Business. This paper purports to show that the various late-trading or market-timing schemes are costing long-term investors in American mutual funds about $4.9 billion a year. The problem is that the paper demonstrated no such thing.

After explicitly acknowledging that there was no direct way of measuring the dilution of long-term fund investors' interests, Mr. Zitzewitz estimated the maximum amount that arbitrageurs or short-term traders could theoretically make from such trading. He then simply assumed that the long-term investors had lost that much in dilution of their shares. But he took no account of individuals' and funds' responses to the behavior under in-

Reprinted from *Wall Street Journal* (January 8, 2004), by permission of Henry G. Manne.

vestigation. Like static tax projections, which fail to account for behavioral responses to a proposed tax change itself, Mr. Zitzewitz's measure wrongly implies that long-term investors or fund managers would sit passively by while returns in their funds were being deeply eroded. Not likely.

The U.S. mutual-fund industry is extremely competitive: 11,000 funds managed by 500 mutual-fund companies. Information about these funds abounds, both that required by law and that voluntarily published. Fund returns, reported daily, are scrutinized minutely by rating agencies and individual and pension portfolio managers, who can quickly and cheaply shift from one fund or management company to another. And even this is but a small part of the total market for investors' funds, which also includes direct stock purchases, savings accounts, insurance, real estate, even consumption. The demand for mutual-fund services is extremely elastic, approaching that for corn or wheat.

A highly competitive capital market will constantly tend to force things into equilibrium, with fund investors receiving a correct rate of return for the risk they assume. Timing practices may indeed occasion some immediate fund-dilution loss—probably significant only if managers are slow to recognize the presence of timers or if necessary adjustment costs are high. But if the investors do not promptly receive the competitive market return, they will simply move their funds elsewhere until they do.

Nevertheless, we know that market timers and late traders have made profits. And, since their activities are not on their face either wealth-producing or wealth-enhancing, we want to know where those profits came from; and, if they came from the funds, whether there were any compensating benefits. But it is certainly not acceptable to assume, as Mr. Zitzewitz did, and as Mr. Spitzer zealously approved, that timers' revenues are actually being squeezed out of long-term investors.

Since the demand by investors for fund services is extremely elastic, any burden from timing costs would rest with fund managers or fund-management companies, according to their respective demand elasticities. Tax consequences apart, long-termers would suffer only a small and temporary loss, if any, since the cost of avoiding any diminution in return by shifting to another fund or to another investment with a higher return is relatively small and transient. But the funds and their managers could shift all or a part of timing costs back to the timers even if investors are locked in by capital-gains taxes. One device for doing this was to charge a high front-end load for all trades. This would spread an occasional one-time cost over a long period for long-term investors but would be prohibitive for frequent traders. Thus long-term investors might reasonably accept a high front-end load as the price of keeping timers out. (So why is Mr. Spitzer complaining about these fees?) Fund companies could also refuse to do business with timers, a solution that several adopted. Others simply specify that only a small number of trades would be allowed in a given period. Some fund managers undoubtedly realized that a high enough net return in fees from having more trades and larger fund assets could make up for any loss from dilution and added administrative costs imposed by timers.

The airline industry provides an analogy. Business flyers, with high time costs, place a higher dollar value on air travel than do most leisure travelers. By charging everyone the same price, the airlines were losing some surplus they could command by charging a differentially higher price for business travelers. The single-price system meant higher total average fares, fewer flights and less leisure travel. The airlines found that they could discriminate between business and leisure travelers by charging different fares for different lengths of stay or for travel over particular days of the week. Business travelers now pay relatively more for their travel, but total social welfare is maximized by this use of differential pricing.

This is very much like the mutual-fund industry where some investors, the timers, could get a higher economic value from funds than others. The funds found a way to charge them a higher price, and everyone but the timers was made better off. The funds and their long-term investors shared in the "surplus" realized only by timers in a single-price system, and the timers were still allowed to do their thing, albeit at a higher price. Fees were set at varying higher levels for rapid traders, who were, of course, far more likely to be the timers. Long-term investors, the leisure flyers of the industry, paid a lower management or redemption fee, or received a higher rate of return for the same fee.

Anyone was free to use either system. This scheme, certainly no secret or concealed fraud, seems to have worked fairly well, judged by the enormous growth in mutual fund deposits while this was going on. However, in

1983 the SEC established what amounted to a 2% cap on regular redemption fees. For some funds, for which the price discrimination device had proved profitable, the cap amounted to a form of price control preventing them from recovering part of the timers' surplus. The incentive was now created for some sort of "black market" to replace the higher redemption fees the funds had previously used as an efficient price-discrimination device. Like all black markets, this one would have higher transactions costs than unregulated markets, but it would still move economic resources in a welfare-enhancing direction.

Various techniques have been used by funds, on the supply side, to accommodate the timers and secure their high-profit business. One was simply to ignore the legally mandated 4 p.m. closing time for transactions (clearly illegal); another was to ignore the funds' own restrictions on the number of trades that could be made in a period of time (perhaps a breach of contract, but hardly criminal in itself). The timers could pay more by "parking" large sums in related but unused funds or, perhaps in cases yet to be uncovered, by making illicit payments under the table.

If the industry had never been regulated, it is doubtful that we would be seeing any of this. Differential pricing and services would be commonplace, and it is even possible that a derivatives market relating to fund shares would have developed. Different firms would adopt different strategies depending on their size, comparative advantage and cost conditions, and the market would have settled on a correct equilibrium. There would be no scandal.

Mr. Spitzer will undoubtedly be surprised to learn that the timing practices he so roundly condemns actually helped investors, and the class-action lawyers will certainly not like learning that any real damages are orders of magnitude less than they hoped. But serious investors can rest secure in the knowledge that they are not fools to continue investing in mutual funds. The fools are the ones who thought they had uncovered a vast swindle when in fact all they had really done was demonstrate that beneficial market forces are always at work.

Regulation "In Terrorem"

Eliot Spitzer's current campaign against major insurance brokers and insurance companies has reaped massive media indignation, just as his "discovery" of a mutual-fund scandal did. No need to wait for messy trials in courts of law or lengthy studies by scholars; the returns are in, at least in the headlines, and Mr. Spitzer has won again.

But what if Mr. Spitzer is wrong, and what if none of the practices complained of was either unethical or anticompetitive? After all, Mr. Spitzer's case against certain practices in the mutual-fund industry relied heavily on one academic study claiming $5 billion a year losses to the investing public. The author of that study now admits that the figure—in any event based on some very dubious suppositions—should have been $2 billion rather than $5 billion. It is probably much less than that.

Furthermore, for all we know, Mr. Spitzer's remedies against the mutual-fund companies may be more costly than the practices complained of. Setting fees by fiat at below-market rates—price controls we call that in a different context—has never worked. Mutual-fund "governance" changes are generally costly jokes for all the effect they will have. Companies never implicated in any wrongdoing have been saddled with costly and unnecessary new regulations. And finally, large fines and restitution have been paid for violations which have been alleged and confessed to, but not yet sustained in a court of law.

Now Mr. Spitzer has condemned the practice of insurance brokers' using

Reprinted from *Wall Street Journal* (November 22, 2004), by permission of Henry G. Manne.

so-called contingent commissions. This was the practice of insurors paying brokers a larger than normal commission if certain contingencies, like good claims experience or more subsequent business, came to pass. This was said to bias the brokers towards influencing their customers to buy more expensive insurance than an ethical broker would recommend. In other words Marsh & McLennan and other brokers were soliciting and taking kickbacks to violate fiduciary obligations to their insurance-buying clients.

Marsh claims that these arrangements were disclosed to the insurance buyers and further that this extra payment was really compensation for various kinds of services, mostly informational, that they provided to the insurance companies. Mr. Spitzer's complaint curtly denies, even scoffs at both these arguments, though no state insurance regulator had ever found anything wrong with the fees, and surely in the hands of sophisticated attorneys each of these arguments could be morphed into a respectable legal defense to charges of deceit and fraud.

Nobel Laureate Ronald Coase once famously showed (*Journal of Law and Economics* 1979) how kickbacks in the so-called radio DJ payola scandal were really a legitimate, albeit superficially confusing, competitive device. Payola was essential, Coase explained, to preserving competition between record companies, and its demise was only sought by competitors who were injured by the practice—not by consumers. There are eerie similarities between the two situations.

If the Coasian analysis is correct—and no serious rebuttal has ever appeared—we may witness the demise of specialized insurance-brokerage firms like Marsh & McLennan in favor of more integrated insurance companies who will do their own marketing. This is already rumored to have begun. Or we may see insurance brokerage firms beginning to acquire and operate insurance companies. In either case we would be witnessing a decrease in market specialization with a commensurate loss of economic efficiency. Mr. Spitzer would have succeeded in making the industry less competitive and less efficient, and insurance buyers will eventually pay higher not lower premiums.

Mr. Spitzer's second charge against Marsh and other brokers is for bid rigging, an explicit antitrust violation. The charge is that the brokers avoided low bidders for some contracts and instead caused the contracts to go to a higher bidder. Mr. Spitzer has by implication, therefore, posited a complex cartel, with higher-than-market premiums for insurance enforced by insurance brokers on behalf of the cartel-member insurance companies.

Anyone familiar with cartel theory will recognize how unlikely this is. Cartels, except in rare and very special cases, are fragile and short-lived entities. The ease with which sophisticated insurance companies could "cheat" on such a cartel makes it extremely unlikely that illicit price fixing was involved. There is another much more likely explanation of this practice.

Let us suppose, for example, that Marsh & McLennan, in order to gain various efficiencies of integration, bought out numerous insurance companies and operated them as divisions of one company. We would call the resulting firm a multi-divisional, vertically integrated company, a perfectly legal way of doing business. There could then be no antitrust concerns about internal decisions to allocate business to one division or another or about allocating costs and revenues internally as they saw fit.

Now suppose that these same economies of integration could be obtained more cheaply by contract, or even by customary norms, rather than through expensive acquisitions and the administration of a larger organization. Certainly there could be no greater economic harm in the latter scenario than in the former. Yet the latter, which is the more likely explanation of what occurred in the insurance industry, is susceptible to easy misunderstanding. What in one case would be seen as internal cost and price management now looks like illegal bid rigging. Of course, it could be, but we cannot assume that from the facts we know.

Nonetheless, in the relatively short time since the civil complaint against Marsh & McLennan was made public, the head of that company has resigned, a torrent of mea culpas has been heard from that and other companies, thousands of employees have lost their jobs, established and successful business practices have been abandoned, and vast sums of money have been earmarked for fines and restitution. A Spitzer blitz, with its inevitable stock price decline, calls for a fast triage response in order to stave off a calamity on the scale of Arthur Andersen or Enron.

In an era of general acceptance of deregulation and privatization, Mr. Spitzer has introduced the world to yet a new form of regulation, the use of the criminal law as an in terrorem weapon to force acceptance of industry-wide regulations. These rules are not vetted through normal authoritative channels, are not reviewable by any administrative process, and are not subject to even the minimal due-process requirements our courts require for normal administrative rule making. The whole process bears no resemblance to a rule of law; it is a reign of force. And to make matters worse, the regulatory remedies are usually vastly more costly to the public than the alleged evils.

No good solution comes readily to mind. We could federalize insurance regulation, though federal regulation did not prevent a "Spitzer scandal" in the mutual-fund industry. And it could, of course, make the situation much worse. Ominously, Senate hearings are now pending on the insurance industry, and we just might get another Sarbanes-Oxley. Or one could hope that the Supreme Court would declare acts like New York's Martin Act unconstitutional for vagueness. But that is very unlikely even with a federal judiciary expected to become more conservative on some issues. Increased activity by the states, tolerated by the courts, is more apt to be the order of the day.

Since Mr. Spitzer wins his cases in the media, where business is now all but defenseless, the best hope is for the American business community to develop its own public voice. The free-market scholarship needed for this purpose is available, though it is rarely availed of in these fights. Too often the corporate defenders conclude, out of ignorance to be sure, that the opposition really has the better case.

But make no mistake: Eliot Spitzer represents, wittingly or not, an attack on the entire corporate free-enterprise system. Clearly we need new or invigorated institutions to defend industries and companies publicly when they come under unwarranted or disproportionate attack. Responsible leaders of the business community should make it a high priority to develop these capabilities before more harm is done.

Insider Trading: Hayek, Virtual Markets, and the Dog That Did Not Bark

"How is the betting?"

"Well, that is the curious part of it. You could have got fifteen to one yesterday, but the price has become shorter and shorter, until you can hardly get three to one now."

"Hum!" said Holmes. "Somebody knows something, that is clear!"

. . .

Inspector Gregory: "Is there any other point to which you would wish to draw my attention?"

Holmes: "To the curious incident of the dog in the night-time."

"The dog did nothing in the night-time."

"That was the curious incident," remarked Sherlock Holmes.[1]

I. Introduction

This Article briefly reexamines the great debates on the role of insider trading in the corporate system from the perspectives of efficiency of capital markets, harm to individual investors, and executive compensation. The focus is on the mystery of why trading by all kinds of insiders as well as

Reprinted from *Journal of Corporation Law* 31 (fall 2005): 167–85, by permission of the publisher.

I am grateful to Stephen M. Bainbridge, George Benston, William Carney, Enrico Colombatto, Stanislav Dolgopolov, Geoffrey Manne, and Larry Ribstein for helpful suggestions and discussions.

1. Arthur Conan Doyle, "Silver Blaze," *in The Adventures and the Memoirs of Sherlock Holmes*, pp. 309, 330 (Sterling Publishing, 2004).

knowledgeable outsiders was studiously ignored by the business and investment communities before the advent of insider trading regulation. It is hardly conceivable that officers, directors, and controlling shareholders would have remained totally silent in the face of widespread insider trading if they had seen the practice as being harmful to the company, to themselves, or to investors. By analogy with the famous article by Friedrich Hayek, "The Use of Knowledge in Society," this Article considers the problem of obtaining necessary information for managers of large corporate enterprises. The suggested analytical framework views the share price, sensitively impacted by informed trading, as a mechanism for timely transmission of valuable information to top managers and large shareholders. Informed trading in the stock market is also compared to "prediction" or "virtual" markets currently used by corporations and policymakers.

II. Background

It has been almost forty years since the publication of my book *Insider Trading and the Stock Market*,[2] and the topic still has the ability to engender heated argument as well as seemingly unending efforts at analytical explication.[3] I apologize at the outset for continuing the debate, especially since I myself thought that it had about run its course. Nonetheless, the topic refuses to die, and it continues to stimulate new hypotheses, one of which is about to be offered.

This taxing of the intellectual tolerance of critics of insider trading may have a redeeming feature for many. In the process of developing this new idea, I have had to reexamine and substantially modify perhaps the most vigorously criticized claim I made for the positive benefits of unregulated insider trading. That claim was the notion that insider trading can be used as an important component of executive compensation. I hope that I am about to offer a much stronger substitute argument.

2. Henry G. Manne, *Insider Trading and the Stock Market* (1966).

3. For an excellent but somewhat dated bibliography, see Stephen M. Bainbridge, "Insider Trading," in *Encyclopedia of Law and Economics* 3:772, 798–812 (Boudewijn Bouckaert & Gerrit De Geest eds., 2000). For the most comprehensive treatise, see William K. S. Wang & Marc I. Steinberg, *Insider Trading* (1996 & Supp. 2002).

Fundamentally, my book made only three basic economic arguments.[4] One was that the practice of insider trading did no significant harm to long-term investors. The other two were claims of positive benefits from the practice: one, the compensation argument, and the other, the idea that insider trading contributed importantly to the efficiency of stock market pricing.

By and large the idea that there is no direct harm from the practice has held up very well, especially the point that no real damage is caused to an investor who engages anonymously on an exchange in a trade with an insider on the other side of the transaction. However, one "harm" argument of feasible merit has dominated the academic literature for some time.[5] This is the so-called "adverse selection" argument. Basically the argument is that since specialists on the floor of stock exchanges (or other market makers) systematically lose money when insiders are trading, they will expand their bid-ask spread in order to cover this greater cost of doing business. In this fashion, it is argued, they pass along the cost of insiders' trading to all outside investors with whom they deal, the so-called "insider trading tax."[6]

The first part of this argument is really just a variant of the idea in my book that short-term traders would indeed frequently lose to insiders[7] (a warning against using the stock market as a gambling casino). I suggested

4. This discussion leaves aside such tangential but important issues as the enforceability of insider trading laws and public choice aspects of the subject, as well as such tangential but economically irrelevant notions as the fairness of the practice.

5. I do not consider the SEC's "official" line on insider trading, that it destroys the confidence of investors and thus lessens both liquidity and investment, to have serious merit. Apart from being a nearly unfalsifiable proposition, it is devoid of the scantest economic or empirical content. It has, however, been enormously important in the propaganda campaign the SEC has waged for years to demonize insider trading.

6. Walter Bagehot (pseud. for Jack L. Treynor), "The Only Game in Town," *Fin. Analysts J.*, Mar.–Apr. 1971, p. 12; Thomas E. Copeland & Dan Galai, "Information Effects on the Bid-Ask Spread," *J. Fin.* 38:1457 (1983); Lawrence R. Glosten & Paul R. Milgrom, "Bid, Ask and Transaction Prices in a Specialist Market with Heterogeneously Informed Traders," *J. Fin. Econ.* 14:71 (1985).

7. Perhaps in some sense long-term traders lose as well, but quantitatively that is insignificant as compared to short-term traders, and even then one must look at various offsetting advantages. *See also* Henry G. Manne, "In Defense of Insider Trading," *Harv. Bus. Rev.*, Nov.–Dec. 1966, pp. 113, 114–15 (discussing a possible harm from insider trading to short-term traders).

that long-term investors[8] had little to worry about quantitatively because of insider trading, and the same thing remains true regardless of the existence of some adverse selection. Furthermore, there is considerable evidence that the harm to market makers exists more in the theoretical world of finance literature than it does in the actual play of the market. Though the argument is theoretically feasible, it seems to be practically irrelevant in the real world.[9]

Of the two arguments that I offered for positive benefits from insider trading, the argument for a strong positive relationship between market efficiency and insider trading has proved to be very robust. I missed the very important and related advantage pointed out by Harold Demsetz that access to valuable trading information may allow controlling shareholders to be compensated for the additional risk they assumed by not being well diversified.[10] This is an especially important factor in corporate governance, since, without a controlling shareholder, agency costs in large corporations, normally dealt with through an exogenous market for corporate control, will be much higher.

There is almost no disagreement that insider trading does always push the price of a stock in the correct direction.[11] This is not to gainsay that

8. This refers to investors whose trades fundamentally represent a rebalancing of diversified portfolios to reflect changed circumstances, or altered weightings in a previously correctly balanced portfolio.

9. *See* Stanislav Dolgopolov, "Insider Trading and the Bid-Ask Spread: A Critical Evaluation of Adverse Selection in Market Making," *Cap. U. L. Rev.* 33:83 (2004). One of the most telling criticisms of the adverse selection argument is that liquidity providers themselves—including the NYSE specialists and the NASDAQ dealers but excluding liquidity providers in options markets—are not generally concerned about the presence of insiders in securities in which they make a market. *Id.*, pp. 108–10, 136–44.

10. *See* Harold Demsetz, "Corporate Control, Insider Trading and Rates of Return," *Am. Econ. Rev.* (*Papers & Proc.*) 76:313 (1986). It is appropriate to note that controlling shareholders perform a valuable management-monitoring function not shouldered by other shareholders, whose incentive would be to free ride, which is the ultimate "separation" problem. Demsetz, however, may have overlooked the extent to which a control block of shares presents agency cost problems of its own, since there are other devices besides inside information by which a controlling shareholder may transfer wealth from minority shareholders.

11. For empirical research arguing that insider trading quickly incorporates the impact of nonpublic information into the market price, see Ji-Chai Lin & Michael S. Rozeff, "The

there are also other mechanisms that play a significant role in stock pricing, such as the explicit public disclosure of new information, sanctioned transmittal of information to financial analysts, and the so-called "derivative" trading that occurs after some form of market "signaling."[12] A vast literature

Speed of Adjustment of Prices to Private Information: Empirical Tests," *J. Fin. Res.* 18:143 (1995); Lisa K. Meulbroek, "An Empirical Analysis of Illegal Insider Trading," *J. Fin.* 47:1661 (1992). The only significant arguments are with the extent and timeliness of a price effect from insider trading. *See* Sugato Chakravarty & John J. McConnell, "Does Insider Trading Really Move Stock Prices?" *J. Fin. & Quantitative Analysis* 34:191 (1999) (offering empirical evidence for the proposition that informed trading by insiders has the same price impact as uninformed trading by outsiders); James D. Cox, "Insider Trading and Contracting: A Critical Response to the 'Chicago School,'" *Duke L.J.*, pp. 628, 646 (1986) (arguing that insider trading is a "noisy" device for communicating the stock value). Research with "laboratory" experiments suggests that inside information is rapidly assimilated into market price and that this may occur even with very few insiders participating in the market, a finding particularly relevant here. *See, e.g.*, Martin Barner et al., "On the Microstructure of Price Determination and Information Aggregation with Sequential and Asymmetric Information Arrival in an Experimental Asset Market," *Annals Fin.* 1:1 (2005); Daniel Friedman et al., "The Informational Efficiency of Experimental Asset Markets," *J. Pol. Econ.* 92:349 (1984); Charles R. Plott & Shyam Sunder, "Efficiency of Experimental Security Markets with Insider Information: An Application of Rational-Expectations Models," *J. Pol. Econ.* 90:663 (1982). *But see* Vernon L. Smith et al., "Bubbles, Crashes, and Endogenous Expectations in Experimental Spot Asset Markets," *Econometrica* 56:1119 (1988) (describing deviations from market efficiency in laboratory settings).

12. The standard reference for this discussion is Ronald J. Gilson & Reinier H. Kraakman, "The Mechanisms of Market Efficiency," *Va. L. Rev.* 70:549 (1984). Without getting into too much detail, there are two significant weaknesses in Gilson and Kraakman's implicit effort to minimize the role of insider trading in this process. One is their failure to reckon with the price influence of insiders' refraining from buying or selling when they have undisclosed information. The other is a certain ambiguity in the concept of "derivative" trading, since it would seem that most of this trading must actually follow real informed trading, especially including insiders' trades. Thus they implicitly underestimated the relative influence of insider trading in making the stock market efficient. That particular ambiguity is gone in the recent update of their piece, Ronald J. Gilson & Reinier Kraakman, "The Mechanisms of Market Efficiency Twenty Years Later: The Hindsight Bias," *J. Corp. L.* 28:715 (2003), but there is still no emphasis put on this fairly obvious feature of market efficiency. This article gives more significance than is due to the impact on market efficiency of behavioral finance and the cognitive bias it posits with noise trading (as if all noise trading was not always seen as a kind of economic irrationality). And they give far less significance than is due to the market inefficiencies created by various bits of securities regulation, though they do emphasize the special problem of the federal securities law's bias against short selling. Unfortunately, that is not the only, or even the

has developed examining the relative impact of these various mechanisms on stock market pricing, but it is fair to say that none of this has seriously damaged the argument of the stock-pricing benefit of insider trading. This is not the right time or place to review that literature, and for present purposes we merely need to understand that insider trading does have the price vector claimed for it, even though this mechanism alone may play less than an exclusive role in making stock market pricing as efficient as it is.[13] The crucial point for present purposes is that, even if only on a few occasions and either by itself or in tandem with other forces, insider trading may be sufficient to move the price of a company's stock.

My second "positive" argument for insider trading, that it could perform well as a part of an executive compensation package, has been the more forcefully attacked,[14] and it is perhaps less robust than I and other proponents[15] had originally assumed. The insider trading compensation argu-

---

most, significant interference with market efficiency to be found in our complex securities regulations.

13. An argument could be made, of course, that all price changes result from new information that someone has traded on profitably. The impact of explicit disclosure is often to confirm that the price reached in other ways is correct. But this argument still allows explicit disclosure an important role in making stock market pricing efficient.

14. Stephen M. Bainbridge, *Corporation Law and Economics,* p. 593 (2002) (stating that insider trading creates the incentive for managers to disclose information prematurely); Robert Charles Clark, *Corporate Law,* pp. 273–74 (1986) (stating that insider trading allows managers to determine their own compensation packages and undo formal compensation agreements); Cox, "Insider Trading and Contracting," pp. 651–52 (stating that insider trading is likely to increase manager tolerance of bad news); Frank H. Easterbrook, "Insider Trading, Secret Agents, Evidentiary Privileges, and the Production of Information," *Sup. Ct. Rev.,* pp. 309, 332 (1981) (stating that insider trading may induce managers to accept excessively risky projects and that insider trading as managerial compensation may be inefficient since risk-averse managers would value trading profits differently than risk-neutral shareholders); Robert J. Haft, "The Effect of Insider Trading Rules on the Internal Efficiency of the Large Corporation," *Mich. L. Rev.* 80:1051, 1053–56 (1982) (stating that insider trading is likely to interfere with the flow of information within the firm); Roy A. Schotland, "Unsafe at Any Price: A Reply to Manne, *Insider Trading and the Stock Market,*" *Va. L. Rev.* 53:1425, 1448–50 (1967) (stating that insider trading is likely to induce managers to delay disclosure and participate in market manipulation).

15. *See* Dennis W. Carlton & Daniel R. Fischel, "The Regulation of Insider Trading," *Stan. L. Rev.* 35:857, 861 (1983) (arguing that "allowing the practice [of insider trading] may be an efficient way to compensate corporate managers").

ment has become especially relevant in recent years,[16] as a great debate has swirled through business, regulatory, and legal circles about the proper way to compensate corporate executives. Much of this discussion has focused recently on stock options, since they were so heavily relied upon to compensate employees of the firms that figured heavily in the market collapse of the early 2000s. The focus on stock options in turn logically implicates the insider trading compensation argument, since the two are undoubtedly the closest substitutes in the compensation arena.

A stock option offers the same incentive to employees to work efficiently that would be provided by ownership of an appropriate number of shares, however obtained, but leveraged by non-recourse, interest-free debt. The indirect incentive effects of this leveraging are very difficult to value for corporate accounting purposes or, for that matter, for the purpose of determining the value of the option to an employee.[17] Thus, even though there is a forward look and a leverage feature to options that cannot be obtained, say, with bonuses, there are still real problems with determining the exact incentive effect of stock option grants.[18]

16. *See* Henry G. Manne, "Options? Nah, Try Insider Trading," *Wall St. J.*, Aug. 2, 2002, p. A8.

17. The corporation's valuation of an option may be quite different from that of the employee, as the debate about the Financial Accounting Standards Board's (FASB) recent requirement that the options be valued as an expense on the corporate books well attests. *See Share-Based Payment,* Statement of Fin. Accounting Standards No. 123 (Fin. Accounting Standards Bd. 2004), *available at* http://www.fasb.org/pdf/fas123r.pdf. *See also* Brian J. Hall & Kevin J. Murphy, "Stock Options for Undiversified Executives," *J. Acct. & Econ.* 33:3, 5 (2002) (arguing that the option's cost to the company "often significantly exceeds the value of the option from the perspective of a risk-averse, undiversified executive, who can neither sell the option nor hedge against its risk").

18. *See* Lucian Arye Bebchuk et al., "Managerial Power and Rent Extraction in the Design of Executive Compensation," *U. Chi. L. Rev.* 69:751, 757 (2002) (noting "firms' failure to use option schemes that filter out stock price rises that are due largely to industry and general market trends and thus are unrelated to the managers' performance"); Michael C. Jensen & Kevin J. Murphy, "Remuneration: Where We Have Been, How We Got to Here, What Are the Problems, and How to Fix Them," pp. 58–65 (Harvard Bus. Sch., NOM Research Paper No. 04-28, 2004), *available at* http://www.ssrn.com/Abstract=561305 (pointing out that many stock option compensation plans often do not take into account the firm's cost of capital or future dividends and hence may create value-destroying incentives for managers); David Yermack, "Do Corporations Award CEO Stock Options Effectively?" *J. Fin. Econ.* 39:237 (1995) (finding little empirical evidence

After the option is exercised, and to the extent the employee holds on to the shares, the executive becomes a (larger) shareholder. Stock ownership obviously motivates a manager to maximize share price, especially if the shares represent a substantial part of the employee's portfolio. However, since the shares will represent only a tiny fraction of the company's outstanding shares, free rider reasons dictate that the induced incentive for risky choices may still fall short of what would be dictated by the interest of all shareholders. In other words, as a number of studies suggest, stock options at best offer no greater incentive than would an appropriate, but difficult to determine, number of shares held by the manager, however acquired, and leveraged by debt.[19] At worst, they may provide real adverse incentives.[20]

When stock options are the primary device used to encourage risky decisions by managers, and to the extent that insider trading is effectively, or even substantially, prevented, the financial focus of corporate officials will necessarily be on accounting information, since the real world events underlying those entries cannot be traded on directly as they occur. The legal flow of information to the market will be via formal, SEC-sanctioned disclosures, including press releases, quarterly reports, 10-Ks, and duly publicized conferences with financial analysts. Since future expected profits cannot be shown on the books, and trading on the underlying information is not allowed, the urge to make the accounting picture look better in order to have it conform to management's current view of the company's prospects—biased or not—may become irresistible. It is at least arguable that

---

for the incentive-alignment rationale of CEO stock awards); David Yermack, "Good Timing: CEO Stock Option Awards and Company News Announcements," *J. Fin.* 52:449, 475 (1997) (offering empirical evidence to support the hypothesis that CEOs "who become aware of impending improvement in corporate performance may influence their compensation committees to award more performance-based pay").

19. It is not surprising that the empirical studies of the incentive effects of options show a mixed bag. This device is arguably most useful in companies with executives who might have difficulty borrowing sufficient money to leverage their own purchases of their companies' shares, as may have been particularly the case with many high-tech start-up companies in recent years.

20. *See* Michael C. Jensen, "Stock Options Reward Management for Destroying Value and What to Do About It" (Harvard Bus. Sch., NOM Research Paper No. 01-27, 2001), *available at* http://www.ssrn.com/Abstract=480401.

this constituted part of the underlying pressure for what occurred at Enron and various telecommunications companies.[21]

Insider trading, on the other hand, does not have these disadvantages. It, in effect, allows insiders to meticulously craft their own reward for innovations almost as soon as they occur and to trade without harm to any investors.[22] The incentive is immediate and precise and is never confounded with stock price changes that are not of the managers' making.

If insider trading were legal and used to replace stock options, there would be no "tragedies" of employees being left high and dry with options way out of the money. There would be no loss of reward when an innovation merely resulted in a reduction of an expected loss. There would be no unearned gain because a company's stock appreciates in line with a market or industry rise. There would be no disappointments about the number of shares optioned or granted to particular employees. There would be none of this absurd business of renegotiating the option plan every time the stock takes a nose dive. And there would be no peculiar problems of accounting, since there would be no reason to put the right of employees to trade on undisclosed information on the company's balance sheet at all; such trading would be entirely extraneous to the company's accounts.

21. This is not an excuse for illegal and fraudulent behavior, but it does reveal a type of unanticipated consequence of securities regulation that rarely figures in the calculus of whether that regulation is desirable or not. One can compare this notion to what Michael Jensen terms the problem of "overvalued equity." *See* Michael C. Jensen, "The Agency Costs of Overvalued Equity and the Current State of Corporate Finance," *Eur. Fin. Mgmt.* 10:549 (2004).

22. A clear statement on this proposition was provided by Carlton and Fischel:

> Insider trading may present a solution to [the] cost-of-renegotiation dilemma. The unique advantage of insider trading is that it allows a manager to alter his compensation package in light of new knowledge, thereby avoiding continual renegotiation. The manager, in effect, "renegotiates" each time he trades. This in turn increases the manager's incentive to acquire and develop valuable information in the first place (as well as to invest in firm-specific human capital). (Carlton & Fischel, "Regulation of Insider Trading," pp. 870–71)

The point about "no harm to investors" does not mean that short-term traders (really gamblers) or market makers trading against insiders will not lose money. They will, however, only lose negligibly more than they would if insiders were not in the market but the price level change (or the release time of new information) was the same.

The SEC's notoriously ineffective, but highly publicized and politicized, efforts to enforce insider trading laws have merely shifted the identity of the people who may trade first on undisclosed information.[23] In the process, they have perhaps prevented the development of an innovative and useful compensation device and unduly encouraged a problematic second best.

Having said that, however, it must be recognized that insider trading cannot be a perfect form of incentive compensation. While many of the criticisms of the practice are vacuous or even tendentious, there are significant problems with the scheme, which many of my critics hastened to elaborate. Valuable information will undoubtedly get into the hands of individuals inside and outside the company who in no sense should be compensated, usually because they will have done nothing to produce the valuable new information.[24] Another problem is that the value of the information cannot be metered to the value of the contribution of a particular individual. And, as was also pointed out, the value of new information will, in many cases, be a function of the financial ability of someone to trade on the information or of their ability to evaluate new knowledge.[25]

Perhaps the most common objection to insider trading as compensation is that it cannot be metered in advance as part of a compensation plan.[26] It

23. *See* David D. Haddock & Jonathan R. Macey, "Regulation on Demand: A Private Interest Model, with an Application to Insider Trading Regulation," *J. L. & Econ.* 30:311 (1987) (arguing that the existence of insider trading regulation benefited "market professionals" in the securities industry). Compare this to the problem addressed by Regulation FD (Fair Disclosure), which prohibited the practice of selective disclosure by issuers to securities analysts and large shareholders. Selective Disclosure and Insider Trading, Securities Act Release No. 7881, Exchange Act Release No. 43,154, Investment Company Act Release No. 24,599, 65 Fed. Reg. 51,716 (Aug. 15, 2000).

24. This argument, like the ones to follow, necessarily reflects only a partial equilibrium conclusion. There are many other positive points that must be included in a general equilibrium solution.

25. Morris Mendelson, "The Economics of Insider Trading Reconsidered," *U. Pa. L. Rev.* 117:470, 488 (1969); Schotland, "Unsafe at Any Price," p. 1455.

26. This criticism may not be quite as forceful as it first appears. If one would grant the distinction between managers and entrepreneurs, referred to in my book, there is still much vitality left in the information-as-compensation argument. A problem with connecting this otherwise valuable economic concept of the entrepreneur, however, is that it allows little useful application since one can never know ahead of time who, in a large company, will be the real entrepreneur. Thus, insider trading has to be allowed either for

is in its very nature a kind of all-or-nothing proposition, since efforts by a given corporation to police its rules about who can trade, and to what extent, will necessarily involve the company in exactly the kind of post hoc compensation calculations that the practice is argued by its supporters to avoid.[27] It is not too surprising then that even before 1968, in the heyday of insider trading in the United States,[28] no company ever announced that certain executives, but not other employees, would be allowed to engage in the practice.[29]

Indeed it is not surprising that there is no evidence that any company ever tried to develop insider trading as an explicit and integral part of an optimal compensation package. On the other hand, our understanding of corporate inaction on insider trading as compensation tells us nothing about the far more startling fact that very few companies in the United States, *prior to the SEC's involvement with the subject,* seemed to have had a rule *against* insider trading.[30] Perhaps even more surprising, there is no sig-

---

all or for none; there is no middle ground. While, for a variety of reasons, I would still conclude that non-regulation is the best solution, I would not deny some force to the argument of those who came down on the other side of the compensation argument.

27. The difficulty of an individual company policing insider trading (assuming that the company thought there was something harmful in the practice) was one basis for Judge Easterbrook's conclusion that the practice should be outlawed and policed by public authorities, something of a non sequitur, since there is no evidence that any company ever actually faced this problem. *See* Frank H. Easterbrook, "Insider Trading as an Agency Problem," *in Principals and Agents: The Structure of Business,* pp. 81, 93–95 (John W. Pratt & Richard Zeckhauser eds., 1985).

28. The first significant judicial holding that insider trading was generally a violation of Rule 10b-5 was *SEC v. Texas Gulf Sulphur Co.,* 401 F.2d 833 (2d Cir. 1968) (en banc), *cert. denied,* 404 U.S. 1005 (1971). However, the SEC's warnings certainly appeared earlier. *See Cady, Roberts & Co.,* 40 S.E.C. 907 (1961) (censuring a broker-dealer firm and one of its partners for executing transactions for their customers on the basis of inside information obtained through one of the employees in his official capacity as a corporate director).

29. I have for years labored—and pressured students—to come up with the outline of a workable compensation plan utilizing insider trading. But, given the constraints implied by the discussion in the text, this has proved to be a fruitless task.

30. *See* Adolf A. Berle, Jr., & Gardiner C. Means, *The Modern Corporation and Private Property,* p. 327 (1932) ("It is known that certain companies, usually under the dominance of some strong individual, decline to permit anyone . . . whether as director or employee to conduct speculative operations in the corporate stock. On the other hand, it is certain that this is not the general practice. . . .").

nificant or convincing evidence of which I am aware that any company, its spokespersons, or major shareholders ever pushed for public regulation of insider trading when it was surely widely known that it was going on.[31] The pre–*Texas Gulf Sulphur* business community was perhaps understandably silent about insider trading as a compensation device, since it probably was not really a feasible practice. However, they were also, far more mysteriously, silent about any problems they might have found generally with the very common practice of insider trading. That is precisely the mystery which can now be solved with a little help from the "dog that did not bark."

III. The Mystery

It is hardly conceivable that officers, directors, and controlling shareholders would have remained totally silent in the face of widespread insider trading if they had seen the practice as being harmful to the company, to investors, or to themselves. And it is equally inconceivable that they would not have recognized some harm if it existed. Insider trading must have been as much a way of life in the U.S. securities markets prior to the 1960s as it is known to have been at a much later date in Japan and other countries. Its existence was so common and taken for granted that there was no need for empirical or even anecdotal evidence for the practice.[32]

And yet no one of significance in the business world was ever heard to complain about the practice, much less declare it to be the moral equivalent

31. An interesting bit of support for the notion that there was no concern about the "evils" of insider trading comes from the fact that, as late as 1939, the New York Stock Exchange and other leading exchanges proposed that section 16(b) of the Securities Exchange Act of 1934, the only provision thought to relate even modestly to insider trading, be repealed. "Text of Exchanges' Proposals to SEC," *Wall St. J.*, Mar. 15, 1939, p. 11. *But see infra* note 33.

32. Classic histories include Henry Clews, *Fifty Years in Wall Street* (1908) and Edwin Lefèvre, *Reminiscences of a Stock Operator* (1923). For evidence of contemporary practices in Japan and elsewhere, see Utpal Bhattacharya & Hazem Daouk, "The World Price of Insider Trading," *J. Fin.* 57:75 (2002); Jan Hanousek & Richard Podpiera, "Information-Driven Trading at the Prague Stock Exchange: Evidence from Intra-Day Data," *Econ. Transition* 10:747 (2002); Richard Small, "From *Tatemae* to *Honne:* A Historical Perspective on the Prohibition of Insider Trading in Japan," *Wash U. Global Stud. L. Rev.* 2:313 (2003).

of murder or rape in the commercial arena.[33] This silence is a mystery that has not been noticed or addressed by modern writers—until now. What can possibly explain this puzzling behavior? Perhaps the practice was thought, as it is today, to be so heinous that no one wanted to even mention it in polite company, as the words "cancer" or "incest" used to be treated. But there is little evidence that prior to the SEC's efforts in this regard insider trading had anything like the connotation of extreme immorality implied by this theory. There is no evidence of any general revulsion by the business community or the public towards insider trading in those "good old days."

One might argue that the adoption of the securities laws of the New Deal, with their ostensible "full disclosure" philosophy, reflected a general dissatisfaction with the state of affairs in securities markets, including insider

33. The few exceptions, primarily academic, that we find today are more notable as proof of this proposition than for suggesting popular revulsion of the practice. *See* Berle & Means, *Modern Corporation,* pp. 223–26, 326 (condemning insider trading as an abuse of access to information in the official capacity and treating inside information as the collective property of the shareholders); Frank P. Smith, *Management Trading: Stock-Market Prices and Profits* (1941) (applying economic analysis to trading by corporate insiders but ultimately condemning insider trading on nonpublic information); H. L. Wilgus, "Purchase of Shares of Corporation by a Director from a Shareholder," *Mich. L. Rev.* 8:267, 297 (1910) (arguing that insider trading "does more to discourage legitimate investment in corporate shares than almost anything else"). More to the point, the Pujo Bill, a comprehensive federal securities statute proposed in 1913 after well publicized congressional hearings, had a provision regulating trading by corporate officers and directors. *Report of the Committee Appointed Pursuant to House Resolutions 429 and 504 to Investigate the Concentration of Control of Money and Credit,* H.R. Rep. No. 62-1593, pp. 171–72 (1913). There were even business witnesses who criticized the practice of insider trading (but did not endorse the proposed regulatory measures) during the subsequent Senate hearings in 1914. *See Regulation of the Stock Exchange: Hearings on S. 3895 Before the S. Comm. on Banking and Currency,* 63d Cong. 152–53, 267–68 (1914). But this was not the central theme of the hearings, and nothing came of the provision regulating insider trading. Again, the lack of any follow-up or of any increased concern after the hearings seems to strengthen the point that there was no serious public concern with insider trading prior to *Texas Gulf Sulphur.*

Perhaps the same can be said about the "minority" common law view that insider trading was improper (though no early case involved an anonymous transaction on an exchange). *See* Wang & Steinberg, *Insider Trading,* § 16.2.3.2.

Admittedly, section 16(b) of the Securities Exchange Act of 1934 was sold to the public as an anti–insider trading provision, but its reach was so limited that it was never thought of as a comprehensive effort to deal with the subject. Even so, the New York Stock Exchange sought repeal of that provision only a few years later. *See supra* note 31.

trading. This would be a serious misreading of that history, however, since that legislation, like most other New Deal regulation, was aimed primarily at preventing or suppressing competition, regardless of what incidental rationalization may have been offered the public for political reason.[34] And while it is true that there would have been considerable "free rider" problems if any one company had tried to enforce a rule against insider trading, this still would not explain the universal silence on the subject. Indeed, if this were part of the explanation, it is much more likely that we would have heard a public clamor for government assistance with the problem, rather than total silence.

It might be argued that, while there was universal disapproval of insider trading, the managers, who were the chief perpetrators, would naturally keep silent about their transactions. This explanation would apply equally to all top managers, board members, and controlling shareholders, and thus it could theoretically explain the universal silence on the subject. This hypothesis is flawed. Top managers or controlling shareholders could not have been the only individuals with access to undisclosed information, and they would have no reason to cover up the trading of others. Accountants would have valuable financial information before the CFO; salespeople and plant forepersons would know of speed-ups in orders and production before the COO; and outsiders would know of pending merger offers before the CEO. Even mid-level executives, to say nothing of secretaries, elevator operators, and office staff, would certainly on occasion have had access to tradable information. Anyone might indeed have had some reason to remain silent about his or her own trading, but that would not explain the silence of the top managers about underlings' trades.

34. *See* Ellis W. Hawley, *The New Deal and the Problem of Monopoly* (1966). Hawley found a real anticompetition motive but a different, publicly stated purpose, in connection with the creation of every New Deal agency except the SEC. The exception Hawley thought he found was clearly an error. *See also* Henry G. Manne, "Economic Aspects of Required Disclosure Under Federal Securities Laws," *in Wall Street in Transition: The Emerging System and Its Impact on the Economy,* pp. 21, 31–36 (Henry G. Manne & Ezra Solomon eds., 1974) (discussing possible anticompetitive motives and consequences of the federal securities laws); Henry G. Manne & Joseph J. Bial, "Questioning the SEC's Crusades," *Reg.,* Winter 2001, p. 8 (hypothesizing a restraint-of-competition motive behind the SEC's initial sally into the subject of insider trading in the 1960s).

Also consider the matter of various employees of a company trading on bad news. One would expect top managers to scream like stuck pigs if underlings traded on information that the superiors did not yet have and that would lower stock price. Such behavior could jeopardize managers' own job security. It is conventional wisdom that top managers of publicly held companies do everything they can to put a rosy hue on any public disclosures and even on the company's financial accounting. Clearly, their interest in survival, as affected by the impact of bad news on the share price, would prevail over any wish to hush up insider trading by others. Thus we could hardly expect that interest to explain their total silence on the subject, since, in this case, insider trading might be harmful to them.

However, what if the top managers were making so much money from trading on undisclosed information themselves that they were willing to acquiesce in underlings' participation in order to avoid killing the gold-bearing goose? This too fails on close examination. Top managers may well have had access to some valuable information before its trading value was frittered away by underlings, but controlling shareholders who were not directly involved in the management of the company would not. If they were being cut out by their managers, there is no reason to believe that they would not complain about it or at least cite it as a reason for putting in new managers. Of course, they too could all have been part of an enormous conspiracy of silence,[35] but the odds are strongly against that.

So it is highly unlikely that corporate managers of the relevant period thought there was a problem with the practice at all. On the other hand, if some (net) advantage to the practice existed of which managers then were even dimly aware, their silence might well imply approval of the practice. Recognition of some benefit to insider trading would still not necessarily result in public discussion of the topic. Silence might still follow because there was no market pressure, and no social, intellectual, or psychological incentive, to open the issue publicly. If any disadvantage from insider trading had been recognized by important business spokespersons of the day,

35. For the far-fetched plea for regulating insider trading to prevent managers from using inside information to "bribe" dominant shareholders to refrain from monitoring (certainly a kind of conspiracy theory), see Ernst Maug, "Insider Trading Legislation and Corporate Governance," *Eur. Econ. Rev.* 46:1569 (2002).

silence would have been unlikely. Conversely, silence could well have been the consequence of approval.[36] Our remaining task then is to see if there was some benefit to the managerial function from insider trading other than the compensation argument that we have already discounted.

IV. The Mystery Solved

One possible solution to this query is suggested by a surprising source, Friedrich Hayek's classic "The Use of Knowledge in Society."[37] In that piece Hayek advances the notion that the most important task of an economic system is not the efficient allocation of goods and services. If the necessary knowledge of relative values were available, those calculations would not in theory be difficult. Though these observations are made in the context of a discussion of central economic planning, his language, as we shall see, seems equally applicable to some of the problems of managing a large corporate enterprise.

The real problem for the socialist planner, as Hayek identified it, is how to manage the necessary information in practice, since "the knowledge of circumstances . . . never exists in concentrated or integrated form, but solely as the dispersed bits of incomplete and frequently contradictory knowledge which all the separate individuals possess."[38] Hayek's argument that "[t]he various ways in which the knowledge on which people base their plans is communicated to them is the crucial problem for any theory explaining the economic process"[39] applies equally well to the problem of managing a large corporation. In other words, the essence of management is not the substance of the information needed for decisions, but rather the process by

36. I have already mentioned that it is highly unlikely that they were merely unaware of the practice or that they could not recognize either an advantage or disadvantage from it.

37. F. A. Hayek, "The Use of Knowledge in Society," *Am. Econ. Rev.* 35:519 (1945).

38. *Id.*, p. 519.

39. *Id.*, p. 520. Hayek makes a distinction between scientific knowledge and the kind of knowledge of the "particular circumstances of time and place," which by its nature cannot enter into statistics such as a central planner would need, *id.*, p. 524, or, it might be argued, into accounting data of the sort to which the SEC gives preeminence.

which information that is somewhere "out there" gets communicated to the decisionmaker.

Hayek compared "central planning," which "by its nature cannot take direct account of . . . circumstances of time and place," to decentralized competition in which the decisions are left to "the man on the spot."[40] The parallels to the managerial problem are very suggestive even if not exact. Top-level managers are regularly beset with enormous problems of getting appropriate, truthful, and timely information for making decisions,[41] decisions which in many ways are similar to those a central economic planner would have to make. And, while the corporate manager, unlike the central planner, cannot leave decisions up to "the man on the spot," Hayek's euphemism for a market process, the manager may have access to a related type of information source unavailable to the socialist planner.

Information comes to top managers, of course, in many forms and through various devices. From within the company, the decisionmakers might receive accounting and statistical data and written and oral reports from subordinates. From outside the company, the managers might enlist various kinds of consultants, auditors, or attorneys. Information can also be gleaned from public disclosures, paid informants, or even books. But even assuming (a real stretch to be sure) the correctness and the relevance of all information obtained through these devices, one critical failing will be found in every one of them. Anything other than information based on first-hand experience (a very limited possibility) will necessarily be somewhat "stale." This is not to deemphasize the fact that much of the information will be erroneous, irrelevant, and/or biased. It is merely to point out that no matter how correct the substance of the information, it will always take time for it to reach the decisionmaker, a delay that in some cases can prove fatal. Information of this sort will always lack the immediacy of what

40. *Id.*

41. For a brief summary of the types of information transmission problems corporate managers confront, see Stephen M. Bainbridge, "Privately Ordered Participatory Management: An Organizational Failures Analysis," *Del. J. Corp. L.* 23:979, 1013–14 (1998). But the "management" literature on the subject of information flows to decisionmakers is enormous, clearly reflecting the seriousness of the problem.

Hayek referred to as the knowledge of the particular circumstances of time and place.[42]

For Hayek, the solution in the case of economic organization was for diffused decisionmakers to utilize the market price of a commodity in their decisions, since that price contained significant information that diffused individual (private) planners need in order to make intelligent decisions. The price of a good or service or commodity was always immediately available and, as a guide to individual choice, inherently correct.[43] But obviously the manager is not a central economic planner, and diffused competition is not usually a feasible alternative way to organize the administration of a single firm. Nonetheless, suggestive similarities remain. As Hayek showed, "[t]he most significant fact about this system is the economy of knowledge with which it operates, or how little the individual participants need to know in order to be able to take the right action."[44]

Consider the plight of a top manager of a corporation considering the expansion of a major division of the company. He has probably received rosy reports about the division's performance even though, perhaps contemporaneously, the price of the company's stock is in sharp decline. We will make the simplifying assumption that all other divisions are known to be steady and the general business conditions have not changed.[45] Clearly, that manager has some unbiased information that things in his reports are

42. Hayek, "Use of Knowledge," p. 524.

43. *Id.*, p. 526.

44. *Id.*, pp. 526–27. "The marvel is that . . . without an order being issued, without perhaps more than a handful of people knowing the cause, tens of thousands of people whose identity could not be ascertained by months of investigation, are made to use the material or its products more sparingly; *i.e.*, they move in the right direction." *Id.*, p. 527.

45. Incidentally, this example strongly supports the use of so-called "tracking" stocks to aid in corporate management. For an example of exactly this scenario, see Joel T. Harper & Jeff Madura, "Sources of Hidden Value and Risk Within Tracking Stock," *Fin. Mgmt.*, Autumn 2002, p. 91. But the scenario, and the others following, is much closer to the ideas implicit in the modern theory of "prediction" markets, the creation of virtual markets in almost any kind of future state. Until recently the system has been used primarily to make election outcome predictions, but it is increasingly finding a place in the corporate world. *See infra* notes 56–59 and accompanying text.

not all they appear to be, and prudence dictates finding out what is really wrong with that division before approving the expansion.[46]

A scenario like that would not be realistic unless someone with information more reliable than that given to the top executives was trading in the company's stock. The manager would not care who got that information or how that person procured it; he would not care whether the trader was an insider or an outsider. He would not care whether the person was a file clerk or an investment banker. What would be important is, first, to stop the planned expansion; second, to find out what was wrong with the division; third, to fix the problem; and possibly fourth, take steps to deal with the producers of the erroneous reports. Each of these represents an important managerial action, and each of them depends on the information first gained through watching the stock's price.[47]

Or consider a manager faced with a well publicized acquisition decision and a stock price that has declined more than such an acquisition should occasion. He should recheck all the numbers and pause before completing the acquisition. Any other course threatens serious litigation, or worse, in the future. The information being impacted into the share's price may have come from insiders or outsiders, but, in any event, someone is betting their own money on the validity of numbers quite different than those the executive has been given.[48] There is great peril in ignoring such information.[49]

46. *See* James B. Kau et al., "Do Managers Listen to the Market?" (Mar. 21, 2005) (unpublished manuscript, on file with author), *available at* http://www.ssrn.com/Abstract=610062 (offering empirical evidence that managers "listen to the market," as they are more likely to cancel investments or merger plans when the market reacts unfavorably to the related announcement).

47. The prototypical *New Yorker* cartoon of a mogul watching the ticker tape in his office implied that he was "playing the market" on company time. But the grain of truth in the office presence of a ticker tape had to be that the top manager was watching primarily his own company's stock price.

48. Yuanzhi Luo, "Do Insiders Learn from Outsiders? Evidence from Mergers and Acquisitions," *J. Fin.* 60:1951 (2005) (offering empirical evidence that market reaction to announcements of mergers or acquisitions predicts whether the companies later consummate deals and that merging companies appear to extract information from the market reaction and later consider it in closing the deal).

49. Or, it might be added, in not having it available because insider trading laws have prevented someone with the relevant information from trading or disseminating the in-

An additional scenario involves a situation that must be common in high-tech fields or others with rapidly changing technology. Suppose that a publicly traded company is riding high with a dominant product in its particular market but not a product that is fully protected by its patents against substitutes. Orders are high, earnings estimates are generous, morale among employees is good, consumer response is enthusiastic, and the managers are about to cash in on their stock options. Just then, for no reason known to the company's top management, the stock plummets. It is in fact being shorted[50] by employees of another company that has developed a far superior substitute product.[51]

Or consider a case of substantial embezzlement and accounting fraud. Top managers notice an otherwise mysterious decline in stock price. This can set off alarms that ultimately lead to discovery of the fraud. But why did the stock price decline? Obviously someone in the know about the fraud decided that stock trading profits were better than the "honor" of whistle-blowing, and, at least this way, other employees of the company may never know who the "snitch" was, thus avoiding various personal embarrassment and recriminations. But why would the top managers care who did the trading or even how those traders knew about the fraud? That knowledge would not be required, nor would it be cheap to acquire, before the managers could take necessary corrective action.

This example suggests a more general use of stock price in the day-to-

---

formation. But I digress; the point of the text is merely that the stock market may convey valuable managerial information either not available or not available in timely fashion anywhere else. A manager might be at some pains to preserve such a valuable source of information and, to repeat the point of the text, not be heard to complain that someone has "immorally" traded on inside information.

50. *See* Stephen Figlewski & Gwendolyn P. Webb, "Options, Short Sales, and Market Completeness," *J. Fin.* 48:761 (1993) (arguing that the feasibility of short selling and the existence of options or futures markets generally improve the process of aggregating information by allowing more individuals to profit on their information and making the market for the underlying security more "complete" and hence more efficient).

51. While there is a great debate as to whether this trading would run afoul of Rule 10b-5, because it is not trading by an *insider* in the usual sense, this example nonetheless still serves to make the point about managers being dependent on stock prices for information they may be unable to secure elsewhere. *See also* Ian Ayres & Joe Bankman, "Substitutes for Insider Trading," *Stan. L. Rev.* 54:235 (2001).

day work of top administrators. If the managers could assume that informed trading was taking place whenever it became profitable—in other words, if managers had acted as though the stock market were "efficient" long before the idea of an efficient market was articulated—they could also have used stock price changes as a kind of confirmation, albeit "noisy," of their own internal financial and other reports. In other words, general insider trading would go a long way towards keeping various functionaries on their toes and honest, since every major error or act of dishonesty would become a potential source of trading profit for someone else in the organization who knew about the problem.[52]

That last idea in turn suggests yet another reason for silence about insider trading, this time by controlling shareholders. The problem of monitoring non-controlling managers was certainly recognized by investors and entrepreneurs long before Berle and Means popularized the notion of a separation of ownership and control.[53] Manifestly, no agency relationship of this kind is feasible without some device for monitoring the quality of work done by the agents. Are large investors who do not directly manage their companies merely to wait until they receive obscure quarterly or annual financials before making decisions about the quality of their managers? And even if they serve or have representatives on the board, can they be assured of speedy and correct information about the real value of managerial decisionmaking? This is the agency cost problem *par excellence*, and a feasible solution is to allow, nay encourage, insider trading in order to assure as fast and accurate conveyance of information as possible via stock price.[54]

52. It goes without saying that we are discussing those cases in which the trading is sufficient to move the price of the company's shares. This implicates the great debate about the effectiveness of insider trading to move share prices. The emerging consensus in the literature seems to be that this mechanism functions rapidly with few trades by insiders necessary to create a substantial movement in the indicated direction. *See supra* note 11. This effect would probably vary with the size and liquidity of the market for the particular company's shares, the number of analysts following the shares, and other factors. But the fact that the scheme may not function well to solve every managerial information problem is clearly no reason for not allowing it generally for those situations in which it is useful.

53. Berle & Means, *Modern Corporation.*

54. This insight makes it particularly ironic that Berle and Means complained that managers of large corporations might engage in insider trading. *See also* Kau et al., "Do

One would guess that these investors would want every bit of market price information they could possibly get, whether it came from stock trading by insiders or the devil. With all the difficulties non-managing shareholders will have in securing adequate information to protect their investment, it certainly comes as no surprise to learn that large shareholders are rarely heard to complain about insider trading. What is more surprising is that they and others with concurrent interests did not mount a more successful effort to thwart the SEC's campaign against the practice.[55]

The various examples given above help explain why managers and others could have been expected to remain silent about insider trading in its heyday. But these same scenarios are also significant because today they could represent actual corporate experiments with so-called "virtual" or "prediction" markets.[56] These schemes typically involve the use of an internally constructed mock or virtual stock market or derivatives market to assess a specific population's valuation (prediction of success) of, for example, a new product or managerial decision.[57] The practice is based on the Hay-

Managers Listen," p. 4 (offering empirical evidence that "firms tend to listen to the market more when large blockholders own a greater share of the firm").

55. *But see* "Text of Exchanges' Proposals to SEC" (showing some concern about section 16(b)). It may well be that the SEC's high-handed method of developing a general rule against insider trading did not allow for such public expression of concern after *Cady*. For those unfamiliar with this history, the *Cady* opinion that interpreted Rule 10b-5 was an administrative adjudication opinion of the SEC. It was the farthest thing from a rule-making procedure, and most observers at the time did not even think that there might be a new rule resulting from it. *See* Henry G. Manne, "Insider Trading and the Administrative Process," *Geo. Wash. L. Rev.* 35:473 (1967). The new rule became more obvious when the Second Circuit accepted that reading of Rule 10b-5 in *Texas Gulf Sulphur*. The SEC may well have taken this approach because they did not want public comment in a rulemaking proceeding, nor did they want to alert Congress to the radical lawmaking in which they were engaged. Given that reading of what occurred, it certainly is not surprising the business community, for the most part, simply let the "dictum" of *Cady* ride, at least until it was too late to really do anything about it.

56. For an excellent description of internal markets for "securities" predicting future sales, success of a certain product, or supplier behavior in such companies as Eli Lilly, Hewlett-Packard, and Microsoft, see Barbara Kiviat, "The End of Management?" *Time*, July 12, 2004, p. A4.

57. *See, e.g.*, Kay-Yut Chen & Charles R. Plott, "Information Aggregation Mechanisms: Concept, Design, and Implementation for a Sales Forecasting Problem" (Cal. Inst. of Tech., Working Paper No. 1131, 2002). The paper discusses, among other issues, the ques-

ekian idea that markets are better organizers of information and predictors of the future than are individuals.

Prediction markets in the corporate world are designed to mimic as nearly as possible the conditions of a real market. Thus they work more effectively if the individuals who bet use their own money and trade to make more money, just as in real markets. The idea is that people with the greatest confidence in the validity of their information will bet more on that supposition than will those who lack such confidence, and the aggregate betting will produce a "price" outcome much more accurate than any one individual could produce, just as Hayek suggested.[58] There are problems with getting the incentive structure right in virtual markets, problems that do not exist in real markets, but the results to date are nonetheless dramatically persuasive of the valuative and predictive powers of such markets.[59]

The similarities and overlaps between the Hayekian "use of knowledge," virtual markets, and insider trading should now be apparent to anyone. They each involve, actually or virtually, one and the same thing, namely a

---

tion of whether the prediction market mechanism can identify knowledgeable individuals and provide an incentive for them to participate, *id.* at 8–9, a problem which does not exist in a real legal market for inside information. *See also* Ajit Kambil & Eric van Heck, *Making Markets: How Firms Can Design and Profit from Online Auctions and Exchanges,* pp. 152–53, 159–61 (2002) (discussing how prediction markets can aid corporate decision-making); Justin Wolfers & Eric Zitzewitz, "Prediction Markets," *J. Econ. Persp.,* Spring 2004, p. 107 (summarizing academic literature on prediction markets).

58. *See also* James Surowiecki, *The Wisdom of Crowds,* pp. 23–39 (2004) (emphasizing the importance of diversity of beliefs among the participants in a virtual or a real market for the "magic" of the aggregation of disparate valuations to work). This is another reason why the exclusion of insiders from the stock market guarantees a less efficient market than would exist otherwise.

59. Readers are most apt to be familiar with the Iowa Electronic Markets for betting on political campaigns. These markets have proved to be considerably more successful than any polling device for predicting the outcomes of American elections. *See* Iowa Electronic Markets, http://www.biz.uiowa.edu/iem (last visited Feb. 5, 2006). The use of prediction markets made headlines a few years ago when the Defense Advanced Research Projects Agency (DARPA) of the U.S. Department of Defense tried to use a virtual market to predict terrorist activities. A popular outcry that this allowed "betting" on terrorism and was a moral hazard forced the Department of Defense to cancel the project. *See* Robin Hanson & Ryan Oprea, "Manipulators Increase Information Market Accuracy," p. 2 & n. 2 (July 2004) (unpublished manuscript, on file with author), *available at* http://hanson.gmu.edu/biashelp.pdf.

market for information. And this market inevitably performs far more successfully than would most any non-market administrative process, whether the latter be socialist central planning, marketing surveys by polls, or mandated financial disclosures such as those required by the SEC. Certainly it should be clear now why corporate managers and others with a real interest in managerial efficiency would not have complained about insider trading when it was widely recognized as a standard practice. Their jobs were—and still are—much simplified with a free and open information market for all possible participants.[60] There never was any need, therefore, to include insider trading in executive compensation packages.[61] Even in this day of regulated, distorted, and corrupted information flows, the smart managers must still keep a weather eye out for unexpected changes in their company's stock price.[62]

60. So much for the argument that it would be "unfair" if an office boy, a janitor, or a secretary were allowed to trade on information that was fortuitously picked up while on the job. *Cf. United States v. O'Hagan*, 521 U.S. 642 (1997) (holding liable a law firm partner not personally representing the company whose options and shares he traded). Management's interest would be just as great in having these low functionaries trade on new information as the highest level executive, so long as their trading added to the accuracy of the stock's price. It is reliable price-effect information they are after, not some puerile ideal of "fairness." This is not to say, of course, that there may not be situations in which it will be in a company's interest to delay information reaching the market, say where this information would be mainly valuable only to competitors. In such a case, however, we could expect the managers to take whatever steps were appropriate to guard the information and not to rely on a general rule against insider trading to cure a rarely occurring problem.

61. This is not to say, however, that no special cases existed where inventors or other entrepreneurs were explicitly allowed, as part of their compensation package, to trade on the value of the information they produced. This might have been especially appropriate to cover such cases as pharmaceutical scientists working on new drug products and betting on their success. A company could enjoy the advantages of a prediction market with the additional advantages of an appropriate form of incentive compensation. This is not the same as a generalized argument for insider trading as part of all compensation packages, which, as we have seen, entails considerable operational problems.

62. It is an open question just how much SEC regulation has distorted the market for valuable information, and the matter has not been addressed by empirical research. Enforcement of insider trading laws is still spotty and ineffective, but whether it is ineffective enough that we still have substantially as reliable and accurate a market for information (net of all the administrative costs of the system) as we would in the absence of the regulation is anyone's guess.

The illustrations used above are considerably oversimplified and describe a kind of event that does not occur every day. In fact, the truly dramatic case of important information being conveyed almost instantaneously by the stock price may be one of the rarer events in a top manager's career. Even so, it would require only a small number of such occasions, experienced directly or only heard about, before managers would understand the desirability of having insider trading–influenced stock prices available. So managers, directors, and large shareholders may have had little or no incentive ever to talk about insider trading as an important managerial tool and certainly none to condemn it. A culture of silence on the subject seems the most likely result. This solves the mystery posed earlier in this Article, and a new defense of insider trading has been described.

V. The Wrap-Up

There are arguments against this new hypothesis in support of legalized insider trading. First, there is the practical point that the stock market is notoriously volatile, and a manager may be hard pressed at any given moment to know whether the stock price change witnessed is a result of informed trading or of so-called "noise" trading.[63] "Noise" significantly complicates the task of ferreting valuable insights out of a stock's price, and on occasion noise makes it impossible to infer any valuable information from a stock price. But the ability to analyze stock price changes should probably be seen as another desirable skill for managers. The fact that "noise" may create some uncertainty with this kind of information and on occasion make it useless certainly does not imply that this information should never be available to managers as well-enforced insider trading laws in effect propose to do.

Similarly, stock markets are always subject to manipulation, and managers relying on stock price to gain new information will regularly be "confused" by others trying to convey false information.[64] While this observation

63. Aggregate market or industry price movements would not obviously have the same value since a general price level change would not implicate the kind of information under examination here.

64. For some suggestion of this kind, see Saul Levmore, "Simply Efficient Markets and the Role of Regulation: Lessons from the Iowa Electronic Markets and the Hollywood

seems plausible, it fails to note that alternative schemes of transmitting information are equally, if not more, subject to the same risks. Even more to the point, however, this argument does not integrate the possibility of "counter manipulators," who can profit by trading on the truth regardless of what their colleagues are up to. All indications are that significant stock price manipulation is extremely difficult to manage, and, ironically, it may actually improve the functioning of the market.[65] This mirrors the point made earlier about the value of insider trading on bad news. In both cases allowing an unfettered market in information creates salutary effects unheard-of in connection with regulatory "disclosure."

Virtual markets possess a special advantage over real markets powered by informed trading. They can be carefully tailored to a very specific query such as, "How will a particular new product fare in the market?" A generalized market for all information, like the stock market, cannot normally perform with this degree of specificity, but on occasion its message will be specific and clear. The fact that this is not always the case is simply one of the conditions of the marketplace; it is not a drawback to insider trading as such.

Of course, since the argument for allowing insider trading presented here is brand new and largely theoretical, little direct empirical or even anecdotal evidence exists to support it. However, we do have a rapidly growing number of reports of experimental work in prediction markets, none of which, needless to say, involve actual trading of stocks on a stock exchange. Additionally, a number of new questions for exploration come to mind. Do managers follow their company's stock price with an obsession suggesting that it contains valuable information (above and beyond their own direct

---

Stock Exchange," *J. Corp. L.* 28:589, 600 & nn. 36–37 (2003). In a somewhat different context, Levmore actually skirts near ideas proposed in this paper, but he seems reluctant to acknowledge any valuable role for insider trading. *Id.*, pp. 598–99. For important studies of the problem of manipulation, see Robin Hanson, Ryan Oprea, and David Porter, "Information Aggregation and Manipulation in an Experimental Market," *J. Econ. Behav. & Org.* (forthcoming 2006); Robin Hanson, "Foul Play in Information Markets" (Jan. 2005) (unpublished manuscript, on file with author), *available at* http://hanson.gmu.edu/foulplay.pdf.

65. *See* Hanson & Oprea, "Manipulators Increase." Levmore also notes that an equilibrium may develop as counter manipulators make profits. Levmore, "Simply Efficient Markets," p. 601.

interest in stock price related compensation plans)? Do we have any evidence that this mechanism has actually discovered problems? Are there other factors that would make stock price monitoring a losing proposition, such as noise, unreliable data, more efficient alternative information transfer devices, or excessive time or other costs associated with the practice?

Even after the SEC began its *in terrorem* campaign against insider trading and required compliance officers nearly everywhere, few top executives of large corporations have made ferreting out insider trading a top priority. In other words, though silence on the topic has not been as complete as it was before *Texas Gulf Sulphur,* complaints about the practice are not deafening. Most of the roar comes from the SEC and its supporters in the academic and media worlds. So, we might wonder, does this signify acquiescence by the corporate elite in the SEC's campaign against insider trading or does it merely mean that the campaign has been simply bluster and headlines, with an extraordinarily low enforcement capability?[66]

All of these are interesting questions that one can ask about the Hayekian hypothesis for insider trading, possibly opening a new area of scholarly research. The hypothesis seems to have enough "bite" that it will have to be integrated into the continuing general argument about insider trading. Because of this hypothesis, we may even begin to see some advocacy of insider trading legality from those whose interest, professional or academic, is in improving management efficiently.

VI. Conclusion

Stock trading by informed individuals can produce information that may be extremely valuable to managers of publicly held companies. Such infor-

66. *See* Ajeyo Banerjee & E. Woodrow Eckard, "Why Regulate Insider Trading? Evidence from the First Great Merger Wave (1897–1903)," *Am. Econ. Rev.* 91:1329 (2001); Arturo Bris, "Do Insider Trading Laws Work?" *Eur. Fin. Mgmt.* 11:267 (2005); Michael P. Dooley, "Enforcement of Insider Trading Restrictions," *Va. L. Rev.* 66:1 (1980); Javier Estrada & J. Ignacio Peña, "Empirical Evidence on the Impact of European Insider Trading Regulation," *Stud. Econ. & Fin.* 20:12 (2002); David Hillier & Andrew P. Marshall, "Are Trading Bans Effective? Exchange Regulation and Corporate Insider Transactions Around Earnings Announcements," *J. Corp. Fin.* 8:393 (2002); Jeffrey F. Jaffe, "The Effect of Regulation Changes on Insider Trading," *Bell J. Econ. & Mgmt. Sci.* 5:93 (1974); H. Nejat Seyhun, "The Effectiveness of Insider Trading Sanctions," *J. L. & Econ.* 35:149 (1992).

mation could result in benefits that are even greater than those stated in favor of insider trading as a device to improve stock market efficiency. That older argument related efficiency of capital markets almost entirely to stock market activities such as investing, stock trading, or transactions in control.[67] Now we have added a corporate governance dimension to the insider trading debate. Indeed, when we view the topic in Hayekian terms, we cannot escape the conclusion that knowledgeable trading in an earlier era did, and probably still does, considerably aid the functioning of the large corporate system. A new question also arises as to whether virtual markets can provide a meaningful alternative to overt legal insider trading, if regulation of such trading has reduced its informational benefit.

There is ample evidence that insider trading simply went underground[68] and there is no need for a substitute. SEC rule enforcement is a mess. SEC policies are arbitrary, capricious, political, and extremely inefficient. Nonetheless, illegal insider trading, no matter how robust, is bound to be more expensive and less efficient than the legalized variety. Thus, it is not surprising that other devices might arise for surmounting the SEC's effort to slow insider trading. If the stock market cannot itself be used to gain certain information because of insider trading restrictions, then managers (though, alas, not outside investors) can create a virtual market to provide some of that same information. Virtual markets even have some benefits the actual stock market does not, such as the ability to segregate specific causes of share-price changes. However, virtual markets will never be a complete substitute for the stock market because of the design and motivational problems mentioned earlier. But these markets can ameliorate some of the costs of the SEC's campaign against insider trading, and we can expect them to flourish.[69]

67. However, the efficient market concept also has some relevance for the executive compensation debate. *See* Carlton and Fischel, "Regulation of Insider Trading," pp. 869–72.

68. *See generally supra* note 66.

69. At least until the SEC decides that a virtual market operated with real money is close enough to the real thing to merit regulation. *See SEC v. SG Ltd.*, 265 F.3d 42 (1st Cir. 2001) (ruling that trading in shares of "fantasy" companies on the Internet—perhaps easily distinguished from a prediction market—is still covered by the federal securities laws).

INDEX

This book is set in Minion, a typeface designed for Adobe in 1990 by Robert Slimbach. It is inspired by the highly readable typefaces of the Renaissance. The display type is set in Myriad.

This book is printed on paper that is acid-free and meets the requirements of the American National Standard for Permanence of Paper for Printed Library Materials, z39.48-1992. ♾